T0269935

THE HILL

OSPREY
PUBLISHING

ROBERT KERSHAW

THE HILL

THE BRUTAL FIGHT FOR HILL 107 IN THE BATTLE OF CRETE

OSPREY PUBLISHING
Bloomsbury Publishing Plc
Kemp House, Chawley Park, Cumnor Hill, Oxford OX2 9PH, UK
29 Earlsfort Terrace, Dublin 2, Ireland
1385 Broadway, 5th Floor, New York, NY 10018, USA
E-mail: info@ospreypublishing.com
www.ospreypublishing.com

OSPREY is a trademark of Osprey Publishing Ltd

First published in Great Britain in 2024

A catalogue record for this book is available from the British Library.

ISBN: HB 9781472864550; PB 9781472864567; eBook 9781472864574; ePDF 9781472864529;
XML 9781472864536; Audio 9781472864543

24 25 26 27 28   10 9 8 7 6 5 4 3 2 1

Author's note

The author wishes to thank Christopher Pugsley and Aaron Fox for their kind assistance in
sourcing the photo of Hargest and his staff at the Platanias farmhouse (page 2 of plate section).

Image credits are given in full in the List of Illustrations (pp. 23–24).
Uncredited images form part of the author's collection.

Maps by www.bounford.com
Index by Angela Hall

Typeset by Deanta Global Publishing Services, Chennai, India
Printed and bound in Great Britain by CPI (Group) UK Ltd, Croydon CR0 4YY

MIX
Paper | Supporting
responsible forestry
FSC® C171272

Contents

Introduction

Individuals in conflict can decisively influence the outcome of a battle. Examples abound. Leonidas and his lonely Spartan defence of the narrow pass at Thermopylae in 480 BC against the might of the invading Persian army; an unknown standard bearer from Caesar's Tenth Legion leaping into the sea off Deal in 55 BC and securing a foothold for the first Roman invasion of Britain; a single cavalry officer carrying a message causing the British Light Brigade to charge the Russian guns at the wrong end of the 'Valley of Death' at Balaclava in 1854; General von Paulus' failure to break out the 6th German Army at Stalingrad in 1942 from Russian encirclement possibly costing Germany World War II. It is the actions of similarly important individuals that resulted in the loss of Hill 107 on Crete in May 1941, the key event that decided the entire campaign to capture the island.

New Zealand forces held this hill in the face of desperate German parachute assaults, which sought to capture the dominating high ground overlooking the only airfield where they could air-land reinforcements to secure the rest of the island of Crete. Hill 107 overlooked the two-thirds of a mile long by one-third of a mile wide primitive red-clay dirt landing strip.

Viewed from the dried-up Tavronitis river bed, the western slope of Hill 107 is high and intimidating, the stepped terraces enclosing small fields. It was spanned by a 130-yard metal girder bridge, perched on concrete piles. Today a modern highway bridge crosses the river alongside. Sections of the metal girders are punctured by ragged bullet holes or peeled back by shrapnel strikes. The steep sides of the west slope rise steadily in undulating fashion towards Crete's southern mountain foothills.

The northern slope facing the line of the aerodrome runway is gentle; its summit slightly higher than the plateau that extends east, a ragged line silhouetted by clumps of olive trees. In 1941, the gently descending slope had open areas, planted with barley and young vines, extending down to the airstrip, which had a soft sandy beach beyond the perimeter. Today there is a multiplicity of olive groves. The summit of point 107, called Kavkazia Hill by the Cretans, is formed by stony red-packed clay, with clumps of dried grass. On its east side, the largely dried-up River Sfakoriako has carved steep-sided gullies in places, overgrown with vegetation, cacti and bamboo shrubs.

Nestled inside the north-eastern side of the hill, the village of Maleme lies due east of an ancient Minoan tomb, only discovered at the eve of the 20th century. Village houses were ugly earth-floor flat-roofed fortress-like structures, opened around the base for livestock, with living accommodation above. An occasional balcony might contain an isolated chair. The main street descended to the sea, and was narrow with tight alleys between houses. Rickety shutters afforded scant protection against radiant heat and bright sunlight. Large families occupied small houses, within a village community numbering about 200 souls.

Creeping villa expansion with brightly coloured tourist holiday homes as well as noisy taverns and night clubs has completely transformed the formerly peaceful idyllic coastline. Originally three churches served the small community and were the only ostentatious dwellings with priests providing social guidance and community leadership. Today only the basement of the original Agia Marina church remains from the war, but the most recent, built alongside, still has one of the original 1941 bullet-scarred venerable icons. Another church and some village houses were relocated when airfield construction started in 1940.

———

Only rarely is it possible to positively identify the decisive point of a battle in modern warfare. Hill 107 was one of these during the night of 20/21 May 1941. Its loss was as decisive as Harold Godwinson's death on Senlac Hill at Hastings in 1066, which irrecoverably changed the future political and social development of England. The battle for Hill 107 likewise decided the entire outcome of this nine-day campaign for the island of Crete.

The book does not seek to comprehensively narrate the Cretan campaign. It deals instead with what was felt, heard or seen, left and right of the 'mark one eyeball', on and around the hill during the battle. At the height of the battle for Hill 107 the New Zealand perspective is from the summit, juxtaposed against the German view, looking up from below. The detail of what was seen was influenced by the azimuth of the sun, moving east to west across the sky. Germans clinging to the western slopes were dazzled during the morning peering up from the shadow of the low ground. During the afternoons the New Zealanders were in the glare, their concealed positions, precisely illuminated by the direct rays of the sun, standing out in sharp relief.

Events are narrated through the filter of key historical eyewitnesses. Each one was either a decision maker or taker. Headings identify the people influencing the major events relating to the subject of that chapter. Two primary perspectives are explored – German and New Zealand – with another, the civilian Cretan view, when caught up in the events.

Drawing upon many original archived New Zealand and German unit post-combat reports and letters, diaries with personal accounts from both sides and supplemented by vivid individual interview testimonies, the three-day battle for 'The Hill' is brought to life.

When the Germans jumped on the morning of 20 May, they had never lost a battle thus far in the war. The New Zealanders, after fighting a succession of desperate rearguards during the evacuation of mainland Greece, had never won one. Success had previously been measured by the ability to break clean in retreat.

Yet, nobody behaved during these three fateful days as they might have been expected to; these were uncharted circumstances for both sides. Mutual surprise is a factor throughout, coming from unseen terrain containing unexpected enemies, a feature common to all airborne insertions. Nobody in history to that date had ever seen a strategic objective conquered from the air alone, and it has not been done since. The actors tell how it was done, peering out from around the summits and within the shadows of Hill 107 beneath.

Prologue

26 April 1941, Central Greece

The ragged stream of German Ju 52 transport aircraft laboured over the craggy southern ranges of the Pindus Mountains in central Greece, seeking the open waters of the Gulf of Corinth. Flying in loose 'V'-shaped threes, the aircraft line stretched back 20 or more miles. Mountain villagers in this bleak region gaped up in astonishment at the spectacular fly-past coming over. The planes seemed virtually to scrape snow-tipped summits and mountain sides at over 6,000 feet and emitted a pulsating roar that throbbed and reverberated around the rocky snow fields and deep ravines below. Flying at 110mph, the sinister shadowy serpent took 20 minutes to pass by before cold mountain stillness descended over the valleys below. *Oberst* Rüdiger von Heyking the air transport chief of *Kampfgeschwader z.b.V. 2** estimated at current progress they had more than an hour to go before reaching their drop zone.

Progress was ponderous. Aircraft rose and fell, buffeted by squally gusting winds that curled up, shrouded in mist from the mountain sides. *Jäger* Sebastian Krug with Kroh's *I Bataillon Fallschirmjäger Regiment 2* in the back of one of the lead transports

---

*The abbreviation *z.b.V.* stands for *zur besonderen Verwendung* which is a special deployment unit.

recalled 'flying low over the mountains at about 5,000 feet, we came into a very heavy hailstorm and could hardly see our noses in front of us'. It was 26 April 1941 and the *Detachment Süssmann* was en route to capture the single bridge spanning the Corinth Canal, over which British and Dominion troops streamed south in retreat. They dropped off fighting rearguards to delay the following German advance in order to reach evacuation ports around Athens and the south Peloponnese.

This was the Balkans, a geographical fault line stretching between east and west Europe. Its historical terrestrial plates, expanding from both directions, constantly butted up against each other. Hitler was intent on moving east. Operation *Barbarossa*, the invasion of Russia, was planned for June that year. Romania had joined Hitler's Tripartite Pact in November 1940, Bulgaria signed the following March. Yugoslavia was persuaded to join on 25 March 1941, but a royalist coup negated this. A furious Hitler, unable to countenance any further fault lines jeopardizing his eastward move from the south decided to invade, and also Greece, to aid the *Duce*, his Italian partner. A British Expeditionary Force landed in Greece the same month. They were outflanked when German troops marched through Yugoslavia in April and had to pull back.

Mussolini's Italy was Hitler's primary Axis partner to the south and was not doing well. The *Duce* had grandiosely attacked Greek Albania in October 1940 after the triumphant German Blitzkrieg romp through France and the Low Countries. During the winter of 1940–41 the Greeks had fought the Italian advance to a standstill in the mountains. The British Royal Navy had meanwhile inflicted crippling losses on the Italian Mediterranean fleet at Taranto in November 1940 and at Cape Matapan at the end of March 1941. Italian forces were also hurled back by British forces in the Libyan desert in December and January 1941. The *Duce* needed help.

By 17 April 1941 Churchill had decided to withdraw British and Dominion troops from Greece. Vital to such an evacuation was the single bridge spanning the Corinth Canal west of Athens, pathway to the southern Peloponnese coast and evacuation by the Royal Navy. An aerial strike force of two reinforced *Fallschirmjäger* (parachute) battalions had taken off from Larissa south of Mount Olympus at first light, 5am, to prevent this.

The bull-necked genial commander of the *Flieger Division 7*, *Generalleutnant* Wilhelm Süssmann, had jumped at the prospect of action. His three-battalion regiment-plus-size task force under *Oberst* Alfred Sturm had been on stand-by at Plovdiv in Bulgaria, poised to invade the Greek island of Lemnos. It was occupied by a British battalion, which withdrew shortly after Hitler commenced Operation *Marita*, the invasion of Greece on 6 April. *Generalfeldmarschall* List's *12 Armee* attacking out of Yugoslavia and Bulgaria had made surprising progress across the Greek mountains and was approaching Athens. The swift capture of the bridge spanning the Corinth Canal would seriously dislocate the British and Dominion evacuation effort, now in full swing. For Süssmann it held the distinction of being the first major parachute insertion since the fall of Holland, almost a year before.

Although the weather became more favourable as the Germans droned south, flying conditions in the mountains remained wintry and hazardous. 'We lost contact with the Ju 52 to our right', Sebastian Krug remembered, 'and discovered later that it had crashed into a high mountain':

> He must have been flying too low. All but two of our fellows were killed in the crash. They must have been standing at the doorway waiting to jump and were thrown out into the deep snow just before the impact.[1]

The plane had swung out of formation. Its two survivors reached a low-lying village after struggling through deep snow; there they purloined a donkey and made it back to German lines with civilian help.

'There were lots of rumours' before the operation 'about places where we were supposed to go into action' recalled *Jäger* Heinrich Sturm, also with *I Bataillon*. Options had been endlessly debated. 'Chaplains of both denominations visited us' two days before. 'Whoever wished to attend a service and take communion could do so.' Immediately after the service they were invited as 'was customary, to write our wills'. Frequent noisy lashings of hail against the corrugated metal fuselages of the Ju 52s underlined the fragility of their futures.[2]

Rearing and bucking aircraft produced airsickness, accentuated by the turbulent air wakes of the aircraft ahead in the stream. Twelve paratroopers, six abreast inside the machines, stolidly regarded each other after the elation of take-off. They sat knee-cap to knee-cap, lost in their own thoughts. War correspondent Hans Rechenberg, embedded with the *II Bataillon* further down the stream, recalled they 'were all loaded up like Father Christmases'. Self-protection on jumping depended on what they could cram inside their pockets and smocks. They would have to fight their way to their all-important weapons containers, released separately by parachute from beneath the Ju 52. 'Above all, weapons and ammunition' were stuffed inside their clothing, mostly pistols, grenades and knives. Veterans often managed to secure a folding stock machine pistol (like a Tommy gun) inside their parachute harness. 'Most were preoccupied with their own thoughts', Rechenberg observed, 'personal past experiences etched across their faces'. Little was said, 'from time to time a snatched word, difficult to discern, which often had to be repeated over the engine noise'.[3]

The force had been stranded since early April at Plovdiv, Bulgaria, the so-called 'Prussia of the Balkans'. Sturm recalled 'tents were put together from pieces of tent cloth, which every soldier carries in his pack'. With 18 to a tent 'conditions were very cramped'. Snow lay on the ground and 'there was a shortage of straw'.[4] Morale was not especially high, Christmas Day had been spent at their Döberitz-Berlin barracks, and they had boarded trains shortly after New Year's Day. Nobody knew anything about what lay ahead, 'nor did we know why we were where we were'. *Oberleutnant* Arnold von Roon commanding the third company of *I Bataillon* remembered 'a primitive tented camp around the airfield, where we froze at night and sweated by day'. Easter had been 'peaceful and shared with the friendly Bulgarian population'.[5] It had followed an interminable 930-mile journey by train and jolting truck. They had rubbed

their hands together to keep warm and dug water run-offs around
their tents amid the dull monochrome landscape and waited and
waited. Rain and sleet had kept them inside their crowded tents
playing endless skat card games. A healthy trade was pursued with
the locals to procure eggs and anything to supplement tasteless and
often insufficient rations.

Soldiers had periodically gathered around the company radio
shack to listen to the latest Wehrmacht special bulletins plotting
the course of the Greek campaign. The news was all good except
it did not involve them. 'Fighting troops in Greece have reached
the Peloponnese in rapid advances', they heard. British troops had
been thrown back either side of Mount Olympus. '*Gebirgsjäger*
[mountain troops] have raised the Reich's war flag at the summit
of Mount Olympus.' Some of the *Fallschirmjäger* were considering
transfer to these more actively engaged units, reversing the previous
trend when veteran soldiers flocked to sign up for the paratroopers
after their dramatic successes in Holland the year before, much
hyped in German newsreels.[6]

When the division commander *Generalleutnant* Wilhelm
Süssmann had turned up at the Plovdiv tented camp there was an
air of expectancy. His long grey leather greatcoat accentuated his
short bulky physique as he was being shown around. He shared a
hot meal and spoke to the troops around the *Gulaschkanone* (mobile
soup kitchen), so-called because its metal smoke stack mounted on
a cart resembled an artillery piece. At least there was a decent stew
that day and his visit portended action. Indeed, a warning order
had been issued to his staff on 23 April, directing the capture of the
Corinth Canal bridge, but still interminable inactivity continued.
Army commander List approved the plan but the *Luftwaffe
VIII Fliegerkorps* commander, the volatile Wolfram Freiherr von
Richthofen, thought the scheme 'unnecessary'. It would 'foolishly'
tie up all the available air transport groups to supply such an
air insertion, resulting in fewer simultaneous attacks on Allied
shipping and retreating transport columns, which would more
meaningfully impede Allied evacuation. Air chief Göring ensured
support for the operation was forthcoming further up the chain of

command, which von Richthofen peremptorily commented was without due 'regard to the situation on the ground'. The mission was beyond Ju 52 range at Plovdiv and would need an intermediate airhead established at Larissa in Greece further south, after it had been seized. Resupplying and moving the force was to tie up almost 400 transport aircraft, because mountain roads were impassable. Süssmann made it happen, by ignoring orders and insisting on holding back two more transport squadrons to do so.[7]

Süssmann had only been in post for three months, upgraded to division commander when *Generalleutnant* Kurt Student took over the newly appointed and expanded *XI Fliegerkorps*. Süssmann had transferred from the police to the newly established Luftwaffe in the 1930s. He was a bomber pilot by trade and had recently commanded a Heinkel 111 *Geschwader*. His technical and staff air force background meant minimal practical experience commanding troops on the ground. Moreover, despite his promotion, he was not an especially lucky officer. He had faced a military tribunal after controversial decisions in Norway resulted in a costly parachute insertion at Dombas the year before. He was exonerated only by the personal intervention of Student, his patron, supported by Göring. He had even had to swim for his life in the icy waters of the Oslo Fjord when the German cruiser *Blücher* was sunk on approaching the capital.

The paratroopers packed inside the Ju 52s had had little sleep, having dozed under the wings of their aircraft at Larissa, after landing the night before. 'Reveille was at 03.00 hours', Heinrich Sturm recalled, 'hot tea was handed out; we buckled our parachutes and emplaned'. Orders had already been given. Süssmann wisely left the planning and execution of the two-battalion drop to *Oberst* Alfred Sturm. He was going to lead the first combined glider and parachute assault of the war. *I Bataillon* would land north of the bridge, and *II Bataillon* on the south bank. A group of six gliders with an assault Pioneer engineer platoon reinforced with paratroopers was to attempt a *coup de main* by landing next to the bridge.

Tension perceptibly increased when the Ju 52 stream began to descend along the lower southern slopes of the Pindus Mountains.

Oberst von Heyking, the transport group commander, had spotted what he was looking for, the open waters of the Gulf of Corinth. The stream altered course to port and was soon skimming over the water, following the southern shoreline. They were now well behind Allied lines. 'It was lighter when we reached the sea', Hans Rechenberg recalled. Looking about he saw 'in every direction, alongside and before us, flight after flight of Ju 52s'. Von Heyking set the force down to almost sea level for the final approach. He utilized the cloaking effect of early morning sea mist, which spiralled behind the transports, raising great spumes of revolving spray that glistened in the early morning sunlight. It was a tangible manifestation of approaching airborne power, inspiring the pilots to skip waves along the shore. Men inside stood up and prepared for action as the doors were opened. 'We almost skimmed the water', Heinrich Sturm observed, glancing down.[8]

Pilots peered through condensation trails streaming around their cockpit windows seeking the tell-tale scar of the canal cut. This was an unmistakable canyon, four miles long with 80-degree-angle carved walls rising perpendicularly 300 feet either side. At 80 feet wide at the base, the canal joined the Ionian to the Aegean Sea, replacing the carved slipway built during ancient times. There was a bridge carrying a road and rail link spanning the gap at a little over half way. It was protected by a random mix of British, Australian, New Zealand and Greek units, each under their own command, dropped off during the evacuation to protect the bridge against possible parachute attack. These were tired men, loosely organized, posted on either side of the canal, looking towards the direction of approach and evacuation rather than in the air. At dusk the night before von Richthofen's *VIII Fliegerkorps* fighter bombers had worked over the defences neutralizing many of the anti-aircraft (AA) guns. When night fell, the 6 New Zealand Brigade passed over the bridge, heading for evacuation beaches further south. At 6.30 that morning another 80 to 100 Me 110s and 109s systematically strafed any visibly defended positions. As von Heyking approached the objective he saw the haze created by dust and smoke from this activity; fighters were snarling past in and out of the approaching formation, descending from a distant swarm of what looked like midges buzzing around the target. Some 20 to 30 descending dots, Stuka dive bombers, were hitting the remaining defences, and black fountains of smoke blossomed up from strikes on both sides of the canal.

The most forward section of the approaching aircraft had steadily climbed to just under 4,000 feet. These were the six Ju 52 transports towing DFS 230 gliders containing 54 men belonging to the reinforced 2nd platoon of *Leutnant* Häffner's assault engineers from *Pionier Bataillon 47*. They released from 12½ miles out and stealthily descended through the smoke and dust created by the bombing and strafing runs. All Allied eyes were transfixed on the menacing gull-shaped Stukas, shrieking down from the brilliant blue early morning sky, dive sirens wailing. Troops scattered in all directions either side of the dusty bridge road, propelled by clanging air alarms punctuated by cracks from flak, and the drumming trails of strafing cannon fire, searching them out. Nobody noticed a glider approach until they involuntary ducked as black shadows swished overhead. They abruptly emerged from smoke and haze like huge birds of prey with outstretched wings. Five of the gliders touched down, skidding and bumping over uneven ground with loud wooden splintering crashes as barbed wire-encrusted skids snatched at the scrub, whipping up enormous clouds of dust. All the birds landed within 100 to 200 yards either side of the bridge. The sixth crashed directly into the foundation block carrying the west ramp of the bridge itself. The forward momentum hurled the pilot and medical sergeant sitting behind him out through the cockpit window into the road ahead, where they lay. All the occupants of this stricken glider were either senseless or seriously injured.

Cockpit canopies and side hatches were discarded and *Fallschirmjäger* in distinctive baggy smocks poured out, many still reeling from the shock of landing. The glider groups immediately fell upon the startled defenders as short bursts from machine pistols became interspersed with the crump of exploding stick grenades. Assault pioneers swarmed over the precarious bridge superstructure more than 300 feet above the canal, and slashed wires and pulled off demolition charges. Four light anti-aircraft guns were disabled, or their crews, taking cover from air attack, were blocked from returning, just as the main parachute stream rose out of the low-lying mist in the gulf.

With a quick surge of power the tri-motor Ju 52 stream lumbered up to 400 feet and began to close in wings of three abreast, with minutes to go before the objective. At two minutes the order '*Fertig machen!* Get ready!' was shouted inside the aircraft. Soldiers stood up and hooked their parachutes onto the wire running along the inside of the aircraft roof; this would pull parachutes open automatically on jumping. Sebastian Krug due to jump on the north bank of the canal with *I Bataillon* recalled 'we met up with some heavy anti-aircraft fire' on the final approach. Ju pilots had now to slow down to a virtual stall, maintain the correct altitude, and decrease speed to just under 100mph whatever the flak, because they were flying in *Kette* formation [three planes flying side by side], virtually wing tip to wing tip. '*Fertig zum Spring!* Ready to jump!' was called with 30 seconds to go. Hans Rechenberg, poised to jump onto the south bank of the canal with *Major* Pietzonka's *II Bataillon*, suddenly saw 'below us land, the hilly landscape on the south side of the Corinth Isthmus'. With that the '*blaaa ... ah*' metallic sound of the jump klaxon sounded. 'Every nerve was stretched' he remembered, readying himself for the exit, jump and landing, then 'thrusting strongly out of the aircraft, throwing arms into the air' in the crucifix position 'and out'.[9]

Total bedlam reigned below. There was no gap between strafing and bombing before gliders and parachutists appeared. 'I will never forget it', recalled Captain K.M. Oliphant with 2/3 Australian Field Regiment, 'the sky was black with German planes ... it was hell let loose – there was not a dozen overhead at a time but hundreds'. German paratroopers jumped so thickly, the officer commanding four guns of the 16th Heavy Anti-Aircraft Battery covering the canal recalled, that the parachutes seemed to touch as they emerged. They jumped so low that some parachutes did not have time to deploy fully, with men seeming to almost 'bounce' on landing. The outer two of the three Ju 52s in each *Kette* flying wing tip to wing tip disgorged troops, while the inner aircraft dropped weapons containers and stores. Separation of containers to troops varied from 100 to 300 yards, resulting in a pause, as with the aid of pistols and grenades they married up.[10]

The first thing company commander *Oberleutnant* Arnold von Roon noticed on leaving the aircraft was relief that there were not crowds of British troops waiting to disembark on the nearby quay at the canal entrance. Kicking his legs into wind, he saw a long column of Allied vehicles stationary on the bridge road. 'They halted at the moment we jumped', he recalled. Drivers dashed through the scrub alongside the road looking for cover. 'Soldiers in khaki were running all over the place, as were civilians seeking cover behind fences and under bushes and trees.' A desultory fire opened up. Once down von Roon observed even more Ju 52 flights bearing down on the objective, with flak bursting ahead of them. 'One didn't want to get too near the bridge', he thought. Distracting flak puffs were encouraging men to jump too soon and eventually a stick of paratroopers came out straddling the waterway itself. It was almost inevitable, he reflected, that some of the 12 would fall inside the 80-feet gap, and three plunged into the 26-feet-deep water below. Weighted down by helmet, parachute and equipment two slipped beneath the water before help could arrive. 'Soldier luck', he philosophically recalled. The whole stick had floated down between 'euphoria and misery, luck and fate, life and death; which in war are inextricably intertwined'.

Hans Rechenberg descending on the opposite south bank noticed the 'occasional suspicious whine of rifle and machine gun fire'. Looking down he saw 'rocky undulating ground' coming up, 'a few fields with young vines crisscrossing the landscape'. The terrain was unsuited for a parachute landing, and with no option but 'keeping his legs tight together' he dropped directly into a ditch. 'It was a heavy landing, unpleasantly hard, but at least he was safely back on earth.' The ditch at least provided some cover as he disentangled himself from his parachute harness. Sebastian Krug had an equally harsh landing on the other side of the canal 'on very stony and uneven ground, which resulted in very heavy casualties'.

Major Pietzonka, the battalion commander, broke his leg and had to hand over command to *Hauptmann* Gerhard Schirmer.[11]

Within 20 minutes some 1,100 paratroopers had landed both sides of the Corinth Canal, and the vital bridge at its centre was fought clear. Then at 7am the bridge erupted in a series of multiple explosions, a succession of sharp cracks sounding out at either side and the centre. The structure briefly rose up like a folding bridge and fell into the canal below under a huge pall of smoke. It killed or wounded almost half of Häffner's engineer group. The canal was completely blocked with wreckage. War correspondent von der Heide had at the same time been filming a section of parachute engineers dashing across the bridge at a crouching run, for the German *Wochenschau* (weekly cinema) newsreels. His final frames ended with the series of multiple explosions that took him and Häffner's engineers into the canal. The camera was found amid bridge wreckage and the exposed film salvaged.

Nobody could say for certain what had caused the explosion. Von Roon's view was that 'explosives were more valuable than gold to engineers' and that they had stacked their treasure trove on the bridge, to be recovered for future use. It was then likely hit by a chance flak round or a direct shot from a stubborn British soldier. Whatever the verdict, the bridge was gone.

Shortly before the bang Sebastian Krug with *I Bataillon* had declared 'well, we soon had so many prisoners that we didn't know what to do with them'. There had been heavy fighting all around the bridge. The attackers were now very vulnerable to counter-measures, as the explosion split *Oberst* Alfred Sturm's regimental-size task group in half, on each bank. Nevertheless, the *Fallschirmjäger* formed pursuit groups and fanned out from both sides, and using captured Allied vehicles and a mixture of daring and bluff netted 72 Allied officers and 1,200 prisoners. Corinth capitulated that afternoon and *III Bataillon* was air-landed nearby the next day. The cost of the operation was sobering, Süssmann lost 63 men killed, 158 wounded and 16 missing.[12]

At midday the same day, *Generalleutnant* Kurt Student, the newly appointed commander of *XI Fliegerkorps*, received an unexpected telephone call from *General* Jeschonnek, the Luftwaffe Chief of Staff. He was informed that earlier that morning the *Detachment Süssmann* had successfully mounted an airborne assault on the Isthmus of Corinth. The operation had been precisely carried out; unfortunately the bridge had been blown but the town and airport at Corinth was in German hands. Student was pleased to be congratulated on the performance of his troops but dumbfounded and somewhat disheartened at the news. Contrary to convention he had received no notice that a considerable part of his force was being deployed, a decision taken by Hitler just four days before. This could be interpreted as a slight against a fresh corps commander, barely three months in post. Süssmann, caught up in the last-minute planning and mounting of the secret operation, had also been required to relocate his headquarters from Plovdiv in Bulgaria to *Luftflotte IV* headquarters at Velos in Greece. There had been scant time or opportunity to inform his commander of what was going on.

More to the point, Student was totally immersed in planning for the invasion of Crete, also agreed by the Führer just the day before. Unfortunately the presence of the *Fallschirmjäger*, not seen since the Blitzkrieg in Holland and the Low Countries, had emerged into the limelight in the Mediterranean. The Allies had not detected any particular strategic or operational imperative. The *XI Korps'* rail move, some 80 to 90 trains, was to begin the next day. Operational security had likely been compromised.

Glider soldier Ferdinand 'Feri' Fink with the *Sturmregiment* remembered they were on a North German exercise area when wireless news 'about paratroopers being used against the Corinth Canal' was announced. Apart from training and preparation for action that never came, and immersed in the expansion process for *XI Korps*, they had been inactive for 11 months: 'We fumed over the report, which led to plunging morale and at times even worse. The envy over those fortunate to be able to demonstrate their capabilities rankled on those unable to participate.' Depression passed when two days later his *I Bataillon* began to entrain at Hildesheim. The trains clattering out from the railheads travelled south-east.[13]

Battalion commander *Hauptmann* Friedrich-August von der Heydte recalled boarding trains with *Fallschirmjäger Regiment 3* 'for a large-scale operation … at last!' They had no idea about the destination. 'Nobody took any notice of our train', he remembered:

> No one waved. Nobody wished us well. The sight of military transport was all too familiar by the end of the second year of the war. People were much too occupied with their own sorrows and their own jobs to worry about the destinies of those who were carried past them to die.

He wrote 30 postcards, all with a different date, to be passed on by his garrison successor saying 'I was fit and well, to my wife'. The aim was that she should not worry and believe he was still somewhere with the garrison, 'but she did not thank me for that' on return.[14]

Von der Heydte, once on the move, was lulled to sleep by the rhythmic throb and clatter of train wheels. When he eventually awoke in one of the saloon cars he saw that 'the train was travelling through flat monotonous country, devoid of people'. His adjutant had set up a portable wireless receiver in the compartment to monitor the war news. 'I listened with only half an ear' at official announcements about the successful conclusion of the campaign in Greece. German troops had marched into Athens the morning of the day before: 'But – what was that? Was I hearing right? In a daring attack from the air German paratroops had occupied the Isthmus of Corinth. Damn! We weren't there. Were we too late?'

He did not begrudge the accomplishment; 'the fight ahead of us was our great adventure', he reflected, 'but we also wanted to experience it for ourselves'.[15]

List of Illustrations

General Kurt Student originated the plan.

Lieutenant Colonel Leslie Andrew commanded the 22
New Zealand Battalion defending Hill 107. (Leslie Wilton
Andrew. S P Andrew Ltd: Portrait negatives. Ref: 1/2-
043326-G. Alexander Turnbull Library, Wellington,
New Zealand. /records/22695917)

New Zealand troops rest at the road side en route to Maleme.
(National Army Museum, New Zealand – DA11043)

Generalmajor Eugen Meindl, the *Sturmregiment* commander,
briefs his battalion commanders at Megara airstrip.

Brigadier James Hargest and his 5 Brigade staff at the Platanias
farmhouse. (Courtesy of A. P. Fox)

This glider has landed on the road embankment just short of the
Tavronitis river bridge.

Generalmajor Julius Ringel commanded the 5. *Gebirgsjäger*
Division.

New Zealand defenders await the German onslaught from their
slit trench.

The approach flight of the first wave, low level over the sea.

German paratroopers grimly sit face to face inside crowded troop
transports.

The New Zealand trench view from below. (National Army
Museum, New Zealand – DA11022)

The Matilda tank *Gnu III* was abandoned after passing beneath the Tavronitis bridge span.

Oberstabsarzt Dr Heinrich Neumann is at the head of the small band of men that took the summit of Hill 107.

Scaling the terraced slopes of Hill 107, thick with undergrowth, was difficult for attackers. (Bundesarchiv, Bild 101I-166-0508-27, Fotograf: Weixler, Franz-Peter)

German soldiers view the aftermath of the failed New Zealand counter-attack from the heights behind Hill 107. (Photo by ullstein bild via Getty Images)

Possibly Andrew's abandoned HQ location, occupied by Stentzler's *II Bataillon*.

The destruction and fires on the airstrip during the air-land convinced Hargest the Germans were evacuating.

The ramshackle state of the German seaborne landings became a debacle.

The New Zealand counter-attack had already run out of momentum by dawn on 22 May when it was subjected to Luftwaffe attacks. (National Army Museum, New Zealand – DA3466)

Generalmajor Ringel's air-landed *Gebirgsjäger* bypassed the New Zealand defence.

Oberleutnant Horst Trebes shouting the order to 'fire!' during the Kondomori massacre on 2 June 1941. (Bundesarchiv, Bild 101I-166-0525-29, Fotograf: Weixler, Franz-Peter)

Leutnant Weixler captured the impact of volley fire bursting upon the 23 assembled villagers. (Bundesarchiv, Bild 101I-166-0525-30, Fotograf: Weixler, Franz-Peter)

List of Maps

Chapter 1

The Decision

BRIGADIER JAMES HARGEST, COMMANDER
5 NEW ZEALAND BRIGADE

30 April–19 May 1941, Western Crete

Brigadier 'Jimmy' Hargest's war in Greece had been taxing, but he and his brigade had come through the experience intact. The first test had been the Olympic pass and mountain. His 21 Battalion temporarily lost control withdrawing south through the Pinios Gorge under German pressure. The brigade, prepared for a virtual Spartan last stand at the Thermopylae pass, was reprieved by the order to break clean for Athens and evacuate through Porto Rafti. 'One of my life's nightmare journeys', he wrote to his wife, describing the two-day withdrawal, 'up hill and down dale, over passes where the best were worse than our very worst New Zealand road'. They drove straight through Athens and left their vehicles, engines running having drained oil sumps, by the side of the evacuation beaches. Evacuation was fraught, with just three ships: the cruisers *Calcutta* and *Perth* and the troopship *Glengyle*. He described the troopship to his wife: 'I went to the Captain and told him we were over 5,000 that we had been told that only 3,000 could get off, but would he insist on taking the lot as there would never be a better chance.'[1]

They worked at it all night; 'open the bosun's quarters', ordered the chief once they were full. A thousand troops were sent over to one of the cruisers. Later it was 'open the hatches' and later still 'open the boiler room' as somehow they managed to cram the brigade on board for the 166-mile journey to the island of Crete. 'I wanted to kneel on the bridge', Hargest recalled, 'and thank God for His goodness.' The Luftwaffe was still snapping at their heels as signalman H. Mohi with the 28 (Maori) Battalion remembered: 'left Greece 4.30am. Disembarked at Crete. Bombed while crossing, two raiders brought down.'[2]

Hargest was confronted with a scene of total confusion as they disembarked from ferrying landing craft. British Military Police were telling his men to pile their weapons at the quayside at Suda. The brigadier was having none of this. 'We will do no such thing,' he shouted at the British officer in charge, 'my men will keep their arms and march off with them!' The officer was insistent he obey the command, a Luftwaffe raid was imminent at any moment. Hargest was derisory, 'I am not surprised that you are in charge of a base area, if this is the way you go on'. Second Lieutenant Geoffrey Cox who witnessed the bad-tempered exchange on disembarking remembered Hargest 'was a combative man who did not look the part': 'At forty-nine his stocky figure was running to fat, and you had to look keenly into his reddish, somewhat pudgy face to see the alert eyes and the resolute mouth and chin.'

Like many veterans, the starting point to the war they were in was the last one they had left. James Hargest had risen from the ranks as sergeant in the Otago Regiment in 1914 to an outstanding battalion commander in his early twenties by 1918. His adjutant recalled his sixth sense in battle, which led him instinctively to the right spot when things were breaking down, rewarded by his DSO and MC. During the intervening 23 years he became a farmer turned politician, a leading figure in the New Zealand National Party, representing the rural Southland seat of Awura. He remained an active Territorial Force officer after the war, commanding 3 New Zealand Infantry Brigade from 1925 to 1930. Inevitably at the outbreak of war in 1939 he wanted a senior command with the 2 New Zealand Expeditionary Force.

This was denied when his medical board diagnosed lingering symptoms of shell shock from World War I. The devastated Hargest personally appealed over the heads of the board to Peter Fraser, the acting Prime Minister, pulling all available political strings. He was confirmed and appointed commander of 5 Brigade.

Hargest joined a select band of leaders, mainly in their middle forties, who had seen intensive action between 1914 and 1918. There were only eight regular New Zealand officers at the outbreak of war and selection for command appointments in the fledgling New Zealand Division was fierce. Outstanding capability at battalion command level in a war fought over two decades ago was not necessarily a guarantee for like success at higher command in the next. Apart from training in New Zealand and England during the height of the 1940 invasion scare, the new leaders had little experience of the sheer totality and pace of operations in modern war. This was now conducted from two dimensions: on the ground with new weapons and now even more intensely from the air. There had been no opportunity to attack in Greece, nor had defensive operations been conducted over a period of days. There had been no real chance to hit back at the enemy. The campaign had been a succession of dispiriting hastily fought pulling back rearguards, one of the most difficult phases of war. They had not been tested in any fast-moving or intense mobile actions. Hargest, identified as potentially psychologically flawed according to the medical evidence, performed satisfactorily in Greece but emerged physically and mentally exhausted, without being fully immersed in the crucible of the new modern methods of waging war.

The 1914–18 experience had taught Hargest and his veteran contemporaries the value of bloody minded 'keep bashing on' – sheer endurance. Geoffrey Cox, an officer on the supreme commander Major-General Bernard Freyberg's intelligence staff, remembered coming across Hargest on the island reading Tolstoy's *War and Peace*: 'A surprising choice for a man who presented himself as a blunt no-nonsense farmer.' 'I have been reading about this fellow Kutuzov', the brigadier explained, 'the commander of the Tsar's army':

> He is the kind of general to study. He knew that in war steadiness and endurance are more important than any amount of strategic flair. You will find that sticking it out is more important than anything else. We were bombarded sometimes in France for 36 hours without a pause, and all you could do was keep steady and try to keep your men steady. Tolstoy knew that.

This was even, he pointed out, when Kutuzov could barely sit a horse, and was so old and out of condition he would fall asleep at the table. The inability to hold successive lines in Greece, despite the suitability of the mountainous terrain for defence, suggested that this new war was more about aircraft, tanks and artillery, not the staying power of infantry.[3]

'You could smell defeat in the air', recalled war correspondent John Hetherington during the evacuation from Greece, 'indeed you could hear it in the arrogant song of the engines of the German bombers swaggering across Athens'.[4] 5 Brigade presented a bedraggled picture on arrival, wearing an ill-assortment of clothing and footwear. Some had webbing equipment and straps, others had none, not all still had their helmets. They did, however, retain their weapons, and did not want to hand any over on disembarking. No tents or accommodation were available on Crete; troops bivouacked among the olive trees on the south side of Suda Bay. Conditions were primitive, cooking was done in cut-down petrol tins with drinking vessels and eating implements fashioned from tin cans and pieces of wire. 'Many men at first were eating and drinking from bully beef or cigarette tins', Geoffrey Cox recalled. 'The round tins which contained fifty Player cigarettes were in high demand, as they made excellent cups.' Men slept fully dressed in the open on the ground to keep warm; there were generally no blankets or greatcoats. There was no hot food and soldiers wandered off into the countryside to forage for themselves. Dark bulbous smoke columns from tankers burning in the bay polluted the blue sky and added to a scene of desolation. The clear nights were bitterly cold.[5]

Soldiers thought their plump and stocky commander genial enough, but as a member of parliament, he was branded a suspect politico. He stood out in contrast to the tall lean young men who surrounded him, habitually dressed in large baggy shorts. Being a politician meant suspect reliability, but here he was, at nearly 50 prepared to compromise his comfortable life and personal advancement to fight with them. Thus far there had been no disasters, but some wondered whether the commander might be a little old for the job. Hargest was ordered by 'Creforce' to deploy his brigade to secure the western exits from Chania, the Cretan capital. Freyberg's Creforce command led a British, New Zealand and Australian Brigade with composite and other forces, to defend the island of Crete. Hargest recced as far forward as Malame aerodrome about ten miles beyond. The mission was to establish a defensive line from Platanias village to the Tavronitis river estuary, just west of the aerodrome. It was a compromise between a lengthy coastal defence and the point security of the airstrip, to guard against an air-land and sea threat. 'Spirited defence' was the key word for an operational scheme backed up with immediate counter-attack options.

Under the benign influence of a perfect Mediterranean spring with ever-increasing sunlight, soldiers rapidly recovered their previous physical rigour. Most thought it only a matter of time before they were moved on to Egypt. Hitler was unlikely to reach across such an expanse of sea. Time in Britain during the invasion scare following Dunkirk underlined the view that islands offered secure bastions, as no strategic ones had fallen yet. Historical examples over the centuries suggested few enemies countenanced pursuit across sea lanes, and an unsupported attack from the air was scarcely imaginable. Over the next two days following disembarkation a constant stream of 5 Brigade troops made their way along the main western coast road to Maleme. Some marched in formation, others straggled exhausted or footsore, often recovering from the effects of the local red wine, which soldiers had characteristically foraged in remarkably short time.

Brigadier Puttick, the newly appointed New Zealand division commander, conducted extensive recces, and advised Hargest that his main body was too far back. 22 Battalion was positioned at the aerodrome, with 23 and the weaker 21 Battalion situated in depth to provide linear coastal protection. 28 (Maori) Battalion was grouped around Platanias three and a half miles back as reserve, where Hargest established his headquarters on 'a lovely little hill' overlooking the village. A daily routine of one-hour stand-to, morning and evening was established, with company positions 100 per cent manned. Sections had one sentry by day and one-third of their strength alert at night.

Meanwhile the Mediterranean sun continued its therapeutic healing process. 'Conditions very pleasant in this peaceful waiting existence', recalled Lieutenant Bassett, the 23 Battalion intelligence officer on the ridge behind 22 Battalion, 'parties bathe in the Mediterranean and bask in the sunshine' as 'orange vendors ply a steady trade'.[6] John Hetherington observed:

> There was naturally a lag of a few days while plans ... were being made and put into operation. In those days men rested, swam from pleasant beaches, roamed the island, picked their way over the Knossos ruins, climbed the mountains, made friends with the peasants. The days grew warmer, sunnier as April drew to an end.[7]

Absolved of the pressures of combat, tension and lack of sleep, the soldiers soon recovered. 'This is the most beautiful place', recalled one Northumberland Hussar tankman:

> We found a lovely little sandy cove, surrounded by rocks about three miles away. The water was crystal clear and just cool enough to be refreshing with a pale blue tint. We sat on the rocks and dried in the evening sun, which doesn't burn you here.

The air was heavy with the scent of thyme. 'It wasn't like a war at all', he reflected.[8]

They had performed well in fast-moving sharp rearguard actions in Greece. But the strain at battalion level on the older World War I veterans had been immense. Their experience had been static warfare on the Western Front, but Greece had subjected them to fast-moving tense actions against mobile armoured columns, requiring uncharacteristically instant decisions. Exposure to overwhelming Luftwaffe air superiority had been an unprecedented shock. They were mentally and physically tired, uncertain what they might face amid the confusing new vicissitudes of modern warfare. The commander of 6 Brigade recalled: 'The lack of rest was a particular severe strain on commanders and staffs. On one occasion some officers were without sleep – without even the traditional "forty winks" – for a period of four days and four nights.'[9]

Officers found it difficult to speak intelligibly on the radio or think logically under such conditions. Geoffrey Cox sensed this suppressed latent torpor visiting Hargest's headquarters, in a farmhouse, a few hundred yards inland from the coastal village of Platanias. It was a lovely evening on the eve of the invasion. They strolled, looking at Maleme some four miles to the west. Dressed 'in baggy shorts and khaki jersey', Cox recalled, 'he looked very much the farmer, which he was in civilian life'. They anticipated a likely airborne attack, and Hargest quietly admitted:

I don't know what lies ahead. I know only that it produces in me a sensation I never knew in the last war. It is not fear. It is something quite different, something which I can only describe as dread.

Cox appreciated what he meant. Hargest had a distinguished 1914–18 record but the enemy he had fought in Greece was nothing like his previous experience, an 'extraordinary phenomenon', he thought, at this early stage of the war. They could not fathom 'the mystique, indeed the mystery which seemed to surround Germany's staggering success in the field'. Moreover this sinister phenomenon was heading their way, added to which the Germans had complete mastery in the air, 'denying those who resisted any place of rest or shelter'. Planning for the defence of Crete was evolving, but Hargest anticipated a bleak outcome.[10]

Hargest's superior was the 49-year-old Brigadier Edward Puttick, who had been the sole regular infantry brigade commander and had effectively and practically commanded 4 Brigade in Greece. Severely wounded during the final German offensive in 1918, Puttick had made his career as a staff officer in the much-diminished inter-war New Zealand army, and was a colonel commanding the Central Military District on North Island New Zealand when war broke out again. He was nicknamed the 'Red Hun' because of his distinctive red hair and meticulous attention to detail and prodigious capacity for hard work. He was appointed to replace Freyberg as the New Zealand Division commander when the latter was chosen to head up Creforce, to defend against an anticipated German invasion. Cox remembered him as 'a talkative man apt to fuss over trifles' but who 'knew his trade'.[11]

Six days after disembarkation Puttick came forward to look at Hargest's 5 Brigade sector. In all, he had 3,183 troops at his disposal and 1,044 Greeks further west at Kastelli Kisamou. His immediate intervention was to push Hargest's command further forward. The key to the position was the hill at point 107 that completely dominated the airfield. Hargest's strongest 22 Battalion, with 640 men, was earmarked to defend it and the aerodrome. The next strongest 23 Battalion with 570 men was set on the ridgeline to the east behind 22 with 570 men, with a much-reduced (from Greece) 21 Battalion with 370 men alongside it further inland to the south, tasked to counter-attack in support. 28 (Maori) Battalion with 220 men remained around the village of Platanias four to five miles away in depth, with Hargest's HQ. He also had a detachment of engineers in the infantry role, filling the gap along the coast between the reserve and the forward battalions. Under command were elements from 27 Machine Gun Battalion and two Matilda tanks from 7 Royal Tank Regiment. Puttick anticipated both air and sea landings, recommending that Hargest position his Vickers machine guns in two groups, one to cover the beaches, the other the aerodrome. Two 3in mortars were sited to cover the northern and southern limits of the airstrip. Puttick then sited 4 New Zealand Brigade behind the 5th, around the junction where the coast road from Maleme met the road leading out of Prison Valley, where he had positioned a scratch-built composite 10 Brigade.

The one great weakness in the 5 Brigade sector was the undefended ground west of the Tavronitis River. The conundrum in defence facing all commanders is that there is always more ground to defend, than troops available to task. Despite its obvious attraction to the enemy as a forming-up point for any attack on the airfield it could not be effectively covered. 1 Greek Regiment ostensibly under command at Kisamos Kastelli further west might be called upon, but they were too isolated and remote from the main objectives to be relevant. Permission from the Greek authorities was also required with no transport to move it, and no defence stores left to entrench, so the vacuum remained unresolved. The only respite for New Zealand officers preparing and planning at this stage was a cocktail party hosted by Major-General Freyberg at Chania on 8 May, in honour of the Greek officers on the island. Some 10 per cent of the soldiers were granted leave and they flocked to Platanias and Chania. Food was limited, unlike the variety of drinks on offer, which led to many soldiers reappearing the worse for wear on return.

On 8 May Hargest convened a meeting of his COs and the heads of the other 14 formations: Royal Marine and naval gunners, RAF ground crew and other miscellaneous units concerned with the defence of Hill 107 and the aerodrome. This was held at the Maleme Court House where the brigadier briefed his aim for the defence to 'be properly coordinated and confusion avoided when an actual attack takes place'. He gave verbal orders followed by a formal defence plan distributed on the 18th. At its heart was the need for 23 and 21 Battalions to not only hold their sectors, but be prepared to counter-attack onto Hill 107 and 22 Battalion's positions, which had to be defended 'at all costs'. A withdrawal plan was not considered.

The Brigade's siting was essentially a compromise between the competing needs of defending the airfield and a long coastline. Neither Puttick nor Freyberg gave any guidance on what was the more important, and Hargest saw no priority for himself. The runway at Maleme was only 800 yards long, whereas a seaborne invasion could unpredictably fall upon any section of a dozen miles of coastline. Whatever happened, some battalions would have to move. Hargest's headquarters, 'set up in a grove of wind twisted olive trees' according to Cox, lay four miles from Maleme – too far. Hargest, being instinctively political, simplified his line of communication to division headquarters at the expense of complicating those to his subordinates. 23 Battalion nearest in line to support 22 forward, was two miles short of the Tavronitis River. In between was the wide Sfakoriako gully, 'wired in' for defence by both sides, which would snag any rapid reinforcement. From these rearward positions, the runway was out of sight, due to obscuration of the shoulders of Hill 107 and screened by thick tangles of bamboo and olive trees. 22 Battalion was therefore rather isolated, like a tortoise head protruding from its shell. 'White-green-white' Verey flare signals were laboriously set up to initiate any 23 or 21 Battalion counter-moves when called upon.[12]

Despite an invasion pending, two of Hargest's four battalion commanders were rotated. Lieutenant Colonel Falconer left 23 Battalion, two weeks after disembarkation, to be replaced by his second in command Major Leckie. The soldiers felt the loss, 'the best colonel we ever had or ever will', remarked one. Replacing an infantry commanding officer (CO) is a major event in any unit's calendar, because soldiers saw professional military competence as key to future survival chances. Company commanders, next down in the chain of command, had also invariably to adjust and think ahead of what the new CO would personally expect from them. This unsettling change was followed on 17 May by the appointment of Lieutenant Colonel J.M. Allen, who took over 21 Battalion from Macky, who had been judged wanting by Freyberg in Greece. Even more unsettling for the men was Freyberg's open criticism of the conduct of their transport column caught by a German armoured ambush on the Larissa road, panicked into flight during the withdrawal from Tempe. The soldiers thought Freyberg was overly critical. As if the soldiers needed reminding of the Greek debacle, Freyberg's debrief coincided with a Stuka dive-bombing attack on Maleme aerodrome nearby. Changes of command on active service could be disconcerting occasions. New leaders were notoriously difficult to predict or read, which might prove vital in a crisis.[13]

Luftwaffe air attacks were steadily increasing and the first heavy bombing raids burst across Maleme on 13 and 15 May. Major Jim Leggat, the second in command of 22 Battalion, recalled 'from about the 8th until the 20th May he [German aircraft] gave us a shake up about every couple of hours'. Repeated exposure to Luftwaffe air raids in Greece had played on minds to the point of obsession. 'The degree to which the nerves of the men of the division had been worn raw by air attack surprised me', Geoffrey Cox remembered, 'when I finally caught up with Division HQ at Thermopylae'. Lieutenant Dan Davin, the intelligence officer with 23 Battalion, had seen the effect of Stuka dive-bombing in Greece:

There was something shameful about the fear of these poor devils, their eyes big and staring, their mouths open and stupid, their reason atrophied. I shall never forget them crouching round the edge of a quarry like terrified animals when I came towards them to offer a drink from my water bottle. It was unimaginable that a plane should need to waste death on these people paralyzed with fear.

A British report remarked on exhausted New Zealanders being sorted into their units among the olive groves around Chania. Many were 'windy' about air attacks and immediately dived for ditches at the appearance of a single German reconnaissance plane, the daily 'shufti kite' from Rhodes. Jim Leggat explained 'you feel terribly naked swimming in the sea if a plane is machine gunning'. 28 (Maori) Battalion also remembered company bathing parades 'had their moments of excitement' when a German plane would suddenly 'swoop out of the clouds and along the beach spraying bullets as it passed'. 'You feel impotent under air attack', war correspondent John Hetherington remembered. 'You can't do anything but curse. Cursing is a safety valve for fear.' Small wonder soldiers were intimidated, 'dealing with a form of attack not only outside their experience, but outside their training', Cox commented, 'nerves became ragged under it'.[14]

There was no let up. The RAF started the defence of the island with eight Blenheim twin-engine fighters from 308 Squadron, six Hurricanes from 33 and 80 Squadrons, six antique bi-plane Gloucester Gladiators from 112 Squadron and a few Navy Fairey Fulmars. They were up against 280 bombers, 150 Stukas, 180 fighters and 40 reconnaissance aircraft from von Richthofen's *VIII Fliegerkorps*. The sole surviving Hurricane was flown out of Maleme on 19 May. One irreverent New Zealand ditty encapsulated the mood of the troops:

'We saw the entire force one day
When a Hurricane hurried the other way.'

Canadian aircraftsman Marcel Comeau with 38 Squadron remembered soldiers cat-calling, substituting RAF for *RA bloody F*, meaning 'Rare as bloody Fairies!' 'It was a hard pill to swallow', he admitted. Although prevailing contempt about the lack of air cover in Greece was not directed against pilots – indeed their efforts had appeared selfless, bordering on suicidal – the ditty remorselessly rhymed:

'When portly Winston aired his views
The RAF are now in Greece
Fighting hard to keep the peace
We scratched our heads and said "pig's arse"
For this to us was just a farce
For if in Greece the air force be
Then where the bloody hell are we?!!'[15]

38

The lynchpin of Jimmy Hargest's 5 Brigade defence plan was spot height 107, the hill overlooking Malame airfield.

GENERALLEUTNANT KURT STUDENT, ## COMMANDER *XI FLIEGERKORPS*

Late April–17 May, Athens, Greece

Kurt Student, the forceful patron and founder of the German airborne arm, was struck down in May 1940 at the very moment his *Fallschirmjäger* concept came of age. During negotiations for the capitulation of Rotterdam he was struck in the head, probably by a German ricochet, when SS troops accidently clashed with the Dutch surrender delegation. 'Suddenly', he recalled, peering out a window, 'I felt a massive blow against my forehead, as if by a massive sledgehammer'. Dreamily conscious he remembered a sequence of events enacted in slow motion:

> I felt a strange, rubbing, splintering, obnoxious noise in my forehead, a bone crunching splintering that produced a singing vibration throughout my skull. I had been struck by a ricochet that split my forehead open to a hand's width, and I sensed my wound was mortal. At that moment, summoning every bit of the life-giving energy I had, I hung onto the table with the last of my strength. My knees were too weak, and I collapsed under it. Total blackness descended.[16]

He would never have thought, he later reflected, that anyone could survive such a wound. Only the skill of a hastily summoned Dutch surgeon saved him. He was conveyed to the German Hansa-Klinik in Berlin, where he was operated upon by a specialist. He lost his speech for a few days and it took nine months to recover. Some contemporaries suspected this dreadful blow must surely have impaired his capacity to command.

The 51-year-old Student appeared outwardly unimpressive, more like a senior diplomat or government official, rather than an intrepid paratrooper. The long convalescence accentuated his pale, wan complexion and his high-pitched voice perceptibly slowed, leading some to assume stupidity or indecision. Lack of exercise during the recovery period produced a degree of businessman flab. Student was, however, driven, focused, extremely capable and totally ruthless in the pursuit of his own goals. As a World War I flyer he had shot down five aircraft over the Eastern Front. Thereafter, his Luftwaffe inter-war service was primarily administrative and technical, steering aircraft development, training and research projects. He cultivated a special relationship with Hermann Göring, the head of the Luftwaffe, who handed him the prestige task of forming the German parachute and airborne forces, while remaining an energetic sponsor. Göring allegedly remarked to Hitler that even if Student occasionally appeared half-witted, he was an intelligent energetic officer who delivered tangible results: 'a man who thinks up the cleverest of things by himself'. Heinz Trettner, Student's chief of staff, remarked on this unusual ability to combine 'the new, the unconventional, even the adventurous' with working methods 'based on meticulous staff work and precise attention to detail'. It was this efficient unorthodoxy that brought him to the attention of Hitler, who regarded airborne troops as one of his potential secret weapons in the early years of the war. A *Fallschirmjäger* contingent had headed up the Führer's birthday parade in April 1939, projecting modern German might.[17]

Student was more the sincere, studious and able soldier rather than combat leader, for which he had no practical experience. He saw the airborne capability he was developing as a strategic force, not irregular sabotage or raiding groups. His concept of air drops and glider landings had cracked open the fortress of Eben-Emael, which could have potentially barred German panzer advances from the Belgian plains beyond. 'Fortress Holland', the Dutch defence concept of retiring behind its moat of canals and waterways, had been simply overflown. Strategic land islands and bridges had been seized and held until relieved by advancing German ground troops. The execution of such attacks was about surprise and instilling panic among the defence, creating floating 'oil spots' of occupied areas before the enemy realized what was going on. The spots, like oil on water, would seep together and be enveloped by the subsequent ground advance. Student was a risk taker in all this, prepared to act even with only rudimentary intelligence. His brusque good humour, irony and drawling speech endeared him to the troops and his staff, who did not see him as a party man or corridor politician. Even so his ruthless ambition and impatience with those not sharing his zealous adherence to airborne ideas did not endear him to high-ranking Wehrmacht officers competing for scarce ground combat resources. Student had sharp elbows.

He was awarded the Knight's Cross for the exploits of his *Fallschirmjäger* in the Low Countries. His severe head wound relaxed the suspicions of many senior competitors, who rated his incapacity as potentially terminal. Yet during convalescence, Student's 7. *Luftlande Division* command was expanded to *XI Fliegerkorps* size, on the basis of its achievements. He had plenty of time in his hospital bed to ponder the goal for such an emerging airborne force, which should be to tackle a strategic objective. This might well be the conquest of the island of Crete from the air alone, following the capitulation of Greece. The genesis of the future attack on Hill 107 overlooking Maleme aerodrome was going to be dependent upon Student's ability to persuade the Führer that he could replicate and surpass the operational success of the Low Countries, by capturing Crete from the air. This was a strategic objective, something that had never been done, or indeed even considered before.

Student flew to the Semmering Pass in Austria on his own initiative, to brief his idea to *General* Hans Jeschonnek, the Luftwaffe Chief of Staff. His headquarters was with Göring at the luxurious Hotel Panhans, with Hitler's special train *Amerika* co-located nearby. They had jointly planned and executed Operation *Marita*, the invasions of Yugoslavia and Greece, from here. Göring, whose Luftwaffe had benefitted greatly in prestige from Student's success in Holland, was supportive. He arranged a special short-notice meeting with Hitler the next day. This was unusual and not welcomed by army chiefs Keitel and Jodl, who wanted to target Malta. Student was competing for resources for a major Luftwaffe operation having barely been at his desk four months, after eight months in hospital. He recalled the fine weather and beautiful countryside as his briefing party took the 12-mile staff car journey from the hotel to the small village of Mönichkirchen, where Hitler's train was lying up, hidden on a steep curve before a 3,000-yard tunnel outside town.

Staff officers and ancillary staff were going about their business along the wooden decking, laid by engineers next to the stationary 15-car dark-green *Reichsbahn* train, when they arrived. Two locomotives, one gently hissing steam, were hitched to the front, on stand-by, ready to puff into the tunnel at first sign of an air threat. Flak guns were installed on sleek, contoured carriages both fore and aft. Hitler had directed operations in Yugoslavia and Greece from here, comfortably ensconced on rails, and linked to the outside world through his signals car, the thirteenth carriage from the front. It was an impressive train, the US Presidential Air Force One equivalent, before its time. When it moved no other train was allowed to run. Nobody knew where *Amerika* was going, or where it had been. Its movements were constantly cloaked in elaborate security measures.

Student's briefing group, including *General* Jeschonnek and *Major* Trettner, his chief of staff, strode alongside the austere yet stylized train acknowledging the salutes of German sentries presenting arms at regular intervals. They climbed aboard the OKW *Vortragswagen* (briefing carriage), where they were met by Jodl and soon joined by Keitel. The car was functional in design, scant decoration with art nouveau furnishing. A rectangular briefing table filled the compartment, with comfortable curved armrest chairs facing inward, curtained windows behind. Maps hung from the walls. Since 12 April numerous conferences and diplomatic meetings with Bulgarians, Hungarians and Count Ciano, the Italian Foreign Minister, had already taken place after the train had arrived. Trettner recalled passing Hitler's coach, third in line from the locomotives, where 'they were busy with diplomatic discussions'. On coming aboard 'the highest-ranking' Luftwaffe generals were already assembled in a neighbouring compartment with Keitel, Jodl and a Kriegsmarine captain.

When Student came in he was immediately questioned by the Luftwaffe seniors what he was going to brief Hitler on. Student told them about the raised readiness of his airborne troops, and said they could attack Malta or Crete. Everyone spoke up for the Malta option.

It was at this point Hitler entered the car, and according to Trettner 'asked Student to lay out his proposal'; Göring had obviously already provided supporting information. Student highlighted the Cretan option, arguing that Malta, being so small, could rapidly deploy reserves against any airborne incursion. As an expert on airborne matters, Student claimed it was possible to take Crete from the air alone. Moreover, he emphasized his elite troops were becoming increasingly frustrated with their forced inactivity, while their Wehrmacht comrades went from victory to victory in Greece. Crete could be overcome utilizing his 'oil-spot' strategy of landing concurrently in many places all at once. Keitel and Jodl had been condescendingly dismissive about Student's scheme, so were taken aback when, as Trettner described:

Hitler considered for a moment, not even five minutes and then commented: 'I wouldn't have believed it possible that paratroopers could attack an island as big as Crete. If you, Student, think that it is possible, then only Crete is in question!'

All the Luftwaffe and Army seniors were taken aback by this spontaneous reaction. Hitler pointed to the need to protect the Romanian oil fields at Ploesti against possible British air attacks, vital to support *Barbarossa*, the planned invasion of Russia next month. Such an operation would further divert attention from the massive build-up of three million soldiers poised to attack eastward. Nevertheless, he still considered the plan too adventurous. Part of the invasion forces for Crete must land by sea, insisting 'you should not stand on one leg'. Moreover, because of the pending Russian offensive, Hitler insisted, 'the attack must happen as soon as possible. Any day sooner is a win, every day later a loss'.

Hitler floated 15 May as a possible launch date, but stated he wanted clarification of additional points before a final decision. This left only three weeks for Student to prepare. Troops now needed to move to be in situ in time. Hitler was adamant he wished to 'further consider the proposal' but agreed Student could at least begin serious preparations. The senior Luftwaffe and Army chiefs chose not to question Hitler's surprising closing comment that 'Crete would be a good finale to the Greek campaign'. Four days later on 25 April, Hitler confirmed his decision with Directive No. 28 for the capture of Crete, given the code name *Mercury*. Overall command was delegated to Student's sponsor Göring; he was to primarily use airborne forces and flying units in the Mediterranean theatre. The following day *Amerika* steamed through the tunnel out of Semmering back to the Chancery in Berlin, the same day Athens capitulated. By the beginning of the month Hitler was relaxing at the Berghof, his mountain retreat in Austria. He saw Crete as a sideshow, the forthcoming attack on Russia occupying all his nervous energy and his entire attention.[18]

Disappointments, however, began to mount up for Student. He was placed under command of the Austrian *Generaloberst* Alexander Löhr, who had been the pre-*Anschluss* commander of the Austrian air force. The dark-haired Löhr, slight in stature, sporting a wispy moustache and arched eyebrows, exuded uncompromising authority. His aircraft had raised Belgrade in April, killing 17,000 civilians. *General* Günther Korten his chief of staff, an ardent Nazi and friend of Göring, made no secret of the fact he considered Student's scheme a sideshow. Löhr was as ruthless as his subordinate *General* Wolfram Freiherr von Richthofen, the nephew of the World War I 'Red Baron'. Von Richthofen was the consummate professional and proven expert of army close air support and commanded *VIII Fliegerkorps*. His record at Guernica during the Spanish Civil War through Poland and the Low Countries to

France, Dunkirk and the Balkans demonstrated resolve rather than just 'terror bombing'. Nevertheless, he never expressed sympathy or concern for civilians who got in the way of a target. He had the piercing gaze of a predator, but never let his feelings affect performance.

Both these generals were sceptical about Student, who with his technical and administrative background had never benefitted from higher-level staff training like themselves. Unsurprisingly Löhr did not accede to Student's request to have the *VIII Korps* placed under his *XI Fliegerkorps* command. Joint planning in the limited time available did not get off the ground. Löhr had his headquarters in Vienna, von Richthofen in the Balkans. Naval planning for the sea leg got under way in Greece under *Admiral Süd-Ost* Schuster. Student, writing the airborne corps plan, incarcerated himself with his staff at Berlin Tempelhof. He did not consult with either of his two division commanders, Süssmann in Corinth or Ringel in the Balkans. Student was obsessively determined to present a fait accompli of advanced airborne planning to the others, to rationally persuade the advantage of his new ideas over traditional norms; that a strategic objective could be taken out by air alone. Each commander was planning in a vacuum.

Further disappointments followed. Student was routinely informed by telephone from Luftwaffe Chief of Staff Jeschonnek that his reinforced *Detachment Süssmann* had – unbeknown to him – conducted an airborne insertion at Corinth. This would alert the Allies to the fact that airborne troops were already in the Mediterranean theatre. Even more unsettling was the notification that his 22. *Luftlande Division*, the only Wehrmacht formation trained and equipped for air-land operations, was unavailable for Crete. It had been committed since March for the protection of the Romanian oilfields at Ploesti, forming part of the security for the Operation *Barbarossa* roll-out plan. It would be replaced by the 5. *Gebirgsjäger Division* under *Generalmajor* Ringel, whose soldiers had never flown before. It was a crack veteran division that had broken the Metaxas Line in Greece, and was already in situ north-west of Athens. It had only two infantry regiments, unlike the *22. Luftlande Division*'s three. This was a psychological blow; 40 per cent of the 22nd's officers and 28 per cent of the men had fallen alongside the *Fallschirmjäger* during the bloody fighting around the Haig in Holland. Both formations were bound by blood and experience.

Generalmajor Julius Ringel's *5. Gebirgsjäger Division* had broken tenacious Greek defence at the Rupel Pass, opening up the main German thrust into the Greek heartland. His soldiers were mostly Austrians and Bavarians and considered themselves the elite of the German infantry and rather resented the pretensions of the Luftwaffe paratroopers. There would be fratricide incidents between the two on the streets of Athens. Ringel was a professional soldier prior to the *Anschluss* and an old Austrian Nazi. Student found Ringel a difficult subordinate, a conventional infantry 'plodder', blind to any subtleties and intricacies the new mode of airborne warfare brought to the battlefield. Löhr, he suspected, secretly favoured his fellow Austrian, whose feet were practically planted on conventional infantry ground; they knew each other well, Ringel had been his pupil at the war academy in Vienna.

Athens was seemingly deserted when the Germans occupied the capital on 20 April. 'The first three days we did not leave the house', remembered 14-year-old Alki Zei, 'the city was paralyzed with shock'. A Volkswagen jeep followed by four Hanomag armoured half-tracks rolled up to the entrance of the Grande Bretagne hotel in Syntagma Square, the former British headquarters. In no time at all the exterior of the beautifully plush Victorian-style hotel assumed a Teutonic appearance, German eagles and a host of red swastika-embossed banners, the new German headquarters in Greece. Outside dense traffic, overloaded donkey carts and overcrowded tramcars once again forced their way through crowded streets, bells clanging, sides festooned with bunches of street urchins.[19]

On 3 May the bustle petered out to make way for the grand German victory parade, which passed the Acropolis and hotel. Ringel attended, a battalion of his *Gebirgsjäger* heading the march past, complete with mules. He recalled a beautiful day, 'summer green trees surrounding the plaza before the old palace bent slightly to the breeze'. The hotel was next to the former king's palace, where 'mixed architectural styles of Paris and Greece merge'. A momentous day, an encouragement to do some sightseeing. The epic scene was overlooked by the classic Parthenon, whose 'walls reflect the bright sunlight'. Behind Ringel's men marched Süssmann's paratroopers, rifles slung, flush with success from their victory at Corinth. Columns of panzers rumbled by the hotel and almost apologetically, at the rear came a battalion of Italians; an embarrassment to Germans and Greeks alike.

As the parade ended a figure emerged from the dispersing throng with an outstretched hand. It was Süssmann, whom Ringel remembered from the Norwegian campaign. He genially clasped his hand and shouted above the hubbub 'to good comradeship in our next undertaking!' Nonplussed Ringel declared he did not have a clue what he was talking about. 'Don't you know?' Süssmann asked, and responding to his blank expression explained 'why the Fifth Mountain Division has been selected for Operation *Merkur* [*Mercury*] – the conquest of Crete'. Chuckling good naturedly at a Ringel lost for words, he moved on. The marvels of ancient Greece and the buffet lunch hosted by *Generalfeldmarschall* List's *12 Armee* Headquarters were banished from Ringel's mind. His driver was abruptly summoned and he sped off to his new headquarters at Euboea in Chalcis to find out why his division had been uselessly ordered to be left 'hanging around'.[20]

John Drakopoulos, a Greek working for British Intelligence, had been planted as an employee in the Hotel Grande Bretagne. During the first week of May he watched as the Luftwaffe appeared to have taken over the entire second floor of the hotel. The ballroom, the centre for ceremonies, festivals and social gatherings, was converted into a carefully guarded war room and access restricted. He recognized Luftwaffe generals Löhr and von Richthofen from photographs, as also the continued presence of airborne division commander Süssmann. Corps staff officers and eventually Student were seen in place. It was obvious an airborne corps operation was pending. Drakopoulos was directed to find out where: Iraq, Malta or Crete? *Where* also remained a mystery to the *Gebirgsjäger* and *Fallschirmjäger* increasingly wandering the tourist sites of Athens, the Parthenon and the deep blue harbours.[21]

Student was hard at work with Trettner and his corps staff to develop a seamless airborne plan to present to Löhr and persuade von Richthofen to accept his scheme of action. Meanwhile his men were set in motion from the Reich to the south-east. Student slavishly focused on the plan rather than oversee his troops through their staging areas, sensing Löhr and von Richthofen would have difficulty with his purist airborne ideas. He was right. Both Luftwaffe generals had attended higher formation staff courses, unlike Student, whom they suspected was an unrealistic idealist. Hermann Götzel on Student's staff recalled *General* Korten – Löhr's chief of staff – greeting Student on arrival at his headquarters at Salonika to begin discussions:

'*Ach* Herr General', he said, 'your arrival is hardly necessary, we can even conquer Crete without you'. The problem with the command arrangement was that no landing attack supremo was designated. Differences soon developed between the *VIII* and *XI Korps* commanders. There was insufficient space for Student's 500 Ju 52 transport aircraft on crowded Greek airfields around Athens, already occupied by *VIII Korps* combat aircraft. This was despite the fact *Luftflotte 4* had already moved most of its airfield commanders and the majority of its signals troops and transport columns east for Operation *Barbarossa*, clearly labelled the priority by Hitler.[22]

Löhr and von Richthofen disagreed with Student's 'oil-spot' strategy of seven simultaneous air drops at Maleme, Chania, Rethymnon and Iraklion, covering the airfields, port and three other landing sites. Student proposed a single psychological shot-gun blast to paralyse the defence, followed up with an air-landed reinforcement. Löhr and von Richthofen saw no

Schwerpunkt or concentration of the main effort. Löhr proposed the island should be rolled up west to east, with the main blow to the west. Von Richthofen argued there were insufficient combat air resources to protect seven simultaneous landings. There was deadlock as debates continued until 16 May, as the Grande Bretagne became a throbbing beehive for *Mercury* planning. Student took quarters there, while Jeschonnek, Löhr, von Richthofen and mountain division commander Ringel came and went. Göring was eventually obliged to impose a compromise on deeply divided views. There would be four drops in two waves, morning and afternoon: Maleme and Suda first followed by Rethymnon and Iraklion. There was backing for Löhr's weightier blow in the west, while some of Student's spread was accepted. Von Richthofen's close air support was to be parcelled throughout the whole day. The solution was an echo of the lack of concentration that had permeated Luftwaffe failure the year before during the Battle of Britain. A *Schwerpunkt* could only be chosen on the second day, depending on whether an aerodrome had been captured at Maleme in the west or Iraklion to the east.

On 16 May *Generaloberst* Löhr chaired the final conference at the Grande Bretagne with the commanding generals and *Admiral Süd-Ost*, coordinating the air and sea reinforcement plan. Logistic difficulties meant the start date must be delayed until 20 May. All the troops had yet to arrive at the airheads around Athens, tactical commanders had yet to be briefed. Fuel supplies for the flight had yet to arrive, impeded by the collapsed bridge in the Corinth Canal, lorry-borne gliders were still being assembled, shortages of communications and transport were impeding preparations. Student was stumbling over these final fences to deliver his strategic aspiration, which was clearly a compromise result. Now he had to deliver.

Student had pored over maps and air photographs to evolve the plan he had briefed at Athens. List's *12 Armee* intelligence section assessed the garrison strength in Crete as one division with two infantry regiments, six battalions, an artillery regiment and remnants of the British and Greek forces, which had managed to be evacuated from Greece. He assumed the British defence would be concentrated along the island's north coast, facing the mainland, and was prepared for an airborne assault. His opinion was that there was likely an infantry battalion defending each of the aerodromes at Maleme and Iraklion, with probably a weaker force around the smaller airstrip at Rethymnon. He was out by a factor of at least 6:1.

Maps had been hastily reproduced from aerial photos; the Greek editions despite their large scale were imprecise and difficult to interpret. They did not project a clear impression of elevation or ground coverage. Most of the competent cartographers had already been relocated east, preparing for the Russian campaign. *Generalleutnant* Student's first sight of the Maleme aerodrome, which he viewed from the air, could be likened to three clay tennis courts, the brown-red runways enclosed within a private triangle. The virtually dry Tavronitis river bed and estuary showed as a clear scar to the west of the aerodrome, traversed by a two-span bridge reaching out to a cluster of houses on the west bank, beyond which was a pronounced bulge of high land. The photographs showed terraces and clearings with neat rows of dots which were likely olive tree groves. Greek maps showed spot height 107 labelled Kavkazia Hill overlooking the airstrip from the south. It had to be one of the primary defending battalion's positions. Maleme village was sited on its eastern slope. The dry river estuary suggested the perfect location for a forming-up point and start line to assault both the airstrip and hill.

Student felt this decisive area for the first blow of the morning should go to the *Sturmregiment*. It was the strongest elite force in the corps, commanded by *Generalmajor* Eugen Meindl, four battalions strong. It had been expanded to regiment size during his convalescence at the Hansa-Klinik, its core being the *Sturmabteilung Koch*, which had captured Fort Eben-Emael the previous year in Belgium. Koch now commanded its *I* (Glider) *Bataillon*. Even as a regiment, Meindl's unit was seen for special tasks directly under corps command. It would be one of the keys to open up the island of Crete from west to east. Student had total confidence that Meindl's crack troops would achieve the sudden *coup d'état* needed to eject the British battalion defending the airfield. A direct glider assault followed up by parachuted infantry supported by heavy dropped weapons should suffice to achieve the objective, and hold it. What he did not appreciate was that he was committing Meindl's 1,860-strong force against 5 New Zealand Brigade, entrenched with a defending force in the area of 11,859 men.[23]

SPOT HEIGHT 107 KAVKAZIA HILL

Early–mid-May, Maleme, Western Crete
Hill 107 rose 350 feet above Maleme aerodrome and completely dominated the length of the red clay runway, 'little more than a stretch of reclaimed beach', recalled airman Marcel Comeau with 33 Squadron RAF. The dusty fighter airstrip had barely been completed. Kavkazia Hill to Greeks was typical of numerous foothills running from the White Mountains, more gently here, at the northern coastline of the island. Hill 107 was the greater of two compacted clay-stony spurs descending to the east–west coast road, with the aerodrome sandwiched between the road and a sandy-pebble beach. Viewed from the metal girder bridge west of the airstrip that spanned the dry Tavronitis estuary, its heights were stepped by open terraces, planted with barley and young vines. 'A wonderful place', recalled New Zealand infantryman Sergeant Major J.S. Pender, with 22 Battalion, 'almost every inch cultivated with grapes, olive groves, orange groves and grain'. Leafy chunky black vine trunks here and there were snares that would trip a man in a hurry. They were planted along the terraced stone banks, interspersed with olive tree groves, some 16–18 feet high. The broken ground made it very difficult to find a spot where the whole of the 22 Battalion area might be observed. It also negated setting up seamless arcs of defensive fire, obvious to Pender's practised eye, as a machine-gun veteran of World War I. Nevertheless, 'to get on the high ground and see the various squares of different coloured

HILL 107

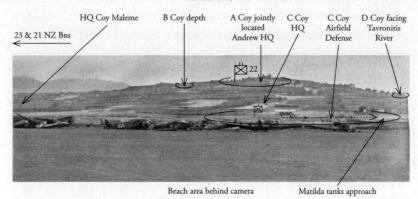

A German photograph taken after the landings shows the north side of Hill 107 taken from the beach showing the 22 NZ Battalion positions almost in their entirety. Note the open areas offering good fields of defensive fire.

cultivation was a wonderful sight'. The whole area was intersected with small ravines, 10–40 feet deep, fanning out from the bottom of the east side of the spurs to the coast.[24]

Cretan locals had been traditionally drawn to such rugged promontories. Kavkazia Hill had been a desirable spot in the past to watch out for Saracen pirates. New Zealand defenders were completely unaware of the Minoan Tholos tomb from the 13th or 14th century BC situated beneath battalion headquarters, which was found and looted at the turn of the 20th century. They were only vaguely aware of the island's turbulent history, which according to one British observer produced 'a burning nationalism, a free spirit and the determination to resist foreign occupation at any sacrifice'. Greeks, Romans, Arabs, Phoenicians and Byzantines were followed by Venetians and finally pitiless Turks. Used to lawless customs, previously directed at oppressors, 'every shepherd goes armed'. Cretans, the observer commented, 'are virtually weaned on powder and shot'.[25]

Maleme village was sited at the lower north-eastern slope of Hill 107, overlooking the sea, to the east of the runway. Its inhabitants were originally attracted by the fresh water stream exit. The name *Malama* meant gold, suggesting the Minoan tomb had been exceedingly rich or gold was locally mined. It was settled by shepherds that originated from Lakkoi, on the southern foothills. Three village churches were in the vicinity of the airstrip. The first, Agiou Antoniou, was built in 1840, and the most recent, a new church of the same name, was inaugurated in the village just three years before. One of the churches, St George, was demolished to make way for the airstrip, still finishing construction. Priests provided much of the leadership and direction within the fabric of Cretan agrarian community. Their buildings with richly appointed interiors offered a capricious form of comfort amid the poverty that remorselessly took the weakest in village society. They prayed daily for relief that was never readily given.

Village inhabitants tended to be crowded together within cheap and ugly flat-roofed houses with earth floors. Faded whitewashed walls faced outward to streets, which the New Zealanders found narrow, dirty and smelly, but ready fortresses. Rough-hewn beams and planks were beneath a layer of trodden earth-covered roofs. This was a hardy agrarian society where an individual's world revolved around family, their village and maybe, because of marriage, the village next door. For several months the villagers had suddenly been obliged to adapt to uncomfortable and unprecedented worldly pressures, tangibly manifested by the increasing numbers of foreign soldiers arriving on their doorstep. Many of the able-bodied men were marooned on the Greek mainland, with the Cretan V Division, composed of men native to Crete and originally seen as its natural home defence. The hamlet of Pirgos, often mistakenly called Maleme, marked the 22 Battalion's eastern boundary with 23. Just like Maleme, myriad streets and alleys ended up in the square housing the church. Dogs abounded, windows were rarely curtained and balconies were mostly empty, with the occasional rough-hewn table and chairs.

Although the British, New Zealand and Australian Dominion troops were island visitors, they had been invited to protect

its inhabitants, because of the enforced absence of the Cretan
V Division. As such they were welcome and afforded pseudo-guest
status. Taverna owners soon recognized the commercial value of
the soldier's insatiable appetite for egg and chips. Grateful Athens
felt that the British had generously compromised on their Libyan
campaign assets to aid the Greeks. Despite being wary of strangers,
Cretans were hospitable to a fault. Guests were offered the best
meal and perhaps the only bed in the house; the owner would go
hungry or sleep on the floor. Guests were also offered protection in
a society where the very wild nature of the terrain put clan feuds
and violence beyond the purview of the law. Unbeknown to the
New Zealanders defending Hill 107, any invader automatically
became the local's foe, who then considered themselves duty bound
to protect guests.

Soldiers simply saw men drinking coffee in the squares watching
their women do the work. War correspondent John Hetherington
remembered:

> The hardy Cretans took this friendly invasion without batting
> an eye. They went quietly on cultivating their vines, ploughing
> the red soil, herding their sheep and goats. They watched with
> unsurprised eyes warships coming and going, unloading troops
> from Greece, loading others and ferrying them across to Egypt.
> The Cretan is not easily moved.

Hetherington appreciated the violent past of the island: 'they have
all the stubbornness of the Greek and when they are roused all the
cruelty of the Turk'.[26]

After the tension and physical demands of closely fought
rearguard actions in Greece, beneath overwhelming German air
superiority, arrival on Crete was a blessed relief. 21 Battalion,
behind 22 Battalion forward on Hill 107, felt their locality was
where they were temporarily staying, rather than a long-term
prepared defensive area. Crete was regarded as a transit camp after
the evacuation from Greece, on the way to Egypt. 'Get everybody

off the mainland first', commented the official battalion account: 'Move on to Egypt, refit, then get our own back on the Italians and Germans now in the Western Desert. That was the program – everybody knew it – and in the meantime, shelter under the olive trees and reorganize.'

Even boot repairs were sent on to Egypt; Crete had no logistic autonomy. Invasion forecasts were from 'jittery prophets on the staff', wrong again as usual. It was all a trick, the soldiers assumed, to get them to dig weapon pits without picks and shovels, which the staff had made them leave behind in Greece. Private Johnston with 23 Battalion nearby felt well rested within two days of arrival on the island, basking in fine weather. 'All we do is eat oranges and swim', he recalled, 'having a marvellous time. God! I'm as fit as a fiddle – a real box of birds!' By the middle of May he wrote again in his diary 'this holiday we are having seems too darned good to last. These swims in the old Mediterranean are great'.[27]

Lieutenant Ed McAra, a New Zealand platoon commander, was dug in with A Company 22 Battalion virtually at the summit of Hill 107. Sitting back and enjoying the vista he wrote to his wife that they were 'holding a ridge from which one looks backwards to purple shadowed sea, blue green in the sun, with its thin line of white, tossing into view above the sandhills'. He could see all the way to Pirgos beyond, 'the little village next to HQ Company toy-like in the distance'. A glance behind him to the south revealed the White Mountains: 'hazily blue mountains, still snow-patched upon the left'. To his front was 'a confusion of semi-cultivated gullies and olive groves'. The hills where 21 and 23 Battalions were, sited in depth, were 'similarly patterned with vineyards, barley fields and bushy plantations'. He could also clearly see the 'shingly river bed' of the Tavronitis estuary with its metal girder bridge carrying the west–east coast road 'that gives one a queer yen for South Canterbury' back home. He painted a picturesque scene for his wife whose colours were 'mainly drab olive green, the richer yellow green of the vines against interlacing stone walls and the sun-blanched pink and white of half hidden villages'. This was the backcloth of the fight to come and he explained it was:

> a difficult type of country to hold against the type of attack we are expecting, and I did a lot of thoughtful prowling around believe me, before we finally decided where and how to site our posts.[28]

They had planned and prepared for war in a veritable Garden of Eden.

Chapter 2

Deployment and Plan

GENERALMAJOR EUGEN MEINDL, COMMANDER
STURMREGIMENT

Early–late May 1941, Balkans and Athens, Greece
Eugen Meindl was short, stocky and barrel-chested with craggy mountain-man features. He had been promoted to command the elite *Sturmregiment* barely four months before and, with the expansion of the airborne division to corps status, he was training it hard. He had formerly commanded a mountain artillery regiment in Poland in 1939 and jumped into Narvik as an artillery adviser, with no formal parachute training, during the 1940 Norwegian campaign. His exacting but humane standards made him a larger-than-life and popular figure among the men. He was a man of action, appropriate to this special unit, whose core had developed from the remarkable *coup de main* force that cracked open the Belgian fortress of Eben-Emael, the opening of the 1940 *Blitzkrieg* campaign across France.

His newly promoted adjutant, *Oberleutnant* Hans-Joachim von Seelen, remembered the regiment being alerted on 23 April, interrupting training on the Bergen exercise area, two days before Hitler confirmed the decision to invade Crete. Meindl was summoned to Berlin for a situation briefing and did not return until 26 April. Von Seelen was given the barest detail. The airborne *XI Fliegerkorps* was to deploy to north-west Romania by rail and then by truck to their respective airheads. All they were told was that they were heading south-east. Such a rapid deployment posed huge logistical problems for the corps and Meindl. They had just 93 trucks because 220 had already been removed to support the roll-out for Operation *Barbarossa*, the intended invasion of Russia. This was barely sufficient lift to get the men to the railway station. It was organized in relays and the trucks then loaded onto flat cars.[1]

Meindl's *I Bataillon* was earmarked for a glider attack role. Up to 100 DFS 230 assault gliders were loaded on trains for Skopje, assembled at airfields and then towed by air to their mounting airfields. *XI Fliegerkorps'* Ju 52 air transport squadrons were flown back to the Reich for servicing, to recover from the intense sortie rates they were subjected to during the Greek campaign. *Oberstleutnant* Conrad Seibt the corps' quartermaster overseeing the complexities of this assembly and move recalled some 80 to 90 trains were employed to transport the troops and their equipment from the Reich. Three thousand trucks had to be found to conduct the final leg of the 2,870-mile journey from Braunschweig to Athens. Fuel for the air transport lifts to Crete was insufficient and an urgent search was conducted to find suitable airfields around the Greek capital to mount the corps attack. Tropical uniforms were unavailable and troops would be reliant on captured British tents for accommodation at Piraeus. Radio and communications shortfalls were critical, much of it having already been dispatched eastward for *Barbarossa*. The blown bridge across the Corinth Canal was a headache, impeding the passage of the vital tanker transporting aircraft fuel for the Ju 52 lift. Seibt and his small staff were under enormous pressure to vaunt these logistic hurdles.[2]

Meanwhile, the soldiers were blissfully unaware of these problems and where they were going. Meindl's *Sturmregiment* was loaded aboard trains at Hildesheim during the evening of 27 April. Locomotives pulled out, hissing steam and belching clouds of smoke at 1.24am the next day. Von Seelen monitored progress as his regimental staff was loaded, and each of the four battalions with four trains apiece followed on over the next four days. The deployment codenamed *Flying Dutchman* was under way, transporting the entire corps from railheads in northern and central Germany towards the Balkans. *Jäger* Fritz Scheuering with *Fallschirmjäger Regiment 1* remembered his dawn departure:

> 'Where are we off to?' The question everyone was asking and nobody knew. 'Perhaps we are jumping into Iran!' offered one. 'I reckon the Suez Canal' said another. So it went on, back and forth, until it got boring, because it was only guesswork.[3]

Hauptmann Walter Gericke, commanding the *IV Bataillon* in Meindl's regiment, likewise had no clue about the ultimate destination: 'it could be the "fortress of Crete", Syria, Cyprus or even the Nile Delta', he surmised. A bull horn sounded along the platform to signal the battalion to board the train, and 'full of impatience the men climbed aboard the carriages'. Gericke's heavy weapons battalion had its transport loaded on flat rail cars while, behind the soldier wagons, the officers had the relative comfort of old French second-class coaches. 'How the emotions welled up inside us', recalled Erich Reinhardt with Scheuering's train, as they 'sang our paratroopers song for the last time'. As they steamed out of Tangermünde 'the atmosphere in the railway carriages was tense'. *Oberjäger* Bernd Bosshammer remembered 'we wore Luftwaffe uniforms without paratroop insignia, our jump suits were rolled up inside our rucksacks – it was all top secret'.[4]

Much of the impatience and tension was a consequence of inaction and hard training since Blitzkrieg the year before, peppered with false alerts. 'It had been a peculiar kind of war, this war of the winter of 1940–1', battalion commander Freiherr von der Heydte with *Fallschirmjäger Regiment 3* concluded. 'A war without fighting and, as it appeared to us, without sense.' Fighting had developed in Libya, Yugoslavia and Greece, all without them. Rumours were flowing, one of their regiment NCOs had heard from the division clerk 'that the Chief of Staff had been extremely busy during the past few days with a map of the Eastern Mediterranean'. Bernd Bosshammer had rigged 'more than 200 parachutes' for a forthcoming operation, 'on temporary tables in a sports hall'. This was at an air base at Stendal, ready equipped for Operation *Sea Lion*, the envisaged invasion of England, which 'was cancelled'. Like von der Heydte, Meindl was well aware 'this waiting for an unknown future was more unnerving than any combat, for both officers and men'.[5]

Von Seelen's *Sturmregiment* unit diary charted the detail and emotion of the long journey south-east through the Balkans. Prague was passed on the first night. Gericke, who had been one of Göring's original police cadet volunteers for the paratroopers, remembered the earliest practice air-land operation ever mounted, which had been at Freudenthal in the Czech Sudetenland. Ju 52 air transports had flown in support of the annexation of Czechoslovakia after the Munich crisis in 1938. Gericke's train paused next to a row of panzers on flat cars from Greece, going the opposite way. Good-natured banter erupted between the black uniformed panzer crews and the paratroopers. 'What do you want to do down there?' they taunted, 'we've already long settled it!' The fresh-faced von Seelen remembered how much the weather improved as the trains steadily travelled through Vienna and Budapest. 'In Hungary the population were very German friendly', he observed, and by the time they reached Romania 'the population greeted us with happy *Heil Hitlers*'. A PK (*Propaganda-Kompanie*) film crew was on board filming the succession of picturesque dawns and dusks as ever more exotic scenery flashed by. The trip developed into a form of military tourism for the newsreel cinemas back home. Soldiers hung out the windows, staring at the passing towns with their completely foreign architectural styles. Countless oil tankers rolled by coming from Romania, heading west for the Reich. At each railway halt Müller and Scheuering remembered 'traders came up to our carriage offering bacon, eggs and other goods'. When they pulled out young dark-haired kids ran alongside shrieking '*Germanski! Bitte* [please] – cigarette!'

The uncertainty about the end game was hard on men who had little else to do apart from sleep, smoke, read, write letters, listen to accordions, play *skat* card games or simply gaze out the window. On open-air flat cars kitchen crews serviced steaming *Gulaschkanone*, mobile cauldrons mounted on carts to prepare hot food for halts. Surrounded by men peeling and the stirrers, feeding ever more ham and vegetables into the kettles, cooks were periodically enveloped in smoke coming from the locomotives up front. 'We changed locomotives twice a day, and food was handed out', Bosshammer recalled. 'We rode south day and night passing through unknown villages.' Gericke noticed the further they clattered south-east 'there were no black-outs'. Peacetime lighting added yet another unreal exotic flavour to their unit odyssey: 'one did not have the impression that we were approaching the front', he remembered.

At various halts *Generalmajor* Meindl could be seen, smiling, cigar in hand, striding along the tracks next to the train, exchanging pleasantries with the men. Dressed in distinctive staff red-striped trousers tucked into high boots with a casual jumper, and accompanied by his adjutant von Seelen, he exuded quiet authority. He was at ease with his men, who had reached a high level of training in preparation for the invasion of England. Every man was an *Einzelkämpfer*, self-sufficient in combat, confident with combined arms harmonization, particularly Luftwaffe close air support. *Jäger* Fink was with the 'Iron Third' company of *Major* Walter Koch's I elite glider-borne battalion. They had burned at the prospect of an invasion of England: 'A sand model showed the battalion objective in every detail, every road, wood, stream, every house and every tree. Every squad knew its precise mission.'

But *Sea Lion* had been cancelled to huge disappointment. They were immensely proud of their DFS 230 assault gliders, 'sticking-plaster steamers' they called them. Priority was given to those skills that produced effective combat benefits, not slavish adherence to bureaucratic tactical army training manuals. Fink's comrades thought themselves 'special', and wore non-regulatory neck scarves to indicate this, not the distinctive four-fingered comet over blue regimental insignia on jump suits. Their legendary commander Koch had emphasized 'we are all equal before death'.[6]

Although Hitler's National Socialist regime sought unquestioning Wagnerian stereotypes in its armed forces, Student's *Fallschirmjäger* spawned unconventional rather than austere Prussian militarist virtues of hard work and obedience. Meindl's *Sturmregiment* took their adapted virtues one step further. 'In every one of us, there was a bit of *Schweinhund* [bad dog]', Fink admitted 'and it all depended on the individual, how much that inner characteristic manifested itself'. They thought themselves 'rebellious patriots', who assiduously served Germany, but used their heads to do so. As Fink expressed it, '*Fatherland und Volk* was not totally ahead of the rogue'. New Zealand troops awaiting them on Hill 107 were told by Churchill that 'the German Air Corps represented the flame of the Hitler Youth Movement, and was the ardent embodiment of the Teutonic spirit of revenge for the defeat of 1918'. The reality was subtler than that.[7]

Fink saw the regiment as soldiers 'with a new face'. Traditional Wehrmacht types uneasy at such rough-and-ready attitudes peddled rumours that Meindl's assault regiment was some kind of penal unit. 'Many of us, it was claimed had criminal records', commented *Jäger* Erich Reinhardt with *Fallschirmjäger Regiment 1*, 'and were serving the rest of our time'. While acknowledging the sentiment, 'I hoped my simple country soul would find some understanding with the paratroopers', he confided, 'which would certainly not have been possible in the old military system fostered in Hitler's Germany'. Communists and Socialists served with *Fallschirmjäger* units like exiles that had gravitated to the French Foreign Legion, to break with the past. With the expansion of the airborne from division to corps size, OKW had intelligently perceived the adventurous spirit that permeated paratrooper recruits. It stipulated *all* applications submitted were to be accepted, whatever the individual's background. Not until 1943 did the *Fallschirmjäger* finally bow to ideological demands to comb their units for Jews. The resulting mix of characters was diverse, with many of them intelligently more perceptive than their Wehrmacht counterparts. *Oberjäger* Martin Pöppel with *Fallschirmjäger Regiment 1* recalled canny veterans were 'always careful to commit some major or minor misdemeanour so they wouldn't get promoted'. These thinking men 'could really give their superiors a rough time'.

Hauptmann von der Heydte identified three 'types' in his battalion. Firstly, blatant idealists, *Hitlerjugend* nationalists, who could quite often break under the rigours of intense combat. Then there were the overly ambitious, a latent hazard to comradeship and morale, because their self-seeking could be dangerous. 'I liked the adventurers best', he admitted, 'you could go horse-stealing with them' and take them on any patrol: 'They were born parachutists. Many of them had committed some offence, only to become honest with us. Others had run away from home solely to prove themselves men.'

Whatever the type, they were rather like Meindl, less National Socialist than committed nationalist serving the regime. 'I liked them all', von der Heydte admitted: 'Whether good or bad, they had grown into my heart. I lived with them and for them.'[8] Many of the so-called men were still virtual boys, with an average age of not more than 18 years. They were to be pitted against older and just as resourceful but more embittered men on Hill 107.

Von Seelen wrote in his log that after crossing the Danube 'the population was poor, ragged and lazy; the men mostly lounged about while the women worked'. On 3 May the regiment unloaded at Rosiori de Verde in Romania and transferred to trucks, heading south into Bulgaria 'across very bad roads, with deep holes, subsidence, alternating between gravel and potholes'. 'We still did not know where we were going, but we no longer bothered our heads about it', recalled von der Heydte. The scenery was majestic as 'we enjoyed the journey through the alien, enchanting land'. As a battalion commander he was lucky, the troops were confined beneath canvas canopies in jolting lurching trucks. Whereas 'driving my car far ahead of the much slower moving battalion column, I felt myself rather on holiday than on a journey into battle'. The drive from the Carpathian Mountains was over 600 miles across primitive roads, negotiating tightly curved mountain passes from the southern edge of Thermopylae to the northern Peloponnese.

Feri Fink with the *I Bataillon Sturmregiment* had liked the train journey, relishing the all-round view he commanded from the observation cupola of a brake van at the rear. By contrast, 'the truck drive was an absolute drudge', he remembered, 'because of the need for security, the canvas flaps at the back were fastened, so only the last two men could peer out'. Evidence of recent fighting came to the fore once they crossed into Greece, and the weather deteriorated to cold rain. German helmets perched on wooden crosses indicated how many men were lost storming the 'famous Metaxas Line' – a veritable mountain 'Maginot Line' – the break-in battle by the *5. Gebirgsjäger Division* into Greece. It was reputedly 'the strongest fortress in the world' and overcome in days. Breached bunkers signposted the course of the fighting: 'The many signs of heavy fighting were still fresh and clear to see. Trenches blackened by flamethrowers, blown bunkers with craters in between.'

Truck convoys lurched along the eastern slopes of snow-capped Mount Olympus. Fritz Scheuering looked out and saw 'majestic Olympus, the peak covered in cloud, with shimmering snow fields'. Weather perceptibly improved the further south they drove, where corn stood taller in the fields. Drivers felt the strain, and complained 'this land contained only mountains, passes and narrow villages'. Bernd Bosshammer with *Fallschirmjäger Regiment 1* recalled:

> The roads were impossible, tracks were not level and the dust and dirt got worse. My job was to keep in touch with the lead vehicles, practically invisible because of the terrible dust. Flat tires and engine ignition breakdowns were frequent. We got down to help and push, then climbed back on board, it was terribly hot.

'A long and tiring road journey', he lamented, 'whose destination nobody knew'.

'Practically all the road bridges had been blown by the British Army during their withdrawal', von Seelen recalled, but 'they were made passable with Engineer emergency bridges'. Mountain passes were wet and rainy, 'vehicles lightly skidded' on negotiating tight curves. Burned-out vehicles littered the roadsides, 'evidence of the Greek and British retreats, where huge bomb craters demonstrated the precise handiwork of German combat aircraft'. German war graves bore testimony to resistance along the way. *Hauptmann* Gericke remembered the 'dead bloated horses raised an awful stench'. Then at last in the distance stood 'Salonika shining, and the blue sea', the city was hardly damaged. Soldiers were quick to appreciate, like Scheuering, that 'trade and haggling is in the Greek blood'. It was not quite what Martin Pöppel had envisaged: 'we'd all learned about blonde Heelenes in our childhood' but 'the people we see look completely different – small, black-haired, more concerned to haggle and bargain than to work. Only the little shoe-shine boys are lively, offering us their "extra top-class Stuka shine" to make us laugh.'[9]

Meindl's regiment reached Eleusis on 10 May, where von Seelen observed 'you could see the clear water of the Bay of Salamis'. By 4pm they had arrived at the Stuka airbase at Megara, where they occupied a tented camp. Fink remembered they were encamped in an olive grove next to the airfield, and were told to keep clear of the locals. Two days later *Generalmajor* Meindl was summoned to Athens for an orientation brief. *Hauptmann* Gericke had meanwhile turned off 'the wonderful asphalt road running along the coast' to Athens. The dusty track led him to the large olive grove housing the newly established HQ. He had observed farmers en route, sitting around village taverns. 'You couldn't believe that only a few days before, the fury of war reigned here. Overall were tremendous signs of life. Peace has already broken out again here.'

His *IV Bataillon* was co-located at Megara alongside Meindl's regimental headquarters. It was a pleasant bivouac site where out to sea they could see the island of Salamis. 'Captured big yellow British tents' were set up, far superior to buttoning together their normal camouflaged ground sheet capes. 'Smoking, sleeping and chatting', Gericke's men 'lay in the shade from the olive trees, which protected them from a merciless sun'. Grasshoppers chirped from the trees as an ass wandered slowly around in a circle, pumping water up from a well, 'so each day followed the other', Gericke recalled as they waited.

Passes were granted so soldiers could visit Athens and the Acropolis. Bernd Bosshammer, bivouacked further north at Topolia, recalled 'we had plenty of free time and very few restrictions – in the shade too':

> All our questions remained unanswered. Rumour number one: we were going to Malta. Rumour number two: by plane to Africa. But somebody asked if a Junkers 52 could get to Africa without a stopover ... This was the calm before the storm and it made us nervous.[10]

Meindl's adjutant von Seelen meanwhile coordinated the rest of the regiment's piecemeal arrival by truck to dirt airstrips at Megara, Eleusis, Tanagra around Athens and Mykene and Corinth. The last packets arrived on 14 May. The day before, Meindl received his warning order from Student, the reinforced *Sturmregiment* would form *Gruppe West* and von Seelen recorded he was 'to take the airfield at Maleme on the west side of Crete'. This would require the capture of Hill 107 overlooking the runway. *Gruppe Mitte* with the corps commander *Generalleutnant* Süssmann and *Fallschirmjäger Regiment 3* was to land in Prison Valley just to the north of Meindl at the same time, as part of the first wave. *Gruppe Ost* would jump in the afternoon, with *Fallschirmjäger Regiment 2* at Rethymnon and *Regiment 1* at Iraklion. Meindl now had sufficient direction to form a plan. His special forces regiment, based on the core that had achieved so much at the outset of the *Blitzkrieg* in Belgium and Holland the year before, was close to Student's heart. Meindl had received the choice mission, the break-in, which he quietly began to formulate. His troops still had no idea where they were going.

Gericke often observed the general, striding around the olive grove HQ area dressed in shorts and a plain white drill shirt, with no rank or unit insignia. Each morning he passed by carrying a collapsible stool and leather map case slung over his shoulder. Meindl was revered by his men, and this typically relaxed demeanour reassured them. He was also an accomplished artist with a particular affinity to animals and nature, more so than humans. But he often took the time to speak with his men. Gericke saw him showing his sketch pad to one of the soldiers, explaining 'that is the mountain over there, the colours are always the same in the early morning light, which I have always found pleasing'. He was, of course, at the same time developing his plan.[11]

He decided the youthful *Major* Walter Koch, a Knight's Cross holder and the hero of Eben-Emael, would be given the task of landing gliders on the west slope of Hill 107, to attack the RAF tented camp and flak positions visible from his air photos. His glider *coup de main* was to capture the airfield from the hill to its south, concurrent with an assault from the west. Koch, now aged 31, had been one of the first police officers to join the *Regiment Hermann Göring* and had participated in the first ever pioneering Luftwaffe jump course. He was a talented, sensitive and creative thinker. One of his Eben-Emael commanders, *Oberleutnant* Rudolf Witzig, remembered he tended to come up with imaginative schemes that others would have considered mad. Koch was a committed Nazi but no 'yes man'; he would take the time to study an order before embracing it. Meindl had full confidence in his ability to pull off a daring spearhead glider assault, and appreciated Koch shared his own view about the need to preserve soldier's lives. He was an aggressive dare-devil, a lover of sports cars and speed. Only Hermann Göring, he was alleged to have said, was entitled to drive faster than he on Germany's new autobahns. Koch was, however, somewhat uneasy that Student's plan called on him to give up two complete glider companies, *Genz* and *Altmann*, to attack two flak positions outside the Cretan capital of Chania. This meant a 50 per cent reduction of his attack force, but Meindl could assure him that two of the regiments' parachute battalions would be jumping virtually alongside.

Meindl's *II Bataillon* commanded by *Major* Eduard Stentzler, a parachute infantry battalion, was likewise obliged to detach a company to clear Kastelli further west, to aid the sea reinforcement. The bulk of his battalion was to support a push along the coast road east to Chania. Stentzler was built like a jockey, and indeed had been the winner of 13 riding and steeplechase competitions. His earlier service had been cavalry, then reconnaissance flying duties.

Somewhat eccentric, he had a long service record, but none of it in combat, and stood out among the men with his penchant to wear long slim cavalry riding boots. He had only been in command since the previous November and was unproven.

Major Otto Scherber's *III Bataillon*, also parachute infantry, was earmarked to drop east of the Maleme aerodrome and attack it from that direction, while blocking the main road leading west from Chania to seal off Hill 107 from any reinforcement. He had been in command just four months longer than Stentzler and was also untested.

Hauptmann Walter Gericke commanded Meindl's heavy support weapons *IV Bataillon*. Like Koch, he had been one of the pioneering police group officers to volunteer for the paratroopers. He was also a legend among the men, for seizing the nearly 2-mile-long Vordingborg Bridge connecting Zeeland to Falster in Denmark in 1940. This had been a daring parachute drop, followed by a spirited dash across the bridge on bicycles. He had fought with distinction in Holland as well as Norway and was clearly a thinker, having already written a book about Germany's fledgling airborne warfare. Meindl had Gericke co-located with his headquarters, valuing his veteran advice and proven competence as a combat leader. He needed to ensure his vital heavy support weapons arrived in the right place at the right time. It was planned for Meindl and Gericke to jump together, immediately west of the dried-up River Tavronitis estuary bridge. His men were to secure the lodgement against any threats from the south, provide supporting fire to Koch's seizure of the aerodrome and Hill 107, and maintain a reserve.

The plan was simple, aggressive and straightforward and nobody questioned the scheme of action. Intelligence was light, as had been the case in Norway and Holland, but Student's high-calibre troops had always pulled it off. Student had pushed his Henschel bi-plane reconnaissance sections hard to produce the information he still felt was lacking. All three of his experienced *Staffel* recce commanders were shot down at low level over the island, seeking the intelligence he craved. Despite good air photos only aspects of the aerodrome defences stood out. Expert *12 Armee* analysis suggested there was only light British security, maybe division strength, garrisoning the island. This meant about six battalions and an artillery regiment holding a land mass 152 miles long by between 35 and seven and a half miles wide. It was anticipated they would be thinly spread, primarily defending the north coast.

Based on identified ship traffic, the Luftwaffe suspected that remnants from the British Greek Expeditionary Force might have been evacuated to the island. The Greeks had already surrendered on the mainland and the population on the island was allegedly pro-German. Indeed, some commented the British may have already evacuated. A number of British fighters had been detected at Maleme airfield, likely wrecks now. All that could be seen was a few flak positions and tented camps on the slopes of Hill 107, and a few light locally constructed bunkers around the airfield itself. Meindl calculated his reinforced four-battalion elite force was facing a British infantry battalion with meagre assets. The British were undoubtedly anticipating an air and sea invasion, so the only achievable surprise was tactical. He felt confident.

Two options were considered: an aggressive airborne assault directly onto the identified positions or an off-set landing, form up in a secure location and mount a deliberate attack. Meindl opted to smother the defences by landing on top of them, using his two most experienced commanders. Koch's glider men would storm the aerodrome and Hill 107, supported by Gericke's IV heavy weapons battalion dropping in tandem to the west of the Tavronitis River. Stentzler's *II Bataillon* would land further west and form up an attack reserve, while Scherber's *III Bataillon* would parachute behind the east side of Hill 107, block it off from Chania and attack from there.

Von Seelen recalled Meindl briefing his battalion commanders on 16 May after the final corps conference at the Hotel Grande Bretagne. He characteristically had his officers seated around a table set up outside his tent. They were dressed in formal uniform and caps, while Meindl took them through the plan dressed in his white drill shirt and shorts. A PK cameraman captured the seemingly relaxed scene, maps and air photographs piled haphazardly across the table, corners curling up with the heat from the bright sun. Meindl indicated points of interest on the air photographs with his pencil, while hand motions and outstretched fingers indicated the direction of attacks. He ordered careful map studies. 'The names of the neighbouring units must be drilled into every man', he insisted, 'so that it must be as though the man was jumping into his own home district'. Meindl was bluff and precise about what they must do, heights were to be swiftly occupied, telephone lines on roads and paths cut – but so they may be repaired again. 'If the population offers resistance, ruthless measures are to be taken, otherwise spare them', he pointed out. There was to be no looting, and all 'transport means were to be immediately requisitioned'. Sub-unit commanders were reminded to lead men as individuals and live humans, not assets. His leadership style was hands-on practical and not textbook. He preferred to communicate orally – brief and talk – rather than issue copious written orders. He even pointed to the orientation value of the RAF aerial masts at the wireless station south of Chania, emphasizing that 'every man must know that point'.

The plan was simple, clear and comprehensive. Officers then briefed NCOs and soldiers beneath the shaded olive groves, using the same tables, piled with maps and air photos. *Jäger* Feri Fink with Koch's battalion recalled that it was 'only beneath the shade of trees before every tent, handing out air photos and sketches, when we realized it was Crete!' Von Seelen observed there was a shortage of maps, which arrived just in time the following day. 'We carefully studied the aids', Fink remembered: 'Topographically they were very precise, the air photos sharp. However, we could only pick out the airfield itself and identify two tented areas with certainty. Other military installations could only be guessed at.'

He was slightly dubious, 'only a half-way certain enemy picture'. Von Seelen commented in the unit regimental diary that 'the mood of all the soldiers was very good and enthusiastic'. They could not fail.[12]

70

LIEUTENANT COLONEL LESLIE ANDREW, COMMANDER
22 NEW ZEALAND BATTALION

Early–late May, Hill 107, Maleme, Crete
Leslie Andrew, commanding the defence of Hill 107 and the
aerodrome it overlooked at Maleme, was a Victoria Cross holder,
and looked the part. Lieutenant Geoffrey Cox on Freyberg's staff
described him as a 'thick-set, reserved man of forty-one, [actually
44] whose deep-set eyes, greying hair brushed straight back and a
black moustache gave him a fine soldierly bearing.'[13]

His men were in awe of him. 'My name is Andrew: A-N-D-R-
E-W', he announced on parade, on meeting the freshly recruited
22 New Zealand Infantry Battalion for the first time. 'There is
no *s* and I'm the boss', he reminded them. Officers, pale in the
face and obviously shaken, were often seen emerging from the
colonel's midday conferences. The tall lean Andrew made certain
his battalion drilled and route-marched like no other unit in the
newly established 2 New Zealand Division. He was a merciless
disciplinarian, maybe too strict, earning the epithet 'February'
due to his inclination to award 28 days' detention to any rules
transgressors. His dogged determination had welded his battalion
into an effective unit, one that more than held its own against the
first German forays to force the Olympus pass holding position on
the Greek mainland, the month before. His men had emerged in
iron-hard condition, prior to deployment, after training in New
Zealand and England.[14]

Brigadier Hargest had set the tricky task of holding Hill 107 and
the Maleme aerodrome to 22 Battalion, following the maxim you
pick the best man for the hardest job. Andrew had won his VC as
a corporal in World War I, wiping out three German machine-
gun posts at Passchendaele. He was not commissioned until
March 1918. Respectful deference was often accorded Victoria
Cross holders, which does not necessarily accord with leadership
capabilities. After the war Andrew gained a commission in the
New Zealand Staff Corps, probably in recognition of his bravery,
and became a professional regular soldier. The appointments that

followed were mainly administrative, and by the time the next war broke out he was a major, then promoted to lieutenant colonel to command 22 Battalion. He had not seen active service beyond platoon commander.

Playing a role in the inception of the newly formed New Zealand Division gave Andrew an acute awareness that if Greece had gone differently, his Dominion country would have lost more men proportionately than any of the other Empire contingents. Politics would always play a role in the commitment of Dominion troops. The same concern applied to Crete. The singular New Zealand experience thus far in the war, on the Greek mainland, was about retreat, hold, and again retreat. Withdrawal to fight another day might become habit forming and was reflected in low morale on arrival in Crete. The first sight of their apparent safe haven was the beached and still smouldering cruiser *York*, crippled by Italian frogmen and finished off by the Luftwaffe. They came ashore at Suda Bay amid palls of smoke from stricken tankers with sunken masts poking out of oil-polluted water. Looking about, Andrew would feel if it all went wrong his battalion would need an exit route. Fighting another day in what was certainly going to be a long-term conflict would enable them to be better equipped and supported, like the Germans. Unlike Leonidas's 300 Spartans facing the Persian hordes at Thermopylae on the Greek mainland, Freyberg had presciently opted to disengage and husband his national force.

Andrew, standing on the summit of Hill 107, considered where to site his companies, and quickly appreciated they would be spread exceedingly thin. Maleme aerodrome was little more than a wide landing strip, abutting a sandy beach, where the largely dried-up Tavronitis estuary dispersed to meet the turquoise-blue Mediterranean. Directly offshore was the island of Theodorou, shaped like a reclining lion, gazing sphinx-like out to sea, the direction of threat. Andrew had insufficient men and heavy weapons to effectively secure an over-large area of responsibility. Below him was the RAF camp, brown tents beneath pines lining the dirt coastal road, housing some 230 or so mainly ground personnel. This part of the northern Crete coastline was criss-crossed by young vineyards interspersed with cleared spaces of withered rye and barley, enclosed by stone walls or hedges of fearsome cacti. Dense thickets of bamboo and luxurious growths of vegetation were everywhere, flowering among the boulders and jutting outgrowths of rock. These hid much of the airfield from the road. Hill 107 had a high and low plateau, which could only be scaled by clambering over loose shale gullies, easily covered entry points to the summit. Terraces along the hill sides provided excellent stepped fields of fire below. Andrew set up his command post in a hollow on the lower plateau, set back from the crest. The problem was the hill configuration and intervening vegetation made it virtually impossible to find a spot to view the entire battalion area. He had to make do with observing parts of the runway, and bits of the bridge crossing the dry Tavronitis and further west beyond.

The topography made him feel isolated. His nearest support was almost two miles back, across the intervening Sfakoriako gulley, even now being wired as an obstacle by 23 and 21 Battalions. These two were sited in depth, connecting the villages of Kondomari and Dhaskaliana, down to the coast beyond Pirgos. The flat-roofed houses enclosed narrow twisting undulating dirt roads, lined by poplars, which led down to the sea. Isolation was further accentuated by the broken nature of the ground above the coast road. It was difficult and tortuous going for infantry and would increase the time taken to conduct counter-attacks at crisis moments, likely under enemy air attack. Likewise, Andrew realized, the going for attackers would be equally tough. None of the supporting battalions had sole responsibility to respond to the threat, should Andrew's position give way. Maleme and Kondomari villages were unfortunately hidden by folds in the ground, when viewed from many points at the summit of Hill 107. The brigade reserve, 28 (Maori) Battalion, was five miles away, sited in a beach defence configuration. Hargest's defence plan issued on 18 May called for 'spirited defence', but there was little detail on the how, and most of his troops faced the sea.

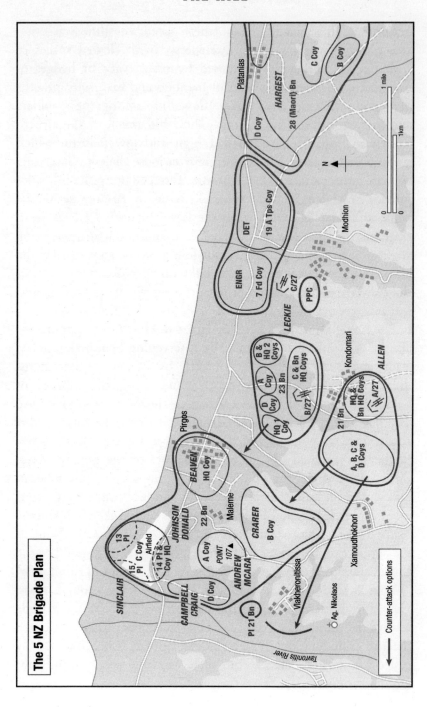

The 5 NZ Brigade Plan

Andrew felt the ten 40mm Bofors providing airfield defence were needlessly exposed. There were two 4in coastal guns on the lower slopes, but they too pointed out to sea; two 3in AA guns were mounted near the hill's peak. The guns, crewed by Royal Marines, were not under his command, but directed from a naval gun operations room in Chania, ten miles away. Andrew complained directly to Brigadier Puttick the division commander, during his reconnaissance on 1 May, about this lack of unified command. He had some 14 navy, air force and ground units involved in the defence of Maleme, nearly all of whom had different passwords. Looking down from the summit, the Bofors looked terribly prominent in their barely knee-high sandbagged positions, broadly marking the outline of the airfield perimeter. He passed a note to Brigadier Hargest, insisting 'unless they are dug in and screened by bushes etc., I'm afraid they won't last long'.[15]

Looking west, the dusty coastal road continued past the airstrip, and curved around the southern edge of the RAF camp, past the

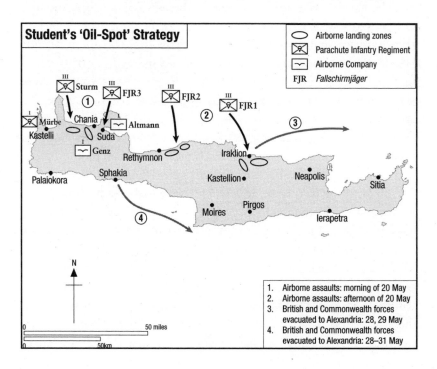

75

hill side and onto the 130-yard long iron-girder bridge mounted on concrete piles that straddled the stony Tavronitis river bed. Further west Andrew could discern low hills covered in olive groves and the village of Ropaniana. This open ground had no defence force, the nearest unit being 1 Greek Regiment at Kastelli, 12 miles away, adding to his sense of detachment.

He had no contact with them. The ground in that direction gradually rose until it merged more abruptly into the craggy heights of the long brown peninsula that stretched northward to Cape Spathia, an obvious pointer for Luftwaffe aircraft seeking Maleme.

Andrew's command inexperience showed in his inability to identify the main point of the defence effort. He was unable to solve the conundrum of which ground to put his boots on, in the absence of heavy weapons able to cover the same. He opted for two companies, 350 men from A and B, to hold the upper and lower plateaus of Hill 107. C Company with 150 men was tasked to defend the airstrip with a platoon facing west, another on the coast and the third at the southern edge of the airstrip opposite the hill. D Company with its 170 men was sited at the western foot of Hill 107, hard up against the river bed and covering the girder bridge. Headquarters Company with 80 men re-roled as infantry secured the village of Pirgos, just east of the airstrip. Significantly, there was no reserve. Andrew was totally dependent upon an aggressive response from 23 and 21 Battalions sited in depth to provide this, from the next ridgeline promontory, two miles to the east. Support therefore depended on Brigadier Hargest's reading of the battle, and he was five miles back in the village of Platanias, with only a Cretan landline telephone and an 'untrustworthy radio link'.

Andrew's overstretched defence configuration was shaped like a paw print, and was especially thin in terms of airfield defence. Only 150 of about 640 troops were actually holding on the aerodrome. With only one platoon of 30 to 40 men on the western perimeter, on an escarpment overlooking the dry river bed, it would be unlikely to absorb or dissipate the first German onrush. Once inside the perimeter, there was little cover or room to assemble or indeed manoeuvre for a counter-attack across the flat coverless runways. RAF aircraftsman

Marcel Comeau thought the airfield defences were meagre: 'The Bofors were badly sited – most of them, standing on flat patches of sand, could not have been more vulnerable to air attack.'

Crews were 'inadequately protected' and he remembered 'some men had rifles, and there were a few Italian carbines and revolvers about'. The New Zealand infantry were well camouflaged, and nowhere to be seen.[16]

During the evening of 14 May, two 11-ton Matilda Mark II infantry tanks laboriously squeaked and crawled into the 22 Battalion defence perimeter, growling and belching diesel exhaust. Having disembarked between air raids at Suda Bay, they had taken almost two days to complete the journey. Their prodigious weight resulted in numerous detours, as far as the beach in one case, because most bridges were unable to support their weight. One of the gear boxes for one of the battered tanks, which had been hastily withdrawn from Egypt, could hardly engage. They were backed into two depressions about 200–300 yards apart, directly opposite the airstrip, at the base of Hill 107. Andrew met Sergeants Gosnold and Marshall in charge of them and instructed them to remain hidden and not use their two-pounder guns, or Vickers and Bren machine guns unless German transport planes landed on the airstrip. Comeau observed 'both had seen long service in the western desert and were minus a few parts, but nevertheless, their arrival was encouraging'. The Germans had no weapons able to penetrate these monoliths.

This was Andrew's sole reserve. The only other heavy weapons available to him were two platoons of Vickers machine guns from 27 New Zealand MG Battalion, and some had no tripods. Just two 3in mortars had been salvaged from Greece, and like the Vickers were short of ammunition. Artillery support was sparse: 27 New Zealand Battery had two English 3.7in howitzers, sited in 21 Battalion's area, three Italian 75mm guns with 23 Battalion and four French guns in the area held by the engineer troops, roled as infantry, holding on the coast road north of Modhion village. Most of the guns lacked fire direction instruments and had to fire over open sights, others improvised markers with wood and chewing gum.

The experience of total air inferiority on the Greek mainland convinced Andrew to be exacting about camouflage from aerial observation. On 7 May, he even persuaded one of the pilots to fly him over his own positions, to spot shortfalls. On return he exhorted his men to even greater efforts. He ordered the digging of deep narrow slit trenches, constructed at right angles to olive tree trunks. The broad canopy of leaves obscured air observation, while at ground level the gnarled and twisted olive trunks left open good fields of fire. Fighting on mainland Greece had demonstrated that trenches dug among the roots gave protection against virtually anything short of a direct hit from a bomb. Platoon commander 'Sandy' Thomas with 23 Battalion behind Andrew, across an intervening gulley, remembered strict restrictions on smoke and movement:

> We were terribly careful, we even wouldn't drop an orange peel or anything at all. We really kept ourselves hidden. Apart from rehearsing, which we always did at times for the counter-attack role. We stayed really hidden to get surprise.[17]

What was coming would be no surprise, but its intensity would take them aback. Frank Twigg with Andrew's intelligence section recalled:

> One day in my rounds at Maleme a group who had a radio informed my section that [Lord] Haw-Haw [broadcasting from Germany] had warned the New Zealanders that the Luftwaffe had a bullet for every leaf and a bomb for every olive tree in Crete.[18]

This seemed much the case to local Cretan civilians. Housewife Mrs Vourexaki-Nikoldaki recalled 'the sky was pitch black' with aircraft over Chania, which had been virtually the case since 13 May. 'You couldn't see anything anymore, just those monstrous things which terrified you.' Aerial bombing of agrarian communities who had rarely seen an aircraft before the war, was incomprehensibly awful. Initially caught by surprise, they had not taken shelter, because none had been dug or prepared. 'You could hear the animals, the dogs and pigeons moaning and screeching with fear', she recalled. It was like a science-fiction alien invasion. 'Even the animals could sense the danger that awaited us.' Eighteen-year old Antonios Markos Kounalakis saw German aircraft bombing: 'everything that was moving; they were coming so low that I remember the olive trees shaking back and forth'. George Psychoundakis recalled aircraft 'came and went like bees in a bee garden', building to a crescendo by 19 May. Nothing appeared to escape their attention, 'it made us grind our teeth to see them hammering away at all the roads and, indeed, wherever they saw so much as a farm animal. "Aaaa! You cuckolds" we cried.' Helpless under bombing, the population simply did not know how to react. Fear was all pervasive. Ten-year-old Electra Petrakogiorgi Gerogianni remembered 'the whole area was literally shaking'. Maleme village on the lower slopes of Hill 107 was regularly bombed and strafed. 'It made people panic', Electra recalled, 'and when we children saw the adults panicking, that fear was transmitted to us as well'. 'Women were screaming', 21-year-old Ageliki Veisaki remembered, 'they were crying so we gathered our children together as quickly as we could and we fled to the mountains, to the caves'. The Maleme community, about 200 strong, fled mostly to shelter with relatives inland, or hastily improvised shelters in foothills to the south.[19]

Lieutenant Colonel Andrew hardly noticed the mini-diaspora. His men were receiving the brunt of the punishing strafing and bombing, while all the time the tension of an imminent invasion was ramping up. He was told by HQ 5 Brigade on the 16th to expect an invasion any day between 17 and 19 May. An airborne attack of some 25,000 to 35,000 troops was likely, supported by seaborne landings with a further 10,000. Air attacks meanwhile increased in frequency and severity.[20]

Ian Rutter, a loader on one of the 40mm Bofor guns positioned so vulnerably around the Maleme aerodrome, recalled these relentless attacks:

First of all you get this red alert, to warn you of any impending attack. Then out on the horizon, you'd see this little dark cloud, and then the noise followed until they were on you. They would

split, there might be 60 or 90 planes, split into three groups –
two would come around behind out of the sun, and the third
would come straight at you.[21]

Aircraftsman Marcel Comeau with 33 Squadron thought the
Messerschmitt fighter attacks the most lethal. 'Cascading empty shells
behind them they climbed out to sea, turned and dropped out of the
sky one after the other, diving headlong for the Bofor guns.' They
deliberately sought to take on and neutralize the airfield's anti-air
defences. 'With a sound as though the sky was being ripped across
like calico, they flattened out', he recalled, 'flashing across the sandy
ground'. Each day there were more casualties among the gun crews,
including sudden surprise attacks, even after sunset. Ian Rutter recalled
a solitary fighter strafing the drome from end to end, with 'the pilot
sitting up in the cockpit, all lit up, like he was driving a car'.[22]

Andrew's New Zealanders likely suspected a seaborne invasion
would be the more challenging threat to their position. They could
more easily identify with the concept. Months had been spent in
England preparing to repel a similar threat from across the Channel,
for which they had laboriously rehearsed counter-attack options.
Viewing the broken craggy ground surrounding Hill 107 did not
suggest the likelihood of any parachute assault. Patchy vegetation
was profuse and there were no obviously suitable landing sites
other than the airstrip itself. Hitler had not attempted an airborne
assault over inviting drop zones in south-east England during
the invasion scare of 1940, and crossing the Aegean would be far
more challenging than the English Channel. Lieutenant Geoffrey
Cox remembered seeing pictures in the American *Life* magazine
of German paratroopers relaxing and smoking after the successful
capture of the Belgian fort at Eben-Emael: 'Under the cowls of their
steel helmets they stared at the camera, hard, relentless, ruthless. I
had asked myself how I would fare if I found myself face to face
with such men in a bayonet fight.'

Andrew's men were early enlisters, with many territorials, who
would fight better among those with whom they had lived and
worked. They signed on for reasons as varied as their backgrounds,

but common to all was that they volunteered of their own free will. Many were hard-bitten tough men, harsh rural and urban children, shaped by the rigours of the Great Depression. They were men whose faces had been prematurely lined by years of arduous physical work on farms, forests and waterfront. To qualify for unemployment relief, they had to labour at road building or similar public works. Some had lived their lives on the edge, 'One Jumpers' Cox called them, men who arrived at the recruiting offices just one jump ahead of the police, or the 'wife dodgers'. 'One man in my platoon I had seen twelve years earlier, when he stood in the dock in the Criminal court in Dunedin charged with the murder of a Chinese prospector in the Central Ortego goldfields.' The man was found guilty of manslaughter, and there he was, 'tall and gaunt', standing as the right flank marker in his platoon.

Others had already fought in the Spanish Civil War, worldly men who appreciated Republicans and Fascists from both sides could be brave and capable. Andrew's battalion had all types, fresh-faced boys mixed with seasoned peacetime territorials. They had joined up with a mix of patriotic responsibility tinged with an enthusiastic desire for adventure and travel. Military service in a world war offered a form of military tourism for many who had never left their home province or even ventured beyond either their North or South Island. Cox described them as 'tough' and 'self-reliant' with a wry sardonic sense of humour.

His own experience before Crete had been with 23 Battalion, now in support of Andrew, 'made up of men from the west coast of the South Island, many of them coal miners and bush workers':

> Studying their weather-hardened, lined, alert faces, under steel helmets, I realized suddenly that they were every bit as tough as these German parachutists, and a great deal more astute and self-reliant, and I felt a surge of confidence that we would, after all, win this war.[23]

Given the right support, Andrew was confident his battalion could more than hold its own against the storm about to break.

Chapter 3

Eve of Battle

GENERALMAJOR JULIUS RINGEL, COMMANDER
5. GEBIRGSJÄGER DIVISION

18–19 May 1941, Athens, Greece
Julius Ringel was the hardy flamboyant Austrian mountain soldier commanding the *5. Gebirgsjäger Division*. He had his doubts on the eve of the invasion. 'We know as good as nothing about the enemy situation', he complained, 'other than rumours, that we could have made up ourselves'. 'Papa' Ringel was a World War I veteran, liked and respected by his troops, recruited from the same resilient Austrian and Bavarian mountain stock. An ardent Nazi during the pre-Austrian *Anschluss* days, he had commanded a regiment in France in 1940. Easily distinguishable by his Austrian fashion full beard and moustache, he was old-school infantry, with feet planted tactically firmly on the ground. He had little time for his Luftwaffe superior Student, whom he regarded as a 'dreamer', obsessed with an unrealistic airborne philosophy, based more on risk and daring than traditional infantry phlegm. Ringel was a dogged mountain soldier, reliant on endurance and the oft-repeated slogan 'sweat saves blood'. Mountain warfare was about spending time and physical effort securing the high ground that would dominate the opposition occupying valleys and gradients below. Earmarked to provide the air-land component for Operation *Mercury*, Ringel's

well-trained veteran soldiers had never flown before, or even seen a stretch of water larger than an alpine lake.

There was understated antipathy between dare-devil paratroopers and their heavier more mature mountain infantry counterparts. Both regarded themselves an elite. Ringel's division had broken the crust of the seemingly impregnable Metaxas Line on the Bulgarian-Greek border, that opened the way for List's German *12 Armee* thrust across the Peloponnese to Athens. Unlike the paratroopers, whom they nicknamed *Saupreussen* (Prussian pigs), the mountain men had fought and marched their way 1,000 miles across much of the Balkan plateau through snow, rain, mud and dust. The airborne had arrived in Athens by train and truck. Cautious and methodical *Gebirgsjäger* tactics, ingrained by mountain warfare, were at odds with the mobile shock-tactics the *Fallschirmjäger* aspired to. Ringel and Student had complete faith in their soldiers' ability to achieve the virtually impossible. 'I know my soldiers could haul the devil out of hell if I ordered it', Ringel insisted. He was to prove a capable yet difficult subordinate.

Ringel set up his headquarters on the top floor of a multistorey building in the Ommonia Square in Athens, a walk or short drive from Student's HQ at the Hotel Grande Bretagne. He began to work the plan – observing his soldiers from the window strolling streets below as tourists – for sea landings and the main air-land operation envisaged at Iraklion, in the *Gruppe Ost* area. 'My attention for the moment lay with the *Leichten Schiffsstaffeln* [light sea transport echelon]', two convoys carrying his *III Bataillon Regiment 100* and the *II Bataillon* from *Regiment 85*. Hitler had insisted the operation could not balance on one airborne leg in isolation in Crete. So on 18 May, Mother's Day in Germany, the mountain troops assigned to the light flotillas made their discreet way through the darkened streets of Piraeus and Chalkis to the docks. Greek crews eyeing them on swaying wooden caique cutters and fishing vessels and the occasional tramp steamer were told this was a transfer to Salonika. They were having none of that, civilian seamen lounging around the harbour retorting in broken German *'Nicht Saloniki – Kriti!'*[1]

One of the convoys was earmarked to land at Maleme, to reinforce the capture of the aerodrome and Hill 107. Boats for the most part were 100-ton twin-mast motor yachts, with wooden hulls, built for coasting or fishing. *Fallschirmjäger* flak and anti-tank guns and all the other heavy weapons that could not be air-dropped or transported by air were loaded aboard. The Maleme contingent were effectively an assault group, but precisely where and how they might be landed across open beaches was problematic. *Konteradmiral Süd-Ost* Karl-Georg Schuster in charge of the sea move had postponed departure until the evening of 19 May, the day before the drop, because of the uncertainty of the whereabouts of the Royal Navy. They were rumoured to be around Melos and the waters of northern Crete, which they needed to cross. The ships in the fleet were too small, mainly unseaworthy vessels that had survived the Luftwaffe's onslaught on the harbour and surrounds of Piraeus before the occupation of Athens. Attempts to mount flak guns made the caiques especially ungainly; almost to a man, the alpine soldiers could not swim.

One medical corporal with the *II Bataillon* of the Krakau Regiment remembered his company commander insisted they 'had to become used to water', which resulted in 'hastily set up water exercises'. They must at least be able to tread water. 'Next we tried to learn how to doggy-paddle, whereby we were drinking sea water as if it was the finest wine'. Empty jerry-cans were tied together as floats, 'which we regarded as especially untrustworthy'. Black humour came to the fore on learning they would disembark, 'sink or swim' with full kit and weapons; this meant doggy-paddle until they reached the water's edge. 'We proudly called ourselves *mountain sailors*.'

Shepherded by two Italian destroyers *Lupo* and *Sagittario*, the Maleme flotilla chugged placidly out to sea, two columns abreast at dusk, each craft lit by a plaintive stern light. Troop lifts per boat varied from 66 to 124, in all 2,331 mainly alpine or heavy weapons *Fallschirmjäger* crews on board, disappearing into the darkness on 19 May, invasion's eve.[2]

'This nonsensical voyage with the "light ship flotilla" caused me more concern', Ringel admitted, 'than the imminent flight of the rest of my units to the island'. He was very apprehensive; intelligence on the island's defences was disturbingly sparse. 'If any officer or man could offer an opinion', Ringel recalled, 'he would rather ten times fly than go over water'. There was no precedent for such an operation from the air, 'it had never been attempted before and there was no experience to support it'. It was a far cry from the 'panther-spring' the glider men and paratroopers had conducted against Fort Eben-Emael in Belgium. Without doubt the paratroopers 'were elite troops in the first range' but the British would not be surprised to receive them on Crete. Moreover, they could not be expected to be rapidly relieved by ground troops like in Holland and Belgium. 'Whatever pressure and help was required to conquer the island must come from the air'. There was enormous respect for the lethal capability of the Royal Navy, who would lie in wait like crocodiles as they crossed the Aegean lagoon. He reflected on:

> Hitler's reluctance against everything that had to go over sea, and be played out from the air. The previous year he had given up the attack against England, even though the comparison of an invasion over the Channel against crossing the Mediterranean, is that of crossing a water ditch.

Ringel was obliged to send two formed battalions into a high seas void, which was 'not only a sensitive weakening of my division, it is a heavy concern for me', he admitted, and with no radio communications between them. But orders were orders and they were committed.

He now immersed himself in the detail of the air-land operation. He travelled to Topolia airfield just to the north of Athens, where he was advised and assisted by *Fallschirmjäger Oberst* Bernhard Ramcke, whom he knew from his time in Norway during 1940. His division was at first due to land at Iraklion, a well-hardened airfield, or Maleme, depending on the success of the first waves. The latter was not an alluring prospect, as he recalled: 'The airstrip at Maleme is only 650 yards long by 150 wide, a handkerchief the flyers would say, and a bit frayed too.'[3]

Ringel's division staff in Ommonia Square pored over maps and air photographs. *Major* Flecker, his intelligence officer, thought the terrain was 'like stepping back into a biblical land', with 'numerous narrow valleys overlooked by mountain heights'. Frontal attacks over such ground would be costly, and he concluded 'surrounding or by-passing despite the terrain difficulties, should always be attempted'. There was little or no precise information about the enemy; reconnaissance pilots only reported 'the island appeared lifeless'. Village houses were 'fortress like', occupying heights and ridgelines. The staff appreciation was 'that here it was going to be a fight of man on man, infantry would be the decisive arm, above all mountain troops'.[4]

As Ringel watched his troops enjoying the tourist sites from his window in a seemingly vibrant peacetime Athens, he was well aware they wondered why they had not already been shipped out by truck or train, because the Greek campaign was long over. Rumours circulated, mainly about Africa or Rhodes, maybe even Turkey, while 'only a minority considered Crete, because it was the closest'. Despite not knowing, *Major* Flecker eyed his veterans, who 'see a hundred tiny details and sense the conclusion'. They knew a major operation was on the cards:

> Every front soldier perceives that peculiarly excitable period that comes before a major attack. Life suddenly takes on a different hue, a different rhythm, with deeper meaning. At the front soldiers are used to belonging and living, recognizing when that moment of uncertainty raises its head.[5]

An *Oberjäger* with *Regiment 85* recalled the announcement of the new mission, 'more daring than all the previous surprises'. All sorts of stories had been exchanged driving through heavy motorized traffic on the main Athens road. 'We're going home', shouted those heading north, 'and we're going to Africa', responded the *Gebirgsjäger* heading south to Topolia airfield. Crete was unexpected. 'Does anyone know what dust is?' they remarked, 'no, only those who knew our airfield and the way to it'. On entering the busy airstrip area everyone was quickly coated in layers; 'in a short time we looked more like miller-boys than mountain troops', the *Oberjäger* recalled. Another soldier with the same regiment remembered they were so dust caked 'they had to look into each other's faces to confirm they were who they claimed'. Caps slapping uniforms 'raised a dust storm'.

They warily approached the Ju 52 transports on the runway for a dress rehearsal of the launch:

> All listened attentively as the platoon commander talked about conditions during the Ju 52 flight. The best news was there would be no puking and the aircraft was able to float for 20 minutes on water. Did some faces change colour?[6]

Oberleutnant Fritz Rosenhauer with *Regiment 100* recalled 'the last days before the operation were spent doing forced marches under a very hot sun'. They had to acclimatize 'to unusual conditions'. Virtually everything would need to be carried, because 'we were taking neither mules nor vehicles to the island'. A few motorcycle combinations would be taken to tow 20mm cannon, but everything loaded on the aircraft would be on their shoulders after arrival. 'They were used to getting tired in the mountains', Rosenhauer commented, 'but not to operating below 35° latitude'. Weak soldiers were thinned from the ranks, 'those unable to keep up were replaced'. Going to war via air transport was a completely new experience. 'We were obliged to reduce all equipment to a minimum', Rosenhauer recalled, 'without lessening the battalion's combat effectiveness'. Light loads were packed in rucksacks; only what was absolutely necessary could be taken by air.[7]

As the blood-red sun set, the sand at Topolia airstrip took on a deep bronze hue as soldiers settled down on straw, laid out for that purpose, near the runways. Fraternization occurred between the mountain soldiers and paratroopers, the imminence of combat transcending previous stand-offs on Athens' streets. Imitation yodels rang out from both sides in the darkness as war stories were exchanged, but 'not a word was spoken about the coming operation', recalled one *Jäger* with *Regiment 85*:

> Everyone only talked about the good things that had happened to them in Norway, Holland, Belgium and Corinth. Some of the blue-green [Luftwaffe] uniformed fellows already had many war adventures behind them. Most crept back to their camp sites very late that night.

Men reflected 'whether new fates would herald the coming day'. Rucksacks provided pillows, with helmet and weapons alongside, a restless night of 'sleep, dreams and waking'.[8]

Ringel had respect for the *Fallschirmjäger* ability to achieve surprise and shock impact, clearly demonstrated at Corinth three weeks before. However, the *12 Armee* commander *Generalfeldmarschall* List had doubts whether jumping into the middle of the enemy, as at Corinth, would work again in Crete. Ringel recognized the innate superiority exuded by every paratrooper, which they were 'burning' to demonstrate at Crete: 'For them there was no enemy whose resistance they could not break, their self-confidence was truly amazing.'

His mountain soldiers were content to go into battle with these 'beserkers'. They had never flown, but adapted to this novel way of entering battle. 'Infantry', he reflected, 'seldom meet the enemy without having to get their boots well-worn first'. First of all they would have to await the outcome of the leading glider and parachute assaults.[9]

Sleep on dusty straw next to runways was fitful, every man anticipating their sojourn would at any moment be interrupted by the urgent shouted commands of 'Wake up, load up, climb aboard!' First to rise were the aircrews, followed by a whine and spluttering uptake of starting propellers. A wall of sound arose from the ever-growing pulsating roar of countless aircraft engines. Dust rose high into the air smudging the emerging emerald blue twilight of dawn on 20 May. The operation was on.

LIEUTENANT ED McARA, A COMPANY
22 NEW ZEALAND BATTALION

19 May, Hill 107, Maleme, Crete
The previous month 35-year-old Lieutenant Ed McAra had been the mortar platoon commander in Greece. As the majority of the 3in tubes were lost, he was re-roled as an infantry platoon commander in Captain Hanton's A Company. On 19 May his platoon held a ridgeline at the summit of Hill 107. Born in Dunedin, he had been a commercial artist before enlisting and was happily married with a son. 'Well dear girl', he had formerly written to his wife:

> I hear the BBC calls the [island] the 'last impregnable fortress of Greece' – I wouldn't exactly go so far as that, but we're about ready now to give him a damned good go for it, particularly as he is not likely to bring tanks.

He was an affectionate husband and father. 'Hug our little man for me', he wrote, 'and buy him something for his birthday from Daddy'.[10]

McAra wrote whimsically as well as factually about being 'installed in my temporary job a mile further back from the beach'. His descriptions of the view from the summit of Hill 107 are vividly atmospheric and usefully differentiate between vegetation coverage in 1941 compared to the more commercially appointed orange and olive groves today. Certainly the topography of the hillside then was more open and clearer than now.

McAra's basic platoon routine was all at readiness for stand-to at dawn and dusk. Reduced sentries by day enabled about three hours' training or instruction. This covered weapons handling, minor tactics and PT conducted in shifts, ending with a daily swim in the Mediterranean. Despite shortages of virtually everything, including field cookers, they slept in the open under trees. 22 Battalion noted in its log on the eve of the invasion that 'the battalion found life pleasant'. Companies had set up their own rudimentary canteens, which meant McAra's soldiers could purchase limited supplies of buns, cigarettes and chocolate from the NAAFI at Chania. Locals were friendly and hospitable and the unit diary further observed that 'a few soldiers struck difficulties in the unexpected potency of cognac'. The men were fit, having recovered from their doleful experience in Greece, and ready for the coming fight. McAra's platoon sergeant, Murphy, encapsulated the type of NCOs he commanded:

> One of those tough, restless souls who can never fit into a peaceful world. Fought first for the Republicans in Spain, then changed to Franco's side just to vary the monotony – a humorous, indomitable fellow whom nothing seemed able to ruffle.[11]

22 Battalion maintained security posts on the coastal road, at the Tavronitis girder bridge over the estuary and in Maleme village. Travellers were interrogated and all vehicle loads checked, which inevitably caused some friction around the villages. Two local bearded orthodox priests were picked up on 19 May and taken to Andrew's Battalion HQ for questioning, protesting volubly and incomprehensibly in Greek. This was a direct consequence of the former 'Fifth column' scare stories that had permeated the Blitzkrieg campaign in the Low Countries and in Britain during the invasion scare and were still current. The battalion pickets bizarrely maintained that these priests had given the unit trouble in Greece. Both of them were arrested ten minutes apart but identified as the same man. On being found innocent the battalion log 'rather guiltily' admitted 'sacrilege had been committed' because 'these young black-bearded orthodox priests, identically dressed, looked very much alike'. Upsetting the priests was tantamount to riling the entire local community, who looked to them for social as well as spiritual guidance. Many of the local inhabitants had, however, already relocated inland to avoid the incessant Luftwaffe bombing for over a week now.[12]

McAra assured his wife 'they were still busy improving their positions':

> The platoon is busy wiring the exit of a nasty little tree-filled gully on our front. Behind the wire I'm putting a small pit for

two men with a tommy gun and a box of grenades, with half a dozen riflemen in pits 100 yards further back to cover their withdrawal if the pressure becomes too great.

Andrew's 22 Battalion had erected obstructions to close most of the approach gullies that led to the summit of Hill 107, and these were covered by fire. McAra's platoon had maintained a section of ten men five minutes to the rear, 'and we will be in, boots and all, as soon as the balloon goes up'. His platoon frontage was easily covered by fire from the high ground and he had focused on 'this one corner' where 'we'll be likely to strike real trouble'.[13]

All this 'peaceful' routine was conducted under relentless Luftwaffe air attacks. Kiwi gunner Allan Jackson positioned nearby recalled 'he bombed and machine gunned all areas hour by hour day by day'. Captain Johnson's C Company defending the aerodrome perimeter had been under bombing and strafing attack 'almost every day and sometimes twice a day for the ten days preceding' the invasion. Aircraftsman Marcel Comeau with 33 Squadron RAF remembered:

By late afternoon [of the 19th] the aerodrome wore the desolate appearance of an out-of-season seaside resort. Wisps of black smoke drifted from the littered beach, across the sandy strip and over the road which curved eastwards towards Pirgos, like a deserted promenade.

Luftwaffe air dominance was disturbingly total. Allan Jackson remembered 'sort of screamer' Stuka dive bombers that continued to swoop and intimidate even when they had run out of ammunition, and 'we had nothing with which we could retaliate'. Despite the cover afforded by olive trees, they were constantly buzzed by an observation plane that regularly flew over. 'If he saw us he would wave and we knew that in an hour the area would be strafed again'. Casualties were, however, surprisingly light. 'After they had gone you could see every tree marked by bullets.'[14]

That same morning, the 19th, McAra's platoon witnessed uncharacteristically determined raids on Maleme aerodrome, clearly visible from the summit. Forty Me 109s were seen to pour out of the sky and whiz across the width of the runways, 'almost scraping the aerodrome with their bellies', as Comeau observed. 'This time the Luftwaffe were out to destroy the guns', he felt, and 'the gunners knew it too and were fighting for their lives'. One by one the Bofors guns were put out of action, with only one still firing after the raid had passed, leaving many of the gun crews lying as casualties.

As evening twilight descended there was every expectation this would bring some respite. An approaching drone, however, led everyone to gaze skyward, and Comeau saw 'sailing over Kavkazia Hill [107] came 18 Heinkels'. McAra's men involuntarily ducked as:

> Formatting on the leader they dropped their bombs in a long stick, and we watched them most of the way. Then the earth erupted suddenly among the New Zealanders up the slope – then down the rising ground toward us. A sudden series of explosions straddled our two gun pits, the world blacked out in a dozen showers of dust and clods of earth.

Each of these aircraft had a payload of 4,410lb of bombs. The 22 Battalion log recorded that '150 bombs were dropped in C and D areas in the space of about five minutes', straddling positions along the Tavronitis estuary and the aerodrome perimeter. Over 200 bomb bursts were counted that day alone. C Company on the edge of the aerodrome lost one man killed and two wounded. Such raids had almost become part of a tense routine. Lieutenant McAra wrote to his wife again, maintaining an understated confidence: 'Our defences are slowly but surely thickening and we're beginning to feel once more as we did after Dunkirk, that soon the blighter will have left it too late.'[15]

McAra's platoon that night was treated to the same remarkable 'blood-red' sunset viewed by the *Fallschirmjäger* on mainland Greece. The purplish hue or dust line just above the horizon turned blue as the red sun dipped into it. Soldiers drank tea and sipped their bully-beef stew, chatting about the chance escapes of the day. Battalion intelligence reports four days before had alerted them to the likelihood of an invasion between 14 and 17 May, preceded by exactly the type of intensive bombing and strafing they had just endured. Overdue by two days, many were starting to believe nothing was going to happen, and that shortly they would be on their way to Egypt.

As stars appeared, McAra described the nighttime view from his platoon position, crouched by a 'bivvy' erected beneath a stone wall at the summit of Hill 107:

> In the hazy light, trees and grasses are stirring; the ridges folding down into the shadowed gullies, the valleys opening upon the cultivated levels by the sea. The only sounds were the 'toot-toot' of some night bird and the crunch of a sentry's boots on the stones, and the long sighs of the distant surf breaking around the bay.

At Galatas village, eight miles inland, in an adjoining valley leading down to the capital Chania, raucous voices emerged from 'Uncle John's' Taverna. The valley was a planned objective for *Fallschirmjäger Regiment 3*. Noisy New Zealand soldiers had to be persuaded it was curfew time and that they had drunk enough wine. The Military Police arrived and the situation turned ugly, until one of the redcaps mounted the bar and announced that the Germans were coming. Everyone was instructed to return to his unit.

Nobody knew with any certainty what was going on. Lieutenant McAra's last penned letter to his wife pointed to the sheer irony of the peaceful scenes he had described, because 'unreal almost in its imminence – is the threat of sudden invasion from the skies'. McAra would not survive the following day's conflict.[16]

MAJOR EDUARD STENTZLER, COMMANDER
II BATAILLON STURMREGIMENT

19 May, Tanagra, North of Athens
On 19 May, 36-year-old *Major* Eduard Stentzler commanding Meindl's *II Bataillon* parachute infantry, with the *Sturmregiment*,

remained unsighted about the date of the invasion launch. His concern was shared by *Major* Reinhard Wenning, commanding *Kampfgruppe z.b.V. 105*, who had driven out to meet him. His 46 Ju 52s were to drop Stentzler's men west of the Maleme aerodrome. The wiry Stentzler, the ex-jockey and cavalryman, had transferred to the Luftwaffe in 1933. Still unproven in combat, his unit had been planned to drop four miles north of Folkstone, as part of the aborted *Sea Lion* invasion of England. His penchant to still wear knee-high cavalry boots tucked into his fatigues was an eccentricity his soldiers seemed to enjoy, and he would jump with them in combat. Wenning, his pilot, knew the final briefing had occurred the day before at the Hotel Grande Bretagne at Athens, but not the outcome. *Oberst* von Heyking, a *Geschwader* chief, who had led the flight for the Corinth Canal coup, had provided some exciting detail. 'The plan was a first in the history of warfare', he enthused, 'the conquest of a heavily fortified island from the air'. He was told his aircraft would fly with the first wave, but not the date. 'Frantic activity reigned on the wide parched runway' at Tanagra, his mounting airfield, 'where some 200 Ju 52s from the various collected squadrons had gathered'. He noticed 12 gliders parked to one side. Vehicles bustling about the airstrip and runways 'raised huge clouds of dust'.

Wenning accompanied by his four *Staffel* commanders was warmly greeted by Stentzler, who had turned up with his four company commanders. They brought maps and air photographs with them to precisely identify the drop locations. Stentzler's battalion needed to be put down west of the Tavronitis River to secure a lodgement area, with one company screening possible enemy approaches from the west and north. They were tasked also to provide the attack reserve. In addition, six aircraft were to parachute a reinforced platoon from *6. Kompanie* under *Leutnant* Peter Mürbe east of a crossroads outside Kastelli, to secure an area to receive the sea landings. Jump sticks were divided among the four flight commanders to ensure troops to task jumped in the order of the agreed plan. With the launch date still undecided, 'tension reached its high point' during this coordination meeting. Wenning had only intermittent contact with his headquarters, which was daily maintained by flying a Fiesler Storch courier aircraft. Stentzler had better communications with *XI Korps* HQ in Athens and was able to finally confirm that afternoon that the launch date was to be the following day. Wenning received Luftwaffe confirmation later that night, but the aircraft could at least be loaded and prepared for the known plan. Stentzler's battalion drove that night to Tanagra airfield, to be ready to mount at first light. Take-off would be at 4.55am, after the last gliders had been towed away.[17]

Tension steadily ratcheted up. Greek civilians anxiously watched the comings and goings at Tanagra. First of all there were Messerschmitt fighter planes and Stukas, then hundreds of transport aircraft. Yiannis M. Vassilas living at Athens nearby observed 'feverish preparations – something very serious is obviously being targeted against our islands'. They noticed 'some wooden aircraft, similar but smaller than standard aeroplanes functioning without engines'. These were gliders – 'we had never seen them before'. The 'funny looking aircraft' were being 'towed by the bombers, one by one and in twos'. Aircraft activity was perceptibly increasing: 'they came and went, landed and took off, transporting swarms of armed forces on our soil'.[18]

Airfields were busy and congested. Von Richthofen's *VIII Fliegerkorps* was already beating up air defences on Crete, and grudged every bit of room for *Generalmajor* Conrad Seibt's *XI Korps* transport aircraft. The latter had ten groups of 50 planes per group that required parking space, nearly as many aircraft as von Richthofen's *VIII Korps* altogether. Ju 52 transport aircraft needed a good take-off run. Ideally the air transport groups and their organic troop cargoes ought to have been combined at one airstrip, but lack of space dictated wide dispersal that impacted upon the regiments, whose battalions, due to lack of space, had also to be split, and take off from different locations. The final seven airfields in use by Student's corps were scattered across 150 miles, from Corinth along the isthmus to Megara and Eleusis, where *XI Korps* HQ was based, and to Phaleron near Athens and Tanagra, Topolia and Dadion north of the capital. Luftwaffe ground and aircraft crews had to improvise their accommodation and messing, supplies were short and fuel had yet to arrive. Perhaps the most dangerous inhibitor, however, was the dust.

The worst affected was the crowded airfield at Topolia, where an enthusiastic army officer had harnessed Greek peasants to plough up the grass on an old lake bed, to create a smooth surface. Grass had previously stabilized erosion, and the three Ju 52 groups based there created a dust bowl, which windmilled dust from propellers to occasionally 3,000 feet in some locations. The Athens fire brigade was summoned to damp down the problem, but over 30°C temperatures and the blazing Aegean sun brought these efforts to naught. *Oberst* von Heyking was tasked to conduct a launch rehearsal to monitor the extent of the difficulties. The problem he recalled was:

> When landing or taking off the aircraft threw up huge clouds of dust hundreds of feet into the air, which afterwards fell to the ground very slowly, because of the high temperatures and lack of wind in the narrow valley.

With 'aircraft wheels sunk in up to the axles', he appreciated, wing take-offs would be seriously impeded. Dust came up and badly obscured pilot vision, 'covering the planes and entering the engines'. Unlike being able to launch wings in minutes, 'seventeen minutes elapsed between one flight taking off and the next getting ready for take-off: this was the time needed for the dust clouds to clear'.[19]

Stentzler and Wenning were well aware of the impact that dust would have on their jointly calibrated tactical plan for the battalion fly-in. Each of the 46 aircraft represented an initial dispersal of his battalion's strength into isolated groups of 12 men. Each stick had to shed their parachute harness, rally on the ground and find their jointly dropped weapons containers before they could even begin to form up as platoon and company groups. All this was, moreover, likely to be under fire, in the air while descending and on the ground. A concentrated orchestrated drop was therefore vital. Wilhelm Rodenbusch with Stentzler's 7. *Kompanie* remembered that not until after arrival at Tanagra 'was our objective revealed and explained to us with the help of maps'. It was all somewhat overwhelming; 'we were all rather light headed', he admitted, 'as most of us were volunteers and it was our first mission'.[20]

Stentzler and the other battalion commanders with senior staff had attended Student's final conference at 11am at the Hotel Grande Bretagne the day before. Staff cars and jeeps arrived all morning, discharging officers of various ranks at the entrance. They were ushered into the large opulent salon that had been converted into a briefing hall. Gestapo officers and armed security guards checked credentials. Outside in the lobby, British agent John Drakopoulos monitored the comings and goings. Student strode in accompanied by his staff and the sheet covering the huge battle plan for the island of Crete was taken down. Everyone now knew the objective. Arrows punctuated with tiny coloured markers revealed the dispositions of each attacking unit. *Hauptmann* von der Heydte was present and described Student's convincing delivery of a plan that all immediately appreciated was likely to be a risky enterprise:

> In a quiet but clear and slightly vibrant voice General Student explained the plan of attack. It was his own personal plan. He had devised it, had struggled against heavy opposition for its acceptance, and had worked out all the details. One could perceive that this plan had become a part of him, a part of his life. He believed in it and lived for it and in it.

Stentzler could see the *Sturmregiment* was being employed in a shock assault role west of the island. It was the spreading 'oil-spot' strategy, to be reinforced by sea and air-landings by the *5. Gebirgsjäger Division*. When *Major* Reinhardt, the corp's intelligence officer, rose to speak, he had everyone's undivided attention. His was a gratifyingly reassuring pitch. Reinhardt put the British garrison at no more than 5,000, mainly around Maleme and Chania. The Cretans would emerge with a powerful Fifth Column to assist the invader, making themselves known by the code word *Major Bock*. This massively understated generalization appears based on optimism rather than hard intelligence. Previously, whatever the intelligence errors, the airborne had always been strong and aggressive enough to win through, whatever the opposition. So far as Stentzler and the majority of the *Fallschirmjäger* officers were concerned, if Student had personally drawn up the plan, that was good enough. Then von der Heydte remarked upon the element of self-serving politicking that could often emerge at such briefings:

> When it came to the turn of unit commanders to ask questions, there were still some whose egos would not permit them to lose the opportunity of posing questions either which they could well have answered themselves or to which no one could provide any answers at all.[21]

John Drakopoulos had hung around the hotel lobby, shadowing a *Major* and his companion, an *Oberleutnant*, chatting amiably nearby. The major reminded the junior officer to surrender his notepad, which he had neglected to do on exiting the conference room. The pad, devoid of writing, was left on the counter, which Drakopoulos casually covered with his jacket. Back in his room, Drakopoulos crumbled charcoal over the imprinted page and smeared it over to reveal doodle patterns, which he blew clean. Holding the page to a light bulb he distinguished five letters, *K*, *R* and *E*, which were quite clear. There was also a faint *T* and a barely recognizable *A*. This spelled *KRETA*, and the symbol *17/V* was also there. He knew the *5. Gebirgsjäger Division* was encamped just outside Athens. The information was clandestinely passed locally and then transmitted by radio to a British submarine on picket duty to the west of Crete, and thence to Gibraltar and London. The clues confirmed what Ultra code de-encryptions were already telling the British Prime Minister. Crete was the objective of this briefing.[22]

The blood-red sunset viewed from the *Fallschirmjäger* encampments on the eve of the invasion launch exacerbated foreboding and concerns about what the morrow would bring. Meindl's adjutant von Seelen recorded enforced rest in the regimental area from 2pm; reveille would be at 3.30am, shortly before dawn. Few with the *Sturmregiment* slept soundly. Gericke commanding the *IV Bataillon* recalled his men 'restlessly fidgeted on straw, nobody could get to sleep quickly this night'. Nerves were taut. At Tanagra Stentzler's *II Bataillon* were assisting aircraft crews to hand pump fuel from oil drums into his 46 parked Ju 52s. Lorry tankers had been driving for three days from Corinth, with the canal blocked by bridge wreckage, and only began to arrive at Tanagra during the final afternoon of imposed rest. This meant they had to work hard late into the night.

Many of the young paratroopers had yet to see action; veterans had trouble sleeping in any case. Young men chatted excitedly across open fires, too enthused and pepped up with adrenalin to rest. Morale was high but folk songs sentimental. Much of the discussion was about girls back home, but many of these teenagers had not even known a serious relationship with a girl. Traditional social habits outside service life created chaperones that got in the way. Many still thought of their mothers. 'No one imagined that this would be the last peaceful evening', recalled von der Heydte at Topolia. He was married, and remembered 'like a passing film, the panorama of my whole life unfolded before my eyes at that moment'.

Twenty-three-year old Jürgen Rothert with *Major* Otto Scherber's *III Bataillon* wrote to his parents. He was a veteran, wounded in Poland, and had transferred to the paratroopers the summer before. 'We probably won't have any more rest until we've put the Tommies to rest', he wrote. They had been at Mykene airstrip, 'lying in the sweltering heat without beer and water'. Von Seelen had to coordinate their transfer to Megara mounting airfield because they had been crowded out by von Richthofen's need for more space for his *VIII Fliegerkorps* combat aircraft. Rothert sent his last field postcard to his mother and father prior to the jump, assuring them 'old Churchill won't know what's hit him'.[23]

It was a bad night for the veterans. 'I was assailed with crazy thoughts', Fritz Scheuering with *Fallschirmjäger Regiment 1* recalled, 'just a year before at the same time, we were on our way to Narvik, and in the morning we're jumping out over Crete!' Like countless others restlessly turning over in their bivouacs at the mounting airheads, there were doubts. Erich Reinhardt was given orders across a sandpit model 'so optimistic, it seemed that the British really did shoot with beans'. Scheuering was similarly uneasy; 'what would the 20th May bring?' he asked himself. 'Would I see a victory or must my comrades shovel a grave for me?' Glider soldier Feri Fink with Koch's *I Bataillon* at Eleusis knew they would make the first contact with the British defending at Maleme. Imponderables outnumbered the very few certainties:

> Would the enemy actually hold Crete? Who was expecting us on the island – just the Tommies? Will the Greeks on the island take up the fight? Was the enemy optimistic? How had he coped with defeat on the mainland? Question after question for the intelligence service, and none answered.

There were last-minute changes to the plan. *Major* Franz Braun, Meindl's HQ Staff commander, was suddenly tasked, with the last nine reserve gliders, to capture the iron-girder bridge across the Tavronitis River. *Generalmajor* Meindl did not want its demolition to delay the immediate support needed to back up Koch's first glider landings, already reduced by half, through Student's insistence to spread his 'oil-spot' glider-borne strikes.[24]

Fink's comrades loaded their gliders 'lost in their thoughts'. *Oberleutnant* Wulf von Plessen, the commander of their 'Iron Third' *Kompanie*, formed his men in a hollow square, framed by an emerging radiant blood-red sunset, to summarize the salient points of the plan. They had two hours to secure the airfield before the *Gebirgsjäger* would begin to air-land, to reinforce the coup. In the middle of this pep talk:

> Von Plessen clasped his arm, seemingly lost in a train of thought, and unexpectedly stopped talking. He bent forward as if to relieve the cramp in his arm. The company continued to regard him silently, not saying a word. We thought it was a premonition. After a moment's silence, von Plessen came back, concluding his talk with a few banal words about soldier's luck and such like.

It was not reassuring. They boarded trucks and drove out to Eleusis airstrip, where they settled inside a huge peach orchard next to the runway. There they waited 'without tents, cover or any rations for this last night'. Max Rauch, one of the company medics, saw the sky 'was speckled with stars'. Turning to his best friends he recalled saying 'if we see these stars again, then everything will have been for the best!' Little fires appeared and groups gathered around singing old school and folk tunes, songs about soldiers dying too early. 'Much was said', Fink recalled, 'every conceivable subject was discussed, but not one word about the coming day'.[25]

In Athens at Student's HQ in the Hotel Grande Bretagne, the heat of the day transitioned to cool night. Tunic jackets replaced shirtsleeves. The previous purposeful hum of activity settled down to a quiet reflective period of waiting. Many of the tasks were done, it was now a question of simple staff routine, re-checking lists, updating map symbols and monitoring aircraft availability. Key staff chiefs retired to their hotel rooms and beds to ensure they were alert for the coming day. 'Second-eleven' shifts took over the various desks and the *XI Korps* HQ settled down to a tense, relatively inactive routine. Logistic desks remained active, fuel was still being delivered late to various airheads and ever more truck-borne tankers were driving along dusty roads through the darkness.

Student retired to his couch. Last-minute issues had required resolution, but most had now been delegated. The plan was issued, execution was now for his subordinates about to cross the start line. Student remained confident. 'In the evening of 19th May all preparations for attack on Crete were complete', he later wrote in the after-action report: 'Leaders and troops had been carefully indoctrinated in their tasks and stood ready at the airfields, eager for action. The command reckoned on a swift and decisive success.'[26]

Shortly before going to bed doubts surfaced over the accuracy of the morning weather forecast. The *Luftflotte 4* meteorologist had identified a disruptive weather front over Spain moving east into the Mediterranean, sufficient to disrupt flying conditions for a successful launch. Student summoned his own meteorologist Dr Brandt from his bed, to recheck his own forecast against that posed by *Generaloberst* Löhr's headquarters. Brandt, having done his homework, predicted on the basis of analysed regional reports stretching back ten years, that disruptive fronts rarely if ever progressed further east than a line drawn from Bari south to the African coast. He minimized the influence of the disturbance, which had now reached Italy, and predicted clear flying and sailing conditions for Crete. There would only be light surface winds over the drop zones, and the weather over Maleme would be clear. Student was the airborne commander so it was his decision. He accepted Brandt's forecast in preference to that of his superior Löhr's HQ, and promptly retired to bed.

Major Trettner, the operations officer, monitored reports while his commander slept. During the night he was notified by the intelligence officer about ominous British Royal Navy developments. The report read: 'Alexandria Squadron of two battleships, one carrier, four cruisers, fifteen destroyers approaching Crete.'

This had disturbing ramifications. If this force happened to station itself off Kithira Island on the Greece–Crete approach route, the massed low-flying vulnerable Ju 52 troop lifts might pass overhead, and be fired upon with devastating consequences. Trettner checked with *General* Korten, Löhr's chief of staff, who agreed it was indeed a grim prognosis. He felt the need to wake Student to share the alarm and perhaps delay the launch. Student was unimpressed, and not prepared to jeopardize such a momentous launch on an unsubstantiated 'maybe'. Trettner was ticked off with the laconic response 'you didn't need to wake me'.[27]

At 3.30am on 20 May, Ferdinand Fink's *3. Kompanie* at Eleusis airstrip was woken up. All they had left for messing was long cold coffee dregs, poured into their flasks the night before. 'We were too uptight for breakfast', he recalled, 'nobody wanted it'. They formed and sat in glider chalk rows and waited. Normal routine. Weapons were checked, then re-checked and checked again, 'how many times already? Hardly a word was spoken'. They were surprised how damp the ground on the runways was when there had been no dew in the peach orchard. The Greek fire brigade had already been hard at work, damping down the dust. The chalks moved off, and 'as we reached the aircraft, the first light of dawn was already apparent', Fink remembered.

Stentzler's *II Bataillon* men had arrived at the airfield the previous afternoon, choosing to bivouac close to the Ju 52s, to ease loading before first light. Their availability meant they were called upon to hand pump fuel from drums dumped on the runway by late arriving fuel trucks. They worked until late into the night, unable to benefit from the imposed rest laid down by Meindl's adjutant von Seelen. When Stentzler ordered the various sticks to board after 3am it was pitch black, a moonless night, illuminated by only pinpricks of starlight. He gazed up to regard a heavenly canopy of stars amid the thunder of windmilling propellers. The weather was going to be good. His only concerns were that Wenning, whose aircraft he was about to board, would get his battalion down in the desired concentrated mass. Moreover, that Mürbe's independent reinforced platoon would get out in the right place. These were fleeting thoughts; overall, he was confident of success in this, his first major combat action.

This was the day.

Chapter 4

The Flight of Daedalus and Icarus

07.00–08.30 20 May 1941, Hill 107, Maleme, Crete
Leslie Andrew awoke to a beautiful blue sky, the 'usual Mediterranean summer's day' on 20 May, as recorded in the battalion log. It was a 'cloudless day, no wind, with extreme visibility'. From his dugout at the summit of Hill 107 they could pick out the craggy detail of the White Mountains to the south, 20 miles away. At 7am the usual 'daily hate' of bombing and strafing by the Luftwaffe rained down. Men were encouraged to remain under cover in stand-to positions, for security from the air and survival. When the drone of aircraft ceased, the men made their way to the RAF administrative building for breakfast, bathed in sunlight, and chatted amiably about their raid experiences. It was normal routine; 'the enemy had drilled us into expecting his bombing at the same time each morning', Andrew explained.[1]

Aircraftsman Marcel Comeau remembered a sergeant wandering about the trenches telling everybody to 'stand-down'. No invasion today, 'if Jerry was coming he'd have been here by now!' was the buzz word. Andrew and his battalion were still locked into the 1914–18 norm that attacks came at either dawn or dusk. Modern warfare had, however, moved on. Enemy approaches now were subject to flight serials and prescribed timings. It took two hours to fly from the Greek mainland, so unbeknown to Andrew's men, the main attack had indeed launched at dawn. It was still on its way as they went to breakfast.

As breakfast began, it was marred at 7.45 by the plaintive wail of the air raid siren that sounded from the mysterious Air Ministry experimental station tucked away in the hills to the east. Captain Johnson on the aerodrome with C Company thought the earlier raid 'was little if any heavier than the regular morning attacks we had been experiencing for a week', except bombing and strafing was over a wider area. Cursing, still-hungry men took cover under trees and in trenches as the first 24 German heavy bombers came overhead.

This time it was different. One eyewitness was convinced the armada's approach could be felt through the ground even before arriving overhead. 'Bombers and fighters appeared very suddenly both from the south and at zero feet from the sea', Johnson remembered, 'in an attack the severity of which left us in no doubt that this was the genuine assault about which we had been advised several days before'.[2] Andrew was familiar with the fly-in route of Luftwaffe bombing raids that had become established over a ten-day routine. They crossed the coast about a mile west of the aerodrome outside Bofor range, after following the line of the Cape Spathe peninsula. Flying inland at 500 feet they wheeled left to Maleme village, skimming the ridgeline held by A and B companies before suddenly diving onto the aerodrome beneath the summit of Hill 107. The spot height had a 3in gun dug in, but the muzzle could never depress sufficiently to engage. The raid was to last 90 minutes as ever larger waves of Heinkel IIIs, Dornier 17s and Junkers 88s flew in, escorted by fighters. An estimated 3,000 bombs rained down on Hill 107 and the airfield. Lieutenant Sinclair commanding 15 Platoon on the western boundary of the airstrip recalled, cowering in his trench, that 'it was not long, about 30 minutes, we realized that this was more than the bombing we had experienced the days preceding'.[3]

Andrew was shaken by the intensity of the raids. He had emerged from World War I exhibiting signs of combat fatigue. The raid brought it all back; he admitted that 'Soldiers of the last war thought of artillery barrages at Messines, Passchendaele and the Somme would rather go through them than see another Maleme blitz.'

He was hit in the temple by 'a wee piece of bomb' which stuck fast to his skin until he pulled it out, 'bloody hot and bled a bit'.[4] Even after unloading their bombs the aircraft wheeled about, air superiority secure, criss-crossing and swooping to strafe targets of opportunity. 'Streams of bullets lashed the olive groves, shredding leaves and boughs', observed one eyewitness, 'setting fire to trees and undergrowth, groping for the men who huddled in the trenches below'. One man heard Andrew exclaim 'we'll go out and get these bastards when the bombing stops'. Sergeant Major Les Young with 21 Battalion on the ridgeline behind Hill 107 remembered 'there was a terrific din and the sky was black with planes'. Bofors gun crew emplacements protected by sandbags which were barely knee high were quickly suppressed. 'Apart from an odd Bren gun, I did not hear any ack-ack fire', he recalled. Soldiers caught in breakfast queues scrambled back up the slopes of Hill 107 to seek the safety of their own deep foxholes.[5]

Sheltering in a slit trench near the dining tent, which attracted strafing and dive-bombing, was aircraftsman Colin Francis with 33 Squadron RAF. 'I decided that the first aid post, which was situated a few feet from the top of Kavkazia Hill [107] was a safer refuge', he recalled, 'and so, along with many others I made my way dodging a hail of bullets as best I could'. The aid post was a cave entrance, partially hidden and protected by a stone wall. Sheltering inside was the unit doctor, an orderly and several others. They were deafened by the cacophony of sound that rolled around the entrance, 'the constant rat-a-tat of machine guns, the bomb explosions, the cries and the never-ending roar of aircraft engines above us'. Leading Aircraftsman Greenhalgh crawled in, 'stone deaf' from a bomb that had exploded in his slit trench, killing some of the occupants. Another aircraftsman stumbled in, 'clothes muddy and tattered', Francis observed,

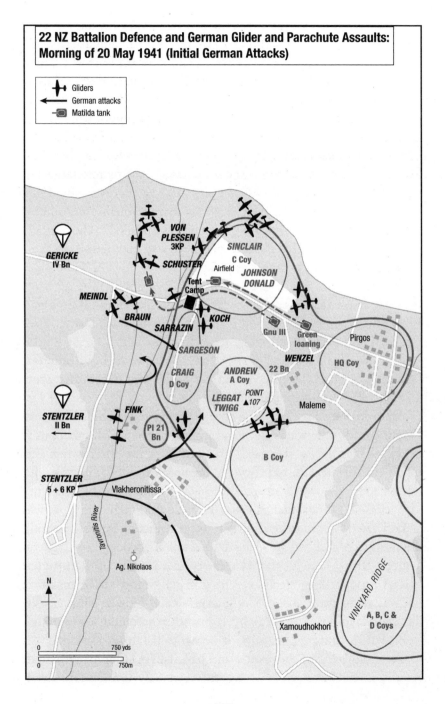

22 NZ Battalion Defence and German Glider and Parachute Assaults: Morning of 20 May 1941 (Initial German Attacks)

Gliders
German attacks
Matilda tank

GERICKE
IV Bn

VON
PLESSEN
3KP

SINCLAIR
C Coy

SCHUSTER
Airfield
JOHNSON
DONALD

Tent
Camp

MEINDL

BRAUN
KOCH

SARRAZIN
Gnu III
Green
loaning
Pirgos

SARGESON
WENZEL
22 Bn
HQ Coy

CRAIG
D Coy
ANDREW
A Coy

LEGGAT
TWIGG
POINT
▲107
Maleme

STENTZLER
II Bn
FINK
PI 21
Bn

B Coy

STENTZLER
5 + 6 KP
Vlakheronitissa

Tavronitis River

Ag. Nikolaos

N

VINEYARD RIDGE

A, B, C &
D Coys
Xamoudhokhori

0   750 yds

0   750m

and 'down his right side we could see where chunks of his flesh had been torn from his body by shrapnel'. His trench had been directly hit, killing three others. The noise was intimidating. 'On all sides I could hear the screaming of the bombs', Marcel Comeau in the tented camp area recalled, 'and the occasional metallic clang of shrapnel as fragments of bomb casing flew in every direction'.[6]

Squadron Leader Edward Howell was pinned on the slopes of Hill 107, cowering at the base of a slit trench. He remembered:

> The bombs struck in twelves, earth sprouted to the heavens, the crump and shock of impact crept closer up the hill. The noise was indescribable. The ground shuddered and shook under us as the bomb pattern passed over and beyond.

Comeau felt 'a violent eruption ahead of me, and through the haze, I thought I saw the bomb lift a man off the ground, but I could not be sure'.

Andrew disorientated by the shrapnel blow to his head had little idea of what was going on and saw even less. Wave after wave of Stuka dive bombers hammered Hill 107 and the edges of the aerodrome. Battalion HQ staff could vaguely make out that C and D companies were receiving the main punishment. Mushrooming explosions could be followed working over the terraces on the north side of the hill back from C towards their HQ. They could not be certain, however, because as Major Jim Leggat the battalion 2IC recalled, the 'air was too thick with dust between my slit trench at Battalion HQ and the drome to see far, but by hearing I think the perimeter and the slopes of the hill got it all.'

Even with normal visibility Andrew could only see just under half of the battalion area from his command post at the summit. He was co-located with A Company, with B nearby. Most of the battalion layout was out of sight in dead ground on the lower slopes to his left, including D Company below to his front. He could see C Company around the drome and parts of HQ Company in and around Pirgos just beyond Maleme village. For the moment he was blind, 'the air was heavy with dust', Leggat recalled, and 'nothing out of the immediate vicinity could be seen'.[7]

'The bombing of the aerodrome and company positions was so severe', Captain Stanton Johnson with C recalled, 'that from company HQ it was impossible to see more than a few yards because of the smoke laden and dust filled air'. His whole position was blanketed with a dense cloud of dust, so that 'we had no knowledge of how 13 and 15 platoons were faring'. The damage around his command post, co-located with 14 Platoon, was bad enough. Five men had been killed and one wounded in trenches that he had insisted should only be occupied by two, mute testimony to the compact density of bomb explosions around them.[8]

Howell still pinned inside his slit trench felt increasingly vulnerable, as each bomb impact physically shook the sides of his shelter. 'We were covered in earth' as a consequence, he recalled:

Our eyes and mouths were full of grit. And still it went on. We were shaken … till our teeth felt loose and we could hardly see. Debris continued to crash around us and the sides of the trench crumbled. We lost count of time.

Towards the end of the 90-minute crescendo, the intensity of the attacks seemed unbelievably to increase. 'Long bursts of cannon and machine gun fire' chewed up the soil around them, Howell remembered, 'as low-flying fighters came in to attack the anti-aircraft pits':

These were already silent under the terrific weight of the attack with the exception of one Bofors gun down by the beach. This went on firing for some time till a host of Stukas and Me 109s fastened on it and shot and blasted it out of existence.[9]

At 9.20am battalion headquarters noted the 'blitz ceased'. Sergeant Sargeson with D Company recalled 'the silence after that was eerie, acrid and ominous'.[10] A pall of dust several hundred feet high was hanging over the hill and aerodrome. Sergeant Francis Twigg,

Andrew's intelligence officer, peering from his trench saw the entire topography of Hill 107 had altered:

> The immediate countryside before, densely covered by grapevines and olive trees was bare of any foliage when the bombing attack ceased and the ground was practically regularly covered by large and small bomb craters.[11]

Corporal Pemberton with D Company remembered 'there was not a tree standing in my area and our trenches were half filled in'.[12]

Down in the tented camp area Comeau was startled to hear 'above me … the sound of rushing air'. A glider swooped low through the curtain of dust, silent and sinister, disappearing westward. Unseen, it was completely unexpected:

> Almost at once there was a crackling and cracking through the olive trees – a second glider was careering straight towards me. I had no time to avoid it. It skidded into the tent, slewed half round, showering me with loose soil and stopping in a cloud of dust with one wing dug into the bank behind me. Another glider piled in close by.

The door of the nearest glider popped open and 'out jumped a dazed-looking German' whom he shot at point-blank range. He fell back inside revealing another figure 'holding his head with his hands'; he shot him too, spinning the man around, and he fell blocking the doorway. Urgently reworking the rifle bolt 'I sent a third bullet into the darkness of the doorway'. Falling back, Comeau was unable to eject the spent casing from his rifle, 'sweating and swearing' he hopelessly wrestled with the bolt action, seeing 'even more Germans racing through the trees from the second crashed glider'. 'It was the longest second of my life', he recalled. At first he could not get away, pinned by a low-flying Dornier 17 'pencil' bomber which sprayed the hillside with machine-gun fire, creating a carpet of dust plumes as it roared by at tree-top height. 'There appeared to be endless yards of it and

I found time to wonder if it would ever pass by.' It did, and he scrambled up the slope, towards the summit of Hill 107, 'clawing at the loose earth' and running for the D Company trenches 'with bursts of rapid fire following me'.[13]

Second Lieutenant James Craig with 17 Platoon D Company lost no one in the bombing but three men 'including a sergeant, broke down and were a bit bomb happy'. Sergeant Sargeson nearby remembered it had 'suddenly became expedient to keep your head down while our slit trenches concertinaed in and out under the grandfather of all blitzes'. Craig observed six gliders skidding and slewing around opposite the company area, throwing up huge clouds of dust:

> Glider crews suffered very heavily in the actual touchdown, and many were killed or injured in crashes. Those who did get down unhurt streaked out of their gliders and took cover very quickly indeed. Unless the glider stopped a burst of machine-gun fire as soon as it came to rest it was very hard to hit the crews before they took cover.[14]

Andrew looking out from Battalion HQ could not see much of this. Johnson with C Company at the aerodrome recalled 'not one glider was seen to land', only his 15 Platoon at the western extremity saw any coming in. 'We were mystified', he later explained, 'by the presence of Germans in both the northern and southern ends of the 15 Platoon area'. Leggat with Andrew on the summit saw gliders 'about 80–100 yards in front, and one on the road [between Malame and Vlakheronitissa] to the right'. Dust obscured their silent approach at the closing moments of the air attack. 'The gliders in our area came down at the end of this and just on the tail of it', he observed. Battalion HQ staff saw the bombing impacts had shifted from the flat areas where they were due to land onto the slopes. Aircraftsman Colin Francis still sheltering in the Battalion First Aid Post had seen nothing. It was only when they began to treat the wounds of the airman lacerated by shrapnel that 'he dropped his own bombshell', remarking on the numbers of gliders that had crashed in and around the camp. 'The news caused a deadly silence for a while', Francis remembered, 'and then everybody began talking at once'.[15]

Andrew had only fragmentary reports to piece together what had happened. Gliders had apparently landed on the terraces, stretching from those he could see from the summit, down to the beach below, north of Maleme village. Some were in the valley behind them, east of the HQ 'but the majority were in the bed of the Tavronitis, both above and below the bridge'. Sergeant Francis Twigg observed the genesis of the psychological strains that were to later afflict Andrew's headquarters. 'Because of the disruption of communications caused by bombing, those in command did appear to be somewhat at a loss as to what the situation was immediately afterwards.' It was not about 'the judgement of the HQ officers', it was more the unsettling effect 'of continual and I suggest unreliable information and rumours'. The outcome 'appeared to me to be a lack of definite orders or plans'. Officers were not so much concerned at their personal safety, more about fundamental responsibilities. Twigg thought 'the OC and 2IC showed signs of strain during the day, and I put this down to lack of news and information concerning their own troops and the position in general'.[16]

Andrew was already struggling to keep calm when at 9.30am the Battalion log recorded 'an angry throb which seemed to make the ground vibrate, heralded the approach of this German air armada'. The rapid and sequential blows the battalion experienced this day was completely outside the formative experiences of the senior officers, most of whom had been of junior rank in World War I. This time there was no solid front. The enemy came at them from every direction out of the sky, front, flanks and rear, separately or simultaneously. In fact, there was no front. The odds even before the arrival of the huge approaching aircraft stream had seemed immense. Based on fragmentary reports, Andrew assessed that 80 to 100 gliders had landed. This suggested he was taking on about 800 to 1,000 German glider soldiers, even before considering what to do with the unknown number in the huge parachute storm about to burst over his positions. His estimate, based on multiple sightings of the same gliders, was out by a factor of three. He was caught off balance right from the start.[17]

MAJOR WALTER KOCH, COMMANDER *I* (GLIDER) *BATAILLON STURMREGIMENT*

Early Morning 20 May, Eleusis Airfield and Tavronitis River Bed Beneath Hill 107
The 31-year-old *Major* Walter Koch, clear-eyed with hawkish features and a receding dark hairline, was on a career roll. He had taken over the *I* (Glider) *Bataillon* of Meindl's *Sturmregiment* the previous summer and trained it hard. A Knight's Cross holder, he was the youngest battalion commander in the regiment and commanded the elite among the elite. As the propellers of his almost 40 Ju 52 tow-transports spiralled dust high into the sky of a blue twilight dawn at Eleusis airstrip, he took stock of the plan he was now required to execute.

The spearhead was programmed to take off first. Although he would never question Student's creative plan, he did harbour some doubts. His battalion was already spread across several separated aerodromes before take-off. Company commanders *Oberleutnant* Alfred Genz and Gustav Altmann were flying two heavy glider raids from Tanagra airfield, to take on flak positions south of Chania and on the Akrotiri Peninsula north of Suda Bay. This meant 24 gliders and 240 men extracted from his overall battalion strength against two widely separated objectives with no prospect of speedy relief from supporting ground forces. Panzers had quickly relieved his men at Eben-Emael in Belgium the year before, whereas Student's 'oil-spot' strategy in this instance had created two near-suicide insertions, if resistance on the island of Crete was not shocked into sudden moral collapse. Koch was daring, but did not risk the lives of his men lightly. He had reservations.

Detaching both companies halved the battalion spearhead combat strength. Despite this, he still marshalled a formidable force of some 41 towed gliders that morning. It was crucial they take off and arrive together, despite the enveloping clouds of dust already obscuring safe vision around the runway at Eleusis. The fighting element of his 3rd and 4th companies under *Oberleutnant* Wulf von Plessen and *Hauptmann* Kurt Sarrazin with Koch's headquarters were to land 36 gliders directly onto the defences of Maleme aerodrome and Hill 107. Five of them would fly in the heavy equipment of Meindl's regimental HQ. Koch's unease at the loss of the two raiding companies was acknowledged by Meindl, who at the last moment included his final reserve force of nine gliders under *Major* Franz Braun, who would bring in his *Stabskompanie* (Staff company). They would land around the Tavronitis bridge. Koch retained some confidence with the plan because he was leading a force of 36 gliders, about 360 men, to directly assault the New Zealand defences. It was the first mass glider assault in history. Only ten had sufficed to bring the impregnable Belgian fort at Eben-Emael to its knees, and just five had captured the Corinth Canal bridge weeks before.[18]

Koch led from the front. He chose to land his personal glider directly onto the slopes of Hill 107, the key ground that dominated the airfield objective. He positively exuded the aggressive energy that harnessed modern technology to succeed on the battlefield, the hallmark of Hitler's National Socialist Wehrmacht. They would ride like Valkyries into the vitals of a strategic objective, never before attempted from the air alone. So long as the Luftwaffe produced the requisite shock and awe required of close air support, the speed and violence of this unprecedented airborne assault should carry the day.

The DFS 230 glider looked like a motorless transport aircraft, but with shorter stubbier wings. Its loaded weight and design committed it to a descending glide, with little or no option to soar. Gliders stealthily landed men replete in section sub-units of ten, not having to disentangle themselves from parachute harnesses or seek weapons containers. The fuselage was a steel tube framework covered with canvas. Care had to be taken on entry and leaving so as not to accidently poke holes with weapons through the thin outer skin. Wings were set high and braced. Wheels were jettisoned on take-off and the glider landed on a central plywood ski-like skid, festooned with barbed wire, to snag as a braking drag. It weighed 2,790lb and carried a cargo of similar weight.

Ferdinand Fink with von Plessen's *3. Kompanie* recalled the tiresome 'passenger list' bureaucracy on boarding, where each man had to sing out his name, rank and home address. Repetitive waiting heightened nerves. Their platoon commander *Leutnant* Musyal gathered them into a half circle and 'drily remarked he hoped to see most of us still healthy after the mission'. The order followed to board their gliders; 'that was it', Fink remembered, 'comrades, there's no going back!'

Inside, a central cushioned bench ran the length of the fuselage. The pilot and five of the glider compliment came in via the cockpit and sat facing forward, the rear four came through the starboard hatch and sat astride the bench, backs to the direction of travel. Fink was the last man. Each soldier had a chair brace to lean back on, and hold onto in front. Knees and boots were pressed against gear stowed under the bench or lashed to the glider walls. 'Our glider was loaded up to our necks with ammunition and a folding motorcycle', Fink remembered. Everything was tightly lashed with hemp rope for crash landings. 'We realized with such a heavy load the glider would descend faster, the landing heavier.' Crammed further into restricted space was a thick life jacket, one for each man. If they ditched the so-called 'freighter' or tow plane would return and throw out a dinghy. 'We would certainly prefer two hours overland', Fink recalled, 'than only have water beneath us.'[19]

'We're starting', their pilot quietly announced. In front was a simple bank of six dials at the instrument panel; the control stick was shaped like an elongated tennis racket, so as to grip and steer. Tightly packed inside, the ten glider soldiers heard the Ju 52 engines splutter as they caught and roared into life. Prop wash slapped and vibrated along the canvas sides. As the 'freighter' revved up nothing could be seen inside, but they could hear the momentary power surges of other aircraft taking off ahead. Glider pilot *Oberfeldwebel* Walter Wachter recalled 'it was still night' as 'the towing aircraft for the first *Kette* were rolling in front of me. Time to take off'. Visibility was hopeless, 'a huge red cloud of dust hung over the airfield', which took some 15 minutes to disperse.[20] There was a jerk, some jockeying and sloshing motion as the tug cable took up the taut. 'The engines howled more loudly', Fink recalled:

and we rolled faster along the ground, a much longer time than we were used to. Uneasy we listened out, finally we lifted, then hard down again, and then another lift and soon thumping down to touch again. That was very unusual!

Wachter also experienced a degree of concern as the 'overloaded glider rumbled along clumsily behind the towing aircraft, and wouldn't leave the ground'. As speed picked up the roller-coaster noise of the wheels blended into prop wash flapping against the canvas sides. 'Slowly we were pulled into the air', Wachter recalled. Fink became so nervous at this interminable take-off that he nervously asked whether they should ditch the folding bike out the hatch. Nobody answered. 'Soon we were off the ground and lazily purred high into the air' leaving huge spiralling dust spumes behind. All that could be heard now was a drumming and low whistle from the wind. Some of the sluggish tugs could only manage 70–75 mph, fighting the restraining drag from their heavily loaded gliders, which considerably increased take-off lengths.

Relief at soaring into the royal-blue sky was soon superseded by the temperature rise that accompanied the early morning glare from the Mediterranean sun. 'Stuck inside their thick jump suits', *Oberjäger* Erich Schuster in Fink's 3. *Kompanie* recalled, stuffy cabins became claustrophobic. They could see other tugs both left and right though the small square portholes. 'Not much was said', Schuster remembered, 'you had to shout to make yourself heard as dust danced in the sunlight'. Fink's friend Horst, complaining about bad air inside the glider, cut a slit in the canvas wall with his dagger, pushing the barrel of his rifle through the rent to prise it apart. 'Precious fresh air flowed around our faces', he recalled. Their plexiglass portholes enabled them to look down upon 'a silver sea narrow, light grey and toned a little violet in the morning light'. When an island came into view, they all agreed 'that must be Salamis'. Shortly they were over the island of Ägina at about 9,800 feet. The sun, the rhythmic drone of the aircraft and the constriction from thick uniforms tightened at knees and elbow by protective pads sent them off to sleep. The flight across the Mediterranean was peaceful, few bothered to look out. 'Suddenly', however, pilot Walter Wachter noticed 'the towing aircraft to our right drew ahead of us trailing a rope, but no glider'. Dispiriting, 'we now had 20 men [from a platoon of 30] – too few'.[21]

Fink, on the verge of dozing off, awoke with a start when he glanced through the plexiglass window to his right: 'I saw a cut-away glider with the tail unit forward diving steeply from our formation, turning steeply and perpendicularly over. This little dance was taking too long and my excitement mounted. Had the pilot completely lost control?' Horrified, he watched as it turned on its head 'revealing its light blue underside' until it stabilized, 'and raced sideways out of my field of vision'. '*A glider has cut away!* I shouted louder than intended.' 'That is the third' came the comment from ahead. 'Poor swine' was murmured along the bench, 'now they're in for a swim, hopefully none of them will drown'.[22]

Fallschirmjäger jargon gave nautical terms to their aircraft. Ju 52 tugs and parachute aircraft were labelled 'freighters' while gliders were 'sticking-plaster steamers'. Good glider pilots were few and hard to find. Tugs created an air pressure bow wave that the glider pilots had to ride, akin to water-skiing behind a speedboat. Mid-air turbulence in the wake of a large aircraft stream caused an occasional trip and fall, parting the tow, producing a heavy rope whiplash smacking against the plexiglass nose. The glider tended to jerk violently downward, and everyone stiffened with fright. A combination of inexperience and weak tow couplings contributed to this observed fall-out rate. New Zealand intelligence officer Geoffrey Cox was subsequently to pick up German glider pilot prisoners, 'just boys of eighteen, who had been sent to Greece at a fortnight's notice to pilot these machines'. Among them were likely *Hitlerjugend* (Hitler Youth) with 'no arms, and wore only mechanics overalls instead of uniforms'. One he recalled, wept at the prospect of being shot for being out of uniform. Experience was everything. *Major* Koch made certain that Heiner Langer, one of the pilots who had landed atop the fort in the dark at Eben-Emael, was the one piloting his glider onto Hill 107. Walter Wachter had survived as one of the five pilots who had landed around the Corinth Canal bridge three weeks before. He had misgivings about this operation, claiming 'it's impossible to compare the Crete attack with the earlier operation'. 'The English knew nothing about it.' Whereas this time:

> We were not told that the attack on Crete from the air would probably yield enormous casualties, but we all felt it – sensed it. It couldn't be otherwise, to attack so large a target only from the air with no back-up.[23]

Koch saw some gliders fall out of formation; fewer men for the vital preliminary assaults. *3. Kompanie* lost a glider from its third platoon and Koch's group with Sarazin lost four. Two landed on islands and two others in the sea, drowning three men. Genz and Altmann's flights lost three each, which meant a total of 110 men had fallen out of Koch's already stretched order of battle. Student's subsequent *XI Korps* after-action report identified weak cable connectors on the tow aircraft, which cost 11 of 53 gliders, 20 per cent of Koch's actual combat strength.[24]

Generalleutnant Süssmann, the *Flieger Division 7* commander, was flying further back in the immense air armada. He and his headquarters were glider borne. Sitting just behind the pilot on the central bench, he watched the majestic stream of Ju 52s uncoiling over the silvery dawn of a Mediterranean sea heading for Crete. For an ex-bomber pilot and now commanding general, his was a somewhat undignified stance, sitting astride a communal bench, gazing out the plexiglass cockpit ahead. As an admirer of Student, he tended to emulate him. An amiable man, he also spoke and attempted to bond with his troops like his superior. He had shared the mess with his soldiers at the muddy bivouac site in Bulgaria, prior to their parachute assault onto the Corinth Canal bridge. Student had sponsored his rise in command, saving him from an embarrassing Court of Inquiry that had attracted Göring's attention over a questionable parachute insertion, which had come to grief in the Dombas Valley in Norway the year before. Süssmann received his promotion to *Generalleutnant* just four days before the Crete operation. He still lacked substantial active service experience, but had overseen the regimental-size insertion at Corinth, three weeks before. He aspired to rise above his present undignified entry into battle, towed along in a 'sticking-plaster steamer', because he was probably on the cusp of a prestigious Knight's Cross, if he pulled off this momentous undertaking. Like Student's inspiring command of the first mass parachute and air landings in Holland the previous spring, he was at the centre of an upgraded corps-strength version. The conquest of the strategic island of Crete from the air alone would be a historic page-turner. Student had flown into the Rotterdam area in a light aircraft 30 minutes after the start of his division's fly-in. Süssmann likewise characteristically insisted his take-off slot should be 30 minutes after the lead *Sturmregiment*.

Spirits soared as they flew over Athens, momentarily shadowing the pillars of the Acropolis, highlighted in a glowing red-golden dawn. Albert Speer, Hitler's architect, was modelling such prestigious government buildings for a future Berlin, on the same classical lines. They would reflect the former glory of Greece and Rome, and now by association National Socialism. Down below the citizens of Athens were awoken by the throbbing vibration of a mighty fly-past, heading, they suspected, for Crete. It heralded a sinister future, as witnessed by American foreign civil aid director Laird Archer, who saw it pass majestically by: 'Since dawn, planes in large formations have been passing over our heads, some low as if heavily laden with paratroops, others towing weird-looking gliders like young vultures following the parent bird from the roost.'[25]

Many of the *Fallschirmjäger* inside watched out for the Acropolis, which they had visited as tourists in the preceding days. They set course for Crete, the birthplace of Zeus in Greek legend. Daedalus the master craftsman had built the legendary labyrinth at Knossos for King Minos, south of Iraklion, now the objective of *Gruppe Ost*. Minos had imprisoned him in it. When he sought to escape back to his native Athens, Daedalus fashioned two pairs of wings from wax and feathers, one for him and the other for his son Icarus. He warned his son to stay clear of the sun, but in flying too high the wax melted, causing him to spiral to his death in the sea below. The legend was a cautionary tale about the perils of hubris, flying too high in the pursuit of glory. Süssmann was at 2,600 feet with the glare from the rising sun producing a silver sheen across the sea ahead. It was becoming increasingly hot.

Süssmann was stirred by this vast panorama of transport aircraft set against a piercingly blue sky with supporting swarms of fighter escorts wheeling by. Distant metallic specks hinted at returning bombers flying in the opposite direction, reassuring him that the close air support plan was on course. The huge stream droned onward and nobody noticed a converging speck growing in size to the starboard side of the tug/glider combination. This was *Leutnant* Paul Gerfehr from *II/Kampfgeschwader 26* intent on overtaking his Heinkel III bombing formation, after being delayed by dust on take-off. He closed at over 240mph, virtually twice the speed of the armada to his front and, seeing a momentary gap, he flew straight through. *Feldwebel* Franz Hausser flying Süssmann's *frachter* or 'freighter', stunned at the sudden appearance of the converging Heinkel to his right dived, jerking the DFS 230 violently downward. Such action normally needed to be synchronized by speaking to Süssmann's glider pilot *Leutnant* Willy Kruppe, who with no warning was unequal to the task. The division commander ought to have been offered the pick of pilots, but Süssmann typically insisted that the spearhead gliders should be the priority. An elasticated twang rang out followed by the slap of the tow rope against the cockpit window, and prop-wash din was superseded by a low humming whistle as the glider broke free.

Kruppe's only recourse was to land on the nearby rocky island of Ägina below in Athens Bay. Pulling back on the control stick he attempted to soar and gain height but the weight and design of the glider was against him. Gerfehr piloting the Heinkel bomber swept over, climbing at over 200mph to get out of the way. His 74-foot wingspan created a whirlpool of air turbulence spiralling behind that snatched at Süssmann's glider. With a dull crack one wing sheared off followed by more snapping tubular steel as the second folded inward also. Horrified onlookers with the rest of the stream watched the carcass of the wingless glider topple end over end all the way down to the ground. Inside was the division commander, both adjutants, an aide, the division medical officer and the hapless pilot. Rigid with fright, they tumbled over and over bombarded by displaced radio equipment shaken free from snapped bindings and a folding bike, which crashed down on top of them. The doctor was the recent replacement for the former senior division medical officer, who had been killed just weeks before at Corinth. Observing from the courtyard of the Convent of the Holy Trinity, the abbot and priests watched the awful spiralling descent of this unknown object that concluded with a huge puff of dust rising from mountainous terrain on the island of Ägina. The fuselage landed near the Temple of Aphoea, with no survivors. Daedalus and Icarus had seemingly returned.[26]

Ahead of the main air transport stream, von Richthofen's *VIII Fliegerkorps* combat squadrons were working over the defences at Maleme and Hill 107. Just after 7am Heinkel 111s from *Major* Friedrich-Karl Knust's *Lehrgeschwader 1* were joined by *Oberst* Herbert Rieckhoff's *KG 2* Dornier-17 'flying pencils' from Tatoi, intensively bombing and strafing the airfield perimeter and the terraces and slopes of the hill. Student recalled *VIII Korps* 'worked a time-table which was precisely worked out in every detail'. Me 109 fighters from *Jagdgeschwader 77* and Me 110 *Zerstörers* with *Zerstörergeschwader 26* flying from Molau and Argos provided escorts during the flight and strafed ground defences on arrival. Stukas from Oskar Dinort's *Sturzkampfgeschwader 2* with Me 110s 'were to destroy and weaken defences', Student noted, 'right up to the arrival of the gliders and lead parachute troops'.[27]

Rieckhoff's Dorniers in the ground support role 'were to engage sighted enemy ground troops, destroy communications and engage traffic behind enemy lines'. Able to come in without disturbance at any altitude they desired, 'hit results', Rieckhoff noted, 'and the observed effects were good'. *Kampfgeschwader* 2 lurked over the target area for up to 90 minutes, which he acknowledged was 'excellently camouflaged' and 'even at low level difficult to detect'. Exit and entry points leading out of Maleme and the surrounding villages were bombed to disrupt communications. The results were better, he emphasized, when *Rotten* and *Ketten* squadrons and flights were given free rein to work over particular sectors. 'The Jericho trumpet sirens of the Stukas had an especially effective morale impact upon the enemy', he reported, 'who immediately took cover'. Despite flying such low-level attacks, his Do 17 aircraft 'were once again seen to be able to absorb considerable punishment'. Rieckhoff kept the subsequent pressure up, flying three sorties per day out of Tatoi.[28]

As the glider formations flew east after making landfall on the west side of the island, they could see plumes of smoke and black aircraft specks against the huge pall of dust rising up from the target area. 'At intervals I could make out the lie of the land between the smoke and clouds', glider pilot Walter Wachter grimly observed, 'it was bloody narrow and steeply inclined', hardly suitable for a landing.[29]

'Kreta in sight', *Oberjäger* Schuster's pilot with von Plessen's 3. *Kompanie* announced. 'Helmets on', the commander ordered, 'final checks!' The tug dived with the glider following and 'a German fighter flashed by', Schuster recalled, and 'the pressure wave threw the DFS like a toy to one side'. They could pick out the dull bangs of exploding flak through the roar of the aircraft engines as the tug curved left, and at the same time the chink of the glider release coupling. 'A hard shock ran through the glider, and all the men were thrown forwards', Schuster remembered, 'then they were in a free glide'. Just for a moment they saw the other two Ju 52s with their platoon in the same curve. Another Me 110 flashed by, its cannon thumping away in the direction of flight. Wachter was now concerned seeing 'a few bushes and trees and hedges were blocking the landing area', they were almost on it 'but too high':

> On the left of our landing site was a dry stream bed [the Tavronitis] running north to the beach. We had to move very swiftly – we couldn't present any target for the AA guns. Everything was happening so fast now.

As Ferdinand Fink's glider approached they could see fighters and bombers hard at work neutralizing the airfield periphery: 'Around the runway clouds of smoke were towering up, steadily dissipating inland. Dive bombers, so small, they seemed like flies to us, were diving perpendicularly in line, one after the other.'

They were at the objective with 'small villages stretching away under us, gardens, fields and trees with wasteland in between'. Breathing heavily they heard the pilot calmly confirm 'we've released'. Flak began to drily crack out and Fink saw a splinter pierce the battery of the folding bike next to him. The glide was taking them low along a valley; 'on the left was soon spot height 107, the bridge and coastal road flashed by under us'. A note of alarm crept into the pilot's calm commentary: 'I can't control the machine now', he announced, the last flak burst had damaged his flaps. Trees emerged and he excitedly blurted out 'I am not going to clear the wood!' 'Then put her down!' bellowed the section commander. They curved steeply to starboard as the pilot warned 'get ready!' With that, the section commander ejected the cockpit chancery while Fink ditched the side hatch. The glider filled with rushing air and the pilot shrieked 'watch out!' Everyone braced, crouching down and ducking down their helmeted heads as low as possible as with a crackling crash they burrowed and careered through vines. 'Thick red-brown earthy dust filled the glider', Fink remembered, 'it was not possible to see'. The glider jumped into the air and crashed back down again, 'at the second impact someone cried out'. Under fire the glider continued to bulldoze its way through the vines until with a final impact it juddered to a halt. 'The dust dispersed and to our surprise', Fink recalled, 'we found the complete interior of the glider was covered in a fine dust, weapons, equipment and clothing, we were all coloured red-brown'. In a daze it took an eternity to find and uncouple their seat belts. Recovering they sprang out through the cockpit and side hatch and immediately went into all-round defence. 'After the loud droning tow, the dull report of flak bursts, the noisy whizzing glide and the crashing sounds on landing, it was surprising', Fink recalled, 'how still it had become'.[30]

Fink glanced at his watch, 'we were three minutes early, probably during all the wheeling about in flak fire, we had lost too much height'. He pulled off some of the fuller grapes from the vines around them, wincing at the sour taste. 'Dear God the world is a great place', he reflected with considerable relief. 'The toasty sun was warm on my back' and it was good to be alive; he was aware of the dusty smell of the surrounding vegetation. Heavy rifle fire was coming from the direction of the bridge, the high ground and aerodrome. Nobody was shooting directly at them, but it was clear from the rising concentration of fire along the valley and from the heights that 'it was not going according to plan'.

After a few tight manoeuvres Wachter saw 'the ground before me'. No machine guns, he noted with relief, 'then they opened up':

> They rattled out as we were a few feet from the ground, but there were not only hedges – there were terraces with hedges on top of them. We flew across them and away, almost touching down – one, two, three terraces – then smash, we landed in a bush.

A tree tore off the glider left wing, shaking up the fuselage 'and stayed still'. 'The second glider hadn't done so well', smashing into one of the terraces, going 'head over tail'. Nearly all the occupants were injured. One of their gliders had been lost at sea and this one destroyed by the terrace; 'now we had only 10 good men out of 30'.[31]

Fink sensed from the intensity of fire and explosions around the airfield and Hill 107 that the plan was going awry. They had landed south of the New Zealand D Company concentration along the line of the dry Tavronitis river bed. The glider crew began to cautiously move north to establish contact with the main landed force. Their company commander von Plessen had force-landed on the beach north-west of the airfield; they extricated themselves bruised but uninjured. The main glider groups containing the 1st and 2nd platoons had landed nearby, careering along bone-shaking clouds of spiralling dust in and along the dried river bed just west of the aerodrome near the outlet to the sea. *Oberjäger* Schuster saw the 2nd Platoon commander's glider crack into a rock 30 yards away and 'burst apart like ripe fruit'. *Feldwebel* Arpke was knocked unconscious, another soldier emerged 'holding an unsupported broken arm'. Schuster took command of the platoon and issued quick orders for an assault on the Bofors gun position in front of them. *Leutnant* Musyal commanding 1st Platoon had his head shattered by a bullet ten yards from his abandoned glider. Both platoons began to attack the western perimeter of the aerodrome under intense fire from New Zealand C Company's 15 and 13 platoons.

Von Plessen led a supporting assault from the north-west against an AA position and was immediately cut down and killed, his pre-flight premonition fulfilled. *Feldwebel* Galla tried to pick up momentum by attacking across the open ground beyond the beach, but his section was cut to pieces in concentrated fire from 15 Platoon, dug in on the western escarpment of the aerodrome perimeter. Schuster made headway, he and his men threw a cluster of six grenades into the first Bofors position. Grenade thumps, shouts, screams and crackling Schmeisser Tommy gunfire signalled its demise. He was momentarily taken off his feet by bullets ricocheting along his helmet and snatching material off his sleeve but rallied, and took out two confused AA gun positions by himself. Despite heavy losses the two platoons cleared much of the western edge of the airfield in a short time. The 3rd Platoon missing one glider came down near the small village of Tavronitis and cleared it after a short firefight, taking 30 prisoners. With all its officers dead or wounded the company medic, *Oberarzt* Dr Weizel, assumed command of von Plessen's *3. Kompanie*, directing operations from the aid post where he was treating the wounded.

Feldwebel Arpke meanwhile regained consciousness and took over the fighting line to the west of the aerodrome. He was nursing a splitting headache and a disabling knee injury from the crash. Intense fire from the heights around Hill 107 had driven the advance back into the cover of the dry river bed. Arpke reorganized, set up a mortar and machine-gun fire base and launched a left flanking attack against the remaining AA guns. These were cleared but from the 40 or so who assaulted, only about 30 were left standing. The early morning sun was in their eyes as they tried to discern movement on the heights and they could not pinpoint the excellently camouflaged New Zealand positions. In any case, there were barely enough men left to hold what they had.

Koch's glider ripped through the guide ropes and tents of the RAF encampment, tearing off shreds of canvas that acted as an effective brake. Two of them were in the midst of the tented camp, while the rest of *4. Kompanie* and the command group gliders landed on the western slopes of Hill 107. Some piled into the south-east Maleme village slope near the New Zealand A Company. Koch instinctively realized with the volume of opposing fire that his plan was unravelling, transitioning to a completely unexpected scenario. The situation had changed. A glider-borne or parachute insertion directly upon enemy positions was akin in control terms to a Napoleonic-era cavalry charge: once loosed, there was no calling it back. Control then exercised by 19th-century bugle, drum, standard or voice could not yet be coherently exercised by 20th-century radio. Koch realized he was dependent upon personal example with control by voice and hand signals.

Gliders curving and wheeling on their final approaches had been engaged with unexpectedly vicious defensive fire and hindered by poor visibility from dust, smoke and column-high black explosions from Stuka dive bombers – still at work even as they came in. This caused wide dispersal on landing. Only 11 of Koch's 15 gliders had made the objective. Hauptmann Sarrazin's glider, the *4. Kompanie* command group, was totally wrecked on landing. He and six others were killed instantly; they included the company doctor, a *Feldwebel* and the pilot. Three radio operators were still unconscious inside the wreckage, unable to be released by the injured survivor. There would be no radio direction.

Koch's after-action report itemized the catastrophic landings of the 4. *Kompanie* gliders. Two were cut away before arrival, four landed in the vicinity of the objective and five were completely in the wrong place, so much so that sections could not attack their objectives. Three gliders were hit and exploded on landing, leaving just eight – 80 men – to continue the attack. Koch was completely surprised to find the British tented camp empty. He gathered his surviving glider crew to attack the nearest height to their landed position. Constantly exposing himself to fire while directing efforts, he was soon spun about by a grazed head wound. He carried on, desperately trying to rally the other dispersed glider groups on broken ground to fight their way up the false crests to the summit of Hill 107. The RAF administrative building at the edge of the airfield was overrun. Koch's next head wound took him down, and it appeared mortal. With the battalion commander out of the fight there were only a few score men on the lower slopes of the hill, with isolated groups cut off above. There were some 30 to 40 men clinging on to the western edge, insufficient to even secure the toehold they had gained.[32]

Now, 25 minutes after the first landings, some of the dust and smoke from the initial bombing started to dissipate. *Major* Franz Braun's nine-glider final reserve began to whistle and hum through the hanging haze to land in a cluster virtually on and about the Tavronitis iron-girder bridge. Braun was Meindl's staff chief and had been given the mission to secure the bridge just days before. The arrival of the final gliders also coincided with a deep throbbing drone, becoming increasingly apparent from the south-west. Hundreds of Ju 52 aircraft from the main stream were approaching the drop zones.

Braun's gliders were spotted from the outset. One pancaked onto the western road embankment leading directly to the bridge. Its occupants swarmed the superstructure seeking the demolition charges that were not there. They were soon pinned by a New Zealand machine gun firing from the opposite bank. A deluge of accurate small arms fire enfiladed these gliders as they came into land, wheeling into their final approaches. *Oberleutnant* Schächter's glider belly-landed in a splintering crash of tearing canvas and snapping tubular steel. Hardly anyone emerged from the dust cloud. Schächter was severely injured. Braun's glider was riddled by machine-gun and small arms fire as it came down and skidded to a halt. The commander and most passengers were dead, still strapped in as they slumped on their seats astride the central bench. About 80 men landed around the bridge, momentarily forcing back the New Zealand D Company's 18 Platoon to an irrigation canal line, just east of the estuary. The machine gun on the east side of the bridge was neutralized, leaving a handful of men rallied by a sole surviving officer, *Oberleutnant* Horst Trebes, who attempted to link with the remnants of von Plessen's *3. Kompanie* nearby. They started attempts to drive a wedge into the New Zealand defence either side of the bridge.

Inside the 25 minutes that heralded the pulsating roar of the arrival of the main parachute stream, Koch's command, the glider-borne elite of the elite, was severely mauled. A and D New Zealand companies were pouring the fire in and had broadly pinned the spearhead of the *Sturmregiment* along the line of the Tavronitis river bed. *3.* and *4. Kompanien* had silenced the anti-aircraft guns at the west end of the aerodrome, penetrated the RAF tented camp and administrative building and captured the Tavronitis bridge. Of over 380 men from some 38 gliders that landed directly on, or adjacent to the New Zealand defences, only about 50 or 60 men were still on their feet on the lower slopes of Hill 107. Perhaps another 30 to 40 were clinging onto the escarpment at the western end of the airfield. Walter Wachter's glider crew was eviscerated by heavy defensive fire from Hill 107, 'and I was wounded', he recalled, 'and as in the paratrooper's song, for eight of my comrades "the sun would never laugh again"'.[33]

Koch's men dragged and pulled at the inert body of their severely wounded commander, blood pouring from his lacerated skull, down the western slope of Hill 107. The head wound looked terminal. They kept to bushes, defiles and any available folds in the ground. Koch was venerated by his men like a mythical Greek hero. They were determined to get him home, alive or on his shield.

CAPTAIN STANTON JOHNSON, OFFICER COMMANDING C COMPANY, 22 NEW ZEALAND BATTALION

08.00–08.30 20 May, Maleme Aerodrome
Thirty-one-year-old Captain Stanton Johnson, an ex-teacher from Auckland, commanded Andrew's C Company. His headquarters was co-located with Lieutenant Haddon Donald's 14 Platoon, next to the coastal road at the foot of Hill 107, that led to the Tavronitis bridge. As the dust from the air bombardment started to dissipate he would soon see the Maleme aerodrome virtually in its entirety, across to the sea. The command post was partially covered by a vineyard on both sides of the road. He was in dead ground to Andrew's Battalion HQ at the summit of Hill 107 above. A previously wrecked British Fairy Fulmer lay to his right, while to the left were lines of sand-filled oil drum aircraft pens. Further rows of petrol-filled drums covered this west side of the aircraft runway. They were to be ignited as incendiaries to prevent enemy air-landings. The command post area had been badly punished during the 90 minutes of intensive bombing and strafing, killing five soldiers and injuring another. Only now were patches of blue sky starting to materialize through the dust shroud that had risen hundreds of feet into the air. Men around Johnson were dazed, as much by cerebral concussion from air pressures generated by multiple bomb bursts, as by all-encompassing fear. 'We just couldn't see a thing for a quarter of an hour or 20 minutes after the bombing ceased', recalled Lieutenant Donald, whose slit trench was nearby, 'because of all the smoke and dust some of us had temporary black outs, and it took a little while to recover from this'.[34]

Squadron Leader Edward Howell RAF around the corner on the western slope of Hill 107 still felt 'numb and unable to appreciate the significance of the scene'. Gliders were nosing through the dust cloud and belly landing on the beach north of Johnson's 15 Platoon and pancaking into the shingly flats of the dry river bed of the Tavronitis, just along the coastal road from Johnson's command post. Howell's experience was common to them all:

Dust was still in the air and it lay thick on everything. Our mouths were dry and full of grit and we were covered in dirt. My ears and head were still singing and I was unable to think clearly... . I chatted about trivialities to the men. They too were badly shaken and automatically shrank down at every aircraft that went over.[35]

Johnson's three platoons numbered some 117 rifles, with seven Bren guns, nine Tommy guns, a Lewis machine gun and six Browning machine guns 'customized' for the ground role having been stripped out of the RAF aircraft wrecks dotted about the aerodrome. Johnson, peering through the smoke and murk to discern what was going on, had concerns. He was instructed to remain in his defensive positions until after the paratroopers – they anticipated – had dropped. Nobody had said anything about gliders; and there was every expectation of further waves of troop carriers, so no counter-attacks until the enemy was down and fixed.

Andrew would request 23 Battalion waiting in depth to counter-attack at the right moment. Meanwhile 14 Platoon, with whom Johnson was co-located, was to block any enemy approaches against the aerodrome from the south-east or south-west, around Hill 107. 13 Platoon was on the sea side of the airstrip to guard against any beach landings. 15 Platoon under Lieutenant Robin Sinclair was his primary concern and Johnson could see nothing in that direction. Sinclair covered the western approach, but there was a lot of dead ground to monitor beneath the escarpment leading down to the dry Tavronitis estuary. His left flank, the interface with D Company to the south, was potentially vulnerable. This was because of the seemingly uncontrolled and uncoordinated RAF tented encampment and buildings, which were in the way. Some 370 Fleet Air Arm and RAF ground crews, naval and marine personnel were even now milling about, effectively denying the ability of D and C companies to close the interface with fire. The necessary defence line would have run straight through the RAF officer's mess, which had been condemned as 'unthinkable!' by the air force.

Sinclair's 15 Platoon was at the most westerly tip of the prized airfield. He had only 23 men to cover a company-size frontage of 1,500 yards. Johnson had surreptitiously 'liberated' vast quantities of small arms ammunition from the RAF camp, sufficient for virtually a box of 1,000 rounds of .303 ammunition for every weapon pit or trench. The Tommy guns had only about 200 rounds apiece and the primitive Brownings were mounted on aircraft segments, which according to Sinclair, were 'a conglomeration of soap and chewing gum on screws for sights'. To repel superbly equipped glider-landed paratroopers the platoon had only jam tin hand grenades, packed with concrete and plugs of gelignite with fuses.

From within the murky dust-screen cloaking the 15 Platoon position, Johnson could hear firing on both flanks. Braun's reserve glider force was attacking west to east around the Tavronitis bridge, while von Plessen's 3. *Kompanie* was attacking Sinclair's seaward flank, and the Bofors positions at the north-west corner of the aerodrome. Sinclair later remembered the shingle deposits in the estuary were 'very undulating where the stream had cut alternate courses from time to time' and these mini courses provided 'excellent cover'. 'We were all more or less pinned to our positions', he recalled, 'as I was fired on from SE, S, SW, W, NW, and NE. It was a queer show, and to understand whether 13 Platoon [on the beach] were firing on us or not.'

Nothing could move and live crossing billiard-table-flat runways. 'Persistent fire on every movement' came from a drain near the south-west corner of the aerodrome. When the dust settled later in the day, Sinclair counted about 14 gliders had landed near his positions.[36]

Johnson had not seen any gliders landing, and what was going on in 15 Platoon area 'remained confused as far as Company HQ was concerned'.[37] All the telephone wires had been cut by bombing leaving only runners, who could not risk crossing any open space. There was no contact with Captain Tom Campbell's D Company to the left, out of sight, around the corner of the lower western slopes of Hill 107, which was covering the bridge and Tavronitis estuary.

Campbell recalled 'vivid recollections of the gliders coming down with their quiet swish, swish, dipping down and swishing in'. He had about 70 men, two platoons, 16 and 17, covering the river bed and 18 Platoon under Sergeant Sargeson holding the right boundary to C Company. Sargeson had no contact with Johnson and was also isolated from the other two platoons. He could, however, hear heavy fighting to his left or south, which was the 21 Battalion platoon positioned as a warning post, to alert its own battalion in the event of landings. Six gliders crashed in front of Second Lieutenant Jim Craig's 17 Platoon, killing and maiming more Germans in the splintering impacts than long-range fire from Craig's men. To their right, or north, they spotted German sections moving from each concrete bridge pylon to the next beneath the superstructure to cross the dry estuary under cover. With the bridge taken, the cutting on its east side began to fill with glider soldiers reassembling as units, having crossed the river. This was potentially a wedge levering apart the uncovered gap between Johnson's own C Company and D. In between, the RAF administrative building had been captured, with many of the relatively defenceless and disorganized airmen and naval groups taken prisoner. The cost to the glider men had been heavy. Craig's 17 Platoon had killed many and 'expected to take part in some sort of counter-attack; they felt most confident about this', Craig recalled, 'and were anxious to start'. They believed they outnumbered the enemy 'and that success was assured'. So far as they were concerned 'it only needed a determined push to drive the enemy right away from the aerodrome'.[38]

The tubular frame canvas-covered gliders proved vulnerable, offering zero protection from fire. Signaller Frank Sherry remembered 'even a .303 rifle made the gliders jump visibly in the air' as they came down, hurling soldiers from benches with the impact of bullet strikes. A number landed near his position and 'out of those five, not many came out alive'. 'They were very flimsily built', agreed Ray Minson:

and this one peeled off and hit an olive tree, and the men started to come out the door. And that was all there was to it. They came out one by one and we shot them one by one. It was too easy – it was like duck shooting.[39]

Peter Butler in Johnson's area remembered seeing:

One man firing a Bren gun from his shoulder, literally tearing a glider to pieces – bits were flying off it. It landed about 20 yards from me and only one man came out. He only made about two steps before he was cut down.[40]

The results of this concentrated fire close up were horrific. Arnold Ashworth recalled one 'pathetic looking German trying to drag his bullet-riddled body behind the glider for a refuge which it could not offer'. On checking through the wrecked gliders 'we heard the most agonizing voice panting over and over again "*shotten, shotten*" "shoot me, shoot me"' it said. They followed the voice direction and found the hapless victim. 'I don't know how he had got so far', Ashworth remembered, 'for half his hip was shot away' after being hit by a heavy-calibre round from a Boys anti-tank rifle. 'I gazed down at his tormented countenance and felt great compassion', he admitted. 'A short while before he had been a fine specimen of manhood' like all the airborne troops, superbly fit. 'Now here he was at my feet pleading with me to put an end to his horrible suffering and wasted life.' They checked over the bodies nearby looking for anything of intelligence value. Ashworth picked up a picture of 'a smart young man smiling at what appeared to be his two children picking flowers'. He was moved to reflect:

I could not help looking down at his horribly distorted form, and wondering if maybe tomorrow someone else would be standing

over me gazing at the few photographs which I carried. It was a
sobering thought and it didn't cheer me up at all.[41]

Captain Johnson had been on the lookout, scanning the skies, for
parachutists as soon as the bombing ceased. He had not seen any
of the gliders from his command post on the coast road, coming
at low level through the smoke and dust. When it cleared 'we saw
them', paratroopers, 'landing in small numbers approximately
50 to 100, between the eastern edge of the airfield and Maleme
village' to his rear, 'and in larger numbers west of the Tavronitis
river bed'. Andrew at the summit of Hill 107 above, likewise
shrouded in dust, detected 'an angry throb which seemed to make
the ground vibrate'. He watched troop carriers skimming across
the hills heading towards Maleme, coming out of the south-west.
Disconcertingly very few Bofors were engaging the low-level Ju 52
transports 'which lumbering along as they did, made an ideal
target'. The gun crews had been effectively neutralized during the
bombing, strafed and bombed in poorly constructed positions; they
were casualties or too far away from the guns in deeper cover to get
back in time. The foremost trenches of D Company by the river and
Sinclair on the western extremity of the aerodrome were the first
to see the transports unload. Sergeant Sargeson near the Tavronitis
bridge recalled 'the planes were literally wing-tip to wing-tip and
all disgorging a sky full of multi-coloured parachutes'. 'Look at that
Bob', he remarked to Corporal Boyd at his side, 'you'll never see
another sight like that as long as you live'. Boyd eminently more
practical and already raising his rifle replied 'Yes – and if we don't
shoot a few of the bastards we won't live too bloody long.'[42]

Lieutenant Robin Sinclair monitored the approach from the
edge of the airfield. 'They came in low', he recalled, 'I estimate
about 300 to 400 feet and dropped the parachutists from roughly
800 yards south of my positions to the sea in the north'. The greater
concentration landed on 'waste uncultivated flat ground' towards
the village of Ropaniano 'in front of me – that is due west'. By
now the Ju 52s were thundering over Johnson's headquarters 'in
a constant stream', he recalled, 'and we guessed rightly that they

were unloading over the hill south of Battalion HQ in B and A Company positions'. Marcel Comeau on the western slopes of Hill 107 saw 'they floated away from the Junkers like soap-sud bubbles, and still more came'. 'Men who were there say there was something hypnotic in the effect when the first Junkers spewed their cargoes of paratroopers out into the sunlight', reported war correspondent John Hetherington: 'They found themselves gaping, staring in wonder, murmuring *Jesus Christ!*'

'There was perhaps a minute's awestruck inactivity', Peter Butler in Johnson's sector remembered, 'while people realized what was going on, then firing started from all over the area'.[43]

Chapter 5

Parachute Assault

MAJOR REINHARD WENNING, COMMANDER
JU 52 WING *Z.B.V. 105*

Early Morning 20 May 1941, Above Hill 107
More than two hours before, on the Greek mainland, *Major*
Reinhard Wenning, the commander of air transport wing *z. b. V. 105*,
had been worried he may not clear Tanagra airstrip at the appointed
time to meet the operational plan. The 33-year-old Wenning had
transferred into the Luftwaffe from the army aged 25, and worked
his way up the promotion ladder to acting major through a series
of training instructor, technical and administrative appointments.
He had assumed command of the wing the previous February. An
adept organizer, he was the right man to lead and coordinate these
hastily assembled Ju 52 groups. His task was to drop *Major* Eduard
Stentzler's *II Bataillon Sturmregiment* west of Maleme aerodrome at
H Hour. But with half an hour to go, the glider tugs towing Koch's
break-in group had still not got away. Wenning had primarily flown
logistic resupply sorties and was not used to the vagaries of last-
minute changes to combat mission flying serials. He had not flown
in support of the airborne operations in Scandinavia or the West. He
was agitated, more attuned to precise military peacetime schedules.
The situation at the Tanagra airhead was outside his control, there
was no option except to wait. Tension built, he recalled, and 'there
was no sign yet of daylight, it was a starlit night with no moon'.

At last the gliders began to be towed off at 5.30am; 'the others followed far too slowly', he remembered, directed by blinking lights and Verey pistol flares. He heard the thumps of jettisoned glider wheels falling away, 'tumbling threateningly close to my aircraft' parked at the runway edge. Dust spewed into the air by assembling and take-off aircraft 'was extremely dangerous', he recalled, and 'soon blanketed the airfield in a thick cloying fog, so that taxiing and starting aircraft could hardly be made out'. Disconcerting news from headquarters was another distraction: 'late last night', Wenning was informed, 'strong British naval units had been identified west of Crete'. They had been ordered to fly low to avoid detection and detour around if necessary, but would remain extremely vulnerable to ship anti-aircraft fire. At about 6am his first aircraft began taking off 'as the first red rays of the morning sun came over the eastern mountains'.[1]

Leutnant Justus von Schutz with *6. Kompanie* in Stentzler's battalion recalled on taking off 'I was quite confident it would be alright and besides this, I was very tired'. They had been hand-pumping fuel into their aircraft until late the night before. 'I asked my boys to wake me up in time so I could take some pictures.' *Leutnant* Horst Grande was doing just that from the cockpit of 'Emil', his Ju 52 transport plane, flying with *Hauptmann* Kosack's *1. Staffel*, directly following Wenning's *Stabschwarm* (HQ Group). He took images of Ju 52 *Ketten* taking off in threes down below. Each aircraft had a trail of thick dust spiralling out behind it, causing some in the *Kette* to break off and take violent evasive action to avoid impenetrable dust clouds ahead.[2] *Hauptmann* von der Heydte flying with *Fallschirmjäger Regiment 3*, due to drop in adjoining Prison Valley, peered through his aircraft window as it rose above the foggy dust:

The hollows of the airfield were sinking deeper beneath us – deep into the dust cloud which blustered and boiled like a dirty sea. One after another the aircraft lifted themselves out of the reddish-grey fog until they had collected like a flight of huge birds and turned in column towards the south.

It took a while for Wenning's 46-aircraft formation to get airborne and assemble. They flew across Athens, 'the town itself was still in the shadow of a light scarf of mist', he recalled. The early morning sun's rays highlighted the Acropolis, suddenly floating into view, 'head and shoulders above the mist'. Many of the paratroopers in the back were looking out for it, 'an unforgettable sight', von der Heydte remembered.

Wenning's spirits were lifted by the sight of the majestic air transport stream flowing south to Crete; 'the coastline of Attika opened up', he recalled, 'the Bay of Athens and then the wide blue Aegean'. It was his first combat mission, as also for many of his crews. Stentzler periodically came forward into the flight cabin to monitor progress. They were soon flying over the mountains of the southern peninsula of the Peloponnese. *Oberfeldwebel* Nowak, Wenning's aircraft captain, almost brushed one of the craggy summits, which caused some consternation, but he managed to haul the overloaded Ju 52 over the underestimated height, 'a case of only a few metres', Wenning nervously recalled. They then descended to between 16 and 32 feet flying low level across the sea, with spray intermittently spiralling behind the aircraft. Now and again small islands emerged from the light mist, causing a start as they so resembled the enemy warships they had been warned against. A fuggy atmosphere inside the fuselages combined with the droning tri-motor engines and uneventful flat views outside soon had the soldiers nodding off. Roaring engines 'became distant', von der Heydte remembered, 'no louder than the humming of bees'. Most were soon asleep.[3]

Wenning set course to a point to some 18 miles off the west coast of Crete, 'aiming to surprise the enemy by coming from an unexpected direction'. *Oberst* Rüdiger von Heyking commanding *Kampfgeschwader z.b.V. 2*, the 2nd Air Transport Wing, led the route, recalling: 'Skimming the water along the east coast of the Peloponnese, they headed toward the western part of Crete, then turned east, crossed the mountains on the west coast of Crete, and descended toward the targets.'

Willi Maue with Stentzler's *5. Kompanie* remembered it was 'a superb flight': 'The sky was completely clear and we crossed the

Mediterranean at somewhere between 50 to 100 metres. From time to time we could even see the bottom of the sea.'

After one hour and ten minutes into the flight, Wenning watched his *2. Staffel* 'take a long curve to the left as at the same time the shadowy western coastline of Crete came in sight'. The island steadily rose up like a cliff out of the glittering sea to meet them. Surf and light sandy beaches were soon visible, 'then already detail – mountains and several houses'. Two flights of Me 109 fighters flashed by, overtaking them, en route to the drop zones, 'as now we fly over the Cretan coastline'. Deep blue sea glinting with the sparkle of early morning sunlight dancing over waves transitioned to milky blue when the transports thundered over the beaches.[4]

Hauptmann Wendorff the *Absetzer* or jumpmaster for Wenning's *Stabschwarm* emerged in the cabin, map in hand, to confer with Nowak 'over the final and decisive flight path' to Stentzler's agreed drop zone. The *Stabschwarm* closed up behind the lead *2. Staffel*, followed by the *4.*, *1.* and *3. Staffeln*, in that order. Down to about 500 feet with mountain summits in close proximity, pilots feathered engines to reduce momentum to about 100mph, virtual stalling speed. This was, as Student's later after-action report emphasized, demanding high-risk flying:

Flying in an unprotected, slow moving cumbersome aircraft at low level, in heavy opposing fire from all calibres, is highly demanding for all crews. Necessary changes in direction, moreover, at low heights in totally strange terrain, with no recourse to curve and fly again, are conditions that place crews under the most difficult circumstances they are liable to encounter.[5]

Many of the Junkers air transport crews were not trained to drop parachutists, having only recently been assembled ad hoc within special-for-purpose air transport groups. Ground visibility in the forward cockpit of the tri-motor Ju 52 is obscured by engine cowlings, left and right, and the forward propeller ring. Crew had to maintain formation in *Ketten* of threes while throttling back and feathering engines to maintain constant dropping speed, keeping an eye on *Schwarm* aircraft ahead while varying speed and distance. They had also to watch the ground coming up to distinguish the vital orientation points to guide them in. All this had to happen as light flak came up, tell-tale puffs of smoke from 40mm Bofors anti-aircraft fire, that concealed bursting shrapnel, mixed in also with distracting lines of incendiary tracer that reached out to hose down the aircraft in front.

Wenning's *Absetzer* flying the lead aircraft of the *Kette* had to display a yellow flag, which is poked up through an opening in the top cockpit window, two minutes out from the jump. This was – *Fertig machen!* – the *Get ready!* signal. Parachutists in back of the aircraft stood up and hooked up their parachutes to the *Sprungseile* or jump-wire, running inside the aircraft below the roof, and turned to face the small exit door on the port side at the rear of the aircraft. When jumping out, the parachute is automatically pulled out from the container strapped to the parachutist's back. With 30 seconds to go the yellow pennant flapping in the slipstream was pulled back inside and replaced with a red and white flag, which signalled *Fertig zum Spring!* or *Ready to jump!* All the parachutists then moved down the aircraft with the first man shuffling to the door. Stomach churning, he bent at the restricted opening, knees inward, holding a hand rail at either side. Facial skin tended to contort in the slipstream as he looked out.

A storm of small arms fire was beginning to rise up from the ground, loud cracks as bullets sped by, breaking the sound barrier. Drum rolls of metallic clacking sounded out when the corrugated sides of the aircraft fuselage were perforated by rounds puncturing on entry and exiting with the same metallic chorus. Wendorff yanked the red and white pennant down inside the cockpit, the signal for *Go!* The shouted *Los!* was accompanied by the klaxon *blaaaa... ah!* of the jump bull horn. Stentzler, the number one, launched through the open door, hands and arms outstretched in the 'crucifix' position, like a high-board diver.

'Seconds later', Wenning recalled, 'repeated jolts from behind in the aircraft indicated successful jumps by our paratroopers'. The need for focused concentration by pilots amid all the attention-grabbing distractions became apparent when Wenning realized they were too close to the port-side aircraft flying in parallel, either side:

> Suddenly with a terrible sound my plane lurched forward and I could see out of the corner of my eye that the right wing of the plane on my left was touching our wing. It could have been serious, because obviously that pilot was concentrating on what was happening on the ground and didn't realize his plane had drifted into mine. We averted disaster by lowering our flap and banking to the right.[6]

The leap into the void by successive parachutists was arrested by a fierce tug as the parachute opened automatically with a five-second delay, after free-falling about 80 feet. The rough jolt was a particular feature of the low-opening RZ-1 German parachute, which tended to fling legs into the air, occasionally causing muscle strain, if the parachute harness had not been heftily tightened. Enormous relief followed. As Stentzler's *II Bataillon* jumped, twisting and turning in the slip stream, each man glimpsed snow-capped mountains to one side and momentarily a view of the sea with its rim of surf on the other. Green hills flashed by in quick succession, squat flat-roofed houses, fields, plantations, trees, rocks and brittle grass until, finally, undulating ground rushed up to meet them. As the sound of aircraft engines receded into the distance the crackling of small arms became ever more intense. The momentary relief of the parachute opening tug was superseded by the feeling of dread at the unexpectedly instant and fierce resistance. Shock was all the greater after seeing the large numbers of Luftwaffe combat aircraft, who were already working over the drop zones on arrival.

Twelve men and four weapons canisters generally cleared the aircraft within 9 to 10 seconds. Casualties or hesitation might impede the doorway and thence the flow. Wenning glanced down as his Ju 52 stream curved to the left out to sea, passing the capital Chania out to the starboard side: 'I saw one parachutist after another landing down there, in an area which I can only describe as very difficult; mountain formations, very rugged and chalky, vineyards, olive trees, and dry fields, with small villages and narrow roads.' All around 'were the countless white spots of parachutes, in trees or on the ground, where the soldiers had discarded them'. Fighting erupted below. The density of resistance visibly escalated and was completely unexpected. *Leutnant* Egbert Freiherr von Könitz's Ju 52 'received many hits' over Maleme and pilots felt vulnerable in unarmoured seats. He recalled the multiple metallic crackling of 'a machine gun burst hit behind the co-pilot's seat, and our on-board mechanic *Feldwebel* Schwörer was hit in the head and seriously wounded'. It also shredded the tyre of their starboard landing gear wheel, which led to a 'circular dance pirouette' when they made an emergency landing at Megara. On inspection they found their starter cable had been shot through, which put the aircraft out of action.

Wenning was trying to control the *Geschwader* stream as 'from the ground, fierce opposing fire crackled up against us': 'Muzzle flash from numerous weapons indicated we were offering a very favourable target to the enemy. Then there was a blow to the aircraft – a strike! Where though cannot be determined.'[7]

'Our Junkers pilot was faced with heavy AA fire', recalled Willi Maue with Stentzler's *II Bataillon*; he did well, 'despite his fear and thanks to his skill as a pilot, he guided us towards the drop zone'. There was no shortage of distractions; 'it was hell!' he emphasized, 'the Ju 52 on our right crashed into a mountain side'. This meant 'our platoon found itself less than a third of its strength' even before the beginning of the battle. 'Our parachutists did not reach the ground in a very tight formation', he remembered, 'on the contrary, they were very spread out': 'A good number of my comrades were wounded before hitting the ground, like my platoon commander *Leutnant* Ulli Kiesewetter, who was hit in the pelvis by a bullet; he was out of the fight.'

Flag-signalling the drop by the *Absetzer* depended upon line of sight from the other aircraft, not always guaranteed. This produced variable jump starts, impacting on the exit flow from doorways and affecting the landing densities on the ground. The distance between each jumper on exit might be anything from 100 to 170 feet, producing a separation of between 460 to 765 yards or so on the ground for a stick of parachutists. This and the fearful tension of doing it under intense fire accounted for the dispersed drops that Willi Maue commented on over Maleme. 'We landed directly in front of the British lines of defence', he recalled, 'where we suffered heavy losses again' on top of those already hit in the air during the 18–30-second descent. 'I jumped near Hill 107' badly dispersed, vulnerable and without immediate access to weapons containers. Once down 'I had to remain under cover and protect my rear' before 'heading east' to rejoin his own troops.

Leutnant Justus von Schutz, who jumped with the *6. Kompanie*, immediately felt vulnerable amid the storm of fire and 'took out grenades from my pocket in case somebody would be there, and try to fight them from the air'. 'We had no weapons', he recalled:

We only had our pistol and grenades, all the other equipment was dropped in containers from the same aircraft, but separately. I thought I would come to the river or the trees. I tried to steer a little bit to avoid them both, and dropped in the pampas [grass] near the river.[8]

Wenning led the Junkers stream into a tight curve to port, overflying 'a tented camp, from which we received heavy fire'. His dorsal gunner mounted behind responded in kind. 'To our right was Chania, the capital of Crete, from which black smoke was pouring from the centre', he noted with satisfaction, 'our bombers had made an impact'. Beneath them were fighters, wheeling, diving and strafing ground targets at low level, supporting them the whole way. Not a single enemy fighter was seen, which 'was icing on the cake', he observed. The formation reassembled after the drop and set off once again at wave-top level back to the Greek mainland.

By 11am they were back at Tanagra where Wenning spent the next half hour watching his aircraft landing. There was considerable relief when he could account for them all. Some, however, were so badly shot up they had to be withdrawn from further operations. All four *Staffel* commanders reported in, assuring Wenning their drops had been accurate. 'Whether that was the case', Wenning reflected, 'we will hear back later from the parachutists themselves'. Ground crews started to patch the damage while air crew headed for steaming field cookers, 'body and soul needing to be refreshed for the second wave'. Paratroopers due to jump at Rethymnon and Iraklion were already loading heavy equipment and weapon containers aboard serviceable Ju 52s. So far as *Major* Wenning was concerned, the operation appeared to be going well.[9]

LIEUTENANT COLONEL LESLIE ANDREW, COMMANDER 22 NEW ZEALAND BATTALION

08.30–11.30 20 May, Summit of Hill 107
'We had a panoramic view of the whole dropping', recalled Andrew's second in command Major Jim Leggat, sharing the battalion command post with him at the summit of Hill 107. He was so excited at the parachutists exiting their aircraft, that he began to shoot at 700 yards, before realizing 'I hadn't put my sights up'. New Zealand soldier Clarence Gordon recalled 'they just floated down':

> They were not high up, two or three hundred feet I suppose. I don't know how long, for the first minute or ten seconds – I wouldn't know – all of a sudden somebody pulled a trigger, and then she was on. The whole thing was on.

Below the headquarters, on the western slopes of Hill 107, every defender fired at every German within range. Aircraftsman Marcel Comeau remembered:

They fell on all sides and it was sometimes difficult to know which target to pick. The dead were probably hit several times over as they fell among the living. The few who reached the ground alive grabbed their parachutes and instantly vanished into the shrubbery.

He saw one aircraft on fire, with 'men leaping out to escape the flames', while near the beach 'a troop carrier hit the sea with a wing and, in slow motion, cartwheeled into the water with a mighty splash'. Andrew's headquarters was virtually co-located with Captain Stan Hanton's A Company, whose men held fire until the descending parachutists were about 100 feet from the ground. Hanton 'saw dozens of corpses on the ground or in the trees'. Twenty-two live Germans who dropped in and around the company area were swiftly accounted for. 'During the lulls', he recalled, 'the men grabbed any German stores that landed near them'. They were amazed at the quality and quantities of equipment thudding down. 'There were canisters of gear, food, motor cycles and even warm coffee from Hun flasks.' Captain Ken Crarer's B Company on the slopes on the other side of the Maleme to Vlakheronitissa road traversing Hill 107 was overflown by successive flights of Ju 52s, 'dropping directly over and beyond us', according to Lieutenant Slade, one of the platoon commanders. 'By this time the Browning [machine gun] was smoking hot', he recalled, 'and I was frantically reloading and spraying the Jerries as they continued the line to circle the drome'. 'One of my NCOs, Lance-Corporal Elliott', Crarer's 11 Platoon commander recalled, 'Took a couple of men despite the standing order that no man was to leave his trench and went down into the valley where several Jerries had landed among the trees, and cleaned them out.'

A container dropped out after every fourth or fifth man, providing rich pickings of machine guns, pistols, Tommy guns and grenades. Comeau came across a wounded *Fallschirmjäger*:

His bared leg was a sickening pulp of red, bullet-shattered flesh and bone. The poor devil must have caught a burst from a Lewis. He was in great pain; agony contorted his sweating face. I felt pity for him. No longer a matchstick man to knock down, a mere clay-pipe target at a fairground, the enemy became a human being for the first time. I heard myself saying: 'all right old chap' as we eased him under a shady bush.[10]

Andrew, as was the case with the men around him, had never seen such an awe-inspiring spectacle as a mass parachute descent, so had problems interpreting what they were looking at. He was still off balance; having overestimated the strength of the glider assault, he now underestimated the number of parachutists that had landed to his front. His battalion log estimated at 09.30 that some '400 to 600 parachutists were landed in our area in this first wave'. Virtually every eye on Hill 107 focused at short range, the nearest landed parachutist or the hint of movement from a nearby bush, or the bizarre. Comeau's eye was caught by 'An isolated parachutist, caught by a thermal, drifted away over the sea, receding from us to a watery death, pulled down by the weight of his equipment.' He thought 'the loss of life must have been fantastic' but those 'who did survive, however, quickly vanished from sight'.

Andrew's visual terrain scan suggested maybe 100 or so had landed near the airfield, 150 behind them to the east and probably another 150 west of the river and near the beach. In fact, over 1,000 Germans had landed unharmed behind the curtain of dust still lingering on the lower slopes of Hill 107, and many of them less than a mile away.[11] Three observers had been dispatched due west to watch out from the heights by the village of Roponiana, but none had returned. If they had, it might have transformed Andrew's perception of this most unusual battle, so entirely different from his experience in 1914–18.

Little or no information, apart from what he could personally observe, was getting through. Several gliders had settled silently between Headquarters Company in Pirgos village and Battalion HQ about a mile away. This did not augur well for the survival prospects of Lieutenant Beaven's small Headquarters force of three officers and 60 men. They were 'cooks and bottlewashers' or administrative staff, not former riflemen. They were isolated. Figures could be seen moving among the buildings, but nobody knew who they were. Beaven tried to send runners to Battalion HQ and B Company just beyond, but none made it back. All telephone wires at HQ were cut; the only conduit for information and messages was runners, who often had to fight to get through.

Isolated groups of Germans were still wandering in the vicinity of A Company nearby. Lance Corporal Chittenden and Private Bill Croft were having a quiet smoke in their trench when Chittenden noticed Croft's 'hands slowly rising and a look of alarm on his face'. Glancing up 'four Germans tommy guns in hand were standing at the end of the trench beckoning to us to get out'. Croft rose and received a full fatal burst of fire. Chittenden grappled with the German leader and was soon rolling over and over down the slope, until stunned by either a heavy blow or shots. When he managed to reach an aid post, no one was convinced there were four Germans in the vicinity, and they were never seen again.[12]

Andrew, worried about the fate of Beaven's weak contingent in Pirgos village behind Hill 107, tried to get down and reach them: 'I endeavoured to contact HQ Company myself, and was fired at by Germans in the valley and under the trees between Battalion HQ, HQ Company and B Company. I went to ground and before withdrawing counted eight enemy.'[13]

Sergeant Francis Twigg, Andrew's intelligence officer, recalled that 'as Battalion HQ was practically in A Company area, we naturally were in close contact with that company'. With B Company just across the intervening village road, I have no reason to believe that we were ever isolated from B Company'.

But dispatch riders 'either to or from Battalion HQ to C, D and HQ Companies were apparently impossible'. All runners inward or outbound 'during that morning' failed to reappear. Uncertainty was exacerbated by a bogus message from 5 Brigade HQ that the enemy was jumping in New Zealand uniforms – an echo of the previous Fifth Column hysteria that had plagued the Blitzkrieg campaign in France. 'Colonel Blimps' at staff were unable to make the mental leap from paratroopers as clandestine operators to an unprecedented mass parachute assault. Andrew sent two runners out to relay this false information to the companies, but both were wounded.

Pandemonium reigned in and around the tented camp and the RAF administrative building on the lower west slope of Hill 107. This was the immediate area of concern for Andrew and his second in command Major Leggat. Sergeant Twigg was sent forward of the command post to block any German infiltration coming up the hill from that direction. Twigg tended to be employed as a roving problem solver more than an intelligence sergeant. Andrew had already shared his concern with Leggat about the vulnerability posed by the RAF camp, which compromised the integrity of the defence line between C Company on the airfield and D covering the Tavronitis bridge. 'There is no doubt', Leggat later recalled, that 'the position of the RAF camp was the weakness in our defence' because 'the camp commanded the bridge, the obvious line of attack'.[14] *Major* Franz Braun's reserve force of nine gliders had landed near the bridge, and Braun was dead, still strapped into the central bench of the glider, like most of the men who had flown with him. Remnants of this force had been rallied by *Oberleutnant* Horst Trebes, and these survivors had sallied into the RAF camp and administrative building and created chaos. One Fleet Air Arm officer in the camp admitted:

We didn't know where our own people were; we didn't know where the enemy were; many people had no rifles and no ammunition … if anyone fired at you, he might be (a) an enemy (b) a friend who thought you were an enemy (c) a friend or an enemy who didn't know who the hell you were (d) someone not firing at you at all.

Trebes and his men were not labouring under any such dilemmas, the imperative was to overcome the enemy if they wanted to live. Marcel Comeau witnessed the unequal struggle: 'single shot rifles were no match for the automatic weapons and hand grenades now turned upon them'. Despite outnumbering the attackers, the contest was unequal. 'Some of the men who had been on their way to the dining tent had only their mug and eating irons with which to defend themselves.' Any resistance was ruthlessly suppressed as one by one most of the isolated defenders were killed or captured. Twigg observing from above viewed the leaderless and haphazardly armed RAF personnel as 'hampering to the battalion and added to the confusion of positions'. Rumours of Germans dressed as New Zealanders added to the chaotic mix. 'Our own troops were suspicious of any unknown personnel', he recalled, and there were scores milling around, making their way to the summit of Hill 107. 'Small parties and individuals moving about in various and incomplete British uniforms were constantly worrying battalion men as to their identity and intention.'

Comeau remembered one young 30 Squadron airman who blindly ran full tilt into the arms of a German glider trooper. 'The German disarmed him before he recovered from the shock, presented him with a packet of cigarettes and three lemons, gave him a swig of coffee, and told him to *beat it!*' Andrew was only too aware of this Achilles heel in the defence. Twigg recalled 'groups of leaderless men' who were 'demoralized and spoke in a defeatist manner'. The overall impact was 'making our troops bewildered and unsure of their positions' which 'inclined to make them distrustful as to the stability of troops on their flanks [and] rear'.[15] Inevitably, as Major Jim Leggat recalled: 'The only place where our perimeter was pierced except for the odd glider man was in the RAF sector, where German troops were in occupation of the olive grove containing the RAF RAP [Regimental Aid Post] above the camp.'

Andrew was soon attracted by 'a definite commotion' according to Twigg, 'heard below the ridge in the direction of the Air Force camp'. The ruthless Trebes was driving up a large party of about 30 to 40 variously uniformed RAF and other personnel, which he was employing as a hostage screen, behind which he moved with a handful of German glider men. Twigg watched them advance 'with hands above their heads, many terror-stricken, all yelling and pleading with us not to shoot'. The bewildered New Zealand defenders looked to Leggat and Twigg for guidance. They could only see two enemy troopers with Schmeisser machine pistols urging them forward. Prisoners were urged to dash for the lower ground coming up, or drop on the order 'fire'. It was kill or be killed. 'Simultaneously, one or more of our troops fired at the oncoming prisoners', Twigg recalled, 'and at least one dropped, shot in the guts'. Leggat explained 'ultimately the first man had to be dropped to see if any Germans were behind. There were not'. Any isolated Germans still standing were picked off or disappeared. 'This action took only a few minutes', Twigg remembered, 'and the position was restored'.[16]

At 10.55am Andrew radioed Brigadier Hargest at 5 Brigade Headquarters that 400 to 600 paratroopers had landed in and around his area. One group jumped out over Maleme village behind his HQ: 'in the narrow streets and on the flat-roofed houses. Street fighting immediately developed with HQ Company trying to dislodge German troops with their Schmeissers and MG 34s from the houses, from the roof tops and from the church.'

The main landings he identified were around Hill 107, one group between the two villages to his south and the largest element along the dried-up Tavronitis river bed, to their front. He was literally enveloped, dismaying for an experienced 1914–18 veteran, accustomed and schooled to contest linear front lines. Concentrations of troops were appearing from nowhere, in strength, and at partially obscured locations all around. This was unprecedented. He asked Hargest at brigade for news about his seemingly cut-off Headquarters Company in Pirgos. There was no contact and he could not see what was going on from the summit of Hill 107. Lieutenant Beaven's 'storemen and drivers' had only two Bren guns and no Tommy guns and were clearly engaged. Noise and fleeting sightings suggested the defence 'was only partial successful'. He was not to know the German incursion into the village had been fiercely contested and Beaven was still zealously holding out. As might be expected Andrew, despite feeling isolated, was characteristically reluctant to admit it. He reported to Hargest that his 'line was still intact and [the battalion] were holding everywhere'.[17]

Andrew itemized his concerns in the battalion log. Although he was holding the line, there was *no front line* in this engagement. Fronts appeared all around. All his telephone lines had been knocked out by the bombing and his radio link to brigade was weak and intermittent. Runners were not getting through to the companies. He also felt uneasy about an apparently growing German presence to his south. Aircraftsman Marcel Comeau on Hill 107 gave fleeting glimpses of what he saw in that direction:

Lying due south of us, Vlakheronitissa, a handful of white-walled houses like grazing sheep on the hillside, appeared deserted, but to our right, near the glider infested Tavronitis, we could make out 21 Battalion's gallant platoon, who were heavily engaged and battling it out in isolation. Two gliders lay across their positions.

Andrew was especially worried about the right flank of D Company, whose 18 Platoon had been driven in and partially overrun. This suggested to Andrew that D Company, lying at the foot of the western convex slope of Hill 107 and therefore in dead ground to the summit, had likely been overrun. However, D Company had already killed plenty of Germans and was expecting to be included in the general counter-attack that they were anxious to see starting. 15 Platoon, Andrew surmised, must surely have been overcome, with the plethora of gliders and paratroopers that had come down immediately to the west of

C Company. Lieutenant Robin Sinclair, the platoon commander, later recalled 'during the morning we appeared to be holding our own despite fire from all directions, and I was not unduly worried'. He remained optimistic:

> Plenty of good targets and an interesting attack provided all the diversion one needed. I had no reason to believe that the machine guns on the Hill [107] behind were not firing because we did not hear them and we certainly did not, or that others were not doing alright, so we just hung on and hoped. New uninitiated troops do not know much fear.[18]

Sinclair was shot in the neck about an hour later.

Andrew was also uneasy about potential German infiltration of the lower slopes of Hill 107 east of the bridge. Although he could see the bridge from his command post, the lower slopes were in dead ground. The ridge to his north and east of D Company was the protrusion along which German parties had twice now attempted penetrations, behind the cover of hostage screens. These cumulative concerns were notable enough to be included in the battalion log. Andrew felt ever more isolated. His intelligence sergeant remembered non-battle-trained RAF and Fleet Air Arm elements 'wandering about and in a panicky condition was inclined to make the battalion area appear confused and made it difficult for all officers and NCOs to know what was happening'.

Rumours of Germans dressed in New Zealand uniforms were rife. Andrew's Regimental Sergeant Major S.A.R. Purnell was killed during the hostage skirmish incident; a mature sounding board for the men's morale had been lost. Andrew had been touchy about the penetration. A section sent up by Captain Johnson from C Company to assist was sent back, with Andrew admonishing 'look after your own backyard – I'll look after mine'. He felt the need to establish a solid line of defence, as he would have done in 1918. But here the enemy was denying him one. In fact, he did not even know where the line was.[19]

GENERALMAJOR EUGEN MEINDL, COMMANDER
STURMREGIMENT

08.30–12.30 20 May, Tavronitis River Bed, Foot of Hill 107
Meindl unusually chose to jump behind his heavy weapons *IV Bataillon* commander, *Hauptmann* Walter Gericke, a useful companion to share ideas with. Gericke had been one of the first members of Herman Göring's paramilitary state police group to transfer into the *Fallschirmjäger* in 1935. He had an illustrious combat record, having seen airborne action in Denmark, Norway and Holland. His big name befitted his considerable height, already a legend with his soldiers. Meindl elected to follow him out the door of the Ju 52, normally the prerequisite of the senior commander, because he explained, Narvik had been his first and only parachute jump. He had never completed the parachute course. Crete was his second jump. He philosophically added that landing in any case was a given, *how* to jump was the issue. 'You jump out first and I'll hop out behind', the general insisted, 'then I can copy everything you do in the air'.[20] The flight gave Meindl two hours to contemplate what was required. It also gave time to exhaustively ponder the plan and bounce any imponderables off the man who was to direct his heavy fire support. The 'cold shower' immersion of the parachutist to instant battle would require quick reactions. Both men were left to contemplate the blank faces occupying the aircraft benches opposite with much on their minds.

Soldiers regarding them, in the back of the lumbering Ju 52s, had few such distractions. *Jäger* Lingg with Gericke's *IV Bataillon* recalled 'sitting on hard bunks, feeling so lonely that we hardly moved'. Gericke had given them the statutory pep talk: 'Germany will be proud of her paratroops', he announced at the final address prior to boarding, expecting 'each man will do his duty!' But after nearly two hours Lingg remembered 'the straps were cutting into our flesh' and 'tension was inexorably building up' although 'none of us ever admitted it'. Gericke stepped inside the pilot's cabin when land started to protrude above the line of their wave-hopping approach. 'Unmistakeably the White Mountains emerged from the sea in a majestic line', he recalled, 'like a glittering diamond climbing into the blue sky'. Lingg felt the aircraft gently bank and enter a wide curve onto a different course: 'We skirted the western end of the island and headed south. Again the aircraft reversed its bearing and headed north.'

By now they had stood up and hooked up. The previous two hours had seemed interminable. 'I looked at the floor', he recalled, 'my stomach as heavy as lead; weird thoughts flashed across my mind'.[21] Meindl had thought through every conceivable tactical ruse that might be employed to surprise an enemy that was obviously expecting them. He directed the stream approach to the drop zones should come out of the south-east. Air defences would then be looking into the face of the Mediterranean morning sun, which should dazzle them.

Gericke was crouched at the door waiting for the jump bullhorn to sound, cheeks quivering in the slipstream, as he peered out looking for orientation points. The sun-baked channels of the dry River Tavronitis estuary were the first markers to stand out, followed by the 'red clay tennis court' runways of Maleme aerodrome. The rest fitted in, the white flat-roofed village houses of Pirgos and Maleme, the bridge over the estuary and blue ocean, visible through the starboard windows behind him. Sharp reverberating cracks from flak came up just before the bullhorn blared and Gericke, arms outstretched in the crucible position, launched himself into the void. He was followed almost immediately by Meindl and *Oberstabsarzt* Dr Neumann. As more paratroopers fell out a storm of small arms fire enfolded them.

Glider soldier Ferdinand Fink at the western edge of the aerodrome below heard:

A noise like a huge swarm of bees, slight at first but soon swelling to a threatening roar filling the air with the familiar sound of many Ju 52s droning by, coming out of the east at about 700 feet and following the coast road.

The noise of their reinforcement was met with enormous relief and satisfaction, 'with the louder roar of the "freighters" enemy small arms fire swelled to an unholy din'. At least there was no heavy Bofors fire, a sign that the 'iron third' glider *Kompanie* had largely silenced them. 'But what was that?' they observed:

> The first paras were exiting the machines over the bridge, far too early we determined. We knew the plan was for them to drop west of the village. So the airborne carpet of Gericke's battalion came out from the bridge on, over woods and villages in the way, up to fields in the west.

Meindl's experience was not much unlike that of *Hauptmann* von der Heydte, who described his jump into Prison Valley further south.

> I pushed with hands and feet, throwing my arms forward as if trying to clutch the black cross on the wing. And then the slipstream caught me, and I was swirling through the space with the air roaring in my ears. A sudden jerk upon the webbing, a pressure on the chest which knocked the breath out of my lungs, and then – I looked upwards and saw spread above me, the wide-open motley hood of my parachute. In relation to this giant umbrella I felt small and insignificant. It was like descending in a lift.[22]

When Meindl looked up about half the men in their aircraft were out, but the rear end of the fuselage was blazing like a torch. The aircraft banked away out to sea trailing black smoke, having been directly hit by flak.

'We were delighted to leave the aircraft, because we thought they couldn't hit us as easy as they could in the plane', *Jäger* Felix Gaerte remembered, 'but that was not so':

> In the air I heard this whistling of bullets around me. But whistling is not so bad to hear, because you know everything

you hear is already past, it can't hit you any more. And then I looked down and saw some soldiers.[23]

Gericke recognized one of his platoon commanders swinging in the air and waved. Holding a machine pistol in his left fist, he attempted to steer his chute with the right. Steering was only achievable by waving arms and kicking legs. A flak burst suddenly perforated his canopy which folded, increasing the rate of descent. He plunged, face first into a barley field, emerging with a bloody nose and severely bruised arm. Winded, dazed and battered, he was unable to disentangle himself from his parachute harness. Somebody crawled over on all fours as bullets hissed and whined overhead. '*Nanu* [aye-aye] what's up here?' the figure asked. He took his helmet off and helped Gericke from his harness; it was Meindl. They immediately took cover behind a wall; the intensity of this fire being directed against the drop was completely unexpected.[24]

Jäger Lingg tumbled over two or three times on leaving the aircraft 'until my parachute opened with a sharp jolt. *Thank God!* Was all I could say'. 'Another brutal jolt' happened in the next instant, accompanied by a sharp blow. *Jäger* Peisker from the same stick had collided with him in mid-air. Winded, 'my helmet fell off my head', the fastening straps had been torn away 'and the rim smashed my nose in the process'. Blood squirted all over his face as he began 'spinning like a dancing dervish'. With horror he realized he was inextricably intertwined with Peisker's parachute. They now entered the sequential 'air-steal' fatal combination of one parachute umbrella repeatedly stealing the air from the canopy above. This resulted in repeated plummeting as the supporting air was lost, 'spinning' and 'bumping into each other all the way' until one of the canopies reflated. The intermittent rate of alarming descent would remorselessly carry on until the entangled pair hit the ground at a rate that would inevitably cause serious injury, or even death. Lingg 'was in terrible pain' and worse still, dangling horizontally instead of 'dropping feet foremost'. Each had the presence of mind to grab the other tightly when they fell past, which meant one of the parachutes collapsed and fell away, leaving them suspended jointly under the surviving chute, no longer starved of air. This all transpired in a matter of seconds. The pendulum drop was ceased when they snagged a tree at the edge of a steep gully, which they rolled into, 1,000 yards from the Tavronitis bridge. They had been totally focused on surviving the unnerving drop, to the exclusion of all else. Only inside the gully did they become aware of the intensity of the fire being directed against them.[25]

Meindl separated from Gericke and left him to move back to reorganize his battalion. Fire support would not be immediately forthcoming. Much of the heavy equipment, suspended by multiple parachutes was unusable, snagged inside branches or hung up on olive trees. Most of the motorcycle combinations foreseen as towing vehicles, were out of action. Lieutenant Craig with D Company opposite saw 'several were seen entangled in trees or else they broke away from their chutes and were destroyed in the fall'. One of two mountain guns landed by glider crashed, killing all the crew members and destroying the gun. Some of Gericke's men had landed too close to Hill 107, and could be seen lying dead nearby, still wearing their parachute harnesses. Gericke glanced up at Hill 107, where 'it looked as though a thick yellow snake was writhing around the summit'.[26]

Jäger Fink at the edge of the aerodrome with the remnants of *3. Kompanie* noted with relief that the carpet of paratroopers from the *II* and *IV Bataillone* landed relatively unscathed to the west of the bridge. 'The enemy had demonstrated with his wild shoot-out', Fink observed, 'how many infantry were dug in from the northern heights [of Hill 107] to the aerodrome, and on the western slope up to the bridge'. It had not been a reassuring sight. 'How long then would our ten men remain unscathed?' he reflected. Gericke came into view, his face covered with dried blood, observing from the road at the olive groves either side of the bridge. 'The man radiated a picture of coolness', he recalled. What was unsettling was that the New Zealanders chose not to engage the reconnaissance patrols sent forward to investigate.

'We realized our enemy was well trained and unusually disciplined'. This did not augur well. 'We began to appreciate it would not be easy to finish them off.'[27]

Propelled by a need to get information, leaders headed towards the important points to find out what was going on. Meindl and Gericke gravitated towards the bridge embankment. Meindl was desperate for situation reports. Radio provision was proving a total disaster. The 80-watt regimental radio set flying in by glider with von Seelen crashed, seriously injuring the indefatigable adjutant and his two operators. Even more serious was the loss of the long-range radio sets. Two gliders carrying the 200-watt transmitter had piled in, killing the entire radio team and completely destroying the set. There would be no communication with Student back in Athens. *Leutnant* Göttsche, Meindl's signals officer, turned up with the one 40-watt transmitter he had salvaged from a wrecked glider and started to cannibalize the damaged sets to hopefully restore communications with Corps. A rudimentary regimental HQ was established in the vicinity of the bridge. There was no radio traffic until mid-morning.[28]

Generalmajor Meindl was aware the *IV* and *II Bataillone* were down, albeit dispersed, because he had watched the end of the landings. He had no idea the regiment had already lost over one-third of its combat strength. With some frustration he strode up and down the bridge road, trying to discern what had happened to Koch's command, which ought by now to be on the aerodrome and in possession of Hill 107. Looking anxiously down the coast road, he anticipated the arrival of Scherber's *III Bataillon*, due to land behind Hill 107. It should be pushing against the aerodrome from the east. Fink watched the *General* just short of the bridge 'striding here and there, with an air recognition flag [red with a swastika in the white circle at centre] in his left hand and pistol in the right'. He was vulnerable, Fink thought, and 'nervous, because he could easily see that the attack either side of the bridge was not going as he had planned'.

Fink's men were quietly directed by Meindl to advance through the bushy terrain north of the bridge, and secure it from any surprises coming from that direction. Fink thought Meindl was reckless going up and down the bridge embankment, 'a wandering target', to get a better view of Koch's progress on Hill 107 opposite. 'Herr General', he called out, 'would it not be better to do that lying down?' 'Don't concern yourself about me, lad', he was told, 'just do *your* things well'. Eight bodies were strewn about Braun's gliders on the near side of the bridge, and on the other side were several more bodies wearing parachute harnesses from Gericke's battalion. Meindl moved again to the dry river bed to improve the view, vainly waving the aircraft recognition panel, seeking to attract Koch's attention on the other side. Koch's command had, however, already been decimated and he himself, felled by a bullet to the head. The only response the exasperated Meindl got was a bullet that creased his hand. Even more frustrated the *General* got up and continued waving until a burst of machine-gun fire stitched across his chest. He had to be recovered by stretcher to the field dressing station, set up in the few houses in Tavronitis village by *Oberstabsarzt* Dr Neumann. Meindl insisted on retaining overall command from his bed, but directed his next most senior officer *Major* Stentzler, commanding *II Bataillon*, to control the actual fighting.[29]

Meindl had already appreciated the need to capture Hill 107, which he saw visibly dominated the aerodrome. Stentzler was directed to penetrate an apparent weak link in the protective girdle around the heights, which was the area between the bridge and the aerodrome to its right. He further proposed a flank envelopment from the south. Meindl's physical condition, however, visibly deteriorated. Dr Heinrich Neumann was already convinced the General's best hope of survival lay in an immediate evacuation flight to Athens, a major operation and then intensive care. Meanwhile conditions in the dressing station set up in a rustic village house were becoming steadily grimmer. Ever more severely wounded paratroopers were being carried or hobbling in, desperate for treatment.

Both Stentzler and Gericke's battalions had experienced dispersed drops and needed time to locate and recover weapons containers.

Much of Gericke's heavy equipment had to be recovered from trees. Stentzler's *II Bataillon* had at least been able to form up without being harassed by fire. Lingg, who had survived his entanglement, 'had to sit down. My knees were wobbly. A "black veil" fell over my eyes'. Many of his comrades who had watched the dramatic episode clapped him on the back, Peisker was convinced Lingg had saved his life. Their weapons container had landed in the river bed, where they recovered their rifles and machine-gun ammunition. 'We were lucky as the spot was in a dead angle, unexposed to enemy fire', he recalled, 'some distance from the New Zealand positions': 'The sun was scorching. It was really hot on this island. I was to cross the dried-up river bed as, in the middle some water trickled, which came in handy to refresh my face.'[30]

Six of Reinhard Wenning's *z.b.V. 105* Ju 52 aircraft had peeled away from the main stream after crossing the coast, heading for the town of Kastelli. They carried the *Kampfgruppe* Mürbe, the reinforced platoon extracted from Stentzler's *II Bataillon*. The 27-year-old *Leutnant* Peter Mürbe had been delighted and flattered to be entrusted with an important independent role in this dramatic corps-size airborne operation. His aircraft were divided into two *Ketten* of three aircraft each: Mürbe's command group and *Feldwebel* Lübker's platoon. They were due to secure a height south of Kastelli, which Mürbe managed to identify and his three aircraft dropped at 8.25am. Navigation had not been easy and in the event they dropped too near the town, north and south of the main road leading into it. They came under immediate fire from Greek soldiers, and unexpectedly from civilians. Lübker's three aircraft flew around more than three times before positively identifying their drop zone, which was under heavy small arms fire by elements from the 1 Greek Regiment.

Mürbe managed to get his 37mm PAK anti-tank gun into action on the main road leading into Kastelli, bringing the area between the town and its cemetery under fire. Fire support went wrong from the very start. Mürbe's mortar could not at first be brought into action because the crew were pinned down, away from the container. Its commander and two ammunition carriers were soon casualties. A heavy machine gun set up to the left of the same road met the same fate. Mürbe was killed 20 minutes after landing and Lübke was mortally wounded trying to man the heavy machine gun. A desperate radio message was transmitted at 11.15am: 'I must break off this transmission for 15 minutes, because I have to get involved in the fight.'[31]

Five miles to the east at the Tavronitis estuary, Fink and his *3. Kompanie* comrades had noticed that *Generalmajor* Meindl was no longer active around the bridge. Then came stunning news, he was severely wounded: 'Angry and truly distraught, I sighed deeply. We had missed that. Now and then I was coming to the realization that the *Kampfgruppe West's* condition was not that good. In fact, its future appeared really dismal.'

They had, however, to continue the mission set by the *General* to penetrate the bushes on the north side of the estuary, and rejoin the surviving elements of *3. Kompanie* on the other side. This meant 'shooing away the many unsettling thoughts going through my mind'. He was not the only one. *Jäger* Lingg with Gericke's *16. Kompanie* 'had other worries' having got over his near-death entanglement experience. 'What would become of us in the next hours?' he reflected. The *Sturmregiment* plan seemed to be unravelling. 'Are we going to win the battle on this island?' he asked himself.[32]

Meindl, growing weaker by the hour, still insisted on directing operations from his stretcher. The operation was faltering, the plan coming apart. Student's 'oil drop' strategy of multiple dispersed landings combining to form a lodgement pool was anathema to conventionally Prussian-schooled commanders, encouraged always to pursue a clearly defined *Schwerpunkt*, or main point of effort. Meindl would have preferred to empty the entire oil can over Hill 107 to gain Maleme aerodrome and secure an air-land reinforcement. He must have rued the day Student insisted he halve his glider-borne elite to send two companies into the heart of enemy territory, lacking close ground support, on the premise there would be a rapid collapse. Optimistic intelligence assessments suggested Student's simple and creative scheme would work.

The volume of fire emanating from Hill 107 had already convinced Meindl that Koch's *coup d'état* had come to nought. But there was still Scherber's *III Bataillon*, landing behind the heights. He anticipated they should appear at any moment on the coast road, effecting a junction with the main force. Meindl started slipping in and out of fevered consciousness. His rapid attack orders to Stentzler and Gericke should facilitate the best means of joining with Scherber. *But where was Scherber?*

Oberstabsarzt Dr Neumann observed the increasing deterioration of Meindl's condition; symptoms of shock and fever were becoming ever more pronounced due to his massive chest wound. If his commander did not receive hospital treatment soon he would die.

Chapter 6

A Battalion Dies

LIEUTENANT COLONEL DOUGLAS LECKIE, COMMANDER
23 NEW ZEALAND BATTALION

09.00–14.25 20 May 1941, Dhaskaliana Ridgeline East of Hill 107
Lieutenant Colonel Leckie was minding Andrew's 22 Battalion's
back, ready to come to his aid if called upon. His was the stronger
of two battalions sited in depth to Hill 107, a much-reduced 21
Battalion lay to his south. 23 Battalion was configured for coastal
defence. Leckie had four companies forward on either side of the
main road from Kondomari village inland to Dhaskaliana and
the sea, with his headquarters and C Company located in depth.
He had good observation towards Maleme from HQ Company
1 to the west and a further vantage point just 100 yards west of
his command post. He had taken command of his battalion just
eight days before, although he had temporarily commanded it in
England in August at the height of the German invasion scare
until March 1941. He had been a school teacher during the inter-
war period and had seen service with the Anzac Mounted Division
during the second half of World War I. Although he had not
actually commanded during the taxing days in Greece, he remained
uneasy, like many of the senior New Zealand commanders, about
total Luftwaffe air superiority there and what would probably
happen in Crete.

It was generally the opinion at stand-to that fateful morning of 20 May that Maleme was receiving more than its normal dose of Luftwaffe hate. This view was shared by observers with 28 (Maori) Battalion, the 5 Brigade reserve, further east at Platanias. 'The area around the aerodrome is being most intensively bombed and machine-gunned by countless planes of all kinds', wrote Private 'Monty' Wikiriwhi in the battalion log: 'Clouds of dust are rising high into the sky turning the whole area into a real inferno of flying dust and metal, and visibility was reduced to almost nil.'[1]

Communications with Andrew's battalion ceased after 7am. Overspill from the Maleme bombing sprinkled Leckie's Battalion ridgeline behind 22 Battalion. Fred Irving was intimidated by the swarms of aircraft – 'we didn't expect the vast number there was', he recalled. 'We were so frightened we were having a wee every few minutes.' Troop carriers then swung into view over the undefended flats beyond Hill 107 and beaches further west. A Jules Verne fantasy unfolded as the sky beyond seemed to suddenly fill with opening black, white and green blossoms. The invasion was clearly on.

It took a while longer before intermittent landings by Scherber's *III Bataillon*, considerably delayed by dust at its mounting airfield, started to descend on the ridgelines to the east of Hill 107. The planes seemed to be flying the south–north dirt roads leading down to the coast. The din from the bombing reached a climax of detonating bombs, which stopped as suddenly as they had started. Irving remembered 'the effect on morale was quite terrific'. Dozens of aircraft had been circling just above the large trees. 'You just prayed', he insisted, 'you literally prayed whether you were religious or not'.[2]

Like Andrew, Leckie too was frightened by the bombing and strafing, which rained down with an intensity outside his experience. Cracks and thuds were superseded by a growing throbbing in the air which reverberated until the ground literally shook. A stream of little white handkerchiefs came from the bellies of the great lumbering Ju 52 transports with little black blobs suspended beneath. The parachute assault was now encompassing the depth positions. Lieutenant 'Sandy' Thomas commanded 15 Platoon with C Company, near Battalion HQ. 'Cripes!' exclaimed Templeton, his platoon sergeant, stumbling over his mess-tin as he stepped back for a better view, 'cripes, they can't be real! They're only dummies!' By the time Scherber's assault came in, '23 battalion were all at their stations and as far as possible under cover from the air'. Thomas estimated they would land about 500 yards away.[3]

Captain Watson with Leckie's A Company on the coast road at Dhaskaliana just short of the canal remembered 'the first lot seemed to curl over us and land on the drome' about one and a half hours before. 'The second lot [Scherber's Battalion] seemed to go over the back of us toward 21 Battalion and we began shooting, though most of these were out of range.' Four plane loads, some 48 men, jumped across Vineyard Ridge near 21 Battalion's D Company; very few reached the ground alive. Two more aircraft dropped on top of Kondomari village, landing in the streets and on flat roofs, where they were picked off, trying to disentangle themselves from their parachute harnesses. Others thumped onto rooftops, became ensnared in trees or were shot as they tumbled over in the narrow streets. The local Greek population immediately waded in, women, children and even snarling dogs. The men shot with ancient flintlock muskets, captured from the Turks a hundred years before, and hacked and slashed with axes, knives and spades. Total pandemonium reigned in the village, with Cretan civilians in the way, felled by crossfire. Of 24 paratroopers that descended over the village only one was captured and two wounded, the rest were killed.

Leckie and most of his men, transfixed by the emerging spectacle over 21 Battalion, only belatedly realized the next Ju 52 *Rotte* (of three) were continuing to shed paratroopers towards the coast. An airborne carpet was laid across the 23 Battalion positions. Watson remembered:

Suddenly, they came among us. I was watching the 21 Battalion area and a pair of feet appeared through a nearby olive tree. They were right on top of us. Around me rifles were cracking. I had a Tommy gun and it was just like duck shooting.[4]

Many of the New Zealand soldiers were from the land, excellent shots and game stalkers, even before they joined the army.

Leckie's men were at once briskly engaged, many not even having to change position, and they wrought terrible damage among the descending paratroopers. 'This is for real boys', Walter Gibbons recalled being told, 'put your bayonets on, it's either you or them'. 'You'd see one go limp', remembered another New Zealander, 'then give a kick and kind of straighten up with a jerk, and then go limp again, and you knew he was done for'. Leckie killed five paratroopers himself from his gully HQ, while his Adjutant Captain Orbell shot two more without even getting up from his packing-case desk.[5]

'The noise built up to a tremendous crescendo', Sandy Thomas recalled:

Machine guns chattered as they plucked at the swinging forms in the sky, men yelled and wounded parachutists still in the air screamed with fear and pain … Above it all, a deep bass rising and falling in intensity but very present, was the drone of aero engines, punctuated by whistling bombs and diving fighters. It was real bedlam.

Whatever the innate skill of New Zealand marksmanship it is still very difficult to hit a descending parachutist, at indeterminate range, oscillating all the way down. The Germans had trialled shooting at descending parachute dummies under peacetime conditions at one of their instruction schools. It was found that it took 185 rounds to hit one at 150 metres and 1,708 to achieve a strike 350 metres away. It is likely the most damage inflicted on Scherber's battalion jumping in contact was due to their need to descend through a cone of fire spitting up from the ground, or being picked off when they were particularly vulnerable, struggling out of parachute harnesses once on the ground. This might take up to 60 to 80 seconds, depending on the frame of mind at the time. 'I think I'll never forget the screaming of the parachutists who thought they were landing in an unopposed area', Thomas recalled, 'as they came down and passing through this tremendous fire'. Some aircraft, appreciating this, veered away and circled around again to make another try. Such isolated aircraft inevitably attracted all the fire.[6]

Leckie lost his second in command Major T. Fyfe, killed in the maelstrom around Battalion HQ. His intelligence officer Lieutenant Dan Davin was also wounded, but not before witnessing the descending paratroopers being lacerated by a storm of rifle and machine-gun fire. 'They were only seconds in the air.' He watched the bullets impact, whereupon 'they doubled up, knees came towards chins convulsively and down again'. The descent at this low level lasted no more than about 14 seconds on average. On the ground they immediately sought cover among olive tree groves. The artificial green of the parachutes was a give-away:

We waited for movement. Suddenly a man, doubled up, began to double along the vine path towards the ridge. We all fired at open sights. The brown dust spurted round him. He fell out of sight in the olives. Up again, he got almost to the ridge. But this time he fell finally. We felt a savage elation.

Thomas was equally uncompromising. 'Shooting that first German, didn't affect me', he admitted. 'Awful to say, there was a sort of exhilaration, you got him first.' Most of those hit in the air were victims of the wall of fire coming up from multiple directions, rather than being individually targeted.[7]

The New Zealand Field Punishment Centre (FPC) was situated on the end of the ridgeline immediately to the right, or east, of Leckie's battalion HQ. It obscured much of the village of Modhion below it. *Oberleutnant* Schulte-Sasse's *10. Kompanie* started lobbing out along the line of the main road leading to the coast and the positions of the New Zealand Engineer Detachment, as they flew over the village. One of the 22 Battalion disciplinary detainees was L.G.J. Follas, who recalled volunteers had been released and quickly armed from the abundance of German supply canisters that had landed nearby. 'Spandaus [machine guns] were used against any plane that came within their orbit of fire.' Schulte-Sasse was quickly killed and his company eviscerated 'by terrific small arms fire' from the Field Punishment Centre that overlooked the line of flight. Follas remembered fire was 'very heavy and almost continuous':

> The ammunition for the machine guns could be clipped together and belt after belt went straight through the guns. Many planes were engaged and the bullets from the spandaus and rifles could be seen going right into them. Two troop carriers came across the front at point-blank range and got the full force of the spandaus; they crashed between the FPC and the beach.

A number of aircraft shied away from the intensity of fire and wheeled around to make a second attempt. Lieutenant Cunningham's platoon with D Company, west of the main road from Kondomari to the coast near the church, engaged one of these 'last drop' aircraft. His Bren gunner had his weapon firing directly through the open doorway of the Ju 52, shredding the emerging figures as they came out; 'few, if any, paratroopers landed alive', he observed. Follas's Field Punishment group spotted another plane coming in low from over the sea and engaged it at fairly long range: 'It faltered, tried to rise again, and then crashed into the sea. Both spandaus kept it under continuous fire until it sank and none of the occupants was seen to escape.'

Lieutenant Sandy Thomas with C Company, was virtually co-located with Leckie's Battalion HQ. He remembered his company commander Major Thomason approaching 'with his distinctive limping gait', grinning and seemingly unruffled by the confusion all around. 'Well young Thomas', he declared, 'here's the war for you, brought right to your doorstep'. Leckie had instructed him to clear paratroopers who had 'dropped wide of their objective'. They could get in the way of any future counter-attacks 23 Battalion may need to push towards the aerodrome in support of Andrew's 22 Battalion. Thomas recalled how he 'looked straight into my eyes, commanding and aggressive' as he instructed, 'move out with your platoon and clean 'em up'.

Once Leckie appreciated all opposition had been suppressed within the company perimeters, he ordered them all to sally out and clear their surrounding areas. D Company cleared west of the Sfakoriako River, A mopped up the main road to its front, B Company and Headquarters Company 2 cleared the north-west while C combed the area to the immediate east. The Germans were given scant opportunity to regroup or gain access to any of the numerous weapons containers scattered about.[8]

As Thomas moved out with his platoon he experienced the distinctive 'clarity when danger expunges all irrelevant worries and crystallizes the brain for that deadliest of all pastimes, the stalking of fellow man'. He killed his first German in an unexpected skirmish, capturing a second 'fair-headed, his face a sickly green'. The German was clearly groggy, dazedly waving a pistol aimlessly around. 'I could see from the saliva oozing down either side of his mouth, and from the gibbering sounds he was making, that there was no fight in him'. He was in close bush country interspersed with stepped stone terraces, and had no idea what he should do with his prisoner. His own soldiers were still closing from some 50 yards away. He thought it best to club him unconscious, but was distracted from doing so when he was suddenly charged by another paratrooper emerging from the undergrowth. He caved in the skull of his helpless prisoner with his rifle butt in the excitement of the moment, just as his German assailant was shot in the temple by one of his platoon. Mercy was neither anticipated nor freely given. 'Before long, every man in the platoon was wearing a Luger revolver and a pair of Zeiss Binoculars', Thomas recalled, 'and our morale was extremely high'.[9]

Leckie was well satisfied that both he and Lieutenant Colonel John Allen's 21 Battalion had delivered a stinging riposte to the German parachute assault, seeking to penetrate the depth and rear of Andrew's 22 Battalion position. He contacted Brigadier Hargest at 11.55am: 'situation in my area in complete control, battalion in high spirits', he radioed. He had no idea of Andrew's predicament, of paramount importance, because he was tasked to support him by counter-attacks if necessary. He sent one of his signallers from the western slopes of his position to gain contact, by visual signals if necessary. There had been no sightings of any white-green-white flares, the agreed signal to initiate any counter-moves. His own observation posts were reporting that Andrew appeared to be holding strongly. His westernmost HQ Company 1 could see that all the aerodrome runways were covered by fire. As no Germans could be seen wandering in the open, it was assumed 22 Battalion was holding firm.[10]

Leckie's own experience suggested Andrew had similarly repulsed the assault. All he could see was the mass of the back of Hill 107. 23 Battalion had fought off four company streams of troop carriers, numbering about a dozen planes each, jumping over and either side of his ridgeline positions. At times the drops had been intermittent and desultory. He could see Andrew's position had seen an absolute Luftwaffe pasting and was still, for the most part, obscured by smoke and dust. They had observed troop transports, but not seen the two concentrated battalion drops on the other side of Hill 107, to the west, and very few gliders. Nothing suggested Andrew's experience was contrary to theirs.

Counter-attack routes had already been reconnoitred, Leckie simply needed to be told to proceed. The intensity of the Luftwaffe close air support that descended after the drops was a deterrent to any movement. Leckie, only recently restored to command, preferred to wait and be told rather than risk any exposed movement forward. Private Follas on the vulnerable ridgeline to his east recalled:

> Messerschmitt fighters came down and roared over from the south to machine gun the 75mm guns of C Troop; they opened fire on the ridge and the stream of bullets would sweep along it until they covered the artillery position just to the north and slightly below the Field Punishment Centre.

Nothing could move. Fred Irving with 23 Battalion felt intimidated by their vulnerability to air attack: 'They must have known we had annihilated their whole unit, and they came over and they fired just everything they had at us, they machine gunned us, bombed us and really just tore us apart.'[11]

Leckie, acutely aware of the consequences should he counter-attack, waited. At 2.25pm he received a message from Brigade HQ which endorsed this calculated hesitation. 'Glad of your message of 11.40 hours', it read: 'Will NOT call upon you for counter attacking unless position very serious. So far everything is in hand and reports from other units satisfactory.'

Leckie relaxed, he was in a strong position. Offensive clearance sweeps had netted a satisfactory grim toll. Lieutenant Thomas's 15 Platoon had killed 30 enemy for the loss of just one killed and two wounded. A small enemy group that had approached Battalion HQ from the south-east had been wiped out by Lieutenant Rex King's 14 Platoon. All attempts to reach or communicate with 22 Battalion's Headquarters Company in Pirgos, however, had been met by fire, despite raising distinctive flat-bowl tin hats accompanied by very English-sounding expletives. No news was good news so far as CO 23 Battalion and Brigadier Hargest were concerned, a view shared by Brigade Major Captain Dawson. He had arrived to deliver messages and orders:

> 23 Battalion at this stage was fairly satisfactory. They had cleaned up all the Huns dropped in their area. Even around Battalion HQ there were bodies everywhere, every ten to twelve yards. One stepped over them as one went through the olive groves – and some very good-looking fellows there were too.

Leckie had only lost seven killed and 30 wounded and was clearly in the ascendant. Lieutenant Gordon Cunningham passed through three companies on his way to Battalion HQ that afternoon, constantly hearing 'the same story that the Huns were easy shooting'.[12]

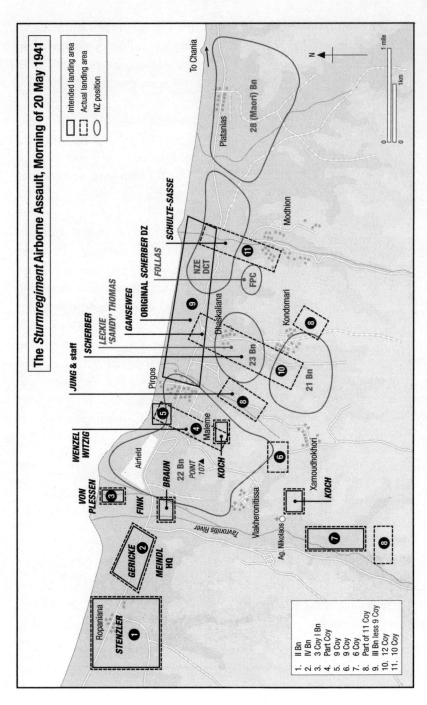

The *Sturmregiment* Airborne Assault, Morning of 20 May 1941

- Intended landing area
- Actual landing area
- NZ position

To Chania

N

1 mile

1km

28 (Maori) Bn

Platanias

SCHULTE-SASSE

Modhion

ORIGINAL *SCHERBER* DZ

FOLLAS

NZE DCT

FPC

11

9

SCHERBER

LECKIE
'SANDY' THOMAS

GANSEWEG

Dhaskaliana

Kondomari

8

23 Bn

10

21 Bn

JUNG & staff

Pirgos

8

WENZEL
WITZIG

5

Maleme

4

KOCH

6

Xamoudhokhori

Airfield

BRAUN

22 Bn

POINT
107

KOCH

VON
PLESSEN

FINK

3

Tavronitis River

Vlakheronitissa

KOCH

Ag. Nikolaos

7

GERICKE

2

MEINDL
HQ

8

Ropaniana

STENZLER

1

1. II Bn
2. IV Bn
3. 3 Coy I Bn
4. Part Coy
5. 9 Coy
6. 9 Coy
7. 6 Coy
8. Part of 11 Coy
9. III Bn less 9 Coy
10. 12 Coy
11. 10 Coy

172

MAJOR OTTO SCHERBER, COMMANDER
III BATAILLON STURMREGIMENT

09.00–Early Afternoon 20 May, Ridgelines East of Hill 107

Two hours after landing, *Jäger* Fink with the *I Sturmregiment* glider men hanging onto the western edge of the Maleme runway 'saw with pleasure a *Staffel* of Freighters coming in from the east at jump height, flying by the aerodrome'. They were relieved, much anticipated reinforcements had arrived. 'The first paratrooper came out of the machine next to Maleme', he recalled, and 'one man somersaulted in the distance all the way to the ground when his parachute failed to open'. The last jumpers came down over the northernmost third of Hill 107. 'A huge salvo of fire embraced this company as soon as the first man was out of the aircraft.' The Maleme vicinity now quietened down, Fink observed, 'but from the east of the airfield and the heights of Hill 107, a thick infantry fire crackled up against them'. They bleakly concluded 'without doubt, this company had landed in the middle of the enemy', another reverse. 'Poor swine', they all thought.[13]

Thirty-six-year-old Otto Scherber had been appointed to command the newly formed *III Bataillon* the previous August and with it came promotion to *Major*. It all formed part of the rapid expansion of the German airborne from division to corps capability. Scherber trained his battalion with a cadre of veteran NCOs and officers, but many of the men were recent transferees from the army and green troops untested in battle. Even so they were motivated volunteers, well trained and superbly fit. Operation *Mercury* was Scherber's first operational deployment and thus far it was not going too smoothly. Five days before his battalion had been supplanted, Cuckoo fashion, from Mykene airfield, edged out to make room for *Stuka Geschwader I* from von Richthofen's *VIII Fliegerkorps*. The short-range dive bombers needed to be closer to their objectives which required Scherber's men to be transferred to Megara. The battalion had now to be inserted within a revised mounting plan, which meant following Meindl's regimental staff and Gericke's IV heavy weapons battalion at the overcrowded airfield. Take-off was bedevilled by enormous dust clouds so that the anxious Scherber and his men, sitting in aircraft parked at the airfield boundaries, soon realized they could be as much as two hours late over the objective. Aircraft *Ketten* lifting off in threes normally took one minute each to become airborne. Frustratingly they were obliged to pause now for five minutes between each take-off until the dust dispersed.

Troops sitting opposite each other in the back of the parked Ju 52s were indifferent. *Unteroffizier* Breuing sat with his friend Jürgen Friedrich Rothert, who had just written to his parents 'old Churchill won't know what's hit him'. 'The mood was great', he recalled, 'we sang and laughed'. Only the pessimists worried. Soldiers were generally confident it was always the other man who got hit first. Eventually, *Major* Krause's *I Geschwader* with transport wing *z.b.V. 172* took to the air, following the huge transport stream that was the first wave of Meindl's *Gruppe West*.[14]

Scherber's uneasiness increased as they flew low level across the Mediterranean. High above were increasing numbers of bombers and fighters coming back, probably their close ground support, returning to the Greek mainland. The two-hour flight gave plenty of time to ponder his assault plan. The *10. Kompanie* was to block the coast road east of Maleme to prevent enemy reinforcements coming up, while *9. Kompanie* would seal the road junction at Maleme and Pirgos, just to the east of the airfield. The other two companies, *11* and *12* would attack Hill 107 and the aerodrome from the east to link up with Meindl's main regimental group on the west side of the Tavronitis River.

Scherber received unsettling news in flight. His primary drop zone, the linear strip along the coast line between Pirgos and the bridge at the river mouth north of Modhion, had been declared inoperable. Prevailing winds from the south would push his soldiers out to sea. His plan had been to drop as a battalion, perhaps profiting from advice offered by veteran jumper *Hauptmann* von der Heydte with *Fallschirmjäger Regiment 3*, who was to drop nearby in Prison Valley. The norm was to jump by companies, but the traumatic Dutch Blitzkrieg experience suggested that cohesion brought resilience, once down on the ground in enemy-infested territory. Limited radio interoperability between aircraft and their paratrooper cargoes meant that Scherber faced difficult and risky options to pass on any new intent to his battalion, already airborne and committed to a rehearsed plan. The change in orders had to be somehow transmitted to the rest of the stream, directed by cockpit-waving flag signals.

The drill was a yellow flag displayed two minutes prior to the jump, which changed to a red and white one with half a minute to go. Both flags waved crossed was the 'don't jump' signal. Instead of flying east to west along the coastline, Scherber's battalion stream would cross the coast and fly east, then turn north and drop the companies short of the sea. This meant the companies would jump their own different drop zones, approaching in four streams of three aircraft abreast. The formations would fly alongside each other in parallel at between half a mile and one and a half miles apart, not as previously ordered in line, following one after the other. Suddenly the imperative became four instead of one primary jumpmaster to navigate and pick the right time to drop, instead of simply following the leader.

The unheralded change of plan in mid-flight was fraught with risk; this was the battalion's first major action. Enemy resistance, however, was thought to be slight. The bulk of the opposition was anticipated around the aerodrome, at most, a battalion strong. The regiment itself was landing three and a half combined glider and parachute battalions, which was thought to be achievable.

9. Kompanie would parachute nearest to Hill 107 and Pirgos. It was commanded by 25-year-old *Hauptmann* Rudolf Witzig, the Knight's Cross holder from *Gruppe Granit*, whose ten gliders had landed atop the seemingly impregnable Belgian fortress at Eben-Emael. Witzig's glider cable had snapped on the approach flight, causing him to abort near Cologne. He recovered the glider and managed to later secure a tow to his objective. Witzig's harum-scarum group of typically high-spirited parachute engineers had been expanded to company size. Few bent willingly to harsh Prussian discipline, the majority were fearless determined individualists.

Platoon commander Witzig had been elevated to captain company commander on the back of his exploits, and for a short period as one of Göring's adjutants. His hard-won experience convinced him of the need to grasp the initiative as soon as they were on the ground. Throughout the flight he was typically working over the plan details.

Oberfeldwebel Helmut Wenzel was three years older and one of Witzig's platoon commanders. He had commanded a section during *Granit* the year before, joining Witzig after being a squad leader in an experimental test unit of paratroopers in 1938. There was bad blood between them because the fiercely independent Wenzel had set up Witzig's HQ for him when he failed to arrive at Eben-Emael, and kept the momentum of the assault going. Command should normally have gone to the next senior, and only other officer, *Leutnant* Delicia, who was the Luftwaffe flying liaison, providing close-in Stuka dive-bomber support. Wenzel answered a ringing phone inside the bunker he captured, and informed the Belgians that the German Army had arrived to take over tenancy. '*Mon Dieu!*' had been the shocked response. Delicia was not infantry trained, and chose to take a back seat during the assault and none of the other members of *Granit* had a problem with this. Wenzel was wounded in the head after Witzig was flown in. When Hitler announced all the airborne officers at Eben-Emael should receive the Knight's Cross, Witzig – ever the traditional conformist – remained circumspect about Wenzel's gallant if unconventional initiative in taking over. The rest of the troops received either the 1st or 2nd class Iron Cross. Wenzel, despite his decisive contribution to success, was precluded from the prestigious award for 'exceeding his jurisdiction'. He never forgave Witzig for this.[15]

Eighteen-year-old *Jäger* Walter Goltz, who had been an apprentice locksmith on the *Reichsbahn* railways, sat alongside his other *9. Kompanie* friends Kurt Hammermann, Heinz Jeremais and Karl Ehrenhofer, all of the same age. They had completed the basic jump course together at Wittstock prior to joining the *Sturmregiment* at Halberstadt. Breakfast that morning at 5 had been coffee and sausages, followed by a test-firing of weapons and a short march to the airstrip at Megara. They had no idea about any changes in drop zones. Goltz had spent the entire flight thinking about his childhood sweetheart Lisalotte, whom he intended to marry.[16]

'*Kreta in sight!*' *Oberfeldwebel* Wenzel was warned off. '*Fertig machen!* Get ready!' was ordered, the men stood up and hooked up their parachutes to the cable running overhead, the length of the aircraft. The door was opened, slipstream buffeting and slapping those nearest the exit, who were able to watch the undulating landscape, rich in vegetation, flashing past below. 'We are still 180 metres above ground', Wenzel reasoned, 'we'll be dangling too bloody long from our 'chutes'. Scherber's four *Kompanie* commanders were in their mid to late twenties; many of the men were still in their teens. The majority were unbloodied. The last-minute change in approach direction was difficult to monitor by map-read landmarks. The dry Tavronitis river bed lay clearly to their left, there was another river and road line to the right. Company aircraft streams tended to navigate by trailing the dirt roads leading north to the sea coming up ahead. Scherber's aircraft flew the line of the main Kondomari to Dhaskaliana road. Green fields with vineyards and olive groves blanketed low-lying hills below, with small houses dotted here and there. The whitewashed houses of the villages of Maleme, Pirgos and Kondomari came into view. Schulte-Sasse's *10. Kompanie* jumpers looking out through their port holes and door could see intermittent lines of the other Ju 52 company streams lumbering along, through the shimmering heat haze streaming out of the port engine. Chania, still smoking after the bombing, was a further marker confirming their position to the right. The first three *Kette* 'Vs' dropped their men across the positions of 21 New Zealand Battalion.

Scherber was out the door first, arms outstretched in the crucifix position, followed immediately by his *III Bataillon* staff. Succeeding aircraft 'Vs' carried on dropping over the houses of Kondomari village at the north end of 21 Battalion. To their left elements of Jung's *11. Kompanie* parachuted onto the Xamoudhokhori to Pirgos road, reassured by seeing the very RAF radio masts Meindl had told them to watch out for at the first briefings. The bulk of Gansewig's *12. Kompanie* jumped into the midst of the 23 New Zealand Battalion north of 21, and *10. Kompanie* came out near the New Zealand Field Punishment Centre north-west of Modhion and into the positions of the New Zealand engineer Detachment on the coastline. Scherber had briefed that this area was likely sparsely defended.

A storm of small arms fire rose up to greet them as soon as the first man was out. Wenzel's first indication of this was 'then I heard a splattering against the fuselage'. As he prepared to jump:

> The fellow behind collapses, unconscious – or dead? No time to think about it. I heave the cycle out and grip my respirator with the other hand, inside is my Leica camera. I couldn't squeeze it under my harness – and I am the first out. As the 'chute opens I hear whistles in the air. Bullets, the *Englander* are expecting and greet us.[17]

Walter Goltz remembered 'bullets peppered the fuselage and the wing was hit with shell fire', causing the aircraft to bank steeply out of control. Fourth in the jump line, he was barely able to maintain balance 'with others shouting and pushing frantically from behind'. His comrades Hammermann, Jeremais and Ehrenhofer had already collapsed in the gangway, felled by the hail of bullets clacking metallically through the metal fuselage, emitting shafts of early morning sunlight. Goltz managed to hurl himself through the door of the doomed aircraft, bullets snatching through the baggy part of his trouser leg, grazing his ankle, knee and thigh. Parachutes struck by heavy-calibre rounds in the air folded like flowers closing at night. On landing in bushes by an old stone hut, he was immediately struck by the odd contrast, everything around him lay still. He was alone. Trailing black smoke, the stricken Junkers arched over the eastern end of the airfield and splashed into the sea.

Wenzel saw he was floating directly over an enemy position spitting up fire. The problem with the German RZ-1 parachute was its single lift suspension at one point over the shoulder blades. This made the jumper hang face forward with no control over direction except to violently fling his limbs about. The spread-eagling this involved could be dangerous as feet and knees needed to be together on striking the ground. Rubber elbow and knee pads were worn to mitigate the inevitable knocks and bangs that occurred as the parachutist sought to 'judo-roll' in the direction of landing. The undulating ground Wenzel was descending towards caused injuries, as the rate of descent was equivalent to jumping off a low wall. He remembered:

> Six Tommies were stood upright shooting at me. The bloody bastards were waiting until I got down. I wriggled myself loose in the harness, so that I was suspended by the upper lift webs, in order to free my pistol. As I raised my arms for a forward roll shortly before hitting the ground, a bullet grazed my chest, passing through the right armpit and exiting close to my neck artery. My braces, tunic, smock and binocular strap were all shot through as also the Leica [camera] strap. I made a very soft landing in a vineyard less than 30 metres from the English position.

Company commander Rudolf Witzig was shot through the lung during the descent; on landing he managed to crawl into a bomb crater screened by bushes. He could only breathe by ramming a field dressing into the holes in his chest to inflate the collapsed lung. He was completely out of the action. He stayed in his hole and laboriously tried to breathe.[18]

The battalion drops came in intermittently and were dispersed across an area of two and a half by one and a quarter miles. Such scattering enabled the whole concentration of ground fire to be directed against isolated clusters of aircraft. 11. *Kompanie* seemed to divide to avoid fire after witnessing the wholesale massacre of 12. *Kompanie*, which dropped directly over 21 New Zealand Battalion and then the 23 further on towards the sea. The parachute assault degenerated into a debacle. Richard Kienzen with *11. Kompanie* recalled his company commander Jung was killed:

> I was wounded during the descent, hit by a bullet that struck between elbow and shoulder. I landed in an olive tree and was hit again, striking a branch so violently I could no longer use my arm. Dangling from my harness and totally defenceless, I was then captured by the British.

Wenzel dropped two approaching Tommies with his pistol, scattering those behind them into cover. This brief respite enabled him to disentangle himself from his parachute harness despite being wounded:

> Now they turned a machine gun onto me, and I squeezed myself into a small hollow in the ground. My small bread pouch was riddled with fire and my water bottle burst apart in a cloud of spray. Tommy thinks me dead and stops firing, but I creep along, tightly pressed up against the earth.

'*Third Platoon on me now!*' he bellowed, seeking to rally his men. Hardly had he shouted when 'a bullet went right through my steel helmet, tearing open the scalp and glancing up against the skull bone'. The concussive blow produced a 'ringing in my head with black and red spots going round and round'. He barely managed to stay conscious, 'gathering every ounce of willpower not to faint, and I succeeded'. His shout was heard and four figures came creeping up. They bandaged him up and Wenzel rubbed soil onto the dressings to make them less conspicuous. A 'hedgehog' all-round defensive circle was quickly formed, but they had no access to weapons containers. Bullets scythed by every moment and Wenzel's boot was almost torn off by another round that passed through his ankle and bone tissue. Half-hearted approaches by the enemy were driven off with hand grenades. Eventually they came across a weapons container, but found it full of the battalion's signals equipment. Nevertheless, it did yield a single rifle and a machine gun. Until then they had been solely reliant upon pistols and hand grenades.[19]

Examination of aircraft returns suggest that *Major* Otto Scherber probably jumped with about 430 men. Only seven of the 493-strong Ju 52 aircraft first wave failed to get back to the Greek mainland after dropping *Gruppe West*. Four to five of these may well have been carrying Scherber's men. Many of the approach runs by single planes, or in twos and threes, were subjected to dense concentrations of defensive fire. One aircraft was seen to fall out of control, sweeping away a group of descending paratroopers, one was seen in flames and another splashed into the sea. One Ju 52 force-landed near Chania, with one of its aircrew dead on board and a fifth crash-landed on return to Topolia. Only two of the four companies jumped as a compact group.[20]

Jürgen Rothert with *9. Kompanie* did not survive. 'He never wanted to become a commissioned officer', his friend *Unteroffizier* Breuing recalled, because 'he said this would have been at the expense of comradeship'. Rothert was one of the individualists, popular in the company, an early member of the *Wandervogal* ramblers movement, which was wound up in 1933 and superseded by the Hitler Youth. His wish was to be a farmer. 'This terrible Nazi Germany', he once complained. 'I've got to get away. I'll go to Africa. I won't have to worry about anything there, only about whether my pigs are fattening nicely.'

Breuing remembered the final evening, before they boarded the aircraft for Crete: 'On the last day before the show the company gathered round a big campfire. We sang our paratrooper songs. Moritz [Rothert's nickname] and I took turns to accompany them on the guitar.'

Now he was somewhere amid the carnage later discovered by another *III Bataillon* eyewitness:

White panels from parachutes were spread across the olive trees, rigging lines completely entangled. Dead paratroopers were hanging in the branches in full equipment. Dead all around!

Those that had managed to free themselves from their 'chutes, were hit or shot nearby – singly or in groups – they lay in the grass or on the road. Materiel was scattered all about: hand grenades, helmets, rifles. A dagger was stuck upright in the sand. Boxes of ammunition and among them a mountain of empty cases, the sun playing on the metal. A few Englishmen also lay in the grass. Burning heat raised clouds of blue-black thick flies, buzzing around. That was the massacre of a *Fallschirmjäger* battalion.[21]

It is not certain where Scherber died, but probably somewhere between Kondomari and Pirgos. By the time his body was recovered, it was indistinguishable from the decomposed rest. He perished alongside virtually every other officer in the battalion, likely with his adjutant *Oberleutnant* Arnd-Rudo. Trebes, now with the regimental staff, was the only standing survivor. All four company commanders and their medical officers were killed, and every officer platoon commander was killed or wounded. The battalion was reduced to about three score men and would lose more. It had effectively ceased to exist.

Nothing was to be heard from the *III Bataillon* for 28 hours, until at 1pm the next day *Feldwebel* Zollinger radioed in. His group of 12, six *Feldwebel*, two junior NCOs and four men were just to the south of the RAF Technical Radar Site, 'with two radio masts' near the village of Xamoudhokhori. They had not been discovered and requested machine gun ammunition. Zollinger reported 'no contact with any of Scherber's positions; they had fought free but were surrounded'. Nobody at Meindl's HQ appreciated they were the only formed element left from the *III Bataillon*.[22]

THE CRETANS

20 May
The German signaller with *Kampfgruppe* Mürbe who broke off his transmission at 11.15am to join the fight, never came back on air. Mürbe's detachment had been steadily whittled down by

fire from 1 Greek Regiment at Kastelli and harassed by villagers who joined in the fighting. Stylianos Koundouras, a local doctor, recalled his father rushed into the garden when the attack began, to dig up an ancient Turkish rifle, previously hidden away during the Metaxas Greek government's arms requisition. There was an argument before he was persuaded to hand it over to his son, who sped off to the fighting with the ancient flintlock in one hand and a medical bag in the other. Germans were being knifed or clubbed to death in a series of savage running battles among the olive groves on the main road outside Kastelli. Quarter was neither asked for nor given.[23]

The surviving Germans who were from Stentzler's battalion barricaded themselves in a farmhouse complex after Mürbe and his second in command Lübker were killed. They resolved to hold on behind its thick stone walls until help arrived. The 72-strong force had already lost more than half its strength. They were completely taken aback at the ferocity of attacks by women, old men and children armed with scythes, clubs, axes and hunting rifles, who simply waded in alongside the regular Greek soldiers. As 23-year-old George Tzitzikas near Rethymnon expressed it:

> The general belief was that the Germans would attack Crete. We knew that the 5th Cretan Division was cut off in Albania. We knew there was no army in Crete to fight the Germans. The general population psychologically prepared themselves for that. Our sons fight in Albania, we have to take their place; and take their place they did.

Church bells were rung as soon as the transport planes appeared. Menfolk who had evacuated their families inland to avoid the Luftwaffe bombing, streamed back. 'We did not have many guns then', 18-year-old Mandis Paterakis remembered: 'But still everyone ran to fight, women and men, children, young and old. They went with meat hooks, they went with stakes, whatever they could find.'

Major Bedding, the senior New Zealand adviser to 1 Greek Regiment, which was loosely under 5 New Zealand Brigade command, recommended the Greeks lay siege to the farmhouse. Hunger and thirst would oblige them to surrender. The Cretans refused to be held in check. Many were cut down by heavy machine-gun fire when they broke cover and rushed the buildings. Entry was forced by sheer weight of numbers and the killing inside became indiscriminate. Luftwaffe bombing had enraged the locals who wanted retribution. 'There was no fear, no question about that', George Tzitzikas explained:

> But that fear brought anger, let me tell you. The iron that was coming down and the fire made the Cretan heart harder than the German steel, and the Cretan spirit harder than German fire. And when they came down on 20th May 1941, we Cretan people were ready for that.[24]

Major Bedding managed to establish a semblance of control inside the farm complex. Only 18 of Mürbe's reinforced parachute company were left alive and one was bayonetted by an enraged Cretan nursing a shattered arm when they emerged. The family of Spiro Vlahakis, the old farm owner and elderly wife and two grandchildren, had been killed inside in the crossfire. One of the captured Germans recalled that on the way to the police cells at Kastelli 'the Greek civilians behaved particularly badly, we were beaten and spat upon'. Bedding locked them in the cells for their own safety, 'a confined room in the state prison'. The German further remembered 'rations were bread, water and lemons; the British soldiers behaved absolutely correctly'.[25]

When Stentzler's *II* and Gericke's *IV Bataillone* parachuted across Maleme, Hill 107 and the flats to the west, the local civilians were taken aback at a technological spectacle completely outside their simple agrarian commune existence. One 15-year-old girl Kaliopi Kapetanakis recalled she 'had no idea what I was seeing'. She had climbed an olive tree to watch the parachutes come down. 'I told my friend the whole sky is full of umbrellas', she recalled. It stirred a virtual ant's nest of frantic activity. 'There were cries from everywhere: the Germans are coming!' remembered 17-year-old

Chrissa Ninolakis. 'The Germans are here and are being dropped. It was a fascinating spectacular sight.' Twenty-two-year-old Sifis Papagiannakis 'vowed the sky people would not succeed in enslaving us'. 'I ran with my older brother who had fought in the Albanian war. He was on furlough. He quickly managed to capture a German rifle.'²⁶

The local Greeks reacted throughout the 5 New Zealand Brigade area. Michalis Doulakis saw parachutists thumping down into the streets and gardens of Maleme village. 'A couple of parachutists landed in my uncle's yard,' he recalled, 'right outside in fact'. The jumpers were dazed, struggling to disentangle themselves from parachute harnesses, armed only with Lugers. 'He killed one of them outright with his cane.' Many were overwhelmed or shot by Andrew's Company men before they could react. 'Most of the time they were dizzy or they would land on a tree. They would fall everywhere, some even fell on the roofs.'²⁷

I. D. Mourellos south-west of Maleme remembered:

I saw strong young men in our village Palia Roumata running as if competing in an athletic event, some with guns, others with sticks; and when asked where are they going without guns, they said 'we will take them from the Germans'.

John Marridakis, a 13-year-old boy, came across one dead paratrooper hanging in an olive tree. He saw 'around his neck he had an automatic gun, and he also had a camera'. 'I said, I'm going to take these for sure. I took them. I also took a wireless radio and gave it to an English soldier. He gave me a watch in exchange. I still have this watch today.'²⁸

Marika Markantonaki watched the drop some distance away from the capital at Chania. Her maid had come running, shouting 'Madame, come and see umbrellas, umbrellas!' These were the overshoots from some of the Ju 52 transports emerging from Prison Valley, who then flew out to sea. 'My goodness', she recalled, 'it was a sight I'll not forget'. A dangerous moment too, as Stuka dive bombers flew out over them in close support 'bombing and machine gun firing'. 'The villagers got their own back then. Bodies hung upon the trees like grapes. It was awful.'[29]

George Tzitzikas wryly commented 'they expected to take over Crete the first day, they had a big surprise'. At Modhion Schulte-Sasse's *10. Kompanie* from Scherber's *III Bataillon* was sprinkled across the village and into the prepared defences of the New Zealand Engineer Detachment manning the coast. Old men, women and children set upon isolated paratroopers with rocks, shovels, pitchforks, scythes and old shotguns. New Zealand defenders in the village had constantly to lift or shift fire so as not to hit civilian mobs. Drops continued further north into the village of Gerani, where they were decimated by defensive fire. The wounded and missing were picked off by the local Cretans. 'Out of the sky the winged devils of Hitler were falling everywhere', future insurgent courier George Psychoundakis observed. The guns the Cretans carried into the fight were what 'anyone would have sworn were taken from some museum', he recalled: 'And they would not have been far wrong, for the villagers had kept them hidden for many years in holes and caves and now, all eaten up with rust, they really were almost archaeological specimens.' The old Martinis he saw were in such a state of disrepair that every cartridge had to be extracted with a ramrod, before it could be reloaded. It reminded him of the old Greek war of independence saying, when they were using muzzle loaders – *'stand still Turk, while I reload'*.[30]

Sifis Papagiannakis recalled one 80-year-old man who fought alongside his brother was armed with 'just a little pistol':

> Can you imagine a man with a Luger trying to fight someone with a machine gun? We said to him 'where are you going with that little Luger? They will kill you!' 'Listen to me' he said, 'I'm an old man, it doesn't matter.'

He was killed in fact, and Papagiannakis remembered when the others witnessed his bravery 'and the life he sacrificed, they suddenly became giants like him'.[31]

The Germans were surprised and shocked that the local civilian population should so vociferously take up arms. It had never happened before in the war. The security of any wounded German soldier immediately became in jeopardy, and as such it had an insidious effect on tactics and, at times, the subsequent course of the battle. Although the veterans who had faced the Greek regulars on the mainland may not have entirely swallowed the 'Major Bock' codeword briefed at Athens, that the Cretans would be sympathetic, they were taken aback by the sheer emotional ferocity of the resistance. Once Gericke's *IV Bataillon* heavy weapons *16. Kompanie* landed to the south of Hill 107, it was immediately pinned down and besieged in the village of Vlakheronitissa by 'ongoing battles with *Freischärlern* (guerrilla) fighters'.

Generalleutnant Student later accepted the total failure of the German intelligence estimate, 'which endangered the *XI Korps* attack and caused unusually high bloody losses among the troops'. He concluded: 'The Cretan population were called up for a sniper war, after a month-long hearts and minds propaganda operation, for a "bandit war" organized and equipped by Cretan and English officers.'[32]

The appearance of female fighters was even more dismaying. Women were accosted by paratroopers and shoulder straps on dresses torn away to seek any tell-tale bruising from rifle recoils. One paratrooper recalled one 'warrior-like human form' leaping out 'from behind thorny bushes like a wild animal' and shooting two of his comrades in the stomach with five rifle shots. The figure slithered 'away into the bushes like a snake' and with his own seven months of rigorous combat and parachute training in the Berlin area 'the way he slid his body along the top of the soil had impressed me'. They managed to surround the fugitive and grenade him into submission. 'Honestly his way of fighting had excited me.' They cautiously closed in on the mortally wounded figure, who even managed to injure another paratrooper.

When in pulling off the kerchief [binding his head] in order to lie him down, half a metre of long black hair tumbled down.

It was then I realized it was a woman. I was dumbstruck. It was something for which I was not prepared. I felt the lump in my throat choking me.[33]

German concepts of a 'fair and honourable' fight, extolled by wartime propaganda, did not fit the Cretan mode. Indeed, paratroopers later complained they were unfairly engaged, hanging helplessly in the air before reaching the ground, a seemingly outrageous violation of the rules of war. Civilian resistance in all the German conquered territories thus far in this war had been passive at worst and grudging at best. Now every isolated German soldier was vulnerable, particularly the wounded. This had the tactical effect of making even simple actions manpower intensive, because active and indeed fierce resistance might be encountered at every turn. Soldiers 'missing' held immediate and sinister connotations. German morale plummeted; they had come to expect their chosen enemies would promptly cave in at the first approach. The exact number of German troops lost to civilian participation in the fighting is unknown, but official reports hint that the majority of the 'missing' had likely been lost to *Freischärlern* or guerrilla activity. In the case of the *Sturmregiment*, this could be as many as some 118–120 men. Even during the subsequent occupation the German mindset was never able to fully comprehend the wild nature of the Island of Crete. It was inimical to law and order, a land of mountains and villages, which seemed to sustain a population of outlaws. They had never yet encountered a civilian community that hated them enough to join the fight.

It was unsettling.[34]

Chapter 7

Command Dilemmas

LIEUTENANT COLONEL LESLIE ANDREW, COMMANDER
22 NEW ZEALAND BATTALION

11.30–18.00 20 May 1941, Summit of Hill 107
There appeared to be a lull in Luftwaffe air activity. Von Richthofen's *VIII Fliegerkorps'* main effort *Schwerpunkt* for close air support switched to the second-wave drops, assisting *Gruppe Ost* at Rethymnon and Iraklion. An occasional raid came in, but the Luftwaffe seemed to be drawing breath. Lieutenant Colonel Andrew found it hard to encompass this sudden immunity, which was broken by a heavy Stuka raid at noon on the summit of Hill 107. Constant bombing produced 'bomb happy' cases of post-combat stress, and men around Andrew were feeling the acute psychological pressure. It was like the Greek mainland all over again, but more vicious in its intensity and duration.

Aircraftsman Marcel Comeau was preoccupied assisting a wounded Ginger Hutchinson from his own squadron, blocking an intestine oozing through a bullet hole just to the right of his navel. 'Is it because this bandage is so tight that it hurts so much?' Hutchinson gasped. Fully immersed by what he was doing, he did not notice the dive bombers gathering overhead. His fingernails 'dug into my arm', Comeau recalled, as 'the great noise drowned out my words'. Stuka sirens 'harmonized with the nightmare screaming of the bombs' screeched down as a succession of 1,110lb and lighter 110lb bombs straddled the summit of Hill 107:

> A dark, cordite stinking tunnel imprisoned us, cutting us off from the world outside. Then there was a loud explosion and a terrifying gust of wind and I was hurled to the ground and pelted with stones and thrown one way and blasted back again. I was hanging on to the edge of the world by my fingertips. The ground opened beneath me and my mouth filled with grit.[1]

Andrew had already been struck on the head by shrapnel during the first preliminary air bombardment that morning. His command post trench was proving too vulnerable a shelter to control this battle. Heavy German mortar fire searching the summit convinced him of the need to pull back battalion headquarters 200 yards into his B Company area. Increasing pressure produced a sense of isolation that steadily built throughout the day. C Company attempts to support Sinclair's 15 Platoon clinging to the western edge of the aerodrome had been completely neutralized by the intensity of German fire. The battalion log plotted the deteriorating situation. 'Position became progressively worse during the afternoon', it read, 'due to attacks from the southwest and to heavy fire right along the ridge from machine guns and mortars west of the Tavronitis'. Many of A Company's forward positions became untenable and Lieutenant Fell was killed. *Major* Stentzler's *5.* and *6. Kompanien* from *II Bataillon* were starting to attack across the Tavronitis valley and turning east, seeking to work around the rear of Hill 107. Gericke's *IV Bataillon* meanwhile strove to enlarge the wedge around the RAF camp fought between C and D Companies at the bridge.[2]

At 10am Andrew had managed to gain wireless communication with Hargest's 5 Brigade, reporting he was under heavy attack. Fifty-five minutes later he added he had lost contact with his forward companies. Andrew had been spooked by the Stuka raid and complained about his 'battalion being subjected to almost continuous bombing'. It was in fact an isolated raid; Luftwaffe impetus had shifted to the east end of the island. Many of those on the summit had already worked out 'the basic rules' of surviving enemy air activity, as Comeau explained:

> When strafed it is usually better to run in the direction of the attacking aircraft than away from it, or, if an enemy bomber is overhead you are as safe as houses. It's the man a mile away who should start worrying.

During the late morning two Ju 52s lined up for an approach and landing on Maleme aerodrome. Johnson's C Company was amazed as they coasted in low and touched down. This was Luftwaffe *Major* Snowadski with his small staff and radio station, earmarked as the administrative commander of Maleme airfield. 'All weapons opened up', Johnson recalled, starring plexiglass cockpit windows with bullet strikes and producing a metallic hail of clacking penetrations through the corrugated fuselage of the aircraft. 'The planes swung out to sea at zero feet', barely making it off the runway. Snowadski immediately appreciated his presence was somewhat premature. 'Our small arms fire was returned by small arms fire from the body of the planes', Johnson observed. The mid upper gunners were firing back for all they were worth.[3]

Andrew got through again to Hargest at 2.55pm to relay 'battalion HQ has been penetrated', and again an hour later to announce 'left flank has given way and the need for at least some reinforcements is now urgent'. He had the general situation under control, but white-green-white flare signals were fired into the air to warn Leckie on the ridgeline behind, with 23 Battalion, that the pre-arranged counter-attack should now be executed. Nothing happened. At 5pm Andrew appealed directly to Hargest, urging 'when can I expect the pre-arranged counter-attack?' The response was dismaying. 'The 23rd cannot carry out your request', Hargest advised, 'because it is itself engaged against paratroops in its own area'. Andrew immediately sent a runner to Captain Johnson's C Company headquarters on the coast road directly below Hill 107. 'At 17.00', Johnson recalled, 'the long and eagerly awaited order to counter-attack with the support of the two I (Infantry) tanks arrived from BN HQ'.[4]

Two Matilda tanks, *Gnu III* commanded by Sergeant Gosnold and *Greenloaning* with Sergeant Marshall's 7 Royal Tank Regiment, emerged snorting diesel exhaust from their camouflaged hide depressions, located 300–400 yards apart at the base of Hill 107. They crossed the filled-in irrigation ditch between them and the airfield and turned west, locking and squealing tracks as they began to laboriously trundle along the coastal road towards the Tavronitis bridge. Their rattling progress could be followed by dust and exhaust clouds from the summit.

Captain Johnson had held them back thus far; they were earmarked to be used against aircraft landing on the runway, which could be shot up and bulldozed. After discussion with one of the sergeants he explained 'that since the Germans would have no anti-tank weapons capable of hurting the Matilda, they feared nothing except enemy personnel on top of his vehicles'. As Johnson recalled, 'he asked therefore that I see that his tanks were kept sprayed with small arms fire'. Lieutenant Haddon Donald, his co-located 14 Platoon commander, was instructed to lead the attack, 'forlorn before it even started'. It was reinforced by an artillery lieutenant with eight more men, from the AA battery, the small group now numbering '28 blokes'. Two of the gunners according to Johnson were 'in an advanced state of shell shock – bomb happy is probably the best description'. So, despite countless recces of counter-attack routes by Andrew's 22 and Leckie's 23 Battalions, the most important offensive action of the day was to be conducted on an ad hoc basis with a slack handful of men. Donald was understandably concerned: 'we hadn't talked [to the tanks] or made a plan', he recalled. They had 'one section on the right of the road, one section on the left of the road, and the other section on the road itself' running behind to catch up with the tanks. The Matildas rattled past Company HQ even before Donald had a chance to confer with the troop commander. His company commander was assured all they had to do to speak with tank commanders was 'press a bell [on the hatch] and the tank commander would open the tank and talk'. He tried to do this as they set off 'but there was no response to the bell'. Donald 'got the NCOs in a little huddle as we ran down toward these tanks', he recalled, 'and told them what we had to do more or less'. It was not a good start.

Andrew on the summit of Hill 107 was an observer rather than active director of this attack. His log suggests he believed the force to be about '40 men' strong, less than two-thirds the reality. At first progress was encouraging. The metal colossi squealing down the road were impervious to the dust puffs of machine gun and rifle fire that raked them down, 'being shot at in every direction', Donald recalled. 'Both plan and execution were perfect', Andrew observed, 'and the surprise effect of the appearance of the tanks must have been enormous', as indeed it was. Lieutenant Robin Sinclair at the western periphery of the airfield saw the first tank approaching 'and I thought, and hoped, it was coming to us'. Andrew watched as 'the attackers crossed the drome with no casualties, and it seemed this first essential step in the re-establishment of our defence of the Maleme area would succeed'.

Donald viewed it differently: 'it was pretty hopeless because it was broad open daylight', he remembered. When his men broke cover the rear of the two tanks was 100 yards ahead of the infantry group and the lead Matilda a further 100 yards beyond that, already half way to the Tavronitis. 'It was like the First World War – over the top in broad daylight, no show at all'. Sergeant Gosnold's *Gnu III* in the lead trundled down the embankment into the river bed in a cloud of dust, enfilading the German line with fire as it did so, and soon passing beneath the bridge piers. Donald saw it 'shooting away with their machine gun, but not the two-pounder, which was pretty useless anyway'. Sinclair hoped to direct it 'having gone over the ground in front countless times as an attacker myself'. Once the Matilda came out from under the bridge and 'onto my front' Sinclair saw 'it came to a halt'. Its sudden appearance certainly unsettled the opposition. 'The place was seething with enemy, plainly visible in the long grass' and 'they appeared uncertain as to what they were to do'.

Andrew thought success was in his grasp but 'ill fortune precluded it'. Donald's men closing up on the rear tank, which had also halted, were lashed with small arms fire. 'We hadn't caught up with the tanks at all', he remembered. One man was killed, others on the right had collapsed wounded, while the lead section to his left had already been reduced by half. The lead tank in the river bed remained motionless, swept by a metallic hail of small arms and low-calibre anti-tank fire. The men inside were choked by dust, cordite and diesel fumes and deafened by the crackling metal on metal rain of bullet strikes bouncing off the metal hull. Shortly after, the turret hatch was heaved open and Sergeant Gosnold and the crew came out with their hands up.[5]

Lieutenant Donald tried to contact the second Matilda, Sergeant Marshall's *Greenloaning*, but was pinned to the ditch by the side of the road. Johnson could see 'their position was hopeless', withdrawing soldiers were 'using the lee side of the tank for shelter', which 'was under withering fire from the front and southern flank'. It had turned around and started to make its way back along the road. Johnson had not seen it fire a single shot. Donald was frantically pressing the hatch bell and, when that did not work, he waved at the driver through the visor and climbed up onto the front of the tank. Marshall warily peered out from under the hatch and told the platoon commander he was pulling back, his turret could not traverse. 'The cowling round the turret had been torn apart', Donald observed, 'and bits of steel were sticking up'. A shell strike had effectively jammed it by ripping the cowling at the turret base. 'We were being shot at all the time', the exposed Donald recalled. 'I got a bullet through the leg and several of my platoon boys were wounded, one or two killed.' The tank ferried his wounded back on the rear engine cover. The artillery lieutenant who had joined him was dead. 'Unfortunately, I never learned the English officer's name', Johnson later commented, 'he was killed in this attack, after pleading with me to let him take part and lead a section'. *Gnu III*, it transpired, had bellied itself on one of the boulders in the dry river bed. 'I think we finished up with eight who weren't wounded or killed out of that 28 that we started with', Donald remembered.

'We knew that it was hopeless to do anything further with the few resources we had', he concluded. 'It was futile to start with.'[6]

The thrust had fallen far short of the brigade counter-attack envisaged in Brigadier Hargest's 5 Brigade defensive plan. Andrew despondently noted 'of those who managed to withdraw to C Company HQ, only three were unwounded'. The failed counter-attack left Johnson's company on the vital aerodrome in a critical condition. He sent a runner to Andrew with an urgent request for reinforcements, explaining:

> My company's position was deteriorating rapidly. 15 platoon [Sinclair] and the western section of 13 platoon appeared to have fallen. 14 platoon [Donald] was practically finished and the cooks, stretcher bearers and company HQ staff could not hold the inland perimeter of the drome for long.

Johnson reckoned he could probably hold until dark, but would have to be reinforced by then.

Andrew was uncompromising, ordering them to 'hold on at all costs'. Andrew felt his predicament was untenable. His superior, Brigadier Hargest, was assessing his unknown situation from four miles away. He had not even come forward at least to 23 Battalion, on the ridgeline behind Hill 107, to see for himself. No brigade counter-attack had materialized; indeed Hargest had said there would not be one. Andrew felt totally isolated. Headquarter Company, positioned on the vital coast road at Pirgos, had not been in contact all day. Large numbers of paratroopers had come down in their area, they had been possibly overrun. A Company nearby was intact, but fighting hard. He himself was co-located with B Company, who appeared to be blocking increasingly heavy probes from the south-west. Johnson had informed him that C Company was virtually decimated. Andrew therefore could only count on two of his five companies. The battalion log mirrored his concerns. The enemy was established in force between the two villages of Vlakheronitissa and Xamoudhokhori to his south and rear. German paratroopers were also starting to probe between his command post and C Company below. If he did not move off Hill 107 he would be surrounded and cut off from 23 and 21 Battalions to his east. If he did not get out during the night, daylight Luftwaffe close air support and rolling ground attacks would force him off the summit in the morning.[7]

At 6pm he contacted Hargest at 5 Brigade and told him 'I must withdraw unless reinforcements reach me soon'. The aerial bombing, isolation and the failure of his optimistic weak tank-supported counter-attack had sapped Andrew's spirit. The intention was not to abandon the position but fall back onto B Company's position on RAP Ridge. In daylight, however, this ridgeline would be overlooked by the summit of Hill 107. Holding it would be untenable. In so doing he was surrendering the vital ground that overlooked and dominated the aerodrome, a compromise that might unravel the whole defence. This was to be the precursor to a form of 'blind man's buff' that would characterize the manoeuvring and skirmishing around the summit of Hill 107 all night long. The prize was the possession of the all-important Maleme aerodrome, the only conduit left for German reinforcement of the, by now, faltering attack on the island of Crete.[8]

BRIGADIER JAMES HARGEST, COMMANDER
5 NEW ZEALAND BRIGADE

07.00–18.30 20 May, Brigade Gully, Command Post, Platanias Village
The day of the invasion had not begun well for Brigadier Jimmy Hargest. The normally taciturn, frank yet friendly chubby commander was not well when he woke up. 'No breakfast', he announced to Captain Bob Dawson, his brigade major, 'feeling a little tired, so I'll take things easier today'. Dawson saw he was 'not well' and went to Battle HQ by himself. Bofors guns were starting up in the background, heralding yet another series of heavy Luftwaffe raids, which descended at 7am. Hargest's HQ was located in a farmhouse in a gully, a few hundred yards inland from the coastal village of Platanias. Maleme airfield lay five miles to the west, where noise and smoke were perceptibly increasing. Just a little further east along the coast towards the capital Chania,

Lieutenant Geoffrey Cox, Major-General Freyberg's intelligence officer observed: 'Away up the coast, where the reddish sand strip that was Maleme airfield showed in the mist, the Bofors guns were thudding away, baying like huge dogs in a cloud of dust and smoke which grew steadily thicker.' The attacks reached a climax when five bombers laid a line of 1,000kg bombs from the Galatas ridge down to the tented hospital encampment by the sea. 'Great brown geysers of earth sprouted up, noiselessly for a second' until 'then came the noise and blast.'[9]

Jimmy Hargest's day got worse. Fighter after fighter roared over Platanias, machine guns blazing. Emerging from the village, he had to dash and crawl through a storm of strafing cannon and machine-gun fire to reach his slit trench in the HQ gully. From there, he could observe Maleme. Communication links to his parent battalions began to break down in this storm of air activity. It seemed 5 Brigade got special attention from enemy aircraft every time a wireless message was passed. This disconcerting inability to communicate emphasized the totally intimidating Luftwaffe mastery of the air. Gliders were spotted by his staff, coming in low overhead and veering off towards Maleme. Reports about crash-landing gliders and paratroopers trickled in. Cox along the coast saw 'the white of a parachute' which 'I took to be a pilot bailing out of a hit aircraft' but soon there were very many more. They soon saw streams of Ju 52 transport aircraft which 'moved in columns of three abreast' coming over the shoulder of the mountains inland and 'handful after handful of these white shapes were flung into the air'. Telephone lines became inoperable and wireless contacts gradually petered out, becoming progressively weaker until they died. Hargest was not necessarily disconcerted. This happened during attacks in war, and had when he was serving as a battalion commander in 1918. He remained relatively confident. His strongest battalion positions were those around Maleme aerodrome and on Hill 107.[10]

Hargest was not only unwell, he was still worn out from the 'touch and go' withdrawal he had endured on mainland Greece. Blanketed by overwhelming Luftwaffe air superiority, his brigade had barely managed to escape intact. He had shared his sense of impending dread with Geoffrey Cox the night before. Both anticipated yet another German 'avalanche' coming as Cox expressed it 'in an even more novel form to descend on us':

> I had experienced a year earlier in France the deadening of the will, the paralysis of initiative which had seized a whole nation as its army had disintegrated before those grey German tanks and grey German planes and grey-clad infantry.

Worst of all was the enemy's mastery of the air, 'denying those who resisted any place of rest or shelter'. The invasion had now begun. 'We knew things were confused', Hargest's brigade major Dawson admitted, not helped by a complete dearth of practical information. 'We knew 22nd Battalion was taking a hammering', he and the staff accepted, 'but we did not feel that they were bad'. Hargest recorded in his diary a few days later that the infantry around him 'seemed cheerful except 22nd, which was badly knocked about'.[11]

None of the New Zealand commanders that day acted like they might typically have been expected to; Hargest and 5 Brigade were no exception. Andrew, the inspiring and resolute company commander of 1918, was not performing confidently as battalion commander. Resolve and optimistic energy was transcended by pessimism. Hargest had the reputation of being one of the outstanding commanding officers in the 1918 New Zealand Division, but the same qualities did not necessarily translate well to the higher brigade level of command in this war. A consummate inter-war politician, he diplomatically chose to site his command HQ nearer his superior, Brigadier Puttick, the acting division commander, rather than the key ground he and his subordinates were tasked to defend. Andrew, commanding his strongest battalion, was nearly five miles away at Maleme. Hargest had little or no news to share with Puttick. Andrew had to command from a slit trench on the south slope of Hill 107, strafed by planes and under constant ground fire, so vulnerable, he would shift location to B Company, on the reverse slope. He only managed to achieve momentary radio contact with Brigade at mid-morning, unable to speak to his own men, who had no wireless sets, except by runner.

At first Hargest received optimistic reports from 23 and 21 Battalions describing heavy casualties inflicted on enemy landings. Then the news got worse. Just before 3pm Andrew got through to report his headquarters had been penetrated. An hour later came word his left flank was giving way and he needed reinforcements. At 5pm the 22 Battalion request for 23 Battalion to mount the pre-arranged counter-attack was refused, an obscure response, because Leckie had already assured Brigade he was in the ascendant and in firm control. This was inexplicable, because Maleme was one of only three vital airfields on the island. Hargest was responding sluggishly, confidence ebbing away alongside his energy levels. He was neither re-grouping nor reinforcing following urgent requests for support, most definitely his remit as brigade commander. He preferred to wait and defer to decisions made by subordinates on the ground, rather than grasping the initiative to drive through the priorities he had set out prior to the landings. 21 Battalion was originally earmarked to move up alongside Andrew to the south, to respond to any parachute landings identified west of the Tavronitis River. One of its platoons was already in situ, to provide observation and guidance for such a move. It was now under attack by German glider troops. 23 Battalion, the next strongest unit, had always been considered the immediate response to Andrew getting into trouble on Hill 107.

Hargest's pre-invasion orders were verbose, but less clear on the main points of effort. Ill health may well have compromised a willingness to execute the complex re-grouping orders that would be required if he put 23 Battalion into the attack. Its primary role was coastal defence and a seaborne invasion force was anticipated at any time. 21 Battalion would have to move forward to take on this role, all the time under incessant Luftwaffe air attack, should this occur by day. Hargest chose not to share these dilemmas with Puttick, his division commander, preferring the safer 'wait and see' option. The lack of clear priorities passed to battalion commanders and a 'hands off' command style had given considerable individual lassitude to his subordinates for individual action. Hargest was generally ready to defer to their decisions, often already made on the ground; his passive stance was such that at no stage did Hargest go forward to confer with his commanders, particularly the increasingly isolated Andrew. The 5 Brigade battalions had fought well, inflicting painful reverses on recently landed parachute troops. Greater overall coordination was now required of Hargest at brigade level to reap the benefits of these local successes.

There was a noticeable disconnect between the way his soldiers regarded the course of the battle, compared to that of Hargest and his staff cocooned in the Platanias HQ gully. Machine gunner Steve Moss manning a Vickers machine gun recalled:

> Then over came another crowd and once more we hammered them. They reckon about 10,000 troops were landed. I think the big majority of them dead ... We're doing pretty good. Everyone quite happy and waiting to see what is going to happen.[12]

Only when Andrew unexpectedly announced the failure of his local tank-infantry counter-attack did Hargest start to realize he might have to re-assess and act.

Hargest sought to hold onto his reserves as long as possible, so as to maintain a resolute defence against an envisaged German seaborne landing. Moreover, further parachute or glider troops might materialize at any moment, from an enemy who appeared to have an inexhaustible supply of them. Brigadier Inglis, commanding 4 Brigade in reserve nearby, was having doubts about Hargest's grip on the Maleme battle, despite only favourable reports received at Puttick's HQ. He met a war correspondent at 2pm returning by Bren carrier from a visit to Platanias village. According to him 5 Brigade HQ was 'out of touch with its units' and 'flapping'. All that Puttick at division and Major-General Freyberg in overall command at Creforce HQ knew, as dusk approached, was that the Germans were in the Tavronitis river bed and ridge to the west of Maleme airfield and were attacking Hill 107. Another substantial force had landed in Prison Valley and was threatening

General Kurt Student originated the plan. Seen as the father of German airborne forces, he was obsessively determined to prove his newly constituted all-arms airborne corps could capture a strategic objective like Crete from the air alone.

Lieutenant Colonel Leslie Andrew commanded the 22 New Zealand Battalion defending Hill 107. A competent soldier and VC holder, he was dismayed by events but stuck to faulty personal judgement as the 5 Brigade plan unravelled around him.
(Alexander Turnbull Library)

New Zealand troops, spent after the fighting withdrawal from Greece, rest at the road side en route to Maleme, after disembarking at Suda Bay.
(National Army Museum, New Zealand – DA11043)

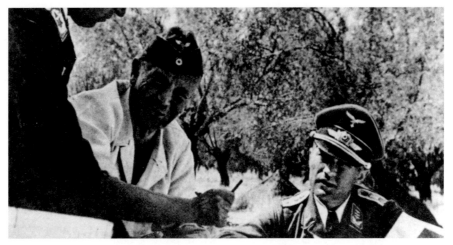

Generalmajor Eugen Meindl, the *Sturmregiment* commander, briefs his battalion commanders in shirtsleeves at Megara airstrip from the map table outside his tent. To his right is *Major* Stentzler, his *II Bataillon* commander.

Brigadier James Hargest (centre) and his 5 Brigade staff at the Platanias farmhouse. Andrew is looking over his left shoulder in the back row and Lieutenant Colonel Dittmer, commanding 28 (Maori) Battalion, stands to his left. (Courtesy of A. P. Fox)

This glider has landed on the road embankment just short of the Tavronitis river bridge. The dry river bed is visible just beyond. The open terrace nature of Hill 107's western slope can be clearly seen in the background.

Generalmajor Julius Ringel commanding the *5. Gebirgsjäger Division* was a committed Austrian National Socialist. The air-land by his mountain division at Maleme turned the tide of the battle.

New Zealand defenders await the German onslaught from their slit trench, dug into the lee of one of the stone wall terraces.

The approach flight of the first wave, low level over the sea.

German paratroopers grimly sit face to face inside crowded troop transports; they had two hours to reflect on what was to come.

The New Zealand trench view from below; they have yet to open fire. (National Army Museum, New Zealand – DA11022)

Below The Matilda heavy infantry tank *Gnu III* was abandoned after passing beneath the Tavronitis bridge span seen behind. The appearance of the two heavy tanks caused consternation because the German paratroopers had no effective means to stop them.

Oberstabsarzt Dr Heinrich Neumann (glasses), seen on the right at foreground, is at the head of the small band of men that took the summit of Hill 107, for which he was awarded the Knight's Cross.

Scaling the terraced slopes of Hill 107, thick with undergrowth, was difficult for attackers. Despite the cover, defenders had the upper hand, because the *Fallschirmjäger*, seen here, had to move to approach. (Bundesarchiv)

German soldiers view the aftermath of the failed New Zealand counter-attack from the heights behind Hill 107. Their own advance would cross the same coastal plain laid out before them. (Getty Images)

Possibly Andrew's abandoned HQ location, occupied by Stentzler's *II Bataillon* paratroopers, who quickly established a defensive screen on Hill 107.

The destruction and fires on the airstrip during the air-land, convinced Hargest the Germans were evacuating rather than reinforcing.

The ramshackle state of the German seaborne landings became a debacle when hunted down by Royal Navy destroyers and cruisers during the night of 21/22 May. Ten ships were sunk, casting 1,800 men into the water.

The New Zealand counter-attack had already run out of momentum by dawn on 22 May when it was subjected to paralysing Luftwaffe air attacks and obliged to withdraw. (National Army Museum, New Zealand – DA3466)

Generalmajor Ringel's air-landed *Gebirgsjäger* bypassed the New Zealand defence by crossing the mountainous terrain to the south, following his maxim, 'sweat saves blood'.

Oberleutnant Horst Trebes (pith helmet and shorts in the foreground) shouting the order to 'fire!' during the Kondomori massacre on 2 June 1941, photographed by *Leutnant* Franz-Peter Weixler. (Bundesarchiv)

Weixler captured the impact of volley fire bursting upon the 23 assembled villagers. Two men can be seen running off to the right. There was only one survivor. (Bundesarchiv)

Galatas village, key for entry into Chania. They could in time cut the coastal road leading to Maleme behind Hargest. Major parachute insertions at Rethymnom and Iraklion had been largely beaten off. Puttick had a generally positive picture of the fighting around Maleme aerodrome, and Pirgos to its east, while 23 and 21 battalions had bloodily repulsed all landings. 'Upwards of 80%' of the glider and paratrooper attacks 'were destroyed before they reached the ground', Puttick was assured.

Freyberg, forewarned by the Ultra decrypt system about the date, time and locations of the German airborne attack, was a picture of self-contained calm when they arrived. He was breakfasting on the terrace of his coastal villa outside Chania, and able to look across to Maleme, when the first drops occurred. He allegedly grunted, glanced at his watch and remarked to those within earshot that the Germans were 'dead on time'. One aide Monty Wodehouse visiting the HQ recalled the general 'seemed mildly surprised at German punctuality'. Watching the German blitz at some distance through his field glasses, Freyberg was 'enthralled by the magnitude of the operation'.[13]

He had impressed upon his commanders the urgency and immediate need to counter-attack newly landed paratroops. Regimental-size parachute assaults at Rethymnon and Iraklion were shot to pieces when the second wave arrived late afternoon to the east of the island. Both assaults were decimated in intense defensive fire. At Rethymnon two Australian battalions led by Lieutenant Colonel Campbell immediately pitched into a hill feature momentarily captured overlooking the airstrip. Brigadier Chappel commanding the British 14 Brigade kept the invaders well clear of the airfield at Iraklion. Freyberg quickly released the island's force reserve to Brigadier Puttick within hours of the landings, to enable local counter-attacks to be immediately mounted. The reserve, however, remained stationary throughout the rest of the day, notwithstanding repeated appeals from local commanders in Prison Valley to clear out the large concentration of German invaders, despite being severely mauled on arrival. From the very start of the planning processes to defend the island of Crete, Freyberg had impressed on his subordinate commanders the value of aggressively counter-attacking straight away. Only the New Zealand commanders, despite the obvious tactical successes of their soldiers, failed to emulate the Australian and British example to implement this stated will to the full.

Two commanders were responsible for the defence of Hill 107, which dominated the vital Maleme aerodrome: Andrew at battalion and Hargest at brigade level. At this stage of the battle, Puttick at division had not been informed about the true situation. Both officers had been selected for command despite recognition that they both shared signs of delayed shell shock after their distinguished World War I experiences. Hargest had even reversed his medical decision by appealing over the heads of the board to the acting Prime Minister Peter Fraser. His appointment to command 5 Brigade was political favouritism. Throughout the day, the two men acted sluggishly and at variance to normally aggressive temperaments. Hargest was unwell at the start of the day and Andrew uncharacteristically pessimistic. They had been shaken by the intensity of the Luftwaffe air attacks. Andrew, hit on the forehead by shrapnel, admitted that men who had experienced mind-numbing World War I artillery barrages at Messines, Passchendaele and the Somme 'would rather go through these [again] than see another Maleme Blitz'. Hargest that morning had to sprint through intense strafing just to reach his brigade command post. There is little doubt that these traumatic experiences resurrected bleak memories of the previous war. Lieutenant Geoffrey Cox located nearby recalled his days under 'the mental impact of intensive and prolonged attack from the air' on the Greek mainland, and what it meant: 'Heavy bombing and strafing not only physically and mentally shook nerves as well as smashed bodies. It also drained away mental energy, inducing a lethargy and exhaustion which inhibited the consideration of issues and the taking of decisions.'

Andrew had to confront some alarming decisions from the confines of an open slit trench on the summit of Hill 107, repeatedly bombed throughout the day. 'It could numb thought', Cox explained, 'it could weigh like lead on the powers of decision, weakening the will not through fear, but through mental fatigue'. What transpired were the decisions of tired men. Cox had already highlighted Hargest's 'dread' at what he knew was coming 'which inhibited initiative – and particularly initiative in a situation which was unclear'. Precisely the interaction going on between these two key command players.[14]

Hargest in May 1941 was fighting a different war. Veterans tend to rely heavily on what they learned the last time. Both Andrew and Hargest drew upon their 1914–18 experiences, with their imperative to maintain defensive lines. Andrew told his superior at about 6pm with dusk approaching that he had no option but to withdraw from the summit of Hill 107 to the B Company ridgeline below it. This would not be defensible in daylight. Hargest, thinking in terms of an intact line that might conceivably be regained, deferred to his man on the ground; after all, he was a VC holder. Like many New Zealand senior commanders, he failed to appreciate that in this new air age, the pace of fighting had perceptibly increased. Counter-attacks in a battle in which the enemy can be supplied and supported from the air had to be swift and as immediate as their unexpected insertion. Hargest was not unique in misunderstanding the problem of command and control during the mixed scrappy fighting that accompanies airborne landings. The Germans were to face the same dilemma in Normandy in 1944, when scattered parachute landings made it exceedingly difficult to identify the actual enemy force concentrations. This was the problem on Crete that first day. There had been heavy drops on top of and west of Maleme village and the dry Tavronitis river bed. Glider assaults had also been made on the Akrotiri Peninsula on the other side of Suda Bay and south of the capital at Chania. A major parachute insertion had occurred in Prison Valley between the Aghia reservoir and Galatas village followed by regimental-size parachute assaults at Rethymnon and Iraklion to the east of the island during the afternoon. Staff officers were unsure of what they were marking up on their situation maps, displaying clusters of enemy activity that lacked any conventional coherence. There were no lines in this battle.

When at 6pm Andrew finally managed to relay to Hargest that he had to withdraw unless reinforcements reached him soon, the brigadier was nonplussed. He had not assimilated the urgency of Andrew's repeated calls for support throughout the day. Hargest had played the politician, maintaining a calm optimistic demeanour throughout, reporting as much to Puttick his superior. But he was clearly uninformed. The credibility gap between Hargest and his favoured and likely best battalion commander – a VC holder – could only be bridged by a personal encounter. Hargest neglected to go forward the not inconsiderable five miles to achieve one. The protection of Maleme aerodrome, the only airstrip under serious threat that day, was vital to the successful outcome of this battle. Holding Hill 107 above it was key, and now Andrew was telling him he was about to move off the summit. Neither Puttick nor Freyberg had accorded it and the airfield absolute priority over the defence of the coast, but it was a key 5 Brigade task, and could not be ignored. Clearly Hargest was taken aback, and he responded somewhat petulantly 'if you must, you must'.[15]

He would, however, have to react. Minutes later he radioed back: 'am sending you two companies, A Company 23rd Battalion and B Company 28th (Maori) Battalion'. Andrew was temporarily mollified at this volte-face on the brigadier's part, but assumed the promised support would arrive within the hour. Both companies were not ordered to depart from their parent battalions for another one and a half hours. They were only two companies, hardly a brigade-level counter-measure, eliciting scant notice from Puttick, who had been assured all was in control.

GENERALLEUTNANT KURT STUDENT, COMMANDER
XI FLIEGERKORPS

10.30 20 May–Early Morning Night Hours 21 May 1941, Hotel Grande Bretagne, Athens
Kurt Student, unlike the primary New Zealand decision makers, was able to consider his options amid the late-baroque splendour of the opulent Grande Bretagne hotel in Athens. Extended in 1842

from the luxurious Dimitrious mansion it overlooked Syntagma Square, next to the former palace of the king. Most of Student's senior officers had a spectacular view of the Parthenon from their balconies. The ballroom where the headquarters was established was 'over-pompously furnished' according to one of his officers, and was as far removed from a slit trench as one could get. Previously used by the British General Staff, it had formerly served as one of the central meeting places where Greeks and foreigners shaped the political, social and economic life of the country. Now Germans exclusively occupied its sumptuous apartments, Italians had to make do with the third best hotel – The Splendid – because the Prince George was likewise reserved only for Germans. Student had set up around the broad table in the centre of the room surrounded by field telephones, according to one of his staff officers: 'Amid a confusion of wires, a stack of papers, two black files, and, in the centre, a large ash-tray piled high with stubs and the remains of half-finished cigarettes.'[16]

The day began with considerable confidence, Student and his staff believing they 'had taken every possibility into consideration'. When the skeleton night staff was replaced by the primary shift, an ordered air of bustle descended on the room. Tunic jackets came off in the heat and heavy ornate curtains were drawn to deflect the worse of the sun's rays. The operation appeared to be going to plan. Most of the returning empty first wave aircraft were down between 10.30 and 11.00am. Losses were slight, just seven aircraft lost. Crews on landing reported successful flights and drops. 'Shattering news' then came from the commander of the glider lift that *Generalleutnant* Süssmann had fatally crashed on the island of Aegina, in sight of Athen's Piraeus harbour. Süssmann had been sponsored for division command by Student. It was a personal as well as damaging command setback.

Student was revered by his staff and paratroopers as the *Papa* of the German airborne arm. He had a very personal emotional and ideological stake in the outcome of this operation, at the pinnacle of proving what his airborne concept was capable of, conquering a strategic objective: the island of Crete. The pinnacle was starting to wobble, despite sharp elbows having been deployed to get to this point. Student had personally sought Göring's patronage and through him personal contact with the Führer. Holland the previous year was a pyrrhic victory of sorts, costly and hard-fought. Student had been well forward and grievously shot in the head. The reward for this *Nibelungen* of a battle had been the Knight's Cross and personal recognition from the Führer. There were those in the room from *Generaloberst* Löhr's *Luftflotte 4* and *Generalmajor* Ringel's *Gebirgsjäger* division staff who were looking askance at a commander barely four months recovered from a severe head wound, heading up a suspected reckless operation. It was at the minimum a huge risk. Even some of Student's backers suspected his personality may have changed with the head injury perhaps influencing mood swings. He was, however, the same man, with unwavering ambition. His *Fallschirmjäger* needed to be used in order to be proven. They had been excluded from the glorious advances across the Balkans and were not earmarked for any particular role in Operation *Barbarossa*, the forthcoming invasion of Russia. There would be no recruits without glory. Success on Crete ensured a future.

By mid-morning there was no definitive news on progress. Student was waiting for the clarity of information that would bring confirmation he had been right to propose the airborne attack on the island outlined to Göring a brief month before. Göring had bathed in the reflected Luftwaffe glory of Student's accomplishments in Holland the year before. The first intimation in the ballroom HQ that things were going wrong was *Major* Snowadski's radio report that he had been fired upon as his two administrative command Ju-52s had attempted to land at Maleme airport. This ominously suggested the aerodrome was not in German hands. Four and a half hours had passed since the landings yet no ground commanders had reported in.

Then, at 11.15am, a quarter of an hour after Snowadski's unsettling transmission, the first situation report was radioed by the *Gruppe West* first wave: 'The enemy have been cleared from the airfield and flak positions' but 'is still sitting on the hills to the south'. They were under artillery fire and 'the commander of *Gruppe West* [Meindl] is wounded, but still leading'. 'We are attacking', the *Sturmregiment* reported, and 'request the situation of *Gruppe Mitte*'. This was clearly bad news. After convincing themselves they had considered every possibility, Student's staff were suddenly wrong-footed. Only 45 minutes were left to confirm the launch of the second waves against Rethymnon and Iraklion further east, but the situation had fundamentally changed. Maleme airfield had not been captured and there was no immediate plan B. No planning revision options were discussed, there was no clarity about the extent of the setback. No flying back-up command headquarters was launched to replace the radios that had obviously failed following the morning insertions. During this period of indecision elements from the second wave began to take off, flight serials were still delayed by the pervasive dust on the airstrips and the labour needed to hand-pump refuelling Ju 52s. It became impractical to recall the second wave, driven by the need to coincide with the arrival of von Richthofen's *VIII Fliegerkorps* close air support over the drop zones, flying out from different airfields. Student's carefully conceived concept and plan was unravelling under the remorseless pressure of events. Unlike in Holland, he could not get forward to see for himself.

Student had also taken risks on the basis of poor intelligence in Holland the year before and got away with it. He only briefly considered reinforcing the apparent setback at Maleme, because his men had always managed to persevere somehow and had never let him down. Re-routing or hesitating with the second wave would dislocate the air transport roll-out and reduce the impact of close air support. There was no *Schwerpunkt* or point of main effort; his airborne concept was rather an 'oil-spot' distribution of force, seeping into the enemy's defences at multiple points to panic them into collapse. The *Seestaffel* (sea contingent) amphibious landings by the mountain battalions at Maleme should, in any case, restore the situation. Second-wave aircraft gradually lumbered into the air, delayed by dust and the need to re-role jump serials into serviceable aircraft to replace those lost or damaged during the first wave launch. They headed for Rethymnon and Iraklion, and would arrive by late afternoon at 4.15 and 5.30 respectively.

All that remained for the staff to do now was anxiously wait again, as snippets of bad news still trickled in from Maleme. At 3.20pm *Gruppe West* radioed alarmingly that they were under tank attack from Maleme 'over the airfield and river bed'. Meindl's command urgently requested anti-tank ammunition to be dropped on the beach just west of the Tavronitis bridge, as 'the attack has been halted for the moment'. The news did not get better. At 6.10pm came another request, the critical need to fly out a seriously wounded *Generalmajor* Meindl, whose condition was deteriorating.

By 7pm that night, the atmosphere in the headquarters was heavy with foreboding. Tension became all pervasive. One officer recalled:

> On the wall, in semi-darkness, was the large map of Crete dotted with little paper flags marking the positions of the German and British units according to the latest information, while in the bottom right-hand corner were arrayed further ranks of little flags like companies awaiting the order to march.

Student sat at the broad table 'which was illuminated with unnecessary brilliance'. Coffee cups and discarded cigarette stubs continued to pile up. 'A headquarters on such nights is a beehive', the staff officer recalled:

> Orderlies come and go, bringing telegrams, receiving orders, and taking messages to the signals department. Typewriters chatter, telephones ring, teleprinters rattle. Groups of officers stand in subdued discussion around table-maps, while down the corridor orderlies hurry with files, maps or cups of coffee for their fatigued superiors.[17]

By now a rudimentary situation outline could be assessed. Seven thousand men had landed on Crete without a single objective being gained. The second wave failed to take the airport at Iraklion and was repelled with heavy losses. They moved onto the defensive. There was no radio traffic at all coming from Rethymnon. Chania had not been reached and heavy losses had been inflicted on the landings at Prison Valley, which also went onto the defensive. Maleme aerodrome had not been captured and the *Sturmregiment* had taken fearful losses. Transport aircraft lost transitioned from seven that morning to 26 destroyed and 27 damaged by dusk, a total of 53 lost on operations. Many commanders were down, including the Division and *Sturmregiment* chiefs. Maleme was the only location where a small bridgehead had been achieved with troops still in the attack.[18]

Generaloberst Löhr and *Generalmajor* Ringel joined the staff that evening, neither of them overly well-disposed to Student. The weight of responsibility for a potential debacle weighed heavily on Student, with some officers perceptibly shying away from association with such failure. More Germans had been killed on this single day than on any other thus far in this war. The number of senior commanders killed and wounded suggested exceedingly heavy casualties overall. Hope that the severe reception at Maleme implied Rethymnon and Iraklion must only be lightly held were soon dashed. Löhr and Ringel viewed proceedings with vulture-like restraint; 'heavy hours', Ringel called them. They would not hesitate to withdraw the battered survivors if the tactical situation was not turned round. Löhr was driven more by the need to conform to the pending demands of the invasion of Russia than Crete. Ringel, dubious from the start of the operation, could scarcely be expected to hazard his men on an operation that had already decimated the 7 Airborne Division, without attaining a single viable bridgehead. Student's fortunes were at a total nadir. If he accepted defeat he would have expended one of the Führer's most cherished and glamorous formations, and let down Göring, his superior, protector and sponsor. He would be utterly discredited.[19]

At midnight the ack-ack guns around Athens opened up as Allied planes were heard attacking the air transport mounting airfields to the north. It reflected the prevailing nervous and pessimistic mood in the headquarters. 'A tense hour passed', one staff officer recalled, 'before news arrived from the airfields that the damage done was, thank God, negligible'. A lesser man might have lost his nerve. Student, unlike some of his contemporaries, possessed a fresh unconventional approach to problem solving. He kept his head and logically analysed the problem that appeared to be slipping out of control. 'At no point', Student later observed, 'did we succeed in completely occupying an airfield': 'The greatest degree of progress was achieved on Maleme airfield, where the valuable assault regiment fought against picked New Zealand troops.'[20]

During the late evening *Oberst* Bernhard Ramcke telephoned Student's staff from Topolia airfield, where he had been assisting Ringel's mountain troops to master the technical skills needed to air-land at Iraklion that day. Aircraft losses and damaged 'non-airworthy' Ju 52s had played havoc with aircraft chalk list seat allocations. Many parachutists were left behind as a consequence when the second-wave aircraft took off. On his own initiative, Ramcke gathered some 550 men at Topolia and formed an ad hoc parachute reserve. This was manna from heaven for the staff, because Student had committed the whole force up front without a reserve. Everything had gone to the second wave 'vertical envelopment', which had been the tactical driver all day. Student's staff had almost run out of resources.

'I decided to concentrate all our forces against one spot', Student wrote afterwards. 'We selected Maleme because here, at least, we could see a glimmer of light', which was where the newly accumulated reserve would be committed. 'The night of May 20th/21st was critical for the German command', he remembered. If Meindl's men could cling to their sparse bridgehead this night, they might yet prevail: 'I had to make a momentous decision. I decided to use the mass of the parachute reserves still at my disposal for the final capture of Maleme airfield.'[21] Forces cut off at Iraklion and probably also Rethymnon would have to fend for themselves. A *Schwerpunkt* was to be concentrated west of the island, which would much simplify von Richthofen's *VIII Fliegerkorps* air support.

Student's staff sent a message to *Gruppe West* during the late evening to 'clear the airstrip from enemy and hold space for an air-landing by two mountain battalions from 6.30am'. They were to be re-roled from Iraklion and would be preceded by six Ju-52s carrying resupply. Assurance was given '*VIII Fliegerkorps* would engage the enemy artillery south-east of the airfield'. They were also asked: 'When is the landing by the *Seestaffel* [sea contingent] possible?'[22]

Student then sent for *Hauptmann* Oskar Kleye, 'a bold go-getting character on my staff', he recalled, and tasked him to fly a Ju 52 'to land at Maleme in order to get a personal feeling of how things were going with the *Sturmregiment*'. Kleye was a skilful and daring pilot, attached to corps headquarters under a bit of a cloud, having upset his squadron commander with *6/KG z.b.V.* His corps commander now offered a form of redemption. He was to personally report back on the situation, with, if possible, an input from *Generalmajor* Meindl. He took off at 3am from Athens.[23]

A combination of initiative and chance was opening up previously irredeemable options. Student retired to his bed, but it would be a sleepless night. 'On the night of the 20th May', he confided much later, 'I waited with my pistol continuously by my side, ready to use it on myself, if the worst came to the worst'. He knew in his own heart what *he* would do if he was the New Zealander commander – squeeze the German bridgehead until it was no more. As he acknowledged: 'If they had launched a counter-attack, (which they did not) from high ground 107 overlooking Maleme, then the situation would have been critical for us. We would have been overthrown.'[24]

Chapter 8

Victory by Chance

HAUPTMANN WALTER GERICKE, COMMANDER
IV BATAILLON STURMREGIMENT

*10.30–23.00 20 May 1941, Sturmregiment HQ, Tavronitis Bridge
Below Hill 107*

The 34-year-old *Hauptmann* Walter Gericke was a highly respected competent combat leader, revered by his men. His radio net was characteristically the first to function at 7.50am, swiftly linking to his regimental commander *Generalmajor* Meindl, located nearby. Once Meindl was critically wounded in the chest Gericke took command and rallied the surviving elements of the badly mauled *I* (Glider) *Bataillon* alongside his *IV* (heavy weapons) *Bataillon*. Meindl, still conscious, had directed Stentzler's *II Bataillon* to get across the Tavronitis river bed and start to surround Hill 107 from the south-east. Progress was laborious. His *5.* and *6. Kompanien* were fighting around the village of Vlakheronitissa, clashing with 21 New Zealand Battalion platoon seeking to push on into the rising folds of Hill 107 south of the summit. He was pinned by A and B Company of 22 Battalion to the lower ground beneath the summit ridgelines.

Gericke had stabilized the tiny bridgehead around the bridge and was seeking to expand the wedge that had been driven between Andrew's weakened C Company at the airstrip and D Company on the south side of the captured RAF camp. D Company was still repelling all efforts to cross the dry river bed. Gericke set up his headquarters in an olive grove, partially screened by the road embankment, directly behind the still intact bridge. Scanning the heights of Hill 107 with field glasses he assessed that maybe 'three-quarters of the northern slope was occupied by weak [German] detachments', according to his late afternoon radio report to regimental headquarters. 'Request attacks from the *II Bataillon* against these heights', he asked. It seemed he was not in contact with Stentzler.[1]

Much of Gericke's *IV Bataillon* manpower was taken up crewing heavy weapons systems. The summit of Hill 107 was subjected to heavy machine gun and mortar harassing fire, while other men were crewing 37mm anti-tank guns in support. There was little infantry in the battalion that could be pushed up the slopes to attack. Gericke was constantly forming ad hoc combat groups from separated paratroopers that appeared back in their lines, who were redirected to attack. 'Tommies still sat in their well-constructed bunker positions and trenches, fortified with sandbags', he remembered, 'well camouflaged amid the gnarled roots of olive trees'. Attacking *Fallschirmjäger* attempted to work their way up, covering each other in leaps and bounds:

> The first to fall was a *Gefreiter* [Corporal] who was shot in the head just as he was about to take aim with his rifle. Then a Berliner went down, a shell fragment split his stomach open. A third was wounded and bled out with long-lasting moans. It was awful.

The setback was reported to Gericke at the bridge; his storm group was pinned down: 'What can one do?' he recalled:

> The commander cannot dispatch reinforcements. All the combat capable men were needed to man the heavy weapons needed to provide effective fire support to take out to some extent, or neutralize the Tommies.[2]

The azimuth of the sun started to have an increasingly important tactical impact on the fighting. *Generalmajor* Meindl had calculated his flying approach and drop should come out of the east so that the British would be dazzled by the sun as they came over. *Jäger* Ferdinand Fink, the glider soldier from von Plessen's decimated *3. Kompanie* taking cover at the western extremity of the airstrip, noticed once 'the sun was high in the sky, it created dense shadows, inside which it was difficult to discern anything'. Not only that, 'garish shining flat areas blinded tired eyes and strained eyesight'. During morning daylight hours, glider men pinned down on the western slopes of Hill 107 were blinded by the sun as they looked up at the New Zealand positions. 'This affected sight at short distances', Fink recalled, 'hindering attackers who felt unsafe'. The enemy had the sun at his back, 'which enabled him to pick out where we were in every detail'. This likewise hindered the sight picture for Gericke's support weapons crews, 'making it hardly possible to make out their positions and give clear precise fire orders'. Midday heat imposed an undeclared 'siesta' period of quiet over the battlefield until the angle of the sun changed. As the afternoon wore on 'the enemy positions became easier to distinguish, clear fire control orders could be given, which meant they could be more effectively engaged'. The *Fallschirmjäger* could now hide in the shadows and 'now our heavy weapons firing across the valley could excellently work over the enemy, who was now blinded'. The advantage of shadow and glare shifted from defender to attacker as the azimuth of the sun shifted between morning and afternoon.[3]

More insidious than the changing angle of the sun was the impact of unexpectedly intense May heat. The paratroopers had jumped wearing the same uniforms worn during arctic conditions in Norway the year before. *Oberjäger* Schuster in Fink's company had already cut his trouser legs to produce shorts. 'The sun burned so hot over the position', he recalled, 'that the stones positively glowed with the heat'. A myriad of flies swarmed about them, irritatingly touching all the sensitive areas of the body, eyes, ears, nose and mouth, while the intensity of incoming fire punished any movement to get rid of them. The sun sucked energy out of them, so that 'soldiers lay apathetically in their holes', Schuster observed. When the angle of the afternoon sun shifted they could at last benefit from the shade they craved. Jump rations, the same as those issued for northern climes 'melted together in shapeless clumps'. *Hauptmann* von der Heydte described the unappetizing mix as 'an extraordinary pot-pourri of melted chocolate, smoked bacon, spiced sausage and rock-hard rusks'. It was eat that or starve, and as von der Heydte commented 'when the devil is hungry, he will eat flies'.[4]

Gericke may have felt he had a flimsy grip on perhaps three-quarters of the northern slope of Hill 107, but these were simply pockets of dispersed paratroopers holding ground where they had come down. They were unlikely to be, as Andrew assumed, enemy who had worked up the eastern slope. The value of such resistance pockets was that they fought on, reassured from what they gleaned from their own radio traffic, which the New Zealanders did not have. But they did not have the strength or ammunition to press on.

Oberfeldwebel Wenzel, wounded and still cut off, had formed a defensive 'hedgehog' with his four surviving companions. 'Our spirits remain unbroken, and at no time do we think of surrender', he recalled. 'The heat is unbearable', they had no fluids, and 'we chew on vine leaves, which taste very bitter, an unfavourable substitute for that precious commodity water, which we are denied!' Enemy fire kept them pinned down amid sharp rock and brittle grass virtually the entire day. 'Our Stukas, bombers and fighters circle and watch throughout the day, but can't make out friend or foe.' They saw the British were decoying German resupply drops onto their own positions. Wenzel was steadily deteriorating. 'My chest wound has not been bandaged – nor seen to all day and is emitting a pungent stink.' As the light faded at dusk they decided 'it is time to move on, to avoid capture'.[5]

Exposure to the sun's heat produced a trance-like quality to all movement. 'Most of my friends were completely worn out', *Jäger* Fink remembered:

Their sweat-stained faces were encrusted with dust, and two days' stubble made them look wild. Despite red cheeks from the heat, they remained noticeably pale. Eyes looked alarmingly dull, the consequence of sleep deprivation, physical over-exertion and hunger and heat.

Sweat-soaked shirts were stiff with salt, grimy hair sticky with dust. Gericke had to send ammunition resupply parties of eight men up the slopes of Hill 107, heavily laden with ammunition and iron rations, spare water bottles with wine and water, and dragging behind a water container. The men for this had to be roused out of the basements of the few houses, where his aid post had been set up behind the bridge. 'The men were totally apathetic and exhausted', he saw, they moved in slow motion and 'they couldn't care less about anything'.[6]

They were suddenly snapped out of the mindless torpor by the sound of approaching tanks. The shout of *'Enemy tanks!'* was taken up and passed along the line at the base of Hill 107. Gericke heard one commander call out 'Nonsense – they're trucks!' But the approaching metallic-rattling clamour suggested otherwise. A counter-attack of some sort had been expected all afternoon. 'Several men jumped up and ran back', Gericke recalled, 'a panic was threatening to break out'. The cry was relayed *'Tanks from the east! Tanks from the east!'*

The first colossus, a Matilda infantry tank, was engaged by the 37mm anti-tank gun positioned at the bridge approach. Contemptuously nicknamed the 'door knocker' by its crews Gericke acknowledged 'that fighting these tanks with the small 37mm would have little effect'. Nevertheless, it continued to fire shot after shot, the crew held in place by the commander's cool fire commands.

Fink was out of sight and could not see what was going on. 'We had the impression from our position that the fight was being played out on the short stretch between the olive grove and bridge', he recalled, 'but we had no visibility'. An indication of the panic caused by New Zealand Lieutenant Donald's counter-attack is the sheer variation in accounts by Germans who witnessed it. Gericke quoted four tanks knocked out in his radio situation report to regimental headquarters at 5.30pm, which he repeated in his memoir. Fink refers to two.

Schuster's section in the river bed north of the bridge had a better view. 'Four machine guns fired on the halted and shooting steel colossus', he remembered, panning across tank vision slits. The attacking infantry were pinned down, separated from their tanks. Mortars opened up and he observed three successive direct hits on one vehicle, each one clanging like a 'cracked bell'. Eventually the turret opened on the stalled tank, motionless in the river bed, while the other drove back down the road past the 'red tennis court' that the aerodrome was already being called. The tank attack was a low point for Gericke, who admitted that 'everyone knew that if these tanks were not settled, then the fight here on Crete was lost'. As he reflected on the murderous first day he appreciated 'their intelligence and capability which had already reduced to a meaningless level, had been shattered to pieces flying into the iron block of Crete's defences'.[7]

Dusk approached, failing golden sunlight snatched at leaves on top of trees and with it a considerable temperature inversion. 'It quickly got cold', Schuster recalled, immediate relief after a stiflingly hot and laborious day. With the change in temperature came balmy wind gusts. 'After an hour', however, 'the cooling effect became uncomfortable, and an hour later, they began to suffer with the cold'. Gericke gazed through 'olive branches, a symbol of peace, silhouetted against the setting sun'. The creeping cold at dusk heightened the aura of vulnerability. He watched the sun descend, 'sinking in a sea of blood, an omen', he depressingly reflected, 'the whole world was sinking in blood'. As the wind dropped Fink recalled the all-pervasive sweet-sour smell of death. It reeked near the corpses, he could smell it on his clothes. His eyes straining in the darkness were able to detect:

Many dead still lay, friend and foe in the bottom of the valley and strewn along its sides, where they had died. The heat of the day had worked on them, cruelly much faster than we from central Europe could imagine.

Gericke remained uneasy. Several hundred New Zealanders were criss-crossing the summit and reverse slopes of Hill 107 that night, but no sign of even probing attacks had emerged. It was too quiet. He later admitted that they 'would not have been able to withstand an energetic counter-attack in battalion strength'. The remnants of his *IV Bataillon* and Koch's *I Bataillon* glider men were literally clinging to the lower western and south-western base of the hill, by the bridge and at the western edge of the airfield. 'Every single sudden unexpected noise', he recalled, 'shook everybody up'. Stentzler's *II Bataillon* were nudging against the area between the New Zealand A and B Companies, but a long day fighting and marching across uncompromising hilly terrain around the village of Vlakeronitissa had exhausted them to a standstill. Schuster was convinced an attack would be forthcoming; 'if they don't come tonight, when we haven't reinforced, then they never will', he confided to a comrade. 'They are certain to come!' He doubled up on security, every second man in the line was on watch.[8]

Movement near their own lines was often stragglers or cut-off detachments, making their way to safety. Sounds were magnified at night, penetrating the stillness. 'Suddenly in front of me, to the right, I heard rustling noises', recalled *Oberfeldwebel* Helmut Wenzel exfiltrating his small group towards the Tavronitis river bed:

> and then more noises to the left. Everybody freezes – listening with every inch of our bodies – blinded by the blackness of the night and our own terror. It must have been a Tommy approaching and passing us in the next row of vines. Damned close! Too close for comfort.

Hauptmann Witzig, wheezing from a shot-through perforated lung, was carried in by some of Scherber's *III Bataillon* survivors. Rumours spread not to expect any assistance from the east. With an all-out counter-attack expected, precious few commanders were still standing, able to receive it. Virtually every glider battalion subordinate commander was either dead or wounded. The chief

medical officer Dr Neumann, who had jumped alongside Meindl
and Gericke, had taken over the mixed *Kampfgruppe* consisting of
I and *IV Bataillon* men south of the bridge. Another medical officer,
Dr Weizel, had assumed command of *3. Kompanie* north of it.
Feldwebel Arpke, Schuster's platoon commander in the company,
motioned rearward with a meaningful glance and commented
'there are none left [back] there, who give orders'.⁹

At 9.35pm Gericke received a heartening signal from Athens
suggesting they may make it if they could survive the night.
Student was ordering 'clear the aerodrome of enemy and hold
open an area from 6.30am for an air-landing by two mountain
infantry battalions'. They were promised a logistic support and
ammunition drop off by 'six resupply aircraft'. The transmission
exuded a confidence that Gericke did not share. '*VIII Fliegerkorps*
was to engage the enemy artillery southeast of the airfield.'
The message finished with 'report when the sea landing will be
possible'. Gericke, who was a veteran of the Rotterdam landings
the year before, had seen what can happen when transport aircraft
try to land in the teeth of enemy anti-aircraft fire. If they did
not clear Hill 107 and the immediate surrounds bordering the
airfield, there would be no air-landing and a prisoner of war cage
would beckon.¹⁰

LIEUTENANT COLONEL LESLIE ANDREW, COMMANDER
22 NEW ZEALAND BATTALION

*18.30 20 May–Early Morning Night Hours 21 May 1941, Summit
and Environs of Hill 107*
Lieutenant Colonel Andrew at the summit of Hill 107 was both
dismayed and perplexed by Brigadier Hargest's 'if you must, you
must' petulant response to his decision to withdraw. As he saw
it, his battalion had been badly mauled and was under serious
pressure. D Company forward of the summit had been wiped
out, he believed, and Headquarters Company to his right rear had
been overrun and ejected from Maleme village. C Company on the
aerodrome was decimated, A Company was mostly intact, as was

B, but heavily engaged from the south. He felt he was about to be surrounded and cut off from the rest of the brigade.

Information on D Company came from a fugitive who claimed they were all dead or taken prisoner. They had in fact lost 40 per cent of their strength, but were holding. Platoon commander Second Lieutenant Jim Craig remembered at this time that 'The men all thought they would be counter-attacking after dark, or at least that their company area would be the pivot of a counter-attack; they were most confident of the outcome.' Craig's primary complaint during the fighting was 'at being left all day on the 20th without any news whatsoever'. Johnson's company on the aerodrome were likewise 'in excellent heart in spite of their losses'. He recalled 'They had *not* had enough. They were first rate in every particular way and were as aggressive as when the action was first joined.'[11]

Hargest had temporized a few minutes after cutting Andrew off, promising two reinforcing companies would be dispatched, one from 23 Battalion and another from 28 (Maori) Battalion. None of these had appeared three hours later and Andrew resolved to move back to the B Company ridgeline to his rear.

Johnson down below on the aerodrome had been unable to make physical contact with Andrew using runners, but various reports after midnight 'convinced me that the battalion was no longer holding its positions'. They had likely withdrawn. He now faced a conundrum that 'as long as I held my position on the airfield perimeter no aircraft could land'. If he remained 'my few remaining men on the island side of the drome would be unable to withstand the dawn attack that the Germans must make if he wanted the drome'. German patrols were active all around the copse housing Company HQ, their southern defence next to the airfield. He watched two German patrols 'numbering approximately 10 men each' moving along the coast road towards Maleme village further east. 'We could hear them infiltrating', recalled the wounded Lieutenant Haddon Donald with Johnson:

To the east of us, there was a mob of Germans. We were finally surrounded, and at that stage I suppose we only had about ten or a dozen fighting troops left that weren't wounded or been killed. Some were signallers and stretcher bearers and that sort of thing, so it was fairly dicey. We hung on for quite some time, not actually being attacked but we could hear that there was an attack being mounted and we knew that we would be for it.[12]

This was likely the probe being mounted by *Oberstabsarzt* Dr Neumann, which was attempting to scale the northern slope of Hill 107. Ian Rutter, an Australian AA gunner, was assisting manning a New Zealand listening post on the lower slopes. Like in mainland Greece, the Germans tended to call out in the night, in English, hoping to elicit a response that would enable them to pinpoint a position. 'Somebody had to wriggle out there and just listen', he remembered. 'You could hear them talking, one German calling out, "*Hello, Charlie? Is that you?*" It was eerie that close to them.'[13] 'We were the obvious remaining strongpoint on the aerodrome', Haddon Donald recalled, 'and not a very strong point; and fairly apprehensive'.

Having agonized, Andrew was convinced he had made the right decision to pull out and itemized the reasons in his battalion log for doing so. He was outgunned, short of officers – eight of 20 were down, his best NCOs had been misdirected to Egypt as part of the battalion rear party – communications had failed, as had the Matilda tanks, and their own artillery, with no sights, was reduced to shooting off the map. The two main reasons, however, were the apparent incomprehensible abandonment of the brigade counter-attack plan, and that overwhelming Luftwaffe air superiority had 'made the daylight movement of troops a most hazardous undertaking'. Frank Twigg, Andrew's intelligence sergeant, explained 'it was difficult and in parts almost impossible, for officers or others to move about to observe and contact troops or positions' under 'very heavy strafing'. Twigg, close by with Andrew in the command post throughout emphasized the feeling of abandonment by 5 Brigade: 'I am sure practically all in the area were expecting the counter-attack to eventuate and non-materialization I think, increased the feeling of bewilderment and isolation that was apparent among all the troops and officers.' 'Practically all news', he claimed, 'was unreliable rumour' and 'I am sure this feeling and non-appearance of the 23 Battalion had a great effect on all'. Nobody knew what was happening beyond their own immediate vision, so that 'no one knew how anyone beyond our own A and B Companies were faring'. These two were the only sub-units to be reliably informed about the battalion commander's decision to pull off Hill 107.[14]

After 9pm Andrew started to move his main force off the summit, beginning with the rearward elements. Withdrawing while in contact with the enemy is one of the trickiest phases of war to conduct. Platoons had to move across terraced and undulating ground in darkness to company rendezvous points where they were checked before being passed onward through manned battalion checkpoints to form a battalion 'snake'. Secrecy and deception from the enemy was paramount, but above all firm leadership and control was required. Men were surprised to be pulled back. 'Up to that time we had no indication that the position was so serious', remembered Corporal Andrews with 16 Platoon B Company. Despite being weary, thirsty and hungry, they knew they had been successful. It was Greece all over again. They were irked to leave prepared positions they had hotly defended, and resented having to leave the seriously wounded behind. As they made their tortuous way back, evidence of their success lay all about. 'Indeed, every few yards we passed dead paratroops', recalled Captain Ken Crarer, commanding B Company, 'and even then they had begun to stink'. The sweet-sour reek of decay appeared to linger even on the soiled uniforms of the living.[15]

Exhaustion and lack of sleep impacted upon vigilance and the ability of leaders to assimilate and understand information. Decision making and even simple tasks took longer; Lieutenant Colonel Andrew, subjected to physical and mental strain all day, made mistakes. He ordered the intelligence officer to lead the walking wounded under the medic, Captain Longmore, into

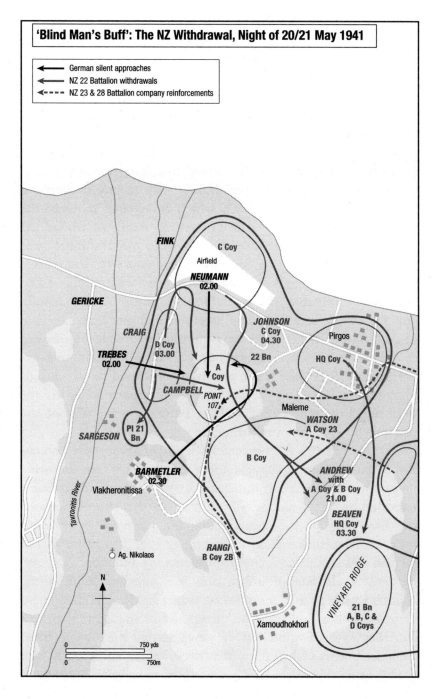

'Blind Man's Buff': The NZ Withdrawal, Night of 20/21 May 1941

German silent approaches
NZ 22 Battalion withdrawals
NZ 23 & 28 Battalion company reinforcements

FINK
C Coy
Airfield
NEUMANN
02.00
GERICKE
JOHNSON
C Coy
04.30
Pirgos
CRAIG
D Coy
03.00
TREBES
02.00
22 Bn
HQ Coy
A
Coy
CAMPBELL
POINT
107
Maleme
WATSON
A Coy 23
PI 21
Bn
SARGESON
B Coy
BARMETLER
02.30
ANDREW
with
A Coy & B Coy
21.00
Vlakheronitissa
BEAVEN
HQ Coy
03.30
Tavronitis River
RANGI
B Coy 2B
Ag. Nikolaos
N
VINEYARD RIDGE
21 Bn
A, B, C &
D Coys
Xamoudhokhori
0   750 yds
0   750m

Maleme village. Twigg protested, reminding him no runners had been able to reach the village all day, so they were led off to a high point west of the B Company area. They were to wait all night, apparently forgotten, until at dawn they were cut off.

Andrew, in the midst of the complicated withdrawal procedure, tying up rendezvous and checkpoints, while trying to avoid enemy patrols, was distracted. He had one eye on pulling back and another on what they should do on reaching the B Company ridge. When they reached this easternmost point, A Company was under pressure dealing with enemy infiltration, (from Stentzler's *II Bataillon*), which threatened to close the withdrawal route to 23 and 21 New Zealand Battalions. At this stage Andrew appreciated the extent to which this area was totally overlooked by the summit he had just left. The chosen area proved completely bare and open, too rocky to dig in and would be vulnerable to Luftwaffe attack and ground machine-gun fire in the morning. His battalion had given up the vital ground, and it would now be a question of recovering instead of keeping the asset, counter-attacks instead of maintaining a prepared defence. Just at the point when his tired mind resolved to continue retreating beyond the B Company ridge to the next ridgeline held by 23 and 21 Battalions, the first of the reinforcement companies turned up.

Captain Watson's A Company from 23 Battalion arrived on the B Company ridge at about 9.30pm. Ironically, it was following one of the pre-recced counter-attack routes. Andrew's strength increased by more than one-third in an instant. It also increased the likelihood of the second company promised by Hargest from 28 (Maori) Battalion turning up as well. The arrival of 250 men in two contingents could transform the situation. Andrew's strength would have doubled. This was sufficient for a strong counter-attack or as a minimum a firmer hold on Hill 107. No German aircraft could land on the aerodrome so long as they held it. Andrew's tired mind was, however, fixated on moving back, convinced he had taken the correct decision. He was a VC holder, used to lesser experienced commanders deferring to his judgement.

Much later, back in Egypt, he was to explain in the final comment in the battalion war diary:

> The withdrawal from Maleme aerodrome and the surrounding country was carried out following a wireless report to Bde HQ and was made on my recommendation. The position was such that if I had not withdrawn my small force that night I would not have been able to do so the next morning. Even if the position could have been restored by a counter-attack it could not have been held even by a fresh battalion. Looking back now and knowing more of the facts I am convinced that the withdrawal at that time was the only possible action to take.[16]

Colonel Andrew ordered Captain Watson, commanding the reinforcing 23 Battalion company, to cover his withdrawal by taking up a screen position in Captain Hanton's old A Company area. He needed a guide and Lieutenant Ed McAra immediately stepped forward, saying 'that's my area. I'll take you in'. This was the same McAra who had written so eloquently to his wife Jill back home in New Zealand extolling the wonderful views visible from the top of Hill 107. As he later led one of the platoons into position a German machine gun opened fire at short range, cutting him down fatally and wounding the platoon commander and sergeant major he was guiding. A note penned to one of McAra's last letters to his wife read:

> Killed on 20th May after the first day of fighting, while showing another officer round, who was taking over his duty – something that is usually told by word of mouth, but Ed did that little bit extra and so was killed.[17]

Four hours after receiving the first reinforcing contingent, Andrew came across Captain Rangi Royal's B Company from 28 (Maori) Battalion on the Xamoudhokhori road. It numbered 114 men and had been following a serpentine route for over 12 miles, having skirmished with and killed more than 30 Germans along the way.

They had gone through Pirgos without seeing HQ Company, stopped just short of the airfield with no sign of C Company and had found the old 22 Battalion Command Post, abandoned, but empty. It had still not been occupied by the Germans, despite the summit of Hill 107 having been deserted by now, for nearly four hours. Andrew was surprised to see them and on hearing about their 12-mile odyssey to reach him, commented 'you are damn lucky to be alive'. Andrew's withdrawing units were by now approaching the 23 and 21 Battalion line in depth. Royal was told to return back to his unit. Andrew was neither disposed to counter-attack nor re-occupy his abandoned position. He had made Hargest's decision for him. As Leckie's 23 Battalion outposts became aware of a long line of figures approaching their positions through trees coming from the west, they were surprised and dismayed to see their friends from the 22nd.

Both 23 and 21 commanders were taken aback and totally ignorant that a withdrawal was happening. A hasty meeting took place at 3am between the commanding officers: Allen, Leckie, Major Phillip commanding 27 Battery and Andrew, who had got in barely an hour before with 250 of his men. Three companies were missing. No record of the meeting has survived. Andrew was apparently largely silent, monosyllabic and somewhat subdued. The other COs were looking for guidance and advice from the more experienced VC holder. No decision was taken to initiate a re-occupation of the empty position, which appeared the case from the most recent information; or mount a counter-attack, despite two and half hours of darkness still remaining. Major Jim Leggat, Andrew's second in command, was sent back to Hargest's 5 Brigade HQ in a Bren gun carrier, to report that 'we were officially off Maleme'. Still unwell, Hargest was roused from bed in pyjamas, completely surprised and unprepared for the shocking development. All that came out of the tri-battalion conference, of which Hargest was not a part, was resolve 'to hold our positions next day'.

While the three battalion commanders were discussing what to do next, the summit of Hill 107 remained empty. Two

Headquarters Company runners picked their way among wrecked gliders, shattered trees, past sweet-smelling bodies of dead and dying and stumbled over bomb craters to reach it. With a start they realized that the sandbagged emplacements and slit trenches lay empty. They reported back to Lieutenant Beaven, who began to make preparations to pull out. By 3.30am the last elements of his men had abandoned the outskirts of Pirgos, moving east.

Captain Stanton Johnson with C Company on the aerodrome and Campbell's D Company on the lower western slopes of Hill 107 had also found the summit deserted while searching for Andrew. Second Lieutenant Jim Craig with Campbell recalled news of a withdrawal 'had been heard before and discounted'. Once it was confirmed 'the morale of his men had fallen flat after they learned that they had been left by their battalion'. Campbell even 'thought that my company position might be wanted as a sort of pivot round which a counter-attack could swing'. But none of the wounded left on the summit knew anything about a counter-attack, so 'I decided to pull out. It was 3am'. An urgent shout of 'every man for himself' prompted independent platoon withdrawals, difficult because D Company was the most exposed of the companies along the lower western slope of Hill 107. Campbell managed to get out with Company HQ and 16 Platoon following a track that ran due east. Aircraftsman Marcel Comeau was fortunate enough to be woken up as they passed en route. He shouldered his Lewis gun and joined the column. It was gruesome progress passing through the carnage that had been inflicted on the enemy during the day. 'A stink of blood and ersatz coffee pervaded the air', he recalled:

> overpowering even the aroma of the shrubs that everywhere pervaded the Cretan scene. Crumpled German corpses littered the countryside, lying in the strange individual attitudes where sudden death had overtaken them. We stumbled over them in the darkness, treading on stomachs, gargling hollow moans from lifeless lips. A few bodies hung from trees, twisted in their harnesses; unpleasant, yielding, fleshy obstacles to blunder against in the darkness.

His companion Jock Fraser came across a young parachutist on the ground, still alive 'with dreadful stomach wounds'. The boy begged for water, but they had none. '*Wir haben kein Wasser*', Fraser guiltily murmured in his schoolboy German. He gathered up a parachute to pillow his head and felt 'he saw a look of gratitude in his eyes'. Further on a New Zealander emerged from the darkness and assured them 'the youngster would not last the night out'. Fraser sensed the man had shot him in the first place.[18]

Sergeant Sargeson's 18 Platoon remnants opted to go south, while Craig's 17 Platoon tried to move along the river bank, but was blocked by the density of German outposts. They had no recourse but to go to ground near the summit, and hope the situation might clarify as first light dawned. It did, they found themselves surrounded by a succession of German probes.[19]

The last company to leave was Johnson's C Company on the aerodrome. A succession of his runners had been unable to make contact with either A, B or D companies for over three hours. This convinced him that by 4.20am he should withdraw. 'The Germans', he assumed, 'were in occupation of the Battalion HQ site'. There was German activity all around his position. 'I ordered every man to remove his boots and hang them around his neck.' At 4.30am they moved off in single file, abandoning the seriously wounded, but keeping the walking wounded interspersed in file along the line of march. Johnson recalled their tense and tortuous progress:

> Past the snoring Germans on our right, through the vineyards which separated C Company from A Company's reserve platoon and HQ area up to A Company's deserted HQ, onto the road, up the hill past a grounded glider, until we reached the forward boundary of B and A Company's position.[20]

They picked up sleeping members of 22 Battalion on the way, unaware they had withdrawn, eventually coming across Campbell's D Company element and Lieutenant Beaven's HQ Company contingent. Beaven attached himself to Johnson's force, which had also picked up scattered RAF personnel and light AA gunners.

The light was growing as they struck east across country to reach 21 Battalion on Vineyard Ridge. With the light came German planes. A single Ju 52 droned by along the coastline and suddenly made a surprise landing in the half light, not long after they had left the aerodrome. Many in the column ruefully reflected that would not have been physically possible less than an hour before.

OBERSTABSARZT DR HEINRICH NEUMANN, ACTING COMMANDER I BATAILLON STURMREGIMENT

01.00 20 May–Dawn 21 May, Northern Slope Hill 107
The 34-year-old *Oberstabsarzt* Dr Heinrich Neumann was the only officer left standing in Koch's *1* (Glider) *Bataillon*. The soldiers were shocked by the numbers of commanders that had already fallen; many known since the very inception of German airborne forces. *Major* Walter Koch, the hero of Eben-Emael, had been recovered from the slopes of Hill 107 with a near mortal head wound. *Oberleutnant* Wulf von Plessen commanding *3. Kompanie* had fulfilled his depressing premonition aired in the final brief before take-off that he would not survive, cut down by machine-gun fire as he exited his glider. *Hauptmann* Kurt Sarrazin with *4. Kompanie* was killed as his glider crash-landed, while *Major* Franz Braun, the last-minute *9. Kompanie* reinforcement provided by Meindl, was found dead, still strapped to the bench of his bullet-riddled glider. Meindl the regimental commander was seriously wounded, slipping in and out of consciousness. Neumann had just left him, handing over command of the regimental medical staff to his deputy. He was all that was left to command the disparate surviving remnants of the *1 Bataillon* with *Oberleutnant* Horst Trebes, who had been attached to the regimental staff from the now-shattered *III Bataillon*. Trebes did not yet know that 16 of his brother officers from the battalion were dead.

It mattered little that Neumann was a medic, he was far senior to Trebes, whom he regarded a wayward rogue, a *schneidigen Hund*, courageous but a 'zealous bastard'. Trebes had proven an uncomfortable chief to be in an attack with; on more than one occasion urging doubters onward at pistol point. It was his idea to storm the summit behind the cover of a pressed RAF hostage screen. Soldiers feared his savagely fierce nature as much as they respected him. Trebes was a recent convert to airborne forces, having joined in 1939. He had been awarded an Iron Cross 2nd class in Poland and the 1st class in Holland the following year. Both he and Neumann were to become unlikely heroes on Hill 107.

Neumann and his nervous men clinging to the lower slopes of Hill 107 had sensed considerable enemy activity going on during the night on the upper terraces. Andrew had departed the summit by midnight leading out some 250 men, two reinforcing companies, more than 200 men had marched up in two contingents between 9.30pm the previous night and 1am. There was movement around the summit and lower slopes south of the Tavronitis bridge, and on the main coastal road between Maleme and Pirgos. All the signs suggested a night counter-attack was in the offing. The British were setting themselves up for the final *coup de grâce*, which would sweep them off the airfield perimeter. Neumann admitted later, if they had come 'we should have had to fight them off with stones and sheath knives'. Their position was immensely precarious.[21]

Neumann had jumped into Crete from the same aircraft as Meindl and Gericke. He was an intense-looking, slim, dark-haired officer with a determined cleft chin and high cheekbones, the epitome of the Wagnerian hero, except for innocuous steel-rimmed spectacles. He took himself seriously as a soldier, somewhat at variance to his professional role as senior doctor, at which he excelled. In 1932 he was conscripted into *Reichswehr Infanterie-Regiment 9*, during which he completed his medical studies and was appointed a doctor in 1934. The same year he transferred to the clandestine Luftwaffe, forming up secretly under Hermann Göring, contrary to the Treaty of Versailles following Hitler's assumption of power in 1933. Neumann was a notorious unit disciplinarian, and readily embraced National Socialism, signing up for the *Legion Condor* in

July 1937, to combat Soviet Bolshevism during the Spanish Civil War. Despite being a member of the medical staff, he attracted the ire of his Chief Medical Officer Dr Schmift by flying 20 combat missions with *Jagdgruppe 88* as a rear gunner in Heinkel biplanes, for which he was posted out in April 1938. Undeterred Neumann completed parachute training at Stendal in early 1939 and was appointed to command *Fallschirm-Sanitätsabteilung 7*, which jumped into Rotterdam in May 1940.

German medics operated with weapons and Neumann was awarded both the 1st and 2nd classes of the Iron Cross in Holland. He was well known in Meindl's *Sturmregiment* as highly decorated for a doctor, holding also the Spanish Cross in Silver and the Civil War campaign medal, as also the bar for the occupation of the Sudetenland. On 14 May 1940, his was the only medical unit that Göring deemed to visit in Holland. Neumann therefore assumed command of the much-esteemed glider battalion in Meindl's command with little trepidation or regrets – it was a destiny moment. He had, in any case, been at the heart of decision making on the ground in Crete, treating the feverish Meindl as he tried to steer a favourable outcome on Hill 107, using Gericke's *Kampfgruppe*. The hill overlooking the airstrip was the key to unlocking reinforcements, and had to be taken, to enable mountain troops to air-land.

The *Sturmregiment* had made it clear by radio to Student's headquarters that night that Stuka support would be vital, to neutralize the 'bunker line' on the northern edge of the aerodrome, if the envisaged landings at 6.30am were to succeed. This was quite possibly the silhouette of Andrew's command post that had been identified during daylight hours. Bombing support should start '600 metres east of the western edge of the airfield, and continue on to the small wood to its east'. Stuka support was also requested two hours after this message was sent, to combat British artillery near Maleme, shelling the aerodrome. 'Transport aircraft must taxi to the south end of the airstrip, which would provide cover against artillery fire.' *Gruppe West* also strongly advised 'that all the remaining airborne left behind should be set down or landed to the west of the big [Tavrontis] bridge'. Clearly, the appreciation from the ground was that any landings east of the aerodrome would be hotly contested.[22]

All these preparations were unseen to the *Fallschirmjäger* grimly hanging onto the lower western and southern slopes of Hill 107. The wounded *Oberfeldwebel* Wenzel was still crawling with his small party of three men across the undulating and spikey bushy terrain, seeking to reach Maleme village. An occasional flare rose up, and:

> The silence of the night is suddenly broken by a wild burst of small arms fire. The enemy must be firing at each other – lucky, we moved on! Onward we go – crawling through the thick undergrowth, over rocks and stones – alerted to meet the enemy at any moment, head on.

They were disorientated; instead of coming out at Maleme, they emerged on the slopes to the west of the airfield. 'My vest and shirt are soaked in sweat and blood and my arm feels dead', Wenzel recalled. They paused inside a gorge, where his companions tried to patch him up again. Up ahead came the sounds of figures approaching. 'Our request for the password is answered with a hail of bullets'. Engel, one of their number, who was ahead and to the left was shot in the head. 'A careless moment perhaps, and he dies without so much as uttering a word.' All Wenzel heard was the 'metallic-sounding click as his helmet hits his rifle'. The enemy too was obviously on the move: 'All hell is let loose. About half a mile away to the west we can hear our machine guns and small arms fire picking up. I decided to make a daring dash to our positions.'[23]

Hauptmann Gericke further down beneath the lower slopes recalled at 'about 2.30am the alarm went, it seemed it was starting up again'. He suspected 'Tommy was attacking from the coastal village at Maleme and down from point 107'. Likely probing attacks, 'Tommy could only force small break-ins' because in the night the *Fallschirmjäger* had dug further down, strengthening and camouflaging positions. He was convinced of the need to aggressively counter-attack, but in reality all they could do was mount counter-probes. A British night attack had not yet seriously developed. Peering up at the darkened slopes he was right to surmise there was indeed movement. New Zealand units had been criss-crossing above for much of the night. German remnants from earlier jumps were laboriously making their way down as their own patrols pushed up and frequently clashed, with each other and with New Zealand stragglers. It was a form of blind man's buff. Gericke had to establish fire support anchor positions further up the slope, so that he could support a general counter-attack to clear the high ground, in concert with the Luftwaffe air support that would come with the dawn. Much of this probing leap-frogging forward was best conducted under the cover of darkness.[24]

Wenzel meanwhile frenziedly stumbling down the slope was being engaged by 'some of the enemy' whom he could see 'standing upright, firing wildly at me – but missing! It is like hare shooting!' He was probably being shot at by elements from Campbell's retreating D Company. Wenzel suddenly found himself in a stand-off with a lone New Zealand soldier, armed with a rifle, whom he covered with a pistol, 'but neither of us fire'. After a few seconds of 'cautious watching' they both sped off in opposite directions. 'Immediately a fusillade of bullets from the German position forces me to take cover again.' His other companions closed up and 'it takes quite some time to make them understand who I am'. They made it as far as the dried-up Tavronitis river bed before Wenzel finally collapsed unconscious; it was the German line.[25]

Oberstabsarzt Neumann began to ascend the northern slope on his own initiative having assembled 20 or so soldiers. A note was allegedly sent to the bemused combat commanders at regimental headquarters that he intended to capture the hill. He could exude an air of self-importance, so this latest mission pronouncement promoted a degree of ironic eye rolling. Once again their doctor had assumed his warrior personae to seek out some form of personal vainglory *Götterdämmerung*. Neumann took with him a mix of men from his *I Bataillon*, some of Gericke's *IV Bataillon* and headquarters personnel. Coincidentally, but likely uncoordinated, *Oberleutnant* Horst Trebes had also set off with similar fierce determination up the western side of the feature, with part of *3. Kompanie* and soldiers from Meindl's headquarters defence platoon. His objective was the two enemy Bofors anti-aircraft guns seen at the summit during the day. Stentzler's *II Bataillon 7. Kompanie* under *Oberleutnant* Barmetler was also on the move, steadily climbing up in leaps and bound from the south. Gericke's heavy weapons remained on defensive stand by, vigorously suppressing any muzzle flash they detected from the top of Hill 107, but there were few winking lights. The various groups blindly made their way towards the summit.

Gericke recalled 'machine guns hammered away giving fire support' as the fragmented advance made its way upward. A bitter fight was anticipated at the top, but according to one witness: 'The nearest English trenches are empty. They jumped forward further, cautiously moving from position to position. No Tommies were in the trenches. There – a dugout, also nothing moving. A few grenades inside – onward.'

Smoke poured from the earthen dugout entrances following the subdued *dumpf* of grenades detonating among sandbags. 'The fellows have definitely cleared out', shouted a platoon commander as they broke into the main positions. There was hardly a sound from either side. Scattered shooting broke out when Trebes' group closed up on Neumann's, which cost the life of a *Feldwebel*. 'From practically every fold in the ground ghosts rose up, who threw their helmets and weapons away.' New Zealanders started to emerge in the dark, from Craig's platoon in D Company, with their hands up. Barmetler's company came up the reverse of Hill 107 and clashed with some retreating New Zealand stragglers, possibly from Johnson's C Company, which had negotiated the same tracks retreating the other way less than an hour before. Neumann and Trebes were to receive the Knight's Cross for this exploit, when the primary antagonists simply passed each other in the night. Even so, Neumann's citation was not necessarily inaccurate: 'The decisive decision by *Oberstabsarzt* Dr Neumann to attack the north-west side of Hill 107 with weak forces, eliminating the threat to the airfield from the flak on the heights, was decisive to the battle.'²⁶

Oberst Ramcke, who later recommended the award, claimed it was for pushing off an 'enemy rearguard'. Hill 107 was the gatepost to entry for Maleme aerodrome and later proven to be of strategic worth. After the painful casualties absorbed in the fight for it, the unexpected abandonment was an anti-climax and an embarrassment as the three groups that took it fired upon each other at various times. The whole episode is cloaked in a degree of unproven controversy, different accounts offer a mix of heroism, chance and luck. German accounts do not accord with New Zealand narratives, but nobody questioned the gallantry of the attack. The three commanders Neumann, Trebes and Barmetler were all awarded the Knight's Cross, for this and other related actions. Such prestigious awards transcended any doubts about the achievement. Neumann the 'fighting doctor' made good copy in National Socialist press propaganda back home; after all, he had excelled at both. In reality, on the ground, there was scant desire by either side to engage in any further fighting worthy of *Nibelungen* lore. After the horror and terrors of the day, there was a persuasive inclination by men of both sides to live and let live. Unknown to them all, the fall of Hill 107 was to be the turning point in the battle for Crete.

When Wenzel regained consciousness he recalled seeing 'a British soldier bending over me with a big pair of scissors in his hands – cutting away my hair!' Surrounded by English soldiers he weakly asked 'am I a prisoner?' 'No, No', came the quick answer from somewhere, '*these* are all our prisoners'. He briefly came to again when being treated by a German doctor at the Maleme airfield first-aid post: 'Whoever attended to your wounds? They saved your life! We have no medical dressings left. He didn't even take my dressings off.'

Wenzel never knew the English doctor who saved his life. One of his friends, *Unteroffizier* Linde, found his bullet-pierced jump helmet encrusted with his blood and hair and on reading the name inside, assumed the worse. The situation regarding dead and wounded or who had been recovered was chaotic. He sadly took the helmet back to Germany to give to his wife, but was confusingly reassured by her that she had received a hospital card from Vienna indicating proof of life. It reduced him to tears to know he had survived. 'My wife', Wenzel later explained, 'now possesses two battle-scarred jumping helmets – one from Eben-Emael, the other from Crete!'[27]

Gericke, looking out to sea as the dawn came up, saw on the shiny strip where water and horizon met 'a dark something or other moving toward the coast'. He reflected on how interesting it was that 'when one is in danger, when every nerve and sense is stretched', you see more. 'Normally he would not have noticed this dark spot on the horizon.' As it magnified in size, he saw it was an approaching Ju 52 transport. *Hauptmann* Oskar Kleye had taken off in darkness just outside Athens and was nearing landfall. '*Good grief*, surely not the mountain troops?' Gericke thought. There would be no chance of landing on the disputed airfield. But it was only a solitary Ju 52 lining up for its approach run, sinking deeper and deeper. No flak spat out from Hill 107, now in German hands.

Fink and the *3. Kompanie* survivors at the western end of the runway were amazed. 'Out of the west he came in very low over the water, flew along the beach, past us and over the airfield and turned east away from Maleme.'

Horrified and knowing full well the aerodrome runway was completely covered by enemy machine-gun fire, they did not know C Company had pulled out about 50 minutes before, in semi-darkness. 'What would the flyer do?' they debated. He then made a 'cheeky' landing in the far western corner of the aerodrome, on the beach, guided in by flares. Fink and the onlookers anticipated a 'fearful accident'. Gericke thought the same: 'he jerked up again just over the tips of the olive trees and set down intact behind our own lines on the beach, in the middle of deep sand'. Men ran to the machine, opened the side door and began to unload and stack cases of ammunition on the beach. One of Gericke's company commanders called across to allay doubts: 'the aerodrome is ours', he announced, 'only the English artillery can hinder landings'.[28]

Kleye leapt down from the aircraft and was quickly briefed on the situation as ammunition was taken off and wounded carried on. Even as they finished the three engines were roaring at maximum power as the Ju 52 taxied for take-off. Large stones were hauled out of the way and shovels used to clear piled sand from the tyres, human muscle was applied to get the wheels moving. With all engines bellowing the aircraft slowly lumbered back into the air amid a huge cloud of swirling dust and sand. It banked out to sea, where it set course for the Greek mainland, skimming the surface of the water.

Somebody had remarked that the cluster of sand-filled oil drums only hindered the western corner of the airfield. Nobody had noticed any artillery detonations among them, and they were unscarred by shrapnel. It dawned that this western corner of the aerodrome must lie in a blind zone to incoming artillery fire. Kleye had appreciated this during his approach run to the airfield. It opened up practical options for a successful air-land. Neumann's occupation of the summit of Hill 107 had indeed been decisive.

Chapter 9

Daedalus Returned

*20 May–18.00 21 May 1941, Topolia Airfield North of Athens to
Maleme, Crete*

The 52-year-old *Oberst* Ramcke was tasked by Student to assist
Ringel's mountain troops in preparing for an envisaged air-land
at Iraklion airport, east of the island, on the second day of the
operation. The war for him had thus far been frustrating. Fleeting
action in Poland was followed by a succession of training and advisory
appointments, which led him to transfer to the *Fallschirmjäger* the
previous year, despite his advanced age. His early life was shaped
by service with the Imperial German Navy, joining as a *Schiffsjunge*
(cabin boy) at 16 in 1905. In 1915 he transferred to the Marine
Infantry and fought in Flanders. His was an intense trench war,
wounded five times with 18 months in hospital. Unusually, in the
Kaiser's army, he was commissioned from the ranks, having won
both classes of the Iron Cross and the prestigious Prussian Golden
Merit Cross, the highest decoration that could be awarded an NCO
in the Imperial German Army. After the war Ramcke served on
with the *Freikorps*, combatting the Bolsheviks in the Baltic States,
where he was again wounded.

An ardent supporter of Hitler, he subscribed to the 'stab in
the back' National Socialist belief that politicians had betrayed

the army into surrender at the end of World War I. This new war against the same foe had got off to a slow start and he burned to get actively involved. Sponsored by Student, he volunteered for the airborne and transferred to the Luftwaffe. The mandatory six-jump parachute course to qualify applied equally to senior officers, and 'Papa' Ramcke completed his in three days. This same zeal and energy was applied to assisting Ringel's *Gebirgsjäger* at their mounting airfields. He made himself indispensable to the division commander with hands-on tuition at Topolia airfield, teaching soldiers how to rig and stow heavy loads in the assembled Ju 52 transport aircraft and promptly exit. Ringel, Ramcke recalled, 'quickly assimilated the basic principles, because he had had air-land experience in Norway before'. He dispersed his staff to school mountain troops at the other mountain airfields thereby earning Ringel's respect as a competent and efficient operator.[1]

Short and stockily built, Ramcke radiated energy and enthusiasm. Promotion in the peacetime over-subscribed *Reichswehr* had been laboriously slow, and he, a newly promoted *Oberst* with the Luftwaffe, was just beginning to grey at the temples. Tradition-conscious mountain troops were often mistrustful of the 'flashy' over-confident newly formed *Fallschirmjäger*, but were confident enough with the avuncular granite-faced 'Papa' Ramcke. He gave useful technical advice in addition to navigating junior commanders through the complexities of a tactical air-land operation.

Ramcke recalled watching 'the last of the Ju's circling the air base in diminishing light' at the end of the first day, 'seeking to find a hole in the dust and haze in which to land'. Chaos and hurried confusion at Topolia had started even before the take-off of the second wave in the afternoon. Although most aircraft returned after the first wave, many, as *Oberjäger* Pöppel at Tanagra noticed, 'had large bullet holes in their wings and fuselage'. More aircraft dropped out with serviceability problems than were shot down. *Gefreiter* Erich Strauch on stand-by to fly to Iraklion with the second wave recalled watching the aircraft land: 'they were not all there, our fears were confirmed'. Before fitting new weapons containers 'the first dead were lifted out of the damaged machine', he recalled, and 'the aircraft chief didn't say much'. Urgent hand-cranking of fuel pumps was needed to replenish tanks. Soldiers had to join in. Aircraft drop-outs meant there was insufficient space for everyone allocated to fly the second wave. Quarrels over seniority for the priority of these places broke out, and soldiers had to drop out. Score of vultures at Topolia overlooking the pandemonium around the planes began to wheel and flutter down at the airfield periphery. Noticed by departing men from *Fallschirmjäger Regiment 1*, they seemed to portray a bleak portent of what may happen. As darkness fell, the confusion worsened with the final returning aircraft landing. Despite this, the heavy weapons for the mountain troops were loaded in the failing light, so that at dawn, they would be ready to air-land at Iraklion. 'With highly stretched nerves we awaited the *go* order', Ramcke recalled, 'which could only happen if the paratroopers opened the way with an airport on Crete, to create the air-land conditions'.

Chafing at the delay in take-offs Ramcke found himself surrounded by frustrated left-behind groups of paratroopers. Many of them were known to him as former pupils at the parachute school and they crowded around, urgently begging for orders. 'From every direction on the runway', he remembered, 'leaders reported in, *Fallschirmjäger* who had not got away because of delays caused by the build-up of dust'. He identified as many as 550 men, at least three full companies. 'The keen youngsters were literally howling with disappointment at not being with their comrades on the embattled island.' Ramcke reported their presence to *Generalmajor* Schlemm, Student's chief of staff, who directed him to form a reserve battalion. 'Half an hour later', he remembered, 'I received the order to jump with this battalion west of Maleme, to fight free the important aerodrome, which was still in enemy hands'. Immediately he set off to unload the *Gebirgsjäger* already set for an air-land, and re-rigged the Ju 52s back again into the parachute role.[2]

That same night Luftwaffe pilot *Leutnant* Egbert Freiherr von Könitz heard 'depressing rumours about huge losses by our paratroopers'. His own aircraft had already been severely shot up dropping the first wave at Maleme and he had to land back at Megara on just one wheel. 'It was even said Operation *Merkur* might have to be abandoned', he recalled. Knowing the radio frequency and code for *Gruppe West* he sat monitoring radio traffic inside his repaired Ju 52. He and the crew monitored repeated requests for ammunition resupply and that a 'severely wounded *Generalmajor* Meindl needed to be flown out to the mainland at the earliest opportunity'. Von Könitz sought official permission to get him out. The *Geschwader* chief Wilke was not prepared to officially sanction this but agreed to turn a blind eye. They located a replacement for their flight engineer, who had been wounded that morning, and were soon roaring down the runway fully laden with 2½ tons of ammunition.

As with Oskar Kleye an hour or so before, they approached Crete at low level in the half light of dawn. When they neared the bay formed by the Rodopos peninsula with the airfield at its head, von Könitz put the aircraft into a steep climb of 250 meters. Nothing ahead seemed to stir and they spotted a red swastika marker flag laid out at the east end of the runway. Gliding in from the west he recalled 'when we were about 50 metres high from the dirt landing strip, we saw small rising clouds of dust'. 'Artillery fire!' he realized; pulling back on the control column he rose and then picked out 'a landing place, behind the airfield, on the beach west of the Tavronitis River' about 250 yards away. This meant flying over the English positions to the east 'with all our explosive freight', to make a 'masterly landing' on a narrow beach, covered in stones and sand, sloping steeply down to the sea. Paratroopers rushed up and began frantically unloading the aircraft.

'I had myself taken to the first-aid post', von Könitz remembered:

It was hellishly hot, the wounded were lying under trees. The badly wounded General Meindl's heart had been grazed by a bullet and his arm shot through. He opened his eyes for a moment in a semi-delirious state, recognized me and whispered 'youngster, it's pretty bad snow, lots of snow'.

By loading eight stretcher cases on board, they had to leave their newly joined flight engineer behind on the beach, to reduce weight. Paratroopers had meanwhile lifted the larger stones clear of their ad hoc runway. An anxious pause ensued while each of the three engines had to be hand-cranked as the power cables had been shot through the day before. 'At this time shells were bursting behind us and to the sides, getting nearer and nearer. We were well pleased when the third propeller was finally turning.' All three engines howled inside the huge plume of dust they windmilled into the air but the overweight aircraft seemed unable to achieve sufficient speed to lumber into flight. Von Könitz pulled back sharply on his stick; the aircraft pancaked, but achieved just enough momentum to lurch into the air on the bounce. With a low banking turn they flew out into the bay and set course for Athens. They reported in-flight and ambulances were waiting for Meindl and the wounded at Phaleron. When they got back to Megara, *Gebirgsjäger* clambered aboard once again and began to re-rig the Ju 52 for air-landing.[3]

Intrepid fly-ins by Kleye and von Könitz provided game-changing information for the joint staffs gathered at the Hotel Grande Bretagne. Hill 107 had been secured and the British had not counter-attacked. Student observed later in his after-action report that Kleye 'came under heavy infantry small arms fire on landing and take-off from bunkers on the north side and church yard west of Maleme'. Not only that, 'shortly after artillery fire came down at the airstrip'. They could not see from where, but it started as soon as the aircraft approached. Von Könitz likewise reported interference from artillery fire and that there was a protected blind-spot on the beach west of the aerodrome. 'Due to these reports', Student wrote, 'the staff decision to land the mountain battalion, already prepared' early that morning, 'had to be postponed'. That said, Student recalled, 'the air-land at Maleme would happen on the 21st May, whatever the conditions'.[4]

Student was working his operation hand to mouth. The intention was to break the British hold at Maleme and Pirgos and clear the airfield by dropping his newly constituted parachute reserve to the east and west of the aerodrome. Because the Ju 52s had now to be re-rigged from air-land to para, and then back again, the new H Hour for the parachute assault could not be before 3pm and the air-land no earlier than an hour later. Löhr and von Richthofen were less than pleased at yet another postponement, especially with the operation clearly tactically teetering on being called off. Kleye could report the British had not counter-attacked during the night. Time was clearly of the essence. Combat flyers with *VIII Fliegerkorps* felt Student's frequent probing and weighing up suggested perplexity and hesitancy. Von Richthofen railed at the delays:

> With this putting off, the predicament of our people at Maleme grows steadily worse! *Ja!* Instead of attacking they let themselves be pushed back. Nor does *Luftflotte 4* [his superior Löhr] do any ordering! … blood flows and hours pass uselessly by.

Ringel, commanding 5. *Gebirgsjäger Division*, was equally impatient. 'The day appears hopelessly lost', he complained. Acutely aware of the tension and frustration among his mountain troops being unloaded and changed around again by paratroopers, he voiced his doubts. 'It will be a hard race against the time', he declared:

> The eerie build-up of dust on the mainland airfields would go on again. Will it actually work with delays between transports at five-minute intervals to land, unload, and again get into the air? In that case it will take a battalion four hours to get down!'[5]

Löhr and von Richthofen were setting Student up for a fall, and already lining up Ringel – a Wehrmacht army general – to supersede him. Student's credibility was dependent on gaining the airfield for an air-land. The precocious hold on Hill 107 still cast its shadow over Maleme aerodrome. Student had this in mind selecting Ramcke to be his airborne foot on the ground, to achieve something decisive, before Ringel air-landed and assumed overall command. The airstrip had to be cleared.

At about 7.15am the first reinforcement drop droned in from the west as 42 Ju 52s dropped a company and a half of *Fallschirm-Panzerjäger Abteilung 7*, from an anti-tank battalion, left behind on the first day. They descended safely west of the Tavronitis bridge, but only a few of the heavy dropped 37mm anti-tank guns and recoilless weapons suspended beneath a canopy of five parachutes were useable. Many of the motorcycle towing combinations were also wrecked on landing. Three soldiers drifted out to sea and were drowned. By 11am the force had assembled around Tavronitis. Gericke directed Hauptmann Schmitz their commander to detach four guns to provide fire support for his *Kampfgruppe* attack to clear Maleme village, before the anticipated air-land later that afternoon. As they motored across the bridge at full speed, one of the gun crews was toppled from his vehicle by a New Zealand sniper. Gericke's unit was due to assault through the village and link with another force due to drop east of Maleme and Pirgos at 3pm. This pincer movement was designed to clear the airfield and secure its eastern edge to facilitate the mountain troop landings.

Generalleutnant Student's airborne doctrine had yet to prove itself. Despite the decision to concentrate in the west, the tactics he employed remained an 'oil-spot' ploy to split and fragment opposition. *In Rücken des Feindes*, 'take the enemy in the rear' remained the watchword. The skill was to identify where the rear actually was. No news had emerged at all from any unit that had dropped east of Hill 107. The *Sturmregiment* was already advised by radio early that morning to commit any parachutists left behind from earlier drops to the west of the Tavronitis bridge. Student, mistakenly assuming the New Zealand line ran through Pirgos and Maleme, surmised the area west of Platanias must be clear, and that the Allied defenders could be encircled. Strong New Zealand positions, however, remained in place along the coast, anticipating a sea landing.[6]

Jäger Franz Rzeha was with *5. Kompanie Fallschirmjager Regiment 2*, which alongside *6. Kompanie* was to drop along this apparently empty stretch of coastline. They formed the eastern claw of the proposed pincer. They were briefed that morning, as Rzeha recalled:

'The 5. *Kompanie* was to jump to the west of Platanias, advance towards the aerodrome at Maleme, secure it and make contact with the *Sturmregiment*. It was as simple as that.'

Major Reinhard Wenning at Tanagra with *Kampfgruppe z.b.V. 105* had been warned off for his third parachute mission. He was to transport *Oberleutnant* Thiel and *Oberleutnant* Nägele's 5. and 6. *Kompanien* reinforcement drop near Platanias. These were veteran parachutists, who had already had significant casualties during the jump on Corinth, three weeks before. 'All the other groups today', Wenning recalled, 'are on the first air-land, on the airfield at Maleme, that the *Fallschirmjäger* would have conquered in between'. 'Bad news arrived from Crete', Franz Rzeha recalled, preparing to board, 'not a good sign, but morale, nevertheless, was good. We were going to help our comrades'. After painstaking checks of weapons and parachute equipment 'we climbed aboard the aircraft, hearts beating'. The sun was at its zenith as they set off at 1pm, once again climbing out of the huge dust clouds shrouding the airfield. Transports dropped to wave-top height, giving 'the impression of touching the sea', they observed. Reassuringly they could see 'our escorts, Me 110s on both sides' through their aircraft windows.[7]

Wenning's group of 24 Ju 52 aircraft approached the coastline near Platanias 'on schedule', he remembered: 'The more we drew near, signs of warlike activity stood out. One could see numerous large and small columns of smoke and striking reddish-brown dust clouds, from vehicle units on the move.' They curved in towards their drop zone, 'where fighting on the ground was visible'. 'Everywhere in the area were countless points of light showing up, from the parachutes left behind by yesterday's jumpers.'

On flying over the island of Theodori, just off the coast at Maleme 'we could hear and see bursts from AA shells, which perforated the skin of our Junkers', Franz Rzeha recalled. It was going to be a hot drop zone. 'Looking out the window we could see two Junkers which had been damaged, and returning to the mainland. One had an engine on fire, the other had fuselage damage.' 'Break a leg!' they muttered to each other, paratrooper epithet for 'take what comes'. Bull horns sounded and they launched themselves through the door. 'The jump from 70 metres up', Rzeha recalled, 'was a jump into hell!'

'One paratrooper standing in the door about to jump was hit by fire from below and seemed badly wounded', Wenning remembered, 'but jumped in any case'. When everybody had cleared the aircraft, a single parachutist remained, who 'for some reason does not want to jump'. They had already flown the drop zone, which meant Wenning would have to do so again, while all the other aircraft in the group headed for home:

> OK, once again out to sea, curve back in to the coastline and down to 150 metres jump height. Naturally the entire ground defence concentrated on us, but despite this, we succeeded in reaching the exit point. The man jumps and we turn heading at full speed out into the open sea. Flak riddled our plane, but without causing serious damage.

Two companies and two parachute medical platoons dropped inside and along the length of the coastal defence boundary of the New Zealand Engineer Detachment and the western edge of 28 (Maori) Battalion. Part of the drop straddled the mined beach area, where hollow-sounding explosions mixed with the screams of the wounded and dying and staccato crack and thump of machine gun and rifle fire. Rzeha with 5. *Kompanie* recalled:

> I could hear the sound of bullets. We had the impression of being expected and were getting shot at by the enemy positions. But we had to get through. A lot of comrades were killed or seriously wounded, still attached to their parachutes.

Rzeha's company was virtually wiped out. *Oberleutnant* Thiel, the company commander, was killed, alongside the medical platoon, similarly cut down with its chief *Oberstabsarzt* Dr Hartmann. Only the *6. Kompanie* element jumping between the sea and coast road survived with some remnants from the 5. *Kompanie*. Survivors were rallied by *Oberleutnant* Nägele, who gathered up about 80 men, many wounded, who reached Pirgos where they fortified some houses to await the night. Yet another parachute reinforcement had proven ineffective. The aerodrome and Maleme could now only be approached and cleared by Gericke's reinforced *Kampfgruppe*, attacking from the west.

Rzeha and a group of about a dozen fugitives captured some New Zealand trenches situated on higher ground. 'On the field nothing moved', he recalled. The drop was a catastrophe. He was taunted by a persistent cry for 'Medic' nearby. 'He was younger than me', he remembered, lying inside the enemy's arc of fire, and could only be approached by crawling. 'His face was bloody and his legs were covered in dried blood.' Rzeha attempted to dress his wounds, but had no water, everyone's water bottles were empty. 'I put a few drops of lemon juice on his lips to calm his thirst' and speaking softly, he tried to comfort him. 'My head is so heavy', the wounded man complained, so Rzeha nestled his head inside the crook of his left arm. 'He looked at me with big eyes', he recalled, 'and murmured *Mutti, Mutti*, Mummy, Mummy' before he finally expired. 'I covered his face with a rag.' They were in a tense situation; 'all the NCOs were dead', he remembered, 'as well as the company commander *Oberleutnant* Thiel'. The 5. *Kompanie* had ceased to exist. Rzeha poignantly regarded the corpse of the youngster he was unable to save; 'his distant mother would never hear her son's words nor see his terrible and lonely death'.[8]

Oberst Ramcke at Topolia had spent the best part of the day overseeing the re-rigging of aircraft from air-land, back to the parachute role. The same aircraft would have to be rejigged to air-land again on return. It was in the midst of this all-consuming activity he received the unexpected directive from Student to assume command of the ad hoc reserve parachute battalion he had created and jump with it, to take command of the *Sturmregiment* at Maleme. 'Distracted by the plethora of orders and reorganizations coming my way, I had no time to think', he later explained. He had neither a parachute nor jump equipment to hand. 'At the last moment before boarding I had to pick up an unknown 'chute.'

It did at least have the distinctive red band attached to it, which indicated it had been properly textbook packed and checked. He was, nevertheless, hardly in the frame of mind or prepared for a parachute descent, 'which I had to do in riding boots, without knee protection, straps or steel helmet'.

As he climbed aboard, the start flag dropped and propellers started to turn. Clearing the interminable dust cloud they were soon out into the bay of Athens skimming the surface at virtual wave height. Ramcke remembered 'sitting near the open door keenly studying the map'. He was well conversant with the flight route and knew they would drop west of the airfield, but: 'What would it be like? How is the battle going? Where are the friendly forces, where are the enemy? Vainly I sought to picture the situation. Everything is unclear and unknown.'

Over an hour later the mountains of Crete rose up from the sea. The predominant colour as they approached was a smoky, dusty, sun-baked brown with parched green shining out in places. The aircraft commander throttled back while the crew chiefs shouted 'Fertig machen zum Absprung! Get ready to jump!' 'Beneath were dark-green olive groves', he recalled, 'light green stretches lay ahead of the approach route. Aa ha vineyards!' The scene was a mix of dusty green and dirty sandy yellows, whitewashed houses and mud-coloured dwellings. Some fifty or so Ju 52s flew in an impressive stream in columns of threes, spewing out a blossoming flow of parachutists, tracking along the coastline west of Maleme aerodrome. Ramcke jumped out as the bull horn sounded, with 550 parachutists gathered by him from the airfields surrounding Athens. They included the almost complete 4. and 12. *Kompanien* from *Fallschirmjäger Regiment 1*, who had failed to jump at Iraklion.

We jumped at the lowest height, to offer the enemy as brief a target in the shortest time possible. I had a good landing between rows of vines … then quickly out of my harness, pistol in hand, looking about. There was no sign of the enemy. Overhead follow-up Ju 52s droned past.

One flight of Ju 52s veered too near the sea and about 35 parachutists came out over the water. Ramcke watched:

> Some Ju's exited too late. Several parachutists were driven out to sea by a mercilessly hard offshore wind. The brave paratroopers sank in the blue flood, dragged down by their heavy equipment. The poor brave youngsters.

Only about ten of the 35 could be rescued, despite Fink and some men from *3. Kompanie* stripping off and swimming out to try and save them. 'We knew only too well', he recalled, 'that a paratrooper would be lost in deep water, as he would not be able to free himself from his 'chute'. Not having eaten for three days, they did not have the energy reserves to achieve much. As they swam out, the parachutes filled with air on the surface of the water and dragged the men further out to their deaths. Those found floating were drowned before they could be reached.[9]

When Ramcke reached the cluster of houses at Tavronitis he received a quick orientation brief from *Leutnant* Göttsche, the *Sturmregiment* signals officer, the man who had salvaged communications with Athens. 'Glad you are here *Herr Oberst*', he said, 'we urgently need direction':

> *General* Meindl is severely wounded, and went out with the first transport. One of the battalion commanders is dead, another wounded. *Major* Braun on our staff has fallen, the regimental adjutant severely injured on the jump. Many officers are dead. We have had heavy losses in hard treacherous fighting. The aerodrome is, however, in our hands.

He was told Gericke was attacking with the combined unit survivors east of the airstrip, and fighting hard on both sides of the coast road. *Major* Stentzler with *II Bataillon* had a screen on the south-east side of Hill 107. The *Gebirgsjäger* had just begun air-landing, but the airstrip runway was under enemy artillery and infantry heavy weapons fire. Student had picked the right man with Ramcke. In fact, he was the only senior airborne officer standing with practical infantry experience. He had already demonstrated swift and decisive leadership at Topolia. Ramcke later acknowledged Göttsche had delivered 'a shocking but clear situation report'. He was now in overall command at Maleme.

Jäger Feri Fink and the survivors of *3. Kompanie* were shortly lined up to be received by Ramcke. They were unimpressed, feeling Student had sprung him upon them. Taking over command in the midst of a tight situation is generally as unsettling for subordinates as it is perilous. '"Why then?" we grumbled inwardly, "Stentzler with Gericke had coped well, good enough!"' Ramcke was regarded with a little resentful mistrust:

> Standing before us was a wiry little man dressed in a fantastic uniform. The only regular form of uniform was the cap on his head, otherwise he was dressed in khaki-coloured riding trousers with thin waders stuck in high black boots, with his skinny frame covered in a light brown shirt of unknown origin.

Ramcke's precisely clipped formal morale-boosting pep talk was ill received: 'With cutting pithy words and sparing gesticulation he spoke of Flanders and 1917, and that his daily bread there was what we had just endured on Crete.'

While speaking, the soldier's attention wandered over his shoulder and fastened onto a magnificent blood-red sunset that produced a glorious majestic glow behind; 'and his speech ran off like water from the rubber apron the doctor was wearing when they had seen him at work in the village shortly before'.[10]

Ramcke had much to do.

BRIGADIER JAMES HARGEST, COMMANDER 5 NEW ZEALAND BRIGADE

Dawn–18.00 21 May 1941, Brigade Gully Command Post, Platanias Village

James Hargest was woken up about an hour before dawn by Andrew's second-in-command, Major James Leggat, to be told that 22 New Zealand Battalion was off Maleme. He stood in his pyjamas in the farmhouse, just a few hundred yards inland from the coastal village of Platanias, surprised and unprepared for such news. The 'dread' he had admitted to Lieutenant Geoffrey Cox on the eve of battle at the almost 'mystical' ability of the German Army at this stage of the war to achieve virtually anything rose up again. German air power seemed to be completely unassailable. Between 5am and 6am Lieutenant Colonel Andrew turned up at the farmhouse on a Bren gun carrier to confirm the 'terrific intensity' of the blitz his men had undergone and the 'havoc' caused by German light guns and mortars from west of the Tavronitis. Both men had been diagnosed with the lingering effects of post-combat stress earning the DSO in Hargest's case, and VC by Andrew in World War I. Andrew did not describe being wrestled off Hill 107 by sheer weight of numbers, more by the psychologically intimidating impact of intense bombardment. It would have been resumed even more intensely at first light. Andrew was down to four officers and two companies remaining in the battalion, maybe 250 men. The two commanders understood each other, there was a wordless acknowledgement such crippling casualties had occurred in the 1914–18 war. Hargest did not question the decision to withdraw, nor did he go forward to confer with his commanding officers, who had essentially convened a brigade conference in the night, and taken the key decision in his absence. The decision to flesh out 21 and 23 battalions with the remnants of 22 was confirmed. Hargest disingenuously wrote in his diary that night that Andrew decided 'to fall back a little off the prominent feature above the aerodrome'. Command of this new defence was delegated to Andrew, who moved back to Vineyard Ridge, behind Hill 107 with Dawson, the brigade major.[11]

Puttick was informed at Division HQ that Andrew had withdrawn shortly before the latter turned up in person at Platanias. Gentry, the Division Chief of Staff, found the loss of Maleme 'hard to believe in the light of the reports from 5 Brigade during the [previous] day'. He recalled 'Puttick was very angry when at last Andrew reported to him':

> In my opinion there is little doubt that a vigorous counter-attack on the first night with the forces available in 5 Brigade would have been successful. [Puttick] thought and still thinks that whatever the reason, 5 Brigade at Maleme on the day of the attack almost completely failed to carry out its role and in fact lost the aerodrome with little more than one fourth of its infantry force employed.

Hargest accepted Andrew's view that replacing 22 Battalion with another would not change the situation. It needed additional force. Despite Puttick's irritation, he also meekly acquiesced. His World War I field experience was not as distinguished as either Hargest's or Andrew's. Puttick was more highly regarded for fastidious attention to administrative detail and an almost inhuman staff work ethic. Hargest had also wielded considerable New Zealand political influence between the wars, better then to let his actions speak for himself. Puttick neither censors Hargest's inactivity, nor does he offer either of the two battalions from 4 Brigade he still has at his disposal. He was more concerned with dealing with anticipated German seaborne landings. Major-General Freyberg the Creforce commander immediately comprehended the seriousness of what had happened and went forward to confer with Puttick at Division HQ. Meanwhile, as the official history of Andrew's 22 Battalion commented '5 Brigade sat like a man bemused when the fate of the invasion of Crete, in the words of German commanders concerned "balanced on a knife edge"'.[12]

'Why had we given up such a commanding entrenched position without a fight, on what we all thought, was the eve of victory?' asked aircraftsman Marcel Comeau, who had withdrawn with the final remnants of 22 Battalion. They could only assume the pull-back was part of a larger scheme to launch a strong counter-attack. 'Even Jerry can't go on losing men at this rate', one of his companions argued:

> If we push him now, he's had it chum. He's got no reserves – unless there's another bunch of silly flakers in Greece waiting

to commit suicide like they did yesterday. Wait and see chum, Jerry's right up the flaking creek without a paddle.

Lieutenant 'Sandy' Thomas with 23 Battalion remembered 'there was a glow of confidence on all sides'. All around was evidence of German failure, with parachutes draped in trees, 'some of them still had their soldiers held in harness, swinging to and fro from the branches'. His platoon expected their order for the pre-recced counter-attack at any moment: 'Even though we had left our carriers and most of our mortars in Greece, thought the battalion, we could still make Jerry sit up and take it. The men were ready for anything.'

But then early that morning, 'when the men of the 22nd Battalion began to stream into our lines, I realized the order never would be given', Thomas recalled. 'Yet without any doubt, the initiative up to that time was ours for the asking.'[13]

The seemingly passive attitude of Hargest's 5 Brigade command had an insidious effect on morale. Andrew's battalion was divided up between 21 and 23 Battalions. 'Throughout the morning our chief discomfort came from the air', remembered Comeau: 'We began to dread the Stukas. At the slightest movement, the ugly bent-winged Junkers circled the spot with their oil-stained bellies turned towards us. One by one, in leisurely fashion, they peeled off, screaming down in a vertical dive.'

Morale further plummeted in the newly sited 22 Battalion, having to endure constant aerial attacks around Kondomari, lacking both slit trenches and the means – apart from helmets – to dig in. They were dive-bombed and 'dive-strafed', Andrew's log noted:

Even when not bombing or machine gunning, groups of about six Me 110s would continually circle our positions – a 100-kilo bomb on each wing. Occasionally a burst of fire on a dive or on an identified target, with or without firing to endeavour to start a rush for cover, which would discern positions.

Having pulled back once, withdrawal was now on everyone's minds. 'Throughout the day, nerves were kept on edge by some reports of penetration', the battalion log recorded. 'Without fixed positions on a dug in line, there was necessarily some ebb and flow.' 'Sandy' Thomas was reluctantly accepting the battle was swinging 'in favour of the side with enterprise' with a steady build-up and 'such air supremacy' that 'I began to see that the battle of Crete might go against us. I felt very bitter'.[14]

In an age familiar with aircraft and air transport it is difficult to comprehend the impact of air invasion on men in 1941. Most had never flown and hardly any had ever seen a parachute descent. The sheer spectacle of a massed fly-in and parachute assault was like something out of H.G. Wells' fiction. Brigadier Hargest was coping with the wildly unfamiliar. Both his brigade and Lieutenant Colonel Andrew's intelligence staff were unsighted at the concept of airborne warfare. Andrew's intelligence sergeant Frank Twigg never once mentions any familiarity with German airborne practice in his post-war correspondence. He could never offer analysis of what might happen next. During the overwhelming spectacle of a dramatic parachute assault, nobody coolly head-counts the number of men exiting, or ten to 12 men per aircraft, to identify unit strengths on landing. Skilful German pilots seemed able to land anywhere, even on a beach; on main roads as in Holland the year before. There were no tactical manuals to explain the modus operandi of German airborne troops. Despite extensive interrogations of captured German parachutists and documents in Holland in 1940, nothing was published for troops until after the invasion of Crete. Gliders with similar wing spans to Ju 52s, carrying a similar number of troops, are mistaken for air transports. Ju 52s accordingly, it was assumed, could land virtually anywhere.

Important tactical decisions in this new technological environment had to be taken within hours, not half days or more as had been the case with static 1914–18 trench warfare. The combination of parachute landings bringing with them their supporting Luftwaffe 'flying artillery' in support of offensive operations was entirely unprecedented and completely unpredictable. Brigadier Hargest and his 5 Brigade staff were more attuned to witnessing gradual military build-ups, which could be detected coming and prepared for. A hostile air-landing was like a cancer, which had to be swiftly cut out before enemy toe-holds could spread. This was instinctively appreciated at ground soldier level: in with the bayonet and Tommy gun before the enemy was given a chance to assemble. The Australians at Rethymnon and the British at Iraklion to the east on the afternoon of the first day did just this before landings had a chance to consolidate. But to the west of Crete, around Maleme and Chania, senior New Zealand commanders stuck to rigid linear defence and dithered. Air strips were accorded lesser priority to coastal defence, and this was where landed enemy offensive potential was taking root like a tumour.

Hargest was preoccupied with maintaining his more comprehensible coastal defence role while monitoring and dealing with the huge distraction of seemingly inexhaustible numbers of air-landings. These continued throughout this second day. The 42 or so Ju 52 transports that dropped the German anti-tank *Panzerjäger* units at 7.15 that morning were largely unseen. The 22 Battalion withdrawal from Hill 107 had hidden them from view to the west of Tavronitis. Groups of two to three Ju 52s continued to drop detachments of men and resupplies during late morning.

The air menace meant nothing could move in strength on roads and tracks. Single vehicles were taken on by fighters peeling off from a virtual taxi-rank of Luftwaffe fighters circling overhead. Individual runners were strafed and driven into ditches. There was general acceptance that daylight counter-attacks would be impractical. Major-General Freyberg, now aware of the seriousness of the Maleme situation, was conferring with Puttick at his division headquarters. Hargest, intimidated by the sheer intensity of enemy air attacks, remained in his HQ gully at Platanias. He elected not to move the headquarters forward to where the action was. He did send his brigade major Dawson forward with Andrew, to try 'to contact the bits and pieces of 22 Battalion', but this was in itself a dangerous proposition. 23 Battalion had already suffered more casualties than the previous day, with strafing and bombing from the air and constant German shelling and mortaring of their forward positions.[15]

Hargest at Platanias was not privy to the counter-attack options discussed by Freyberg and Puttick at Division HQ. Hargest had accepted Andrew's opinion that Hill 107 could not be held or retaken with 5 Brigade resources alone. Nor could it happen by day. Puttick was likewise cautious. Pressure was building up in Prison Valley to the south of Maleme, where the ad hoc 10 Brigade was resisting attempts by *Fallschirmjäger Regiment 3* to seize the strategic Cemetery Hill, blocking the German advance to Chania. Success by them would cut off 5 Brigade to its rear and all the time there was the persistent threat of anticipated German seaborne landings. Freyberg offered the Australian 2/7 Battalion to fill a coastal defence gap, so that Puttick could dispatch 20 Battalion to 5 Brigade from his own division reserve. It was warned off to mount a counter-attack alongside 28 (Maori) Battalion under Hargest's direction. Hargest, until now completely outside the information loop, was brought into the discussion by a telephone call with Puttick at 11.15am. Freyberg set up a conference for that afternoon with Brigadiers Edward Puttick, Lindsay Inglis with 4 Brigade, George Vasey the Australian commander and Major-General Stewart, the Creforce Chief of Staff, to confirm the detail.

It required two battalions to move in daylight. The Australian 2/7th had to cover 32 miles in a hostile air environment to relieve 20 Battalion, that would then have to cover six more miles to reach the planned brigade counter-attack start line. Delays would inevitably occur to get these forces into position leaving only limited nighttime hours to execute the attack. Hargest at Platanias was not party to this detail, to be confirmed that afternoon, but was expected to lead an operation without contributing to the planning. Dead telephone lines meant, moreover, that Hargest was unable to communicate with his own three forward battalions.

Unlike Student, comfortably ensconced in the Hotel Grande Bretagne at Athens, Hargest conducted his operations from a dugout in the gully at Platanias, constantly under air attack. The tempo of these air operations had steadily increased from 2pm that afternoon. Dive bombers and fighters could be seen swarming over Maleme and Pirgos, visible at distance further along the coast, seeming a precursor to a further ground attack. Inside an hour, yet another formation of 27 Ju 52 transports droned in from the sea and popped up along the very coastline to his front. Over 300 paratroopers belonging to the 5. and 6. *Kompanien* from *Fallschirmjäger Regiment 2* jumped out over the coastal defence line manned by D Company 28 (Maori) Battalion and the Brigade Engineer Detachment. Parachute reinforcement was a constant threat; indeed Lieutenant Geoffrey Cox at Freyberg's HQ nearby remembered 'the General normally sat behind a bare wooden trestle table in his dugout' and 'on the table lay a hand grenade, ready for use against any enemy intruder'. The aircraft roared over Hargest's HQ and began to disgorge masses of paratroopers as the stream, having made landfall, wheeled to the west along the beach line towards Pirgos. Any thoughts about the counter-attack due that night were immediately eclipsed by this latest emergency.

The nearest Germans to Hargest landed in the D Company positions by Modhion around the mouth of the River Platanias, the rest among the Engineer Detachment manning the coast. Crackling rifle and thumping machine-gun fire rose up and the paratroopers dropped into the midst of a close fought melee of Schmeisser machine pistol and Luger against rifle, Bren gun fire and bayonet. 'At one stage I stopped for a minute or two to see how things were going', recalled Captain J.N. Anderson, 'and a Hun dropped not ten feet away':

> I had my pistol in my hand – what for I can't imagine – and without really knowing what I was doing I let him have it while he was on the ground. I had hardly got over the shock when another came down almost on top of me and I plugged him too while he was untangling himself. Not cricket I know, but there it is.

'Our fellows, behaved well and did some sound destruction', Anderson remembered. 'Every man who could handle a rifle did his bit. Officers – cooks – bottle washers – all were in it.'

Oberleutnant Thiel's 5. *Kompanie* was virtually wiped out to a man.

The Maori Company Commander Major H.G. Dyer recalled the savage mopping up action that occurred to overwhelm those of Thiel's men that reached the ground alive. They reached one 'crouched down shamming dead' after firing at them with his Schmeisser. 'I told the Maori to bayonet him', Dyer remembered. 'As he did so he turned his head away, not bearing the sight.' German paratroopers had landed around them 'scattered every 15 or 20 yards.' One had lain prone to fire at him from about 15 yards: 'I took a snap shot with a German Mauser. It grazed his behind and missed between his legs. My back hair lifted, but the Maori got him, (I had no bayonet).'

The fight was a virtual massacre, some Germans sprinting away, others crawling. One 'giant of a man jumped up with his hands up like a gorilla, shouting *Hants Oop!*' 'I said: "shoot the bastard" and the Maori shot him. That was because many others were firing at us and a Spandau [machine gun] from further off.'

It took nearly four hours to completely clear the D Company and Engineer positions with gun battles and hand to hand with the bayonet. By last light about 80 Germans succeeded in reaching the outskirts of Pirgos. In between some groups took cover in isolated houses and bamboo clumps between the road and sea, waiting for the protection of the night.[16]

As Freyberg and the brigadiers were discussing the detail of the impending counter-attack that afternoon, Hargest was dealing with considerable issues in his own brigade area. The Creforce coordination conference agreed two battalions supported by a troop of light tanks would suffice. Hargest meanwhile had to deal with Gericke's *Kampfgruppe*, which had begun its advance on seeing the Ju 52s fly over. Intensive air attacks preceded his thrust through Maleme and into Pirgos. Just beyond Pirgos the advance both sides of the coast road came under withering fire from two defending 23 Battalion companies and suffered painful casualties. They drew back into the village, leaving scores of dead and wounded behind. The *Sturmregiment* had a thin screen from

Stentzler's *II Bataillon* holding the summit of Hill 107, while Gericke penetrated beyond Maleme to Pirgos. The eastern claw of the pincer designed to ensnare the 5 Brigade defence had, however, been destroyed.

Hargest, still fearing seaborne landings in his sector, and concerned perhaps the failed German parachute assault was the precursor to this, was still under severe psychological and physical pressure. By contrast his soldiers remained convinced they were besting the Germans. 'Dead German parachutists lay in their hundreds', the 22 Battalion log recorded, 'some still in their parachutes, others but a few yards away'. They were of the opinion their present dubious situation could be restored. Around them:

> After only two days in the Cretan sun the odour was sickening and the village wells may easily have become contaminated. But the three battalions between them [in 5 Brigade] could not have mustered as many as the German corpses, and moreover none could be spared from the fighting line [for burial duty].[17]

At about 4pm Luftwaffe strafing and bombing activity perceptibly increased. Lieutenant Geoffrey Cox a little further along the coast from Hargest's HQ picked up, once again, the distinctive 'heavy drumming' of multiple Ju 52 engines. A dark stream of about 60 aircraft was detected nearing the coast from across the bay: 'They came in low down across the sea, black specks moving against the grey rocky coastline stretching towards Cape Spathe. Like great bumble bees they circled above the airfield.'

Behind him came the sound of outgoing booming artillery. This was from between four to nine old 75mm Italian field pieces, captured in the Western desert with rudimentary sticking-plaster sights. 'Through my glasses I watched brown earth and dust spurt up', Cox remembered, 'not a square yard of the landing area seemed uncovered'.

War correspondent John Hetherington captured the initial reaction of men on the ground. Unfamiliar with aeroplanes and flying, what was coming towards them seemed like something out of Jules Verne's science fiction. It was an incomprehensible scene: 'No man but a madman would send aircraft to destruction there. No man but a madman would obey an order to pilot an aircraft onto that steel-raked field.' But it was happening. Hetherington assured himself: 'They would not attempt to land. They could not. They dared not. It would be suicidal madness; it would be death. But they circled, they came into land.'[18]

The British and New Zealanders had not encompassed the reckless capability of a modern air-land relying on surprise alone. Specks of sunlight glinted from cockpit windows catching the rays of the setting sun as the serpentine stream wormed its way in across the sea. The reflected light glistened like scales on a monstrous snake, set to coil itself around Hill 107 and the aerodrome at its base. Lieutenant Colonel Andrew likely felt vindicated by his awkward decision to withdraw. He had probably saved what was left of his battalion and could now face their families back home. Hargest watched the approach of this sinister stream, exuding seemingly limitless German air power. Any confidence he had in the ability of his two-battalion counter-attack to reverse this reinforcement during the coming night likely diminished.

OBERST ULRICH BUCHHOLZ, COMMANDER *KAMPFGRUPPE Z.B.V. 3*

17.00–23.00 21 May, Maleme Aerodrome, Crete
The 48-year-old *Oberst* Ulrich Buchholz led *Kampfgruppe z.b.V. 3* and on this day was flying the lead aircraft towards Maleme aerodrome. Perspiration stung narrowed eyes as he sought to avoid the glare from a golden setting sun, beating through the cockpit window. Concentrating, he pursed thin lips, glancing at his co-pilot to the right, also sweating beneath his flying helmet minutely studying the map on his lap. Buchholz was a slight wiry figure in his flying suit and turned his gaunt face away again from the sun. The island of Melos was coming up on their left. Opening the small windows in the cockpit did little to reduce

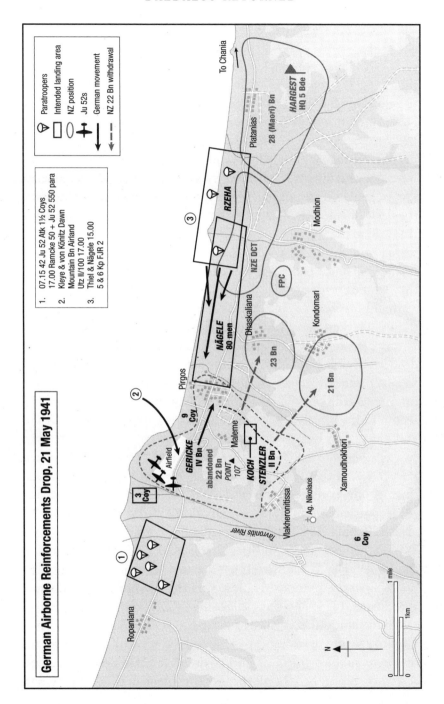

German Airborne Reinforcements Drop, 21 May 1941

Legend:

- Paratroopers
- Intended landing area
- NZ position
- Ju 52s
- German movement
- NZ 22 Bn withdrawal

1. 07.15 42 Ju 52 Atk 1½ Coys
   17.00 Ramcke 50 + Ju 52 550 para
2. Kleye & von Könitz Dawn
   Mountain Bn Airland
   Utz II/100 17.00
3. Thiel & Nägele 15.00
   5 & 6 Kp FJR 2

To Chania

HARGEST HQ 5 Bde

Platanias

28 (Maori) Bn

Modhion

RZEHA

NZE DCT

FPC

Dhaskaliana

Kondomari

NÄGELE 80 men

23 Bn

21 Bn

Pirgos

9 Coy

GERICKE IV Bn

Maleme

abandoned 22 Bn

POINT 107

KOCH STENZLER II Bn

Xamoudhokhori

Airfield

3 Coy

Ag. Nikolaos

Vlakheronitissa

Tavronitis River

6 Coy

Ropaniana

N

1 mile

1km

the heat, despite thundering along at 120mph barely 100 feet above the waves. Behind them sat 12 young *Gebirgsjäger*, facing each other with interlocked knees, rifles grasped firmly between their legs, helmets under their seats. Some had been air-sick from their bumpy low-level passage above the waves. Being at the head of 63 aircraft was preferable to the unfortunates further back in the stream. Aircraft constantly yawed, rising and falling as they negotiated the swirling prop-wash from those in front. They too were hot and sweaty, embraced by suffocating cumbersome cork life jackets and becoming progressively more tense. Those near the door fingered the straps on their mountain rucksacks, perched ready to go at their feet. Additional packs belonging to the men seated near the cockpit were stacked among the heavy equipment in the tail space behind the door. They would be yanked out as they exited the door.

Buchholz was an 'old hand' at this, and knew what he was doing. He had served as an infantry lieutenant in World War I, transferring to flying duties in 1915. Wounded, he had been decorated with both classes of the Iron Cross, the wound badge in silver and a Hessian commendation medal. Returning to the infantry in the post-war *Reichswehr*, he took time out to join the secret Luftwaffe flying programme as a captain between 1930 and 1931. This was seeing the introduction of the first prototype Ju 52s as he finished. By the time he reached *Major* in 1935 he had transferred to the fledgling Luftwaffe. He was a good pilot, rising through the ranks in staff and flying leadership appointments. After participation in the occupation of the Sudetenland he was well used to leading and operating air transport groups. Now as *Oberst* and commander of *z.b.V. 3*, he was flying in the vital air-land reinforcement needed to relieve the battered *Sturmregiment*, tenuously holding its tiny bridgehead at Maleme aerodrome.

Concentration was needed to pilot such a stream at wave-hopping height across an open azure-blue sea to hit the coastline of Crete in formation, at the right place. His final navigation reference point had been the boulder-shaped island of Melos, which they had passed to their left. This was the approximate half-way point, leaving 50 minutes to the objective. On setting up the flight plan, Buchholz's initial reaction had been to follow the route of the day before, and approach Crete from the west. In a subsequent interview he recalled 'to hell with that nonsense, go direct; approach under the lee of Cape Spatha, get the planes down quickly and the troops out'. He was flying *Major* Friedmann's reinforced *II Gebirgsbataillon* from *Regiment 100* out of Tanagra, 30 miles above Athens, with over 700 men and heavy equipment. Time was of the essence because they had heard the runway was under intermittent enemy artillery fire.[19]

Squinting through the glare reflected up from the sheen covering the sea's expanse, Buchholz identified dark specks ahead, rapidly increasing in size. They were spread in uneven lines across the deep blue sea. They passed over a number of motorized wooden sailing boats, Greek caiques or cutters, single- and twin-masted. There were also a few coastal freighters. They belonged to the First Flotilla of the *Seestaffel*, Ringel's so-called 'Argonaut Platoon', the seaborne invasion force. There were some 25 tired-looking vessels of different shapes and sizes, labouring through a choppy headwind towards the coast of Crete. This collection of boats carried the *III Bataillon* of *Oberst* Utz's *Regiment 100*, in addition to *Fallschirmjäger* engineers, anti-tank, artillery, flak and other heavy airborne elements, numbering about 2,500 men. They were shepherded along by the light Italian destroyer *Lupo*, 'the wolf'. Having left Athens 30 hours before, they were delayed at Melos for six hours, where they rested, reacting to reports of a possible British Royal Navy hunter force, lurking north of Crete. As Buchholz flew overhead there were excited waves from below and friendly wing wagging in response.

The caiques still had another 40 miles to go. It was essential they reach the disembarkation zone off Maleme by dusk, when they would forgo the fighter cover being provided by von Richthofen's *VIII Fliegerkorps*. The fly-over was a morale fillip to those down below. Clearly they were headed in the right direction and the aerial armada passing by, dipping wings in recognition, looked overwhelmingly massive. *Generalleutnant* Süssmann, like Icarus, had flown too near the sun and the expectations of *Gruppe West* had crashed to earth. This new armada was trying a new approach: a decisive blow against the defenders of Maleme aerodrome and the consolidation of Hill 107 overlooking it. Daedalus in metaphorical terms was about to return.

Buchholz had received word that afternoon at about 3pm; *z.b.V. 3* had been on stand-by, with some elements committed to a parachute insertion, for much of the day. The first trio of Ju 52 transports was airborne inside ten minutes. It had been a long tense wait for many of the men in the back of the aircraft in the stream. Endless waves of paratroopers had been watched taking off, while they were seemingly pointlessly re-roled from air-land and then back again. 'When finally do they need us?' was the oft-repeated question. *Major* Flecker on Ringel's staff recalled 'impatience grew ever more and the waiting was unbearable'. *Generalmajor* Ringel had watched his men emulate the pilots, creeping into the shadow area under aircraft wings to sleep:

> What to do then? Now and then some fool would be discovered, who would be hung with the squad's water bottles and sent stumbling off with a sullen expression. Drinking too much was also bad. It rinsed through skin like a tea strainer and stuck to the body in a disgusting way.

The temperature at Tanagra was 60 degrees in the shade. When the word suddenly came '*Auf gegen Kreta!* We're off to Crete!', it was unexpected; lively conversations ensued and by the time they were sitting in the aircraft, tension was ramping up.

Ringel was not confident with the decision to commit his division at this tenuous stage. *Hauptmann* Kleye's report of hostile fire against the runway was disconcerting:

> The 'handkerchief' [of the aerodrome], which was already too small for heavy transports had got even smaller due to shell craters and the wreckage of shot-up English aircraft lying

about. It was now rifle and machine gun fire laid down by the New Zealanders, every attempt at a landing would be pure nonsense.[20]

Buchholz decided to fly in north from the sea and set his aircraft down in threes, with a short south–north landing run across the widest western half of the baked earth expanse of the aerodrome. The White Mountains of Crete seemed to rise perpendicularly out of the sea as the order '*Stahlhelm Auf!* Helmets on!' was given. Green orchards and the olive trees on the coastal plain grew steadily larger through his cockpit windscreen as the stream thundered along the line of the Cape Spathia peninsula to his right. On their left was the Sphinx-shaped island of Theodori and then the coastline defended by the 28 (Maori) Battalion and the New Zealand Engineer Detachment. The bare red earth of the aerodrome was easily detectable next to the dried estuary of the Tavronitis River, which extended skeletal riverlet fingers into the sea. Wavetops clearly indicated a steady afternoon breeze blowing from the mainland and he would need to land the formation into wind.

With half a mile to go to the shore the sky ahead was suddenly punctuated by clusters of white-grey puffs of exploding flak. Water geysers shot up from the surface of the sea, creating a seemingly impenetrable screen, but splashbacks passed harmlessly beneath the aircraft. Fingers of light-orange tracer reached up, tracking across the aircraft's nose, trying to snatch them off their thundering course. Metallic cracks rang out as gunfire peppered the fuselage, sounding like gravel striking the corrugated metal sides. Yellow light from the setting sun immediately shafted through punctured holes accompanied by cries of nervous pain from soldiers strapped into seats in the back.

Buchholz turned the flight column and banked towards the north-west side of the field. This kept the runway in sight from his side of the aircraft, making the alignment for landing easier than with the full cockpit view, partially obscured by the forward propellers. By banking hard left into wind Buchholz exposed the belly of his Ju 52, a large 96-foot cross of a wingspan, in the sky directly above Hill 107. It would have been an inviting target previously for New Zealand gunners; thankfully now, Stentzler's *II Bataillon* men occupied the trenches below. Throttling back and feathering propellers, Buchholz rolled out of the turn and rapidly descended. He was on the approach at 90–100mph. A glance over the shoulder confirmed the air transport train was still following him in, and with a jarring shock his main landing gear hit the dirt runway raising a huge cloud of red Martian-like dust.

Oberjäger Erich Schuster watched him come down, 'flying through flak burst puffs of smoke, the thunder from his engines ever louder'. He seemed to come down hard, 'touch down, a few hops, until finally stopping with a hard jerk'. Before departure Buchholz had ordered his flyers to 'land at all costs'. His wingman's aircraft came in with tracer biting off metal chunks from his tail and then bursting into flame after a direct artillery strike. The fiery explosion was inaudible set against the roar of aircraft engines braking and the din of artillery bursts and crackling small arms fire. Schuster saw him come down 'hauling a bright bundle of flame behind him': 'Even while the fiercely burning Ju taxied further, men were jumping out, hitting the ground hard, and many lay there injured.'[21]

Oberleutnant Raither with *Major* Friedmann's *Kompanietrupp* in one of the lead aircraft recalled seeing small puffs of flak bursts around their aircraft as it came into land. 'The air gunner was sending belt after belt out of his machine gun.' The first three aircraft down 'set up a huge red dust cloud, indicating the landing place'. It looked far too short, 'volumes of dust made it almost impossible to see anything'. '*Hold tight!*' the pilot called out and a few seconds later pulled the aircraft in a tight turn to the right and stopped. '*Raus!* Out!' came the command:

> Inside the roar of the engines could be heard the dull reports of enemy artillery strikes. They were on target, right up against our aircraft. A rapid firing cannon was also sounding and machine gun bullets were whipping up red dusty patches. They splattered through the aircraft hull, petrol ran out of the tank – if it starts to burn!

The aim was to exit and unload the aircraft as speedily as possible. One mountain soldier remembered landing with an open door:

> The first man jumped out of the moving plane with heavy rucksacks flying out behind them. The wind of the propellers blew the yellow dust in our faces; the Junkers was already moving again. A mortar bomb burst very close. The crash of the detonation, the noise of the engines, the dust and shouting of the ground crews made our heads swim.

They took cover in an enormous bomb crater nearby. Two men came running up. 'They had almost been taken back [to Greece] but at the last moment they had jumped from the plane as it started up, leaving their packs behind.' More and more aircraft came into land.

> Our Junkers was hardly away when the next one landed right in the middle of the thick dust. A cracking rending sound ensued, more clouds of dust … crash … belly landing. The undercarriage flies in huge bounds into the nearby water.[22]

Buchholz's lead plane was riddled with fire as it waited for space to take off again and burst into flames. He was hit in the leg and the crew hauled him out through the cockpit. *Oberleutnant* Raither's machine spurted even more fuel onto the dirt strip and it was struck again during the unloading process, so that it was unable to restart. Remarkably nobody had been wounded inside the aircraft. He watched, dismayed, as *Major* Friedmann was evacuated from near Buchholz's machine, severely wounded by a shell blast. An unloaded motorcycle combination paused to pick him up and drive off at high speed. Raither had nothing but admiration for the pilots, 'magnificent fellows', he recalled:

> In the midst of this chaos, under heavy enemy fire, obscured by dust and smoke, leaping obstacles – some even on fire – they set their machines safely down on the ground and enabled us,

thereby, to unload our weapons and ammunition. You have our thanks comrades!²³

'We hadn't imagined a landing like this', he later reflected. 'You do not have time to think clearly', remembered *Jäger* Johann Pfefferkorn, 'because you are just trying to avoid getting killed'. Split second decisions governed life or death. 'Courage and anguish do not exist here', he reflected:

Happy times go by and bad memories gradually lose their intensity ... soldiers do not have the sense of victory, like for example a footballer has. A soldier's only purpose is to accomplish his mission. After that he knows he must go and fight somewhere else again. It's a hard life being a soldier.

Landing on this contested airstrip was simply the start point of battle. Feri Fink observing from the *3. Kompanie* positions at the western edge of the aerodrome counted 60 'freighters' coming in, the advance guard from *Gebirgsjäger Regiment 100*. 'Inwardly we celebrated', he recalled; 'from now on, we're over the worst of it', he thought with visible relief, from this point on they were likely to win.

Emerging from the smoke-shrouded pandemonium of landing and crashing aircraft was the bizarre image of a well-dressed Luftwaffe *Hauptmann*, replete with 'plate cap' and white dress tunic. He urged this 'slim and smart' officer 'with blond hair' to quickly get away before even more artillery strikes rained down. His haughty response was 'first I will collect my *Staffel* and then take off in close formation'. Fink was incredulous, 'didn't this bird of paradise appreciate', in his popinjay uniform, 'what artillery shells can do?' At this point the *Hauptmann*'s third aircraft taxied up and caught its undercarriage wheel in a hole, which swung the heavy machine round 'and with a grinding cracking report took the wings off the second and third freighter'. The exasperated officer was still shouting '*whoa ... whoa ... whoa!*' when another salvo of shells howled in amongst the entangled aircraft. Fink dived for cover in one of the perimeter trenches, closely followed by the dismayed figure in white. Billows of smoke and dust palls floated gently out to sea.

Soon more than a dozen crashed Ju 52s were littering the open spaces of the aerodrome. Landing space, often obscured by smoke, was at a premium. Lieutenant Geoffrey Cox, observing from Freyberg's HQ further along the coast, was watching the aircraft circle:

> Then one dived. A moment later it was just a black column of smoke winding up. Others tried, and seemed to be hit too. Then one started down onto the airfield, and, after a brief pause, took off again in a cloud of dust.

He sat alongside an Australian gunner colonel, Freyberg's artillery commander at Creforce HQ. 'Seventy seconds to land and clear its men and gear', he laconically commented. 'An ominous proof of German efficiency', Cox thought.[24]

One mountain *Gefreiter* saw they were just 300 yards off the beach as their Ju 52 roared along the coastline. 'There was a loud crack sounding inside the aircraft and we could clearly hear machine gun fire.' Above their seats the air gunner was firing for all he was worth 'and air holes appeared along the corrugated fuselage'. 'The Tommies have prepared a warm reception for us', they all agreed, and then 'it came thick and fast, a strike, a dull explosion, a splintering cracking and then it was dark all around'. Blazing obstacles and dust clouds on the aerodrome obliged pilots to consider landing on the beaches alongside. The *Gefreiter's* machine had been hit by artillery:

> A shower of water on the neck resurrected my survival instinct once again. Thank God we were still afloat. The little bit of light coming through the window enabled us to find our swim vests. Our gallant bird rocked gently on the waves as the first machine gun bursts whined beside us. *Raus!* Out! The cry was taken up inside the fuselage.

The door was already open and the first were outside. They waded waist deep in water and congregated under the tail. The grizzly veteran corporal took time to stick a couple of dry cigarette packs under his field cap before setting off. Machine gun bursts spurted up spray, 'one man cried out *"I've been hit!"* But it didn't seem too bad'. 'Half an eternity' later they straggled through the gentle surf on the beach, whereupon he took one of his dry cigarettes out and lit up. An Me 110 swooped onto the machine gun 'attacking at low level, burst upon burst fired into the trench'. A Stuka finished him off and 'carefully laid his eggs in the nest'. The assembled men squelched their way to the signalled assembly area, but their weapons had been lost inside the aircraft.[25]

Fink and the *3. Kompanie* survivors were impressed at the steadiness of the *Gebirgsjäger* emerging from the 'pandemonium of a wild boar hunt'. Aircraft had been immobilized by the shell craters on landing, snapping off their landing gear:

> Groups of *Gebirgsjäger* came out of a wall of dust and moved off, trotting in file towards the olive grove, often towing loads and their heavy weapons behind, all with their distinctive rucksacks on their backs. Not a sign of panic from these boys!

He could see that aircraft landing to the west of the runway got away with it. 'In all the machines coming down to the east of the aerodrome', which could be reached by fire from the 23 and 21 New Zealand battalions, 'the mountain troops suffered heavy casualties. Very few freighters came down here unscathed'. Even so, *Oberst* Utz, the commander of *Regiment 100*, who landed with the first aircraft, found casualties low, relative to the enormous risks they had taken. He lost 22 dead and 17 wounded on this day, mostly from crash landings outside the aerodrome perimeter, an amazing accomplishment. When Ramcke took over at 6.15pm that evening, he had Gericke's *IV Bataillon*, Stentzler's *II* and a reinforced battalion from Utz's *Regiment 100* under command. Overall direction still lay with Student in Athens and not Luftwaffe *Generaloberst* Löhr's man. This was the first important step to inverting the ratio of Allied odds to German on the west side of the island.

The *Gebirgsjäger* gathered in an assembly area by the Tavronitis bridge. *Oberst* Utz was unable at this stage, to deploy his regiment's battalion as a whole. His *7. Kompanie* was dispatched forward along the coast road to reinforce Gericke's *Kampfgruppe* thrust in the fight beyond Maleme. *8. Kompanie* was sent south-west to join *16. Sturmregiment* to safeguard the road leading to Kandanos. The two remaining companies were kept in reserve around Tavronitis, warned by von Richthofen's *VIII Fliegerkorps* staff about a possible enemy approach from the south-west, which proved bogus.

Major Snowadski, prevented from touching down earlier the previous day, assumed administrative command of Maleme aerodrome and set about the task of towing and bulldozing wrecks out of the way of landing aircraft. Space would be needed for reinforcements due to fly in the next day. A captured Bren gun carrier and one of the Matilda tanks were employed to begin shifting the 20 or so wrecks littering the landing space. One in three aircraft landing had not made it out.

Ramcke now commanded about 1,500 to 1,600 troops at Maleme, a force to be reckoned with. It would that night be reinforced by the first echelon of the seaborne *Leichte Seestaffel* transporting Utz's *III Bataillon* from *Regiment 100*, and *Fallschirmjäger* engineer and heavy weapons, about 2,500 men.

Kapitänleutnant Bartels from the Kriegsmarine had landed with the first mountain troop transports to identify the precise embarkation point for sea-landed troops, and mark it off with flags and lights. He waited with his staff at Cape Spatha, the peninsula stretching 12½ miles north into the Aegean, west of the aerodrome. As it grew dark he became increasingly nervous, there was no sign of any ships or boats on the northern horizon. He was to direct the landings. Tension rose further when Luftwaffe reconnaissance reported English cruisers with destroyers to the south of Crete, just beyond bomber range. At about 11pm the naval staff on the cape saw a searchlight playing across the water to the north, then a second and third. An 'electric shock' went through the assembled naval personnel when they heard the rumble of heavy-calibre naval guns rolling ominously across the dark water.[26]

Oberst Buchholz, lightly wounded in the leg, had been unable to fly out that day. He and the surviving aircrew from the wrecks strewn about the airfield had given priority to flying the wounded back to the Greek mainland. Stranded aircrew would be lifted back with the returning air-land due in at first light the following day. What they saw on the horizon at sea was echoed by *Hauptmann* von der Heydte, who was observing the flashes at sea from Castle Hill, in Prison Valley to the south.

> What we saw from there was like a giant firework display. Rockets and flares were shooting into the night sky, searchlights probed the darkness, and the red glow of fire was spreading across the entire horizon. The muffled thunder of distant detonations lent sound to this dismal sight. For about 20 minutes we watched, until suddenly the fireworks ceased, and the velvety, star-sprinkled cupola of the night arched itself once more in peaceful repose over the island.[27]

The activity was estimated to be about six to 12 miles off the coast. They knew how dispersed the boats had been, when Buchholz's Ju 52 stream had flown over. Hopefully the British Alexandria Squadron had only come across the lead or rear elements, but the flashes and detonations went on intermittently for another two and a half hours. It was unlikely that any seaborne reinforcements would make landfall that night.

Chapter 10

The Swing of the Force Pendulum

OBERSTLEUTNANT EHAL, COMMANDER
LEICHTE SCHIFFSSTAFFELN

Night 21–22 May 1941, Nearing the Aegean Coast, Western Crete
Oberstleutnant Ehal, the commander of the *III Bataillon* from
Oberst Utz's *Regiment 100*, had chosen the 300-ton antiquated
vessel *Papapopiou I* as his 'flagship'. He was the senior officer
leading the *Leichte Schiffsstaffeln*, the first convoy of the seaborne
invasion force bound for Maleme Crete. *Generalmajor* Ringel, his
division commander, thought the vessel's name unpronounceable,
which is why boats named *Adriatico*, *Patria Eterna* and *Labor* were
designated simple naval serials. Ehal's ship became the *S105*. It
was roomier, swifter and steadier than most of his fleet of some
22 to 25 boats, varying between 80 and 300 tons. On board was
Ehal's *III Bataillon*, two anti-aircraft batteries, the rest of the
non-flying elements of Süssman's *7. Luftlande Division* and the
paratrooper's heavy mortars, anti-tank guns and crews, alongside
vast quantities of ammunition and motorcycle combinations to
tow or haul them. The contingent numbered about 2,300 men,
a decisive reinforcement, enough to tip the balance of opposing
forces at Maleme in the German favour. Ehal's men had been at
sea for two days since departing Athens. When they left, they were
a reinforcement force, now they were attentively monitored from

Student's Hotel Grande Bretagne headquarters as something of a rescue force.

A second convoy had departed Chalkis on 21 May with about 22 boats with the second *Staffel* or echelon. These carried the *II Bataillon Gebirgsjäger Regiment 85* with elements from *Fallschirmjäger Regiment 1*, about a further 1,500 men. Secured in its holds were about 100 vehicles, 180 horses, motorcycles, light anti-aircraft guns and even more ammunition. Following these two convoys was a third Italian convoy consisting of tramp steamers and fishing boats with a strong navy escort. Hitler had insisted on a firm leg on the ground for this invasion, an amphibious force to back up the air-landings. After the disaster that had befallen the Italian battle fleet at Cape Matapan seven weeks before, when they lost three cruisers and two destroyers sunk, and the battleship *Vittorio Veneto* heavily damaged, *Generaloberst* Löhr and Student's staff had few illusions about the risk they were undertaking. Three thousand lives had been lost then.[1]

Few of the mountain troops could swim, and they had felt vulnerable from the start of the voyage. They preferred their feet firmly planted on mountain terrain, having already acquitted themselves well in the fight for the Rupel Pass between 6 and 10 April 1941, piercing the Greek Metaxas Line on the Bulgarian border. Three fort complexes had been carried with heavy Stuka and artillery support, fighting in rain and sleet at heights of over 3,000 feet above sea level. Ehal's battalion was now dispersed across a fleet of wooden leaking caiques, propelled with aged diesel motors, which constantly broke down, with one or two sails. Each boat had a Greek crew overseen by one or two German naval ratings. The whole tramp fleet was shepherded by a single Italian destroyer, the *Lupo*, and straggled into Melos harbour, about the half-way point at dusk on 20 May. They laid up overnight forewarned of Royal Navy activity and set off again before dawn, heading south for Crete with low-flying Ju 52 streams pointing the way. By day two Me 109 fighter planes from *Luftflotte 4* wheeled overhead like buzzards, offering protective observation. At night they would be easy prey for the Royal Navy. Frequent engine breakdowns increased straggling to the extent that the second convoy, theoretically six hours behind, occasionally hove in sight of the first.

Ehal decided to press on to Crete at best speed, leaving it to the stragglers to catch up, otherwise they would not reach Maleme before the onset of malevolent darkness. British fleets had been spotted and attacked by the Luftwaffe both east and west of the Cretan mainland. *Konteradmiral Süd-Ost* Schuster felt the invasion force would be compromised if it carried on. *Leutnant* Schmidt, Ehal's signals officer aboard *Sio5* remembered at about 9am the *Lupo* came sailing up and signalled *Back – Return to Melos*, but 'the reason was unknown'. What followed was hardly a maritime manoeuvre; the wooden ships went about and limped and straggled in a northerly direction back to Melos in a seemingly blind follow-my-leader turn-around.

A six-hour delay then ensued while Ehal gathered his officers to discuss the situation in the officer's mess established aboard *Sio5*. Within hours of being called back, *Kapitän* Heye, Schuster's chief of staff, was besieged by Löhr and von Richthofen's staff to reverse the decision and get moving south again. 'The chart plot of these days offered a wild picture that defied the imagination', Heye recalled. It eventually became clear that no British ships were now south of the fleet, because in daylight, British ships remained south of the island, preferring to stay just outside the Luftwaffe's reach. None of this was known on board *Sio5*. Had Operation *Mercury* been called off? Was the British fleet on their side of the island? Ehal's conference group was convinced the dive-bomber threat would deter them by day. British submarines were less of a threat because of the shallow draught of the primitive caique keels, not dissimilar to barges. Ehal received word to proceed again that afternoon, lifting anchor at 2pm. Admiral Schuster calculated that, with luck, the 16 or so remaining boats of the Maleme flotilla should reach the beaches off Maleme by about 10pm that night. Schmidt recalled his commanding officer assessing they should be in the Chania bay by nightfall 'with unloading possible by about morning the next day'. The Greek crews were less enthusiastic: '*Kreta big. Why go to Kreta? Englishmen there ... inglesi – machen Kaputt!*' Ehal's men were amused, 'we'll show who is going to make us *Kaputt!*' they laughed.[2]

Hauptmann Schlechter with part of his *12. Kompanie* aboard the *Rosa* or *V4*, a 100-ton motor sailing boat, could only make about three sea miles per hour. Sailing into a choppy headwind 'a heavy sea was making the cargo on deck dangerous' and waves were breaking over the deck. Lookouts complained of poor visibility. *Oberleutnant* W. Staubwasser on the 105-ton *T2* or *Adriatico* remembered 'the wind state rose from force 3 to 4 and the German and Italian sailors suspected that a storm was rising, about 25 men were suffering from sea sickness'. Schmidt on *S105* reckoned 'at sunset, the sea which up until then had been very calm began to stir'. The small boats began to violently pitch, 'small engines carrying heavy freight'. Periodically the Italian *Lupo* could be seen shepherding from the flanks and rear with 'water skipping over her deck'.[3]

After 10pm the flotilla was still about 18 miles off the coast of Crete, nearing the bay of Chania. Morale on board Ehal's boat was high; 'the England song', often sung in France prior to the anticipated invasion of England, 'could be heard repeatedly', Schmidt recalled. Troop leaders re-checked landing preparations: inflating life-rafts, taking heavy mountain boots off and putting life jackets on in readiness for going ashore. Landing would be across ramps, improvised at the bows, across open beaches. The arrival of the fully equipped mountain battalion with its equipment and heavy weapons would make a considerable impact on German combat power at Maleme. Schmidt watched Ehal 'sitting at a table with some of his officers in the mess', an atmospheric scene. The duty officer came in 'reporting that all was well on board': 'The smoking lamp swinging in its holder over the table, swung with the momentum of the pitching ship, dimly lighting up the faces of the almost silent officers.'[4]

Leutnant Linder on board remembered the navigation officer saw a shadow bearing down on *S101*, one of the boats off the port bow astern. 'It looks like an English destroyer', one of the flak commanders nearby said, at which point an 'artillery salvo cracked out and the *S101* immediately burst into flames'. 'I heard a loud explosion at 10pm', Schmidt reported:

Immediately *Oberleutnant* Prosinger and I went up on deck. As we emerged a shell landed about ten metres from the ship, to starboard. Splinters struck the deck wounding several people, some of the fragments grazing my left upper arm. *Oberleutnant* Prosinger went straight down to the battalion commander in the officer's mess, while I went to my platoon on the upper deck. In the same instant a shell burst inside the officer's mess. I don't know who was in there, but loud cries came out from the wounded.

Ehal ordered an immediate reversal of course, to clear the bay. 'Make ready the lifeboats!' was instructed. 'Suddenly a shell struck close by me', Schmidt remembered, 'and I was flung overboard with the air pressure'.[5]

Feldwebel Gunter Kerstens, a mountain soldier in Ehal's battalion, recalled 'we were nearing Crete, our destination, when searchlights came on ahead, and heavy guns started to fire':

We could see the English ships getting closer, outlined in silhouette by the flash of their guns. Ships and boats ahead of us were on fire and then it was our turn. The boat alongside exploded and through the smoke came the bow of an English ship. I could not move. Some jumped, but I was rooted to the spot as it came down on us. The boat splintered and was pushed under, me with it. With my last gasp I came to the surface to see the ship continue on with the *Götterdämmerung*.

The leading British destroyers turned towards Crete inshore, blocking off any German approach, and started to pick off targets. They concentrated on the fat ones first, like Ehal's *S105*. Cruisers coming up behind turned shoreward to join in. *Leutnant* Sigrist aboard the *S15* remembered 'the way to the south was blocked by British ships, we turned east' which he illustrated with a sketch map appended to his report, 'and then the engine broke down'.

The aim, having broadly encircled their prey, was to dart in and finish them off. Bill Bracht on the Australian cruiser *Perth*, recalled that night:

> Our surface radar picked up ships, on went our searchlights, there in the beams, about 8,000 yards away were a mass of small boats, low Greek caiques, their decks crammed with men. All ships switched on their searchlights and opened fire. It was a horrible massacre of defenceless men and boats, it had to be done. Soldiers jumped overboard and others were blown to kingdom come by murderous gunfire. The destroyers raced across the area churning the sea into a cauldron. It was soon over and once more the ocean was strewn with burning debris, patches of oil and dead men.[6]

The fortunate boats were the stragglers, well behind like *Oberleutnant* W. Staubwasser aboard the 105-ton *T2 Adriatico*, who saw 'a single explosion which started a sea fight that we observed resulted in seven ships in the convoy burning or sinking'. The first ship had burst into flames at the second or third shot. 'We also were picked up out by a searchlight', he recalled, 'and received a salvo, which dropped short by 30 to 50 metres.' Amid blossoming water spouts and burning wrecks 'the Italian destroyer came between us and the enemy ships'. The *Lupo* shone a searchlight on one of the British cruisers and began pounding away with all guns as well as releasing a spread of torpedoes. The destroyer's outline was soon flashing and crackling as several bruising broadsides were received; hit 18 times by 6in shells, *Lupo* lost two crew killed and many wounded. *Lupo*'s audacious action and the protective smoke screen it laid between its flock and the Royal Navy predators enabled many boats to disappear eastwards – including Staubwasser's *T2* – under cover of darkness.

Staubwasser observed 'that enemy units shot up dinghies with machine guns and flak in the water'. In this mayhem 'rescuing ship's survivors was out of the question with the high sea state'.

Leutnant Hörmann aboard *S-8* was also at the rear of the convoy. They were passed by a cruiser that was so close in the turbulent wake that, despite being illuminated by a searchlight, all that could be depressed to bear were machine guns that raked them from bow to stern. More ships erupted into flames around them as a second British ship raced close by, ripping up the decks with machine-gun fire and snapping off the mast, which fell across the helm and caused the boat to circle. A third ship coasting by raked the sea around them and deck with even more machine-gun fire, enveloping two unfortunates in the dinghy alongside. Hörmann ordered abandon ship, but the crew pinned down by fire thought better of it, and *S-8* managed to get under way again after pushing away the splintered mast.[7]

Schmidt, blown overboard from Ehal's flagship the *S105*, remembered that from the water 'the ship's sails stood out like a magnesium torch, lit up by a searchlight beam'. A big black shadow was gliding past its port side and a broadside flashed out producing 'hits, steel splinters and wrecked timbers with yells from the wounded'. Fresh strikes set the ship alight, men were blown overboard, others jumped to swim to a lifeboat and a couple of dinghies. Schmidt was now some distance from the ship, having been pulled from the water by men on a rubber dinghy. He was the only officer remaining with no sign at all from Prosinger or Ehal, the commanding officer, since the shell had exploded in the boat's wardroom. Many officers were missing. 'Then we heard a huge explosion', Schmidt recalled, 'as a huge sheet of flame shot up high into the air from the ship' as she went under.[8]

Ehal's *III Bataillon* ceased to exist as an operational fighting unit. Ten caiques were sunk and about a thousand men were in the water. *Feldwebel* Karl Riep, who had jumped from *S12*, remembered 'many soldiers in the water cried out for help. The British shot them too'. Ernst Stribny, another survivor, claimed despite showing a white flag 'six British ships opened fire on it and continued to shoot at men who jumped into the water, and tried to swim away'. He was caught up in a maelstrom of heavy machine-gun fire:

> I was wounded in my right shoulder ... we suffered the most from the heavy cruiser, which moved criss-cross amid the shipwrecked, and continuously shot at us. And in its wake many comrades were pulled into the depths by the suction of the propellers. The British did not rescue a single man.[9]

The sleek grey vessels prowled about scanning the surface for over two hours, seeking fresh prey. 'Finally', Staubwasser remembered, 'the searchlights switched off at 2.05am'.

The second convoy that left Chalkis on 21 May, destined for Iraklion, had more luck. Despite being apprehended by another Royal Navy hunter force, all but two of the ships escaped destruction. Again an Italian destroyer, the *Sagittario*, managed to lay a protective smoke screen and they got back to Melos. The news at the Hotel Grande Bretagne was positively alarming, the first convoy was reported destroyed and 1,800 men lost. *Generaloberst* Löhr was genuinely shocked; 'the British fleet make the extremely urgent transport of heavy weapons by sea impossible', he recalled. *VIII Fliegerkorps* were instructed in no uncertain terms to neutralize British shipping around Crete. On the following day two British cruisers and a destroyer were sunk, two battleships and two cruisers damaged for the loss of only six aircraft downed and five damaged.[10]

Feldwebel Gunter Kerstens survived being rammed and run over by a 'big ship'. 'I spent all the next day in the water', he recalled, 'clinging to wreckage before being picked up'. He bitterly resented the Royal Navy 'which made no attempt to rescue us – curse them!' *Jäger* Joseph Würz remembered 'we could neither shoot nor help': 'We just stood by looking on in helpless rage. One of my dearest friends was found dead after 16 hours floating in the sea. Sixty of my company drowned. The survivors were brought back to Athens.'

Remarkably the alarming figures of 20 ships and 1,800 men lost turned around to ten ships sunk and 1,800 men saved. Luftwaffe sea rescue *Rettungsstaffeln* began picking survivors out of the water at first light. One sea plane rescued over 200 men alone, while Italian destroyers and motor launches plucked out the rest. It was still a considerable loss, 304 dead or missing, including *Oberstleutnant* Ehal, who likely went down with his flagship, 100 were wounded. The Royal Navy lost many times these numbers the following day. Ringel lamented the 'adventure' had cost one of his battalions virtually its entire fighting strength. Only 49 of Ehal's *Gebirgsjäger* reached Crete's shores in dinghies or rescue craft. All the heavy weapons and ammunition resupply was lost. Perhaps about 150 from the original 2,250 eventually landed on Crete. The sea invasion was a complete debacle. The third heavy Italian convoy was held in port.[11]

BRIGADIER JAMES HARGEST, COMMANDER
5 NEW ZEALAND BRIGADE

Night 21–22 May, Brigade HQ, Plantanias Village
The start line for Hargest's 5 Brigade counter-attack was almost outside his headquarters in the village of Platanias, just west of the bridge crossing the dry river bed. Hargest, who had been unwell since the start of the invasion, was exhausted and despondent. His brigade had given up Maleme aerodrome and Hill 107, the key high ground that rises above the runways and dominates it. He played no personal part in planning this counter-move, which appeared to ignore the fact the Germans had been reinforced by a contested battalion air-land before dusk. *Oberst* Ramcke, who had parachuted in to take over command from the wounded *Sturmregiment* leader Meindl, was already deploying for an attack himself, amazed a strong Allied counter-attack had not materialized thus far. Hargest, befuddled by fatigue, was neither thinking clearly nor aggressively. Clinging to the same headquarters, located for coastal defence, he had not even gone forward to physically confer with his battalion commanders,

still well forward, despite Andrew's unexpected and precipitate withdrawal from the vital ground on Hill 107 the night before. The aim of this attack was to regain it and the aerodrome.

His start line was on familiar ground, terrain he could see in daylight. The plan had in reality been pressed on him by Puttick, his division commander, and Major-General Freyberg. It paid scant cognisance to counter-attack options laboriously worked out and rehearsed prior to the airborne invasion. No consideration appears to have been given to moving the 28 (Maori) Battalion and soon to arrive 20 Battalion start lines much further forward. A start line at least another mile forward in the vicinity of Vineyard Ridge would be the nearest high ground behind the objective Hill 107, where 21 and 23 Battalions were firmly in situ. Instead attacking units would have to advance in darkness along the coastal plain, characterized by olive groves on high ground with small fields on the coastal flats, bounded by thick belts of bamboo providing wind shelter. These grow in thick clumps along each river and stream bank, enclosing small fields with orange and olive trees. One- or two-storey farm houses were scattered along the roads leading to small villages, whose centre-piece was invariably a church and square. The attackers would be traversing the failed parachute reinforcement drop zones. Isolated pockets of German resistance were here and there, holed up in olive groves, bamboo clumps and the odd farmhouse. Placing the start line so far east meant they were snagged by a trip wire of potential resistance points forward of the main German line beyond the aerodrome, which could harass any advance.

Not only was Hargest outside the planning information loop, he had more than his fair share of concurrent and more immediate distractions. His headquarters had been overflown by the twin company German drop that had descended between Platanias and Pirgos. While this was going on, a message arrived at Freyberg's Creforce HQ from Cairo, as they were conferring the detail for the attack that night. The gist according to Brigadier Inglis with 4 Brigade was 'enemy attempting seaborne landings beaches of

Chania tonight', which was Hargest's sector. 'Navy informed', the message read. A forcible instruction was immediately dispatched to Puttick's HQ reminding them it was their responsibility to blunt such an attack. Pressured by this, Brigadier Puttick insisted on a virtual man-for-man relief of 20 Battalion by the 2/7 Australian Battalion, before releasing it to move to Hargest's counter-attack start line. Impractical timings laid down for the attack meant the inevitable difficulty of moving major units in daylight under aggressive Luftwaffe harassing attacks, which impacted on the planned schedule. In effect the importance of a counter-attack against a functioning German airhead was considered less to that of repulsing as yet unidentified seaborne landings.

Hargest, observing with some trepidation the number of Ju 52 transports arriving at Maleme during the late afternoon, must have wondered whether a two-battalion counter-stroke that night would indeed suffice. He was dealing with two ongoing crises at the same time: possible seaborne landings in his sector that night and delays in forming up the counter-attack force. Neither Freyberg nor Puttick insisted on any task priority: coastal defence versus elimination of the enemy airhead. Hargest wrote in his diary that 'at 8pm Division HQ rang me and told me to counter-attack – they gave me the 20th Battalion and the attack was to be a night one supported by light tanks'.

The agreed plan was an advance from the Platanias start line at 1am to enable a final assault at the Maleme aerodrome for 4am. There were barely enough hours of darkness to achieve this, with dawn due an hour and a half later. 'I did not know that the 20th had to be relieved by the Australians', Hargest wrote, 'then embus and come six miles to me. I was not told till very late'. Not only that, all telephone lines to his three forward battalions were dead. Hargest had no means of effectively coordinating the attack once it was under way. Lieutenant Colonel Gentry, Puttick's senior operations officer, came forward at 10pm to assist and noticed that Hargest was clearly exhausted.[12]

Major Marshall with the 2/7 Australian Battalion had the unenviable task of mustering an adequate number of trucks, sufficient to move the battalion to Chania and relieve 20 Battalion for its counter-attack. Much of this had to be conducted in daylight under Luftwaffe surveillance. 'As we turned a corner', Marshall recalled, we 'found half a dozen planes above with the obvious intention of stopping us somewhere'. This was the prelude to a hazardous cat and mouse running of a Luftwaffe gauntlet. 'It was rather exhilarating', Marshall admitted:

> The planes had now obviously got onto to us, but the road was winding along a valley, and there were a few straight stretches waiting for us ... twice I watched a plane single us out, bank and turn to machine gun us along the straight and I told the driver to crack it up. It then became a race to the curve.

The lead elements did not reach 20 Battalion until dusk at about 8pm, and the final companies straggled in much later, because as Marshall recalled, they had 'streaked along, and I hoped the battalion was following'.[13]

Major Jim Barrow's 20 Battalion had only received the order to counter-attack two and a half hours before. The plan was for 20 Battalion to attack on the seaward side of the main coastal road leading from Platanias to Maleme. 28 (Maori) Battalion under Lieutenant Colonel George Dittmer was to advance on the landward side supported by three light tanks from the 3rd Hussars under Lieutenant Roy Farran, moving along the road in the middle between them. There would be a 30-minute pause in the village of Pirgos before 20 Battalion attacked the aerodrome and 28 Battalion Hill 107. It would link there with 21 Battalion, which would secure the south side of Hill 107, to cover the Tavronitis River, while 28 Battalion secured the high ground to the north. 28 Battalion would then return to Platanias before first light.

At 11.30pm Hargest was at the Platanias schoolhouse, short of the start line, conferring with the attacking battalion commanders. It had been an anxious wait. Planning times had gone completely awry. 28 Battalion had been in situ several hours but there was no sign of 20 Battalion. Lieutenant Farran arrived at Platanias village with his three light tanks. His men were also exhausted, 'since we had been in action almost non-stop for 48 hours', he recalled, 'and I felt that this was almost certain suicide'. Neither was his confidence restored on meeting Hargest.

> Together we mounted the steps of an old farmhouse to receive the orders from the Brigadier. He was a red, open-faced man, who looked like a country farmer and it was obvious he was suffering from acute fatigue. He asked us to wait for half an hour while he had some sleep. Disgusted, intolerant, we sat down on the steps until he was ready.

Farran discovered artillery support would be 'from a few captured Italian guns, which had to be aimed by squinting down the barrel'. Support was hardly encouraging: no mortars, no spades for weapon pits, helmets would have to be used for digging shell-scrapes. They were up against captured Bofors guns which 'would blow large holes in my tanks'. Arguing that 'my tanks were only thinly armoured perambulators and that this was a job for [heavy] Matildas', he was reminded these had been knocked out the day before and 'beggars cannot be choosers'. Nevertheless, he was promised a section of Maoris behind each tank to regulate the pace of the advance 'and prevent Molotov Cocktails from being thrown from the ditches'.[14]

At Freyberg's Creforce HQ, in a quarry a few miles east of Hargest, Lieutenant Geoffrey Cox received a reassuring message that 'the Royal Navy had sighted the convoy' en route to Maleme, 'and were moving in for the kill'. He recalled: 'Suddenly on the horizon away to the north came the flash and thunder of guns, and then the dull red glow of burning vessels. Within a matter of some 20 minutes all was over.'

Hargest and the assembled force were treated to the same sight. Cox remembered Freyberg responded to a remark from Colonel Keith Stewart, his chief of staff, that 'it has been a great responsibility. A great responsibility'. Clearly he was mightily relieved the worst was probably over. 'His tones conveyed the deep thankfulness of a man who had discharged well a nightmarishly difficult task.' It looked very much like the seaborne attack had been routed.

At neither Rethymnon nor Iraklion had the enemy secured a grip on an airfield. At Maleme, the Germans' one remaining foothold, a counter-attack in substantial force by the best troops of the New Zealand Division supported by tanks was about to go in.

Cox felt confident together 'with a feeling of profound thankfulness'. So far as he was concerned 'it indeed seemed that we had turned the corner'.[15]

Despite the clear absence if not reduction of the German threat from the sea, Puttick did not react and speed up the relief process. Planning thus far had resembled a map exercise. Puttick obsessed with the detail had only committed the minimum force necessary for the counter-attack. The red glow apparent to all on the northern horizon obviated the need for 20 Battalion to wait for relief, it could have been brought immediately forward to the start line. The division commander did not display the gambler's instinct the situation needed. H Hour for the advance had been due at 1am, but Major Jim Burrows did not appear with his headquarters and the two lead companies until 2.15am. They had not seen the ground and it was dark, with only about three hours remaining before daylight and with it the marauding Luftwaffe.

'I forget the starting time of the arrival of the [Australian] relief', recalled Lieutenant George Brown with C Company, 'but they were hours late'. When they got to Platanias, Brown recalled his acting company commander Denver Fountain going into 5 Brigade Headquarters: 'I waited outside, and when Denver came out I said to him "What's the story?" and he said "George, you know as much about it as I do."'

They took up position on the starting line. 'The Germans must have known we were there', he recalled, 'we were being machine gunned very heavily'. Private F.W. Carr remembered moving along 'pitch black roads' before filing into a field after dropping their haversacks. 'Good luck, Kiwi, give the bastards hell', the Australians had said, seeing them off. Nerves on the start line were taut. 'God be merciful to me', Carr prayed. 'My heart is pumping ninety to the dozen. I wonder if I'll be afraid or if I'll get out alive?'

The enemy were clearly within earshot. Bursts of machine-gun fire were already spiralling across his field of vision in tracer light flecks. His 'temples were pulsating tremendously, my heart was pounding away beneath my shirt'.[16]

Hargest was far from optimistic, senses dulled by the mental pressure of seemingly intractable dilemmas and physical exhaustion. 23 Battalion, on the left wing of the counter-attack, did not hear it was on until midnight, 21 Battalion next to it, heard 40 minutes later. By 3am the advance was ready to go but they were two hours behind schedule, with just two and half hours of darkness left. Burrows elected to advance with his two companies, relying on his remaining three to hurry and catch up, once they were off the trucks. Hargest, sensing the plan was likely to be thrown out by these successive delays, doubted by now whether it would succeed at all. 'I rang Div HQ', he later recalled, 'and asked must the attack go on – "it must" was the reply, and on it went – too late!' The troops crossed the start line at 3.30am, with just two hours before first light.[17]

'And then, boy oh boy, hell broke loose', Carr with 20 Battalion recalled. Major Jim Burrows remembered 'the distance of our objective was approximately three miles': 'Neither the company commanders nor I had seen the country ahead, though we knew what to expect – olive trees, vineyards, hedges, irrigation ditches, dry water courses with steep banks and the occasional cottage.'

'Jerry fired straight down the depression in which we were lying', Carr recalled. Fire had forced them off a ploughed field as soon as they started, and they piled into a shallow depression along a hedgerow. 'The bullets were only just missing me. I could hear that ominous *sssss* and by raising my eyebrows a whisker, could see the coloured trail of the little messengers of death.' On their left 'we heard hurrahs, shouts, epithets, hakas etc. The Maoris were attacking'.

The advance soon began to clash with stay-behind survivors from the abortive afternoon German parachute landings. The attack developed into an extended series of running small action fights with these outposts. Burrows recalled 'a burst of automatic and small arms fire at close range, a grenade explosion followed by a furious assault' and then 'the subsequent silence'. The scraps were merciless. 'Jerry would file out of houses – after emptying his mag – with his hands in the air', Carr remembered, 'but we'd just mow him down'. 'I was worried all the while about the time factor', Burrows recalled, 'and how much had to be done before daylight'.

Once the battalions crossed the start line, Hargest, in effect, relinquished control. In the absence of effective communications, the battle was to be decided by the battalion commanders, whose control in darkness was also tenuous. 'Strangely enough though, I, who wouldn't hurt a fly, was just as bloodthirsty as the others', admitted Carr.

I seemed to be in a trance for I remember that blood and guts didn't worry me in the least. We had received orders to take no prisoners – not that we wanted to – and we left no wounded. We bayonetted those still living, it was a safety measure anyway.[18]

Farran's light tanks advanced down the coastal road, the central axis of advance. They drove by 'parachutes lying in the trees and there were two dead Germans hanging on the telephone wires, blown up like green bladders'. The tanks sprayed lines of tracer into the darkness ahead of them, hitting an ammunition stash 'which exploded like golden rain at the Crystal Palace'. Distracted by the exuberance of their clattering advance Farran turned back and was astonished to see his accompanying section of Maoris had suffered heavy casualties in the dark: 'I had not even realized that we had been fired at, but the sadly depleted numbers and the bandage around the head of the sergeant were evidence enough.'

Fratricide or friendly fire took a toll in the confusion of dark vegetation and murky blackness. Streaks of fire flashing across the darkened landscape gave away enemy positions. 'Machine gun fire

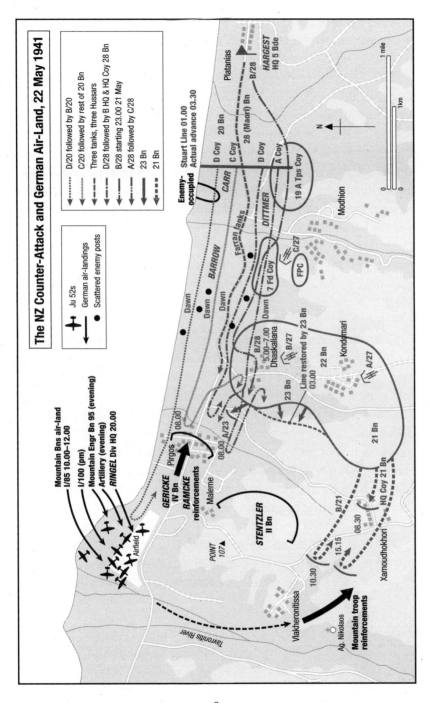

The NZ Counter-Attack and German Air-Land, 22 May 1941

D/20 followed by B/20
C/20 followed by rest of 20 Bn
Three tanks, three Hussars
D/28 followed by B HQ & HQ Coy 28 Bn
B/28 starting 23.00 21 May
A/28 followed by C/28
23 Bn
21 Bn

Enemy-occupied

Stuart Line 01.00
Actual advance 03.30

Ju 52s
German air-landings
Scattered enemy posts

Mountain Bns air-land
I/85 10.00–12.00
I/100 (pm)
Mountain Engr Bn 95 (evening)
Artillery (evening)
RINGEL Div HQ 20.00

seemed terrific', remembered Farran, 'and Tommy guns, pistols, grenades and the shouts and screams of men combined in an unearthly din like nothing they had ever heard before'.

The scattered German units provided an unexpected resistance in depth that soaked up much of the momentum of the advance. Fighting broke out in ditches, behind hedges, in the top and bottom storeys of farmhouses and in fields and gardens all along the coastal road. The leading elements of 28 (Maori) Battalion reached the crossroads at Dhaskaliana as the sky lightened. Pirgos village lay 800 yards beyond and the aerodrome a similar distance beyond that. Tom Beel with D Company 20 Battalion reached the wrecked gliders along the beach approach to the aerodrome, 'where they crash-landed, ploughing into one another in a tangled mass of wreckage'. They could also see burning Ju 52 transport aircraft as they neared the airfield perimeter. 'The sky was now turning grey, heralding the pre-dawn', he recalled. 'We were now well behind schedule.'[19]

Defending Pirgos were about 80 survivors from the abortive jumps mounted the previous afternoon by *Oberleutnant* Nägele and *Oberleutnant* Thiel's *6.* and *5. Kompanien* from *Fallschirmjäger Regiment 2*. With them was Franz Rzeha, who saw they were being attacked by Maoris 'coming from the east from three different directions'. They twice got close, barely metres away. 'We defended desperately, but were running out of ammunition.' A third attack came in, closely supported with heavy mortar fire. 'We fired to the last round', Rzeha remembered, 'until our machine gunner was mortally wounded by grenade splinters'.

The final attack began. A drunk Maori, bayonet fixed, advanced on me. I saw him and could smell the alcohol. I had my P.08 [pistol] in my hand, but the magazine was empty. I could already feel the bayonet on my stomach.

A New Zealand officer stepped between, pushed the bayonet aside and took him by the shoulder. 'Come on boy!' he said gently. He was saved.[20]

It was not always so. Private Melville Hill-Rennie with Lieutenant Upham's C Company saw the first of his actions that was to result in a VC award. It was still dark at the time and 'we could tell by the way the Jerries were shouting to each other that they didn't like the look of the situation'. Upham emerged from behind a tree:

> and hurled three Mills bombs, one right after another, into the nest and then jumped forward with his revolver blazing. Single-handed he wiped out seven Jerries with their Tommy guns and another with a machine gun ... Two machine gunners managed to hobble away in the darkness, but we got them later.

Upham felt just one more hour of darkness would have got them to the airfield. Resistance began to stiffen, because behind Pirgos *Hauptmann* Gericke's *IV Bataillon Sturmregiment* had moved forward, reinforced on their right by air-dropped anti-tank guns. Farran's lead tank had already come to grief nearing the Maleme churchyard. Pushing on ahead, he was engaged by two 37mm guns.

> The first shot holed them, mortally wounding the gunner, but he bravely continued to fire until he had dispatched one of the enemy guns. The tank tried to turn to get out of its impossible position, but another shell hit them in the middle.

This killed the gunner, 'the commander Sergeant Skedgewell was mashed up with the seat', the driver was hit in the foot and 'what was worse', Farran recalled, 'the tank was set on fire'.

How the driver with the tank on fire and a severely injured foot managed to drive out, Farran would never know, 'but he achieved it somehow'. Farran clambered on top and peered at the carnage inside:

> Skedgewell was writhing in mortal agony shouting for us to get him out. I tried to pull him from the top of the turret but his thin sweat-soaked khaki shirt ripped in my hands. He was obviously

beyond all hope and in great pain, so I gave him some Morphia
– perhaps too much – and … he died within 20 minutes.

The sun had now been up for an hour 'and all hell broke loose in
the sky'. A swarm of Me 109s repeatedly strafed them, so that 'hot
flakes of burning metal flew off the inside of the turrets into our
faces' with the incessant cannon strikes. 'Finally, like a wounded
bull trying to shake off a cloud of flies', Farran recalled, 'I crashed
into a bamboo field'. The third light tank pulled back.

'I lost my head', he admitted, 'I was so afraid that I could have
burrowed into the ground'. He frantically dashed away 'crashing
through the undergrowth, tumbling into ditches, and all the
time looking up at the sky at the black crosses on the aeroplanes'.
Running through an open stable door he threw himself inside an
iron feeding manger seeking protection, 'while the bombs carved
a big crater in the road outside'. Drawing breath, he realized once
the raid was over, 'that the other mangers were all occupied by New
Zealanders in a similar state'.[21]

By 7.30am Burrows' 20 Battalion was 'at a dead halt'. C and
D companies had reached the aerodrome, as Lieutenant Peter
Maxwell recalled:

We reached the clear part of the 'drome all right – there were
stacks of aircraft, some crashed, some not. I remember [Private]
P Amos saying 'I've carried this anti-tank rifle all this way and I
am going to have one shot'. He fired two shots into one aircraft
and made a mess of it.

Open ground about the airstrip was enfiladed with intense mortar
and machine-gun fire. D Company had to pull back into the cover
of bamboo groves. Disconcertingly aircraft continued to land,
disgorge troops and take off.

The only option now to continue the attack, having failed to
take the airstrip, was to switch left (south) and carry out a modified
form of the original plan. If the Maoris could get up Hill 107,
Burrows' 20 Battalion could also gain access to these heights and

subsequently move down to capture the airfield, or at least block any landings with observed fire. 28 (Maori) Battalion fought its way to the top of RAP Ridge behind Hill 107, but Stentzler's *II Bataillon*, clinging to the higher ground, repulsed any upward movement with fire. Leckie and Andrew's 23 and 22 battalions perched on the high ground on the left flank of the coastal plain advance had already concluded the attack had shot its bolt. It would be better to stabilize on the line held.

Tom Beel with D Company 20 Battalion had also reached as far as the aerodrome, where he had been wounded by mortar fire. Luftwaffe daylight air dominance had become increasingly intimidating. 'A German fighter plane skimmed over us at tree-top level, machine gunning', catching a soldier nearby, he recalled, 'in a hail of bullets': 'He ran past me screaming, holding his intestines in his hands. My last glimpse of him was the medical officer had thrown him to the ground and was doing what he could do for the soldier.'[22]

21 Battalion, the last to receive the orders for the counter-attack, had begun their own advance at 7am, and achieved significant gains, moving westward immediately south of Hill 107. They reached the village of Vlakheronitissa, as far forward as the D Company 22 Battalion positions, held on the first day of the invasion. This showed Stentzler's *II Bataillon* defending Hill 107 had its southern flank somewhat in the air, and it was being speedily reinforced by air-landed mountain troops, beginning to work their way up into the hills to the south. Hargest's conventional plan of attack along the coastal plain, into the teeth of Ramcke's assembling counter-offensive, had likely missed an opportunity. The weak point of the German line lay to the south, with insufficient infantry footfall to cover it. If the coastal thrust had been a feint, with the weight of force developing to the south of Hill 107, the outcome may well have been decisive. It had indeed been one of Hargest's original brigade counter-attack options, rehearsed prior to the invasion.

Two companies of 21 Battalion went through the village of Xamoudhokhori, brushing aside the German infiltration that had occurred during the night. The Tavronitis river bed was even coming into view. Les Young remembered that as they went in 'we were met with a hail of machine gun fire and a fair amount of mortar fire'. Casualties rose steeply:

> We received orders to withdraw to our previous position but the delay had been fatal – the enemy had appreciated the position and followed through smartly and it became a question of running the gauntlet to get around and over the hills to our original positions.[23]

Lieutenant Colonel Allen, realizing the coastal plain advance had stalled, paused to take stock. He decided to fall back and re-form his battalion on Vineyard Ridge, precisely where he had set out that morning.

Hargest's counter-attack was dying. The late start caused by the amphibious threat delayed battalions reaching the start line. This left precious few hours of darkness before the dead hand of the Luftwaffe blocked any movement in daylight hours in any meaningful strength.

The epic ancestral fighting spirit of the Maori fighting troops could not get them through. One of their company commanders Major Dyer remembered his men advancing 'in a scattered mob' going forward 'crying *Ah! Ah!* and firing at the hip' with 'the Huns with their fat behinds to us going for their lives down the gully and then our job to hold the Maoris in'.

Their ferocity and staying power impressed both sides. One British serviceman, Ken Stalder, remembered handing over a blanket to assist a mortally wounded Maori casualty:

> I was frightened of course. There were bombers and God knows what, and he was lying there. He knew he was going to die, so he took me by the hand. 'Don't be frightened' he said, and *he* was dying. I gave him my blanket to bury him. Wonderful. He was comforting me and he was dying.

Lieutenant Charles Upham remembered 'we had heavy casualties, but the Germans had much heavier'. A combination of overwhelming air attacks and the inability to completely clear the areas over which they advanced cost them dear. 'The real reason that the advance stopped, however, was that there were not enough men left to fight.'[24]

Despite the ferocity of the fighting around the airfield perimeter, two more German battalions were air-landing. Creforce HQ in the quarry just east of Hargest's Platanias 5 Brigade HQ had a grandstand view of the landings. Major Kennedy Elliott standing beside Freyberg and his aide de camp Jack Griffiths watched intently:

> We saw what was the real end – a stream of heavy black Ju 52s was coming in from the sea and landing on Maleme. They came with the regularity of trains and one landed every two minutes. Maleme even at our distance was the best imitation of an inferno that I ever want to see. We could count about seven or eight crash-landed planes on the beach – some of these were burning. The aerodrome was covered with crashed and burning planes. It was obscured at intervals by dust and smoke ... they landed enough men and ammunition and mortars and guns that day to put the decision beyond doubt.[25]

Hargest had the same view but was being unconscionably optimistic. Increasing numbers of German planes over at Maleme suggested to him they were preparing to pull out. There was very little evidence for this. The return of Farran's single tank ought to have at least prompted some foreboding. Neither did Hargest call upon the remaining three tanks of the squadron to go forward, it was too light. Shortly before 8am his Brigade HQ – as if it needed reminding of the air threat – was severely strafed and bombed by Messerschmitts; an ammunition truck was set on fire. Constant air traffic in and out of Maleme was proof the airhead was not yet in the hands of the attacking troops, even if returning wounded and prisoners suggested partial success. Hargest was at the end of his physical and emotional tether. He dallied with the idea that what he was viewing, amid the fires and smoke on the aerodrome, was not a reinforcement but an evacuation. At 10.42am he sent a message to Puttick at division stating there was a 'steady flow of enemy planes landing and taking off. Maybe trying to take troops off', he conjectured. 'Investigating', he added. Captain Dawson and others on the staff disagreed. Eighteen minutes later another message followed:

> From general quietness and because eleven fires have been lit on the drome it appears as though the enemy might be preparing evacuation. Am having further investigations made. Do any other reports from other sources show further evidence of this?

Division HQ was non-committal: 'no other indications as you suggest but it is possible'.

This was wishful thinking and the penalty accruing from poor communications forward. Men were observed running towards planes before they took off, but at the same time, light vehicles and stores were certainly being unloaded. At 11.50am Hargest further reported to division that 'reliable reports state aerodrome occupied by own troops now, held EAST side of drome'. Captain Dawson, the brigade major was sent forward in a Bren gun carrier to confirm, taking the last available 18 radio set. The next message 35 minutes later tempered the previous optimism: 'Recent messages make position confused', it read. Dawson was forward attempting to investigate. 'Troops NOT so far forward on left as believed.' Hargest continued to grasp at optimistic straws, making the same mistake of not personally going forward, which had resulted in the isolated Andrew precipitately pulling off Hill 107. 'Officers on ground believe enemy preparing for attack and take serious view', the brigadier messaged, 'I disagree, but of course they have a closer view'. Dawson was later strafed and sniped, and pinned down until late afternoon. The radio set and carrier were wrecked and he had no recourse but to return to Brigade HQ on foot.[26]

By mid-afternoon Hargest was aware that 20 Battalion had withdrawn in the face of increasing German pressure on his right flank. 28 (Maori) Battalion was holding positions from Pirgos on the coastal plain up to the high ground to its left occupied by 23 Battalion. 21 Battalion was still attacking. 5 Brigade was battering itself against an increasingly impervious brick wall. The arrival of ever more mountain troops was inverting force ratios; defenders were now starting to outnumber attackers. Hargest meanwhile was becoming increasingly uneasy about his rear, fearing Heidrich's *Fallschirmjäger Regiment 3* in Prison Valley might thrust towards Chania and cut the coast road behind him, between Platanias and Division HQ. Despite reporting partial success in the morning, the fact remained the 5 Brigade counter-attack had failed to take Hill 107 and the aerodrome remained a tenuously functioning German airhead.

Hargest equated his own exhausted mental state with that of his soldiers, but they still exhibited undiminished buoyancy. Convinced they could do no more, at 11.07am he recommended to Puttick that 5 Brigade should withdraw that night. This was without any face-to-face discussion with his superior. The decision was taken in an intelligence and situational awareness vacuum. Neither of the two brigadiers had gone forward at any crisis stage. Puttick conceded to his subordinate, and Freyberg, pressing for a stronger last-ditch offensive to carry the aerodrome, demurred to the assessment of his commanders on the ground: 'Maleme becomes [an] enemy operational aerodrome', he cryptically recorded in his diary.[27]

Hargest received the order to pull 5 Brigade back at 1am the next morning. 'Though few of us realized it then', recalled Lieutenant Geoffrey Cox with Freyberg, 'the final chance to hold Crete had gone'. The withdrawal from Hill 107 had set off the chain of events, which could be likened to pulling on a single strand of wool that unravels an entire jumper. Crete was lost from that point. From now on the campaign was to degenerate into a long rearguard action.[28]

Jäger Fink, still at the aerodrome with the *Sturmregiment* glider soldier remnants, observed the scene ahead with some satisfaction:

After dawn on the third day when the enemy attacks on Pirgos and Maleme and also Hill 107 remained pathetically hanging

onto the backs of the hills, he finally lost his head and nerve …
soon after, all the enemy units were on their way back.[29]

Hill 107 was securely in German hands and Maleme aerodrome
had been fought clear.

Inside four days the decision to evacuate would be taken and at
seven, it would be all over.

GENERALMAJOR JULIUS RINGEL, COMMANDER
5. GEBIRGSJÄGER DIVISION

22 May–Dawn 23 May 1941, Maleme Aerodrome
In Athens at *5. Gebirgsjäger Division* HQ on the Omnia Plaza,
Generalmajor Ringel received word for a revised mission: he was
to assume overall command on Crete. Transport for himself and
staff was arranged for 5pm on 22 May. Five Ju 52s escorted by
five fighters to cover the flight and landing would take off from
the Athens Phaleron seaside airport. Originally they had been on
stand-by to fly to Iraklion. Ringel's chief intelligence officer *Major*
Flecker recalled:

> The division staff is to fly to Crete. Thank God the order has
> come, finally we are off! We know we can do this, officers are
> calm and confident, despite this flight into the unknown, laying
> aside the tension of the last days.[30]

The *I Bataillon* from *Oberst* Krakau's *Regiment 85* had been due
to land at Iraklion on the second day. They had been ready to
load at 4am and boarded two hours later. At 9.15am they had to
unload because reports indicated that no landing strips had yet
been fought free by the first assault waves. Things began to look
bad. Several aircraft were lost during the first flights and about
50 rendered unserviceable. Loading plans had to be revised and
some men returned to their old accommodation area, while others
simply bivouacked beneath aircraft wings and slept. On this third
day, 22 May, at 5am the battalion once again received the order

to fly. At Tanagra the first aircraft started to roll between 7am and 8am, with dust impeding the flow, so that the last aircraft were climbing into the air at 10.30. Small wonder that Ringel was having doubts about the efficacy of this operation. Shocking news at the fate of the seaborne *Leichte Schiffsstaffel* coincided with the first good news from Student's Grande Bretagne HQ. Despite appalling *Fallschirmjäger* losses, an airhead had been fought free at Maleme.[31]

Ringel was caught up in the game of 'chess' that *Hauptmann* von der Heydte described typically occurred between airborne Luftlande, Luftwaffe and Wehrmacht headquarters. 'High command', he opined, 'thinks simply in terms of chess men – or so it seemed to us only too often during the war. Manpower will be thoughtlessly sacrificed if there appears any chance of gaining a favourable position in the bloody game.'

General von Richthofen commanding *VIII Fliegerkorps* was impatient with seeming hesitant directives emanating from Student's headquarters. His dive bombers had so mauled the British fleet that 'despite the shock of the destruction of the first convoy, the *Englander* cannot come back today or tomorrow again'. Seaborne reinforcements needed to get moving, 'ever growing numbers of troops on the ground are not attacking and lying about'. Von Richthofen's log noted he:

> presses with all means at his disposal … to have General Ringel sent to Maleme to get the ground fight there firmly organized with a firm hand. Prestige matters arise – Army versus Luftwaffe. General Jeschonnek [the Luftwaffe chief of staff] has been brought on board, even Field Marshal List, C in C Southeast.

Student was on the embarrassing verge of having to explain to Göring that his much-vaunted airborne command had been severely mauled, thus far for only limited return. 'Every military leader is to a certain degree an egotist', von der Heydte explained, 'who thinks only of his own task, his own objectives and his own troops'. Student, he observed, was 'impelled by the passion of an explorer or inventor'. What was at stake for him was 'to prove that it was possible to capture a defended island from the air with paratroops', never done before or even attempted. Von Richthofen was increasingly critical of Student's *Fallschirmjäger*: 'They are not sufficiently trained for ground operations and with no combat experience, poorly disciplined. The huge losses, especially in officers, have weakened them considerably.'

Student was preparing to move his HQ to the improvised airhead he had created at Maleme. His chief of staff Trettner would be left behind to handle and advise on airborne issues. Göring stopped the move to command troops directly from Maleme, insisting he remain at Athens, only he possessed the necessary overview of the situation across the whole island. Quite likely he had been alerted by Löhr and von Richthofen that events were not proceeding to plan. Ringel was Löhr's protégé, a former staff academy pupil. He even saw him off at Phaleron airport, '*Servus* Ringel! Goodbye, make it good!' He wanted a solid Wehrmacht supremo in charge, with feet firmly planted on the ground. Von Richthofen was also satisfied; 'finally General Ringel flies to Maleme, well protected', he smugly recalled: 'The impression now is things can get cracking with the necessary energy, clarity and decisiveness.'

Student was clearly out of favour. 'It is not hard to imagine how this battle tore at his nerves', von der Heydte recalled: 'In Athens it was being whispered that the High Command was threatening to open an enquiry into the reasons why success had not been achieved as quickly as anticipated.'[32]

The desperate air-land operation of the late afternoon and early evening the day before had brought in much needed reinforcements, but left the detritus of 20 or so wrecked Ju 52s strewn about the airfield and beaches. The fly-in on the 22nd was vital, even as fighting raged around the airstrip perimeter to fend off the 5 New Zealand Brigade counter-attack. The aim now was to alter the force ratios on the ground to the advantage of the invaders. If Ringel's future mission was to succeed, the force pendulum of odds needed to swing decisively to the German advantage. Swarms of Ju 52 transports began to approach Maleme from the north by about 9.40am, criss-crossing formations of fighters and Stuka dive bombers, engaging the stalled New Zealand counter-attacks. They were driven back from the aerodrome perimeter to Pirgos and onto the rear slopes of Hill 107 and ridgelines to the east.

Major Reinhard Wenning commanding the *z.b.V. 105* Ju 52 wing recalled 'we were told before take-off that the landing at Maleme on Crete would be in the face of effective enemy fire'. Once again the White Mountains came in sight, a light craggy perpendicular façade rising from the sea. Scanning the approaching mass, Wenning found 'We can slowly pick up the outline of the bay at Chania and in the middle of this, a huge black column of smoke.'

This had to be the Maleme airstrip, 'covered in vast clouds of smoke and dust, with a large number of Ju 52s circling above it'. Kurt Neher, a war correspondent in one of the aircraft behind, attached to *Regiment 100*, remembered their pilot assured them from the outset their 'crate' was 'as safe as a furniture van' or, more relevantly, as 'reliable as your mountain boots'. They had been inspired by their aircraft shadow flickering over the majestic ruin of the Acropolis back in Athens, 'looking history in the face', he felt. Two hours later their radio operator called out from the crew compartment: '*Get ready – Crete!*' To their right was the Spatha Peninsula, which they flew by at low level. Fountains of spray spurted up below as 'British machine gun bursts skim the water', Neher appreciated, 'but fall far too short'.

Wenning now understood why the Ju 52s were circling; 'on the airfield', he noticed, 'which is extremely small, there are a number of crashed planes, some of which are burning'. They were piling up: 'One Ju 52, which is landing collides with one of these wrecks, spins around and lies motionless in the middle of the narrow inadequate landing strip.' This blocked their own landing attempt, so they circled like the other Ju's to await an opportunity. Three times as Wenning's pilot came into land he was stymied by other pilots turning in from the side, barring their approach. 'On the airfield itself we can see shells exploding', he recalled, some aircraft were receiving direct hits as they taxied in, 'causing many dead and wounded; all in all a rotten situation'.

'*Hold tight!*' Neher's pilot shouted as they came in. 'The ground is over us' he saw as they descended, 'a strip of shore, vineyards and spray from the sea' as they appeared to accelerate down the dirt strip. Suddenly he pulled back on the control column, 'there is nowhere to touch down'. 'The Ju lifts itself, floating in a wide curve over the water. Brown fountains erupt and cover the transport aircraft already down with earth, smoke and dust.'

British artillery fire amounted to no more than five to nine old Italian 75mm field pieces, captured from the western desert. Several were faulty and with improvised sights. With the constant harassment from the air, which had great difficulty locating them, as even muzzle flash was well concealed, the best that could be achieved was broadly unobserved desultory fire. The small size of the obscured runway meant only one aircraft could land or take off at a time. Getting a battalion down meant a four-hour ordeal, as each aircraft could be individually engaged. On this day alone one of the Ju 52 groups lost 37 of an authorized strength of 53 aircraft, another unit lost 14. *Major* Snowadski's airfield control party spent the day bulldozing 137 wrecks out of the way. Student's *XI Fliegerkorps* haemorrhaged men and machines at an alarming rate. Despite the interference, the harassed airhead was handling up to 20 landings and take-offs an hour.[33]

'Despite all this chaos', Kurt Neher observed, 'some Junkers still manage to land men, weapons and ammunition, then take off in dense smoke from impacting shells'. Mouthing expletives their pilot came in yet again even as 'machine gun bullets pierce the right wing':

He grits his teeth. To hell with it – the bird *must* land. The Ju just manages to jump over a vine, touches the ground, bucks up and digs one wing into the earth. Grinding with the huge pressure, it snaps in the middle and rips the fuselage with a half turn to the left. Men, packs, life jackets and ammunition all slide forward, torn and crushed. No use to holding onto anything, all control from our bodies is gone, and the Ju is left standing on its head.

Miraculously nobody was injured. '*Raus!* Out!' Someone called.

Wenning's aircraft curved in, intending to land on the beach, where it crashed next to the sea in a shower of dust and spray. 'The right-hand steering column was forced into my body', he recalled, 'and I lost consciousness'. Most of those careering into the beach snapped off their undercarriages. The crew hauled him clear through the cockpit. When he came to, he noticed 'there was another machine lying about 30 metres out in the water from the beach, the waves were practically breaking over it'. 'Even from the air one already had the impression that the landing ground is alive', another eyewitness recalled. 'Small fountains of smoke and dust arise from the earth, and when they have cleared, it looks as though an army of moles has been at work.'

For most of the mountain troops, confined to the backs of aircraft, landing was a series of fleeting images and impressions. As planes touched down 'the roar of the engines' deaccelerating 'is added to the crackling explosions of bursting shells', Neher recalled. 'Splinters rip through cabin walls. A man cries out, grasping his shoulder. He is the first casualty.' Everybody scrambles out the door as fast as possible. The ground perspective is a world apart from what they saw more clinically, from the air:

The fountains of dust which from the air looked so small and innocuous have suddenly grown to enormity, and from their midst there explodes blinding red flashes of light. The crash of the explosions deafens you, yet, in the whining of the shells you seem to hear a sound like the cry of a tortured animal.[34]

Men threw themselves to the ground outside, seeking the nearest available cover. 'The distinctive smell of bursting shells burns your nose and gums', claimed one eyewitness.

One mountain soldier with Krakau's *Regiment 85* leapt out the door, struck by the sudden change from sitting quietly in an aircraft seat for two hours to the cold shower immersion to 'war! Suddenly we were standing in the middle of it'. Kurt Neher likewise recalled that 'only two hours ago we were lying under the shade of our planes on the mainland, now we are being fired at from everywhere'. They grabbed their rucksacks, jumped up, dashed forward a few paces and instinctively ducked when fresh salvos howled overhead. *'Get forward!'* was the shout, 'over there, the overhang, there is cover!' Everybody was looking about, 'where is the enemy?' the soldier wondered. They were waved over to be guided by *Fallschirmjäger* 'with tired fought out faces' which lightened as they came running up. All around parachutes were hanging and here and there dead bodies. They briefly waited while the wounded were driven up to the aircraft on vehicles for evacuation, engines roaring, poised to taxi. 'It was an evil twenty hours', one of the paratroopers said, 'very bad hours'.[35]

Between 10am and midday the *I Bataillon Regiment 85* under *Major* Dr Trek landed at Maleme under fairly punishing artillery fire. It was followed by *Major* Schrank's *1 Bataillon Regiment 100* during the early afternoon. Both battalions moved off to the southern foothills, intending an envelopment of the enemy on the coastal plain to stop the artillery fire. Twelve further Ju 52s landed the Field Hospital for the parachute force, then towards evening *Gebirgspionier* (Mountain Engineer) *Bataillon 95* landed alongside mountain artillery and *Major* Bode's battery of parachute artillery. Student's Corps Chief of Staff *Generalmajor* Schlemm landed just after midday, ostensibly to prepare the ground for Student's arrival. In reality he would provide command muscle to back up *Oberst* Ramcke, who would shortly have to deal with *Generalmajor* Ringel, due in later that evening.

Despite the harassment of the airfield, well over 3,000 reinforcements landed with light artillery, ammunition and equipment. This was to decisively tilt the scales numerically and materially to the German favour west of the island. Hill 107 was firmly in German hands. Even now Ramcke's *Sturmregiment* and *Oberst* Utz, the commander of *Regiment 100*, were conducting field recces, poised to begin a general offensive west to east against the capital Chania.

Generalmajor Ringel was in the air and due to land at 8pm that evening. The flight he recalled was 'tense and full of expectation'. *Generaloberst* Löhr's parting words were clear, the battle was now for him to win or lose. He had the resources and Ringel had been given the go ahead, previously in dispute, to wrap up the island from west to east. *Major* Flecker, his intelligence officer, was enjoying a picturesque and uneventful flight. 'The sea lit up dark blue', he recalled peering from the window, 'and a light breeze reflected up a myriad of shining light spray'. He observed the *General* was 'completely still, summoning strength for what lay ahead, the heavy decisions he would have to make'.

Landing the five transports was no easy task. Ringel recalled 'the Ju 52 that brought us to Crete had sometimes to endure 15 minutes of circling, and the risk of having to fly home with damaged undercarriage and torn wings'. The risks as he later pointed out, were considerable:

> The airstrip at Maleme was already too small for landings and take-offs with heavy machines. Imagine how the pilots with overloaded aircraft had to dive through enormous clouds of dust and murk, meet English shells and machine gun bursts, as the wreckage of 143 of our own and some enemy aircraft built up. More than one landed on fire, others belly-landed because the under carriage had been shot away, without their knowledge. Again others went off the runway onto the beach, *Ja* into the water, overshooting and bursting into flames.

Flecker remembered it took three attempts to get down; 'a masterly landing', all five aircraft safely landed. The command party was swiftly gathered together, 'the general and men shouldering their rucksacks'. Dusk was falling when they reached the olive grove HQ on the Tavronitis, where they were met by *Oberst* Utz from *Regiment 100* and Schlemm, Student's chief of staff. Flecker experienced a nervous night as 'report after report came in'. Ringel thought the information 'was so clumsily encrypted as to be rumour control', the fault of indiscretion by radio operators. According to them: 'The paratroopers in Iraklion and Rethymnon for example had been wiped out or surrendered, over 9,000 *Gebirgsjäger* had perished in the *Leichte Schiffsstaffeln* catastrophe and two new Australian divisions had landed on the south coast of Crete.'[36]

Ringel was sceptical about such reports and refused to be distracted. Flecker remained somewhat apprehensive: 'Maleme is only a tiny island ringed around by the enemy', he reflected, 'and constant reports gave no clarity to the general picture'. The overall island situation was not as grim as thought, but bad enough. *Oberst* Alfred Sturm at Rethymnon with *Fallschirmjäger Regiment 2* was a prisoner, with the final remnants of his command fighting last-ditch stands. At Iraklion, Brauer's *Regiment 1* was stopped in two pieces; Heidrich's *Regiment 3* was still locked at the bottom of Prison Valley. The main English force lay to the east, there were Greeks and guerrilla fighters to the south-west and British warships circled to the north. 'Every hour could bring an attack from all sides', Flecker conjectured. 'Although nothing appeared to be stirring in the pitch darkness outside, we all listened out with half an ear at the stillness: are they coming?'[37]

Ringel convened an orders group soon after landing and divided his force into three battle groups or *Kampfgruppen*. *Major* Schätte's mountain engineers were to be responsible for the aerodrome's close defence and Palaiokora to the west. In addition he was to clear Kastelli, where still no word had been heard about the fate of Mürbe's parachute detachment. All the parachute units would be combined to form a second *Kampfgruppe* under *Oberst* Ramcke and he was to attack eastward along the coastal road and plain. The third *Kampfgruppe* was *Oberst* Utz's three mountain battalions, who were directed to envelop the enemy on the coastal plain from the high ground to the south. Utz immediately set off, enemy artillery fire on the aerodrome had to be stopped.

Hauptmann Gericke and his mixed force of *I* and *IV Bataillon Sturmregiment* remnants, reinforced by the parachute companies dropped the day before, had already pursued the retreating New Zealanders into Pirgos, which he now firmly held. Stiff resistance ahead had stymied further advances. They prepared to attack again the next day, 23 May.

All Ringel had done in effect was to expand the tactical plan set in motion by Ramcke on arrival the day before. 'We could now see the reality and compare it to the picture we had developed [in Athens] over the previous few days', he remembered:

> There was the devastated airfield and the hill behind it, with the amazing heights taken at point 107. So far as could be seen, the hill was bald, burnt out and so remote looking that it looked as though no human foot had been set upon it.

He looked in the distance at the seemingly sheer heights his men would have to scale to secure a breakout. It seemed 'impossible for troops to cross such a merciless stony desert with no roads going east, not even a mule track'. Utz had already picked out a flanking move that would enable them to bypass the Allied line, which only extended a mile and a half beyond. The objective was Height 259 just a mile and a quarter south of Agia Marina on the coast. Penetrating further east would enable them to silence the artillery fire coming at them from depth, near the village of Modhion. The British had assumed this high ground was impassable, Ringel's mountain troops would demonstrate the contrary. They were sensitive to any move over the heights to their flank, which meant they might be cut from the coast and the port at Suda Bay.

Student had labelled Ringel a typical infantry 'plodder', who would methodically wrap up the island west to east. His 'oil-spot' strategy aimed to overwhelm opposition by landing everywhere, exploiting the unexpected. It had clearly failed. Such mountain terrain, for which Ringel's men were trained and accustomed, had to be systematically overcome. First, the heights had to be picketed, so as to dominate the low ground and valleys in between with observed fire. Ringel's men had already done this on mainland Greece, breaking through the Metaxas Line and traversing the Peloponnese. His tactical approach was totally at variance to Student's seemingly reckless assaults, fiercely conducted and with considerable élan. Ringel explained: 'Our basic principle on Crete was based in the first instance that it was better to haemorrhage sweat rather than blood. Better by day and night to march, rather than run against prepared positions with frontal attacks.'

This, however, was no mean task:

> My men had to carry all their weapons and packs on their shoulders and backs, when normally the logistic train or other means were used – the heavy machine guns, infantry and mountain artillery, ammunition, provisions and above all water – had to be taken across this stone desert, where every creature thirsted, who could not live off early morning dew.

War correspondent Kurt Neher with the mountain troops agreed: 'The men carrying mortar ammo had a hellish 66 pounds in their carriers, while the twin legs for the mortars weighed 55 pounds ... "Hot" remarked one of the men, "a lot like Africa with little beer".'

These loads were hauled 'through the hellish heat of the day and the cold at night, which was not much above freezing', Ringel recalled, sending out Utz's mountain battalions that night. 'My men marched', he stressed, 'which meant they tediously crawled through a landscape the devil had created in his anger'.[38]

Early the next morning *Hauptmann* Gericke watching from Pirgos village saw clear signs that the New Zealand battalions were withdrawing. Shortly after, the Ramcke *Kampfgruppe* began their advance. The mountain troops climbed to point 259 and from there were able to dominate Agia Marina on the coastal plain, Ramcke's objective. The mountain soldiers had crossed the rocky spine that separated the coastal plain from Prison Valley to the north, where they linked up with the remnants of Heidrich's *Fallschirmjäger Regiment 3*. Hargest's headquarters at Platanias was overrun on 24 May but they were long gone. Some 8,500 German troops air-landed at Maleme, achieving a clear German superiority to the west of the island.

A combined advance along the coastal plain linked with that emerging from Prison Valley to the south-west led to the fall of the Cretan capital at Chania on 27 May. Freyberg's force reserve was needlessly sacrificed in this fight and he elected to evacuate

Crete the same night. Successive and tenacious rearguard actions enabled the British, New Zealand and Australian troops to break clean, and begin their epic march, mostly on foot, with little water and rations, across the White Mountains to the rocky southern Cretan coastline, but there was no port. Pursued by the Luftwaffe and mountain troops, they were taken off by the Royal Navy from rocky inlets and small beaches next to the village of Sphakia.

Student had decided to sacrifice his parachute-landed troops at Rethymnon and Iraklion further east, so as to establish a decisive *Schwerpunkt* to the west of the island, his only toehold at Maleme, beneath Hill 107. Ringel's subsequent methodical advance from west to east missed the bulk of the Allied withdrawal to the south. Unaware of the British decision to evacuate, Ringel placed emphasis on a rapid eastward march along the coastline to rescue Student's cut-off paratroopers, not realizing Rethymnon had already been abandoned and the British force at Iraklion taken off by sea during the night of 28 May. Only two mountain battalions were dispatched south, to pursue the retreating British, Australians and New Zealanders to Sphakia. These closed in on the evacuation beaches during the night of 31 May/1 June, by which time some 17,000 troops had been evacuated. On 1 June the island was formally surrendered, leaving 12,000 behind to be taken prisoner.

The fight for Hill 107 and the aerodrome at Maleme was the key event that decided the outcome of the 12-day battle of Crete. Hargest's 5 Brigade began the fight with 3,183 men of which about 950 were eventually taken off at Sphakia. Total Allied casualties for the 12 days were 4,051 of which 1,751 were army, the rest Royal Navy. Perhaps 1,500 Greek army and civilians were killed and 5,000 taken prisoner.

Meindl's *Sturmregiment* suffered grievously, 72 of its officers had fallen of which 34 were killed. They lost 1,166 wounded and missing from which 667 never came back. Ringel's mountain troops suffered 580 killed and 458 wounded, the majority in the fighting for the west of the island around Maleme, Prison Valley and outside Chania. Süssmann's 7. *Luftlande Division* had 5,140 casualties with 3,094 killed. 503 Ju 52 transport aircraft had started the landings of which 271 were lost and maybe 147 damaged; the former represented 54 per cent of the whole. These were eye-watering losses. The German airborne arm had been rendered temporarily combat ineffective with these figures.

Generalleutnant Student had finally flown into Maleme on 25 May as a bystander, and Ringel was in overall command. Student made every effort to visit his troops and was visibly affected by what he encountered. *Hauptmann* von der Heydte met him again after the fall of Chania:

> I saw him before the battle at a briefing in Athens and I would say he was a man full of strength, full of confidence when he gave his orders. When I saw him after the battle he had changed absolutely. This battle made him years older, he looked like an old man, like an ill man.[39]

Göring and Hitler were shocked at the extent of the casualties, the highest number of German lives lost on a single day, 20 May, during the war to date. In the middle of July *Generalmajor* Ringel and *Generalleutnant* Student attended a ceremony at the Führer's HQ for Knight's Cross awards won on Crete. During the ensuing chat Ringel presciently remarked, amiably enough, that Crete would make a fine trip for sunbathers in the future. Hitler replied darkly 'for that the Crimea has been reserved'. Operation *Barbarossa*, the invasion of Russia, was already under way and occupied his sole attention. At the same ceremony Hitler remarked to Student that 'Crete has proved that the day of the paratrooper is gone', adding: 'The parachute arm is a weapon of pure surprise. The surprise factor in the meantime has worn itself out.'[40]

There would be no more large-scale airborne operations. Student was not spoken to or included in any meetings involving Hitler or Göring for more than a year. The father of German airborne forces' star was at a nadir.

What happened on and around Hill 107 not only decided the outcome of the battle on Crete, it also conceivably impacted on the future of the World War. The Allies came to precisely the opposite conclusion to Hitler and expanded their airborne forces. Churchill, after the first massive deployment of airborne troops in Holland and Belgium, had announced on 22 June 1940, barely 12 days into office, in a memo to General Ismay at the British War Office that 'we ought to have a corps of at least 5,000 parachute troops'. The Allied debacle on Crete accelerated this process both in Britain and the United States, resulting in a rapid expansion of the Allied airborne arm. This was to have a significant impact on the course and eventual outcome of the war from from D-Day on 6 June 1944 and beyond.[41]

The shadow of what happened on Hill 107 had yet to extend skeletal fingers over the village of Kondomari, two miles behind Maleme aerodrome and in sight of the hill.

Postscript

LEUTNANT FRANZ-PETER WEIXLER,
PROPAGANDA-KOMPANIE 690

2 June 1941, Kondomari Village, Two Miles South-east of Hill 107
On 14 June, two weeks after the cessation of hostilities on
Crete, *Leutnant* Franz-Peter Weixler, a *Bildberichter* (camera
reporter), snapped an image of *Hauptmann* Walter Gericke and
Oberleutnant Horst Trebes receiving the Knight's Cross at Chania,
for distinguished service on the island. Trebes wore his Luftwaffe
service tunic over captured British tropical dress shorts. Weixler
knew them both well, having landed by glider with Meindl's
Sturmregiment in the first assault wave. He was a 41-year-old
Leutnant with *Propaganda-Kompanie 690*, assigned to cover their
actions and photograph the fighting for the airfield at Maleme
and Hill 107. He produced a well-received photo report for the
Luftwaffe magazine *Der Adler* (The Eagle). The article *Hande Hoch!*
(Hands Up!) dramatically showed a British entrenched position
surrendering to German *Fallschirmjäger* after being grenaded into
submission. Readers back home were unaware the whole episode
had been staged, using pressed POWs from the cage established
outside Chania after its capitulation.

Gericke and Trebes were decorated for courage and leadership.
Wearing airborne helmets they looked the part; Trebes with stubble
on his chin smiles into the camera, looking askance into the glare of
the evening sun, with a long shadow behind. Ranks of *Sturmregiment*

troopers are formed to their rear, providing a suitably martial backcloth. Gericke looks like a man at peace with himself. Trebes, the former *Hitlerjugend* (Hitler Youth) 24-year-old, with the sun reflected on his boyish face appears slightly agitated, holding back suppressed energy. Weixler knew he had something to hide. Trebes exhibited many of the classic signs of post-combat stress disorder. Writing in 1945, Weixler commented in a transcribed interview: 'he received the *Ritterkreuz* from Göring for his "braveness" in Crete'. It was meant to be an ironic statement.

Like every good journalist, Weixler was alert to any potential 'scoop' for his wartime reportage. He recalled being approached by the adjutant of Stentzler's *II Bataillon* in Chania; shortly after his commander had been appointed *Ortskommandant* (town commander) of the capital: 'On June 1st or 2nd 1941, I was in my billet in the capital of Crete, Chania, when a young officer told me that that afternoon I would see something very interesting.' Intrigued, he asked for more information. 'He told me that a punitive expedition would be sent against several villages, since the corpses of parachutists, massacred and plundered, had been found.' Göring, alerted several days before, had ordered 'the sharpest of measures', which meant 'the shooting of the male population' in selected villages 'between 18 and 50 years of age was to take place'.[1]

Weixler came from Munich and was much older than many of the paratroopers on Crete. He was a World War I veteran who had worked as a banker between the wars. His more liberal Catholic and Christian-Democratic ideals got him into trouble with the regime. Despite joining the SS and Nazi Party in 1933, after Hitler's assumption to power, he was expelled four years later and lost his bank director job for political reasons. He turned to writing and photography to make a living and became an official army photographer with the outbreak of war in 1939 and an officer with the *Propaganda-Kompanie*, which brought him to Crete.

He was more aware than most about the horrific casualties the *Sturmregiment* had endured on Crete. The German public were not told until five days into the shaky operation, and remained blissfully unaware of the extent of the losses. Operation *Barbarossa*, the invasion of Russia, would be under way in two weeks' time, and would dwarf any meaningful publicity about the catastrophic losses in Student's *XI Fliegerkorps*, estimated at nearly four in ten soldiers. It was also the first time in the war that civilians had actually fought against a German occupation. Gruesome acts of brutality had been meted out to wounded and captured German prisoners by the civilian population. Exaggerated stories had already been circulating among German troops that excessively high *Fallschirmjäger* casualties were caused by Greeks finishing off, and in some cases torturing and mutilating, the helpless or wounded. When Weixler was made aware of likely punitive retribution he appealed to *Hauptmann* Gericke with the *IV Bataillon* 'that I had never seen a single massacred parachutist' having covered the fighting from Maleme to Chania. He had, however, 'seen dozens of dead comrades whose faces had partially decayed because of the tropical heat'. Gericke had his doubts and wanted nothing to do with the business. He had been shocked at the carnage wreaked on his unit and likely felt the Greeks were getting their just deserts.

The whole concept of irregular warfare was anathema to the ordered Prussian mind and its belief of 'fairness' in fighting. Warfare it was felt ought to be conducted along certain established rules, in uniform, and separate from civilian society. *Bushkrieg* or guerrilla warfare had been regarded with outraged disdain during the Franco-Prussian war of 1871 and again during the early occupation phases of Belgium in 1914. There was no place in the ordered German military mind or tactical doctrine to deal with civilian resistance. Indeed, many *Fallschirmjäger* thought it grossly unfair to be fired upon in the air, when descending helplessly by parachute. Irregulars were 'bandits' in German military parlance and treated as such. Student as incensed as Göring at the outrages meted on his men accepted the supreme Luftwaffe commander's edict on 'Reprisal Measure', which he himself ordered. 'I intend to proceed with extreme harshness', Student announced. Maleme and Kastelli were identified as areas where reprisals should take place. 'I put special importance on that – as much as is possible – the retribution is carried out by the actual unit that has suffered under the bestial atrocities.'

Trebes, the only officer still standing in Scherber's destroyed *III Bataillon*, was placed in charge of the *Sturmregiment*'s retribution zone. His group included a Luftwaffe inspector of *Oberleutnant* rank, an interpreter, two NCOs and 25 men from the *II Bataillon*, men who had fought free the summit of Hill 107. They were to head for the village of Kondomari, where the New Zealand 21 Battalion had been based, with Lieutenant Colonel Allen's HQ. During the first drops it was straddled by parts of Jung's *11.* and *Oberleutnant* Ganseweg's *12. Kompanien*, subjected to a storm of fire during the descent. Greeks joined in and even got in the way of the firing. Of 24 parachutists that came down in the village, one was captured alive and two wounded, the rest killed. Many of Trebes' brother officers and friends were killed here. Student considered 'extermination of the male population of entire areas' and 'burning villages' but permission for these 'can only be granted by me' but 'with succinct motivation'. *Generalmajor* Julius Ringel with the *5. Gebirgsjäger Division* had also ordered 'ruthless reprisals were to be taken against any act of defiance or brutality on the part of civilians', virtually as soon as he arrived on 23 May. 'Where a Greek civilian is found with a firearm in hand, he is to be shot immediately', he instructed. It was the conventional, almost predictable, Prussian approach to insurrectionary warfare. 'The same is to be done with attacks on wounded men', he ordered. Measures were to be enacted swiftly, Student directed: 'This whole case is a matter of the troops and not of the regular courts. They are not appropriate for beasts and murderers.'

It is claimed that several senior officers stormed out of the conference at Student's Corps HQ in disgust at this order. *Oberleutnant* Horst Trebes was of like mind to his supreme commander. There were those fresh from the savagery of battle with no compunction about leading or being part of execution squads. Franz-Peter Weixler was not one of them.[2]

Faced with Gericke's apparent indifference, Weixler sought out *Ortskommandant* Edgar Stentzler. He told him that a commission of the German Foreign Office had already flown in the day before to begin the judicial investigation into the alleged massacres of German troops. Stentzler insisted he had his orders. Weixler remembered:

> I told Stentzler that during the first days of the fighting I had seen vultures pick on the corpses of our comrades. I reminded the major that we had seen innumerable half-decayed comrades, but that we had never seen a single murder or massacre, and that I would consider it outright murder to execute Göring's order.

Stentzler rebuked him, reminding him that he had only temporarily been assigned to the *Fallschirmjäger* for the Crete operation, and should concern himself only as a photographer.

'This was none of my business' he was haughtily informed.

Weixler next sought out Trebes, appealing to him not to carry out the order, pointing out that 'blood revenge still existed on Crete'. Trebes bellowed at him in front of the assembled group, waiting to board a number of captured British lorries, that he 'had lost over 100 men of his company because of these swine and had freely volunteered to carry out the retaliatory expedition and would brook no interference whatsoever'.[3]

The young Trebes was schooled in the era of National Socialism and a former Hitler Youth. He had grown into a fierce and uncompromising fighter. He had led one of the early assaults on Hill 107 from behind a hostage screen of unarmed captured Allied soldiers driven ahead and occasionally inspired his men to greater efforts at pistol point. Of the 580 men in his *III Bataillon*, 250 had perished, 135 were still missing and 115 wounded. Trebes found himself the only surviving officer, and suffering from combat fatigue he was consumed with grief and hatred. He wanted revenge – and would have it.

As the trucks turned left off the coast road to Maleme from Chania they drove steadily uphill. Several times they paused to look at dead bodies of paratroopers strewn about, some wearing parachute harnesses, with parachutes draped over trees. 'As a photographer assigned to my division', Weixler recalled, 'I was permitted to accompany this *kommando*'. The sweet stench of decay permeated the olive groves at the roadside. They passed a naked corpse completely covered in crawling maggots, 'again a pillaged comrade!' Trebes insisted, and 'he incited the men against the civilian population', Weixler recalled. He took a total of 41 photographs of what happened next. Sequential exposed photographs from negatives that Weixler had to hand in to the authorities were passed to a friend in Athens, and were eventually found in the Federal German Archives in 1980. They dramatically chart the events that occurred in Kondomari during the brutal reprisal action on 2 June 1941.[4]

Kondomari, just under two miles south-east of the Maleme airstrip, is situated on a ridge, on the next high ground behind Hill 107. The trucks squeaked to a halt in the village and the first photo frames show, as Weixler recalled, 'the men got off, and ran into the few houses of the little community'. From the top end of the main village street, sky-blue sea can be clearly seen ahead to the north. The next few snaps show the village community being rounded up and escorted to an assembly point, set up in a quiet olive grove at the north end of the village, opposite the turning to the local church. 'They got all men, women and children onto the little square', Weixler observed. The older Greek men are dressed in distinctive traditional baggy pants or 'crap-catchers' as the British troops labelled them. Women and children are simply dressed. *Fallschirmjäger* escorts, wearing distinctive airborne helmets, are shepherding them along with rifles and Schmeisser machine pistols, wearing parachute smocks over captured British-issue shorts.

Tension rose when 'a German soldier brought out the coat [Luftwaffe tunic jacket] of a parachutist, which he had picked up in one of the houses', Weixler recalled, 'which had a bullet hole in the back'. He took a photograph of the small group poring over the holed uniform jacket, clearly adorned with officer shoulder epaulettes. It may have been *Oberleutnant* Ganseweg's, whose *12. Kompanie* had jumped into the village and was known to Trebes, or a member of Scherber's staff. 'Trebes had the house burned down immediately', Weixler remembered.[5]

The next sequence of photographs shows younger able-bodied Greek men being separated from old men, women and children. One of them has been singled out, a worried-looking young man with thick unruly hair, wearing a simple jacket over sweater and trousers. 'One man admitted having killed a German soldier', Weixler commented. The other villagers, sitting on the grass-lined ditch next to the road, had identified him as such. Wild scenes had occurred in these streets two weeks before. Paratroopers crashing into rooftops and sprawling onto the roads had been set upon by the enraged locals. New Zealand soldiers had to check fire to avoid hitting civilians in the scrambling melee. German soldiers were hunted through the village houses. Trebes is seen glancing about, wearing a captured British empire pith helmet for its sun protection, like the interpreter interrogating the unfortunate Greek. The suspect admitted fighting with New Zealand troops and shooting a German. He is nervously fingering a handkerchief as a worry bead substitute, his face is creased with concern, knowing that after the burning of the house he was as good as dead. Weixler tried to convince Trebes 'it was not possible to convict any of the others of any crimes or plundering', recommending he 'stop the contemplated action and give the orders to return, taking with us only the one man'. Once feted a hero on the day it happened, the man had given himself up, prepared to die as one.

Trebes was having none of this. Those selected in the round up were told to stand, while as the pictures show, Trebes moved further along the road to address the village crowd, numbering the old, young and women. Through the interpreter it was announced the menfolk would be shot in reprisal for killing five German soldiers. They were instructed to have them buried inside two hours. After this, the main body is shepherded away by *Fallschirmjäger* gesticulating the direction with machine pistols. The pictures show the news has been received with remarkable equanimity, there is no sign of protest or emotion.

Some two dozen paratroopers can now be seen lining up across the road in the next photo and Weixler panned his camera towards the hostages, who are displaying the first signs of agitation, having realized they are about to be shot. The *Fallschirmjäger* are edging around them. They sit looking worried with hands across knees, some have removed their hats and are remonstrating. Told to line up in the little field that forms part of an olive grove they plead in waistcoats and shirt sleeves to be allowed to live, forcefully arguing with the German soldiers. 'When Trebes turned his back for a few moments', Weixler claimed, 'I made it possible for nine men to get away', the teenagers.

Weixler now turned the camera and focused on Trebes and the firing squad, some of whom were kneeling in front and others to the rear standing. 'He had them form a half circle', he recalled, readying weapons and levelling rifles and machine pistols at the hostages.

Trebes seems to be shouting orders to open fire as weapons are raised in aim. Weixler turned his camera to the hostage group and froze the scene in time, men plunging and reeling under the concussive impact of a fusillade of bullets that raises dust puffs in the grass around them and shatters masonry on the stone wall behind them. Two men can be seen vainly crouching behind the thick gnarled trunk of an ancient olive tree, seeking elusive cover. Dust impacts are erupting from the torsos of panicked individuals caught grotesquely in mid-stride as they attempt to dodge, dive for cover or run. To the right of one frame [30] are a number of hostages who have leaped over the low stone wall and are streaking through the olive trees behind them. Concentrated bursts of fire seek them out, lashing repeatedly across the 20 or so inert forms crumpled and piled in the foreground, sprawled in a line from the thick olive trunk that provided initial illusory cover. 'After about fifteen seconds', a long drawn-out cacophony of shooting and cries, Weixler remembered, 'everything was over'. He turned and 'asked Trebes, who was quite pale, whether he realized what he had done'. Dust and grey cordite smoke remains hanging above the crumpled untidy forms, who were repeatedly shot at by the firing squad for some time after the first volley. Trebes replied 'he had only executed the order of Hermann Göring and avenged his dead comrades'.[6]

Two men, Georgios Galanis and Aristeides Vlazakis, despite being wounded, astonishingly got away. They managed to run to an overgrown field about 200 yards away, where Galanis stayed hidden. Vlazakis, however, losing too much blood, attempted to get back to his house and have the wound treated. The Germans followed up the blood trail and after some chasing and shooting, Vlazakis was brought down, having reached his already shot-dead brother's house, next door. The Luftwaffe inspector and a paratrooper can be seen in Weixler's final frame administering *coup de grâce* pistol shots to the head. Galanis was to survive.

After the Germans had boarded their trucks and driven off from the village another survivor was found. Evripides Daskalakis had managed to crawl a few yards from the execution site. He asked for water and died a few moments later. The entire core of the village's young and mature men had been taken, 23 men from just four families. Five belonged to the Daskalakis family, three each from the Vlazakis and Apostolakis and two from the Papadakis families. The youngest was 21 years old, the oldest 47. The following day Trebes and his men sacked the village at Kandenos, where the locals had held off the German advance to the coast for three days. The population had fled, but Trebes killed the eight who had been unable to leave.[7]

The shadow of what had happened on and around Hill 107 was to extend to the Reich. By 13 July the *Sturmregiment* was back in its home barracks in Germany. Six days later Trebes with the other Knight's Cross heroes were received by Hitler in a special ceremony at the *Wolfsschanze* Headquarters near Rastenberg.

The troops were received as heroes in their garrison towns, although the formations of flower-adorned *Fallschirmjäger* were sadly depleted and likely filled out with replacements. The German public were ignorant at the true scale of the losses, which was diluted in the publicity surrounding the invasion of Russia. There was a celebration party for the survivors of the *III Bataillon* at Halberstadt, overseen by their very young newly appointed acting battalion commander Horst Trebes. Like in all these events, there was a recklessly conducted celebratory drunken party, where soldiers were allowed to let off the steam accrued by days of desperate fighting for Hill 107 and Crete. As the party was winding down *Oberjäger* Karl Polzin, one of the original feted heroes of *Stoss-Trupp 4* that had captured the Belgian fort at Eben-Emael with *Sturmgruppe Granit*, was paralytically drunk, and was sleeping it off behind a locked bathroom door. Trebes, equally blind drunk, could not get in and failing to rouse Polzin, fired his pistol into the floor, to gain entry. A ricocheting round killed Polzin, one of the mythical hero figures of Eben-Emael, which Trebes was not. Polzin had allegedly remarked upon Trebes' 'bravery' in Crete and had baited him by alluding to his role in the reprisals that took place afterwards. Nothing was proven.

Despite being the battalion commander, Trebes could not go unpunished. At the subsequent court martial he barely escaped the death penalty, benefitting from his stature as a Knight's Cross holder. *Reichsmarschal* Göring personally interceded on his behalf. Trebes' mother-in-law had been an army nurse in 1917 and had met the young Göring as a fighter pilot, recovering in hospital after he had been shot down. She sought his help to save her son-in-law. Trebes was stripped of his commission and every award, including the Knight's Cross, reduced to the ranks, and sent to Russia. Weixler meanwhile was later dismissed from the Wehrmacht for political reasons and graded 'unworthy for military service', but he had secreted prints of what he had seen in Crete.[8]

The Key Decision-Makers and Takers

And What Became of Them

LIEUTENANT-COLONEL LESLIE ANDREW

The 22 Battalion commander defending Hill 107 whose withdrawal likely unravelled the entire campaign to hold Crete.

Andrew's conduct during the battle was embroiled in controversy, surfacing briefly in Egypt after the evacuation. He never changed his view about the decision to pull off from Hill 107. There was sympathy for his obvious post-combat trauma and the fact his command had been left isolated, and respect for his VC profile. He and 22 Battalion conducted themselves well during the early phase of the North African campaign later that year. When Hargest's 5 Brigade Headquarters was overrun by Rommel's tanks at Sidi Aziz during Operation *Crusader*, Andrew's battalion continued to fight, in the chaos that followed at Menastir nearby. Andrew assumed temporary command of 5 Brigade in a tight spot, for which he was awarded a DSO. He relinquished command of 22 Battalion in February 1942 and returned to New Zealand on promotion to colonel, assuming command of the Wellington Fortress Area, a training appointment. His reputation appeared to remain intact. He commanded the New Zealand victory contingent during the London parade in 1946 and was promoted brigadier, to command the Central Military District. He retired in 1952 and died on 8 January 1969 aged 71.

OBERST ULRICH BUCHHOLZ

Buchholz led the first Ju 52 wing to land at Maleme aerodrome under New Zealand artillery fire during the afternoon of the second day.

Buchholz recovered from his wounds after Crete and was rewarded with promotion to *Generalmajor* in December 1941. He retained command of *Kampfgruppe z. b. V. 3* until the end of 1942, after which he was appointed to be the Air Transport Chief Mediterranean Region under *Luftflotte 2* until April 1943, and then Air Transport Chief Southeast. His wide flying and organizational experience was needed for the Tunisian air reinforcement operations and fly-in of airborne troops and supplies to sustain the German *coup d'état* against Italy in 1943, when the country changed sides. Bucholz was rewarded with the German Cross in Gold and promoted *Generalleutnant* in February 1944. Thereafter he assumed staff and training appointments commanding Pilot Training Divisions 2 and 1. He was captured at war's end on 8 May 1945 and released in 1947. He died in June 1974 at Mölln.

OBERSTLEUTNANT EHAL

The commander of the ill-fated Leichte Schiffsstaffel seaborne German landing force that was badly mauled by a Royal Navy Cruiser hunter force off the coast of Maleme on the second night of the battle.

Ehal's flagship the *Papapopiou* or *S105* was sunk and his body never recovered. He was last seen in the officer's galley.

HAUPTMANN WALTER GERICKE

Gericke commanded the IV heavy weapons Bataillon of the Sturmregiment and played a major role, alongside Stentzler, in capturing Hill 107 and spearheading the advance towards Chania.

Gericke was awarded the Knight's Cross just outside Chania on 14 June 1941. After returning to Germany he fought in Russia

THE KEY DECISION-MAKERS AND TAKERS

during the winter retreats of 1941/42. In September 1943 he led the raid to capture the Italian High Command at Monte Rotondo, after Italy elected to leave the war. He was in command of *Fallschirmjäger Regiment 11* by the following January and in November a much-reduced *Kampfgruppe* Gericke was fighting at the Anzio-Nettuno bridgehead. He was promoted *Oberst* in February 1945 and in command of *Fallschirmdivision 11* until April, never more than a much-reduced battle group. He was captured by the British at Oldenberg on 8 May 1945 after his unit contested the Allied Rhine crossings. He joined the post-war German Army *Bundeswehr* in April 1956 and retired as a *Generalmajor*. He died on 19 October 1991 at Alsfeld/Ghessen.

BRIGADIER JAMES HARGEST

The overall New Zealand commander conducting the defence of the Maleme aerodrome and coastal sector.

Despite being strangely inactive during the crucial fight for Hill 107 Hargest was awarded a bar to his DSO. The following November he and his headquarters were captured at Sidi Aziz in the Libyan desert. Incarcerated near Florence in Italy he escaped in March 1943 and made it across occupied France to reach Spain. He was then attached, as an observer, to the British 50 Division, which landed in Normandy on D-Day in 1944, where he was wounded in June. Two months later he was killed by shellfire, having already lost one of his sons earlier the same year. His experiences in captivity and during his escape gave him an insight he felt he never had before, lacking awareness of his strengths and weaknesses. Writing to his wife before D-Day he claimed she would 'I hope find me a better husband than before'. Like many of the key commanders defending and attacking Hill 107 he had acted uncharacteristically. He had learned a lot, confiding to his wife he had 'never been embittered by any experience' and felt 'life is still very wonderful to contemplate'.[1]

CAPTAIN STANTON JOHNSON

The New Zealand company commander defending Maleme aerodrome.

Johnson, commanding C Company 22 Battalion, was caught up in the 5 Brigade debacle at Sidi Aziz in November 1941 and taken prisoner. He survived the war and was in the regular post-war New Zealand army in 1947, appointed Director AEWS in 1953.

MAJOR WALTER KOCH

The victor of Eben-Emael and commander of the first German gliders to land on Hill 107.

Koch was in hospital for months after Crete recovering from a serious head wound. By early 1942 he was leading his battalion in Russia and by 1943 was promoted to *Oberstleutnant* commanding *Fallschirmjäger Regiment 5*. He was part of the air-land reinforcement of Tunisia, designed to screen the flank of Rommel's defeated *Afrika-Korps* after El Alamein. He was a tough soldier, whose leadership style did not always gel with his soldiers, although they knew he fought with courage and ruthless determination. He often reminisced with old friends over Eben-Emael rather than Crete. His glider pilot Heiner Lange recalled discussing glider landing possibilities on the rock of Gibraltar, and even an attempt to snatch Churchill, landing on the green opposite the House of Commons. Koch was a reckless lover of speed, and decapitated himself in an accident on the Berlin–Magdeburg autobahn on 23 October 1943, ramming the rear of a truck while driving a low sports roadster.[2]

LIEUTENANT COLONEL D.F. LECKIE

The 23 Battalion commander holding the ridgeline to the rear of Hill 107.

Leckie had been wounded on Crete on 25 May, but managed to escape the island with his battalion. He relinquished command of

23 Battalion to command Sub-Area 75 with the Middle East Force in August 1942, remaining until March 1944. He was promoted Colonel and awarded an OBE.

LIEUTENANT ED McARA

New Zealand platoon commander in A Company defending Hill 107.

Ed McAra is commemorated on Face 13 of the New Zealand Athens Memorial. He left a wife and child in New Zealand.

GENERALMAJOR EUGEN MEINDL

The commander of the elite Sturmregiment, *seriously wounded at the start of the assault on Hill 107.*

Meindl remained in hospital for months and was transferred from Athens to Germany. His daughter Ursula remarked 'how heavy a burden he carried, from the severe losses of his officers and men'. He was not complimentary about Student's conduct of the battle, claiming 'we were crucified everywhere'. By the winter of 1941/2 he was fighting a *Kampfgruppe* in Russia, returning home in September with typhus. His wartime record was distinguished, command of *XIII Fliegerkorps* and then the *II Fallschirmkorps* in Normandy. His corps fought the Americans to a standstill around Saint Lô in the Normandy bridgehead and it was virtually destroyed at Falaise. It was re-formed as part of Student's 1st Parachute Army blunting the *Market-Garden* ground advance to Arnhem. He remained a prisoner of war from May 1945 to September 1947. Although his doubts about Hitler's regime rose after Stalingrad, innate nationalism remained. He refused to cooperate, unlike many other German generals, with the post-war US analysis of tactical lessons learned from the war when the Cold War broke out. He died at Munich on 24 January 1951.[3]

OBERSTABSARZT DR HEINRICH NEUMANN

The German medical officer who led the final occupation of the summit of Hill 107.

Neumann accompanied Meindl's Division to Russia as the senior doctor in early 1942 and by autumn he was appointed senior doctor to *XIII Fliegerkorps*. He was active, and showed the same energy and initiative in Russia, ensuring patients were evacuated and cared for during multiple crises on the Eastern Front, including at Minsk in 1943. By war's end he was the senior doctor for the *II Fallschirmkorps*. After the war he practised in Hamburg. In 1959 he joined the post-war German Army, the *Bundeswehr*, and in 1962 was a senior instructor at the German Airborne School at Altenstadt/Schongau, retiring as an *Oberstabsarzt* on the reserve. He died at Düsseldorf on 19 May 2005.

OBERST BERNHARD RAMCKE

Parachuted into Maleme to take the place of Meindl, the Sturmregiment commander was severely wounded on the first day. He turned round the fortunes of the operation with zeal, initiative, energy and reinforcements.

Following Crete Ramcke was awarded the Knight's Cross and assigned to the Italian *Folgore* Division, involved in the plan to seize Malta by air, which was rejected by Hitler. Ramcke was instead sent with a *Fallschirmjäger* brigade to reinforce Rommel's *Afrika-Korps*. In late October 1941 his brigade was caught up in the precipitate retreat from El Alamein. Ramcke effected the escape of his foot-borne unit by hijacking a British supply train in its entirety and driving through 185 miles of Allied occupied territory. The *Fallschirmdivision 2* was formed in France during the spring of 1943 by a promoted *Generalmajor* Ramcke. It was used as part of the German airborne *coup d'état* in Rome, when Italy switched sides during the summer. His command was then switched to Russia and the Ukraine. After the Allied breakout from the Normandy beaches the following summer in 1944, Ramcke held the vital port at Brest with *Fallschirmjäger Regiments 2* and *7*, denying access to the Allies until 20 September, when he was captured. An unrepentant National Socialist and favoured by Hitler, he was awarded both sword and diamonds to his Knight's Cross. Ramcke underwent lengthy and strenuous war crimes investigations, because of excesses against French civilians. He was not convicted, but the French held him until June 1951. He never compromised on vocal right-wing views. He worked in the concrete industry post-war, and writing four books. He died of cancer on 4 July 1968 at Kappeln and was buried near Kiel.

GENERALMAJOR JULIUS RINGEL

The 5. Gebirgsjäger Division *commander who air-landed and took on overall command from Student on Crete, bringing the campaign to a victorious conclusion.*

Ringel was awarded the Knight's Cross two weeks after the British evacuation. In March 1942 his division was in Russia, fighting a series of successful defensive battles on the shores of Lake Ladoga outside Leningrad. He was promoted *Generalleutnant* in 1943 and was on the winter line in Italy during 1943/44 in the mountains south of Rome fighting again alongside *Fallschirmjäger* at Monte Cassino. Four months later he commanded a corps in Croatia ending the war in an administrative command with *Wehrkreis XVIII* at Salzburg. 'Papa Julius' was always relaxed with his men, but drew the line on one occasion when one of his muleteers failed to recognize and salute him, mistaking him for the unit padre, because of the Knight's Cross he wore round his neck. After the war he wrote his memoires in retirement at Bad Reichenhall. A committed Austrian National Socialist, he was unapologetic and investigated by the Allies and Greeks for war crimes. He died in 1967 at Gmain, Bavaria.

MAJOR OTTO SCHERBER

Commander of the III Bataillon Sturmregiment, *which was wiped out when it parachuted directly over prepared New Zealand defensive positions.*

Scherber was given a hasty burial near where he fell. His remains were later recovered and interred at the German military cemetery on Hill 107 at Maleme, overlooking the airfield.

MAJOR EDUARD STENTZLER

The II Bataillon Sturmregiment *commander whose unit parachuted west of Hill 107 and occupied the summit.*

Immediately after the battle Stentzler was appointed the *Stadtkommandant* of the captured Cretan capital of Chania, and he was awarded the Knight's Cross on 9 July. On return to Germany his reinforced battalion was flown to Leningrad during the winter of 1941/42 to combat a Russian bridgehead at Petruchino, between Lake Ladoga and the city. Casualties were heavy and on 3 October 1941 Stentzler was severely wounded, losing an eye. Evacuated back to the Reich he died in hospital two weeks later at Tilsit-Konigsberg.

GENERALLEUTNANT KURT STUDENT

Student commanded XI Fliegerkorps, *the first and only airborne formation to successfully attack and reduce a strategic objective, the island of Crete, from the air alone.*

Hitler and Göring cold-shouldered Student for some considerable time after Crete due to the mauling *XI Fliegerkorps* received. Perhaps one in three or four of its fighting soldiers were casualties and the *Sturmregiment* was rendered temporarily combat ineffective. Hitler dismissed Student's daring scheme to capture Malta in 1942 out of hand. Student's corps was instead committed to both Russia and Italy as a shock-troop 'fire brigade', to shore up fronts in crisis. Its proven training methods and fighting élan meant, despite Hitler's belief that the day of mass airborne operations was over, it was expanded until in 1944 it numbered ten divisions. Student oversaw the Skorzeny glider raid that rescued the Führer's friend Mussolini in March 1944 at Gran Sasso. He was then appointed to raise a new airborne force so as to keep the airborne divisions in Russia and Italy supplied with replacements. Student commanded the *1. Fallschirmjäger Armee* in Belgium and Holland in September 1944, delaying the *Market-Garden* Allied ground advance on Nijmegen and Arnhem. In November 1944 he was named the commander of Army Group H. He was a *Generaloberst* when taken prisoner by British forces at Schleswig-Holstein. He faced eight charges of war crimes, including on Crete, and was found guilty of three. The previous New Zealand 4 Brigade Commander Lindsay Inglis interceded on his behalf and he only received five years, which was commuted so that he was released in 1948. He was therefore extremely fortunate and lived with good health in retirement, revered internationally as the 'father' of airborne forces and regarded as the 'old eagle' living at home in Bad Salzuflen. He had few interests outside the military and died in 1978 at the age of 82.

GENERALLEUTNANT WILHELM SÜSSMANN

The commander of the Flieger Division 7 *attacking Crete, killed in a glider crash en route.*

Süssmann's body was recovered, alongside those of his staff, from the island of Aegina and was buried in the Dionyssos-Rapendoza war cemetery at Athens. He never made it to Crete.

OBERLEUTNANT HORST TREBES

Led one of the groups that occupied the summit of Hill 107 and conducted the brutal reprisal operation at Kondomari village near Maleme aerodrome.

Despite being stripped of his rank and Knight's Cross following the drunken shooting accident that killed fellow paratrooper Polzin, Trebes commanded a company with the *Sturmregiment* in the Russian winter fighting of 1941/42. He was emotionally shattered by the court martial episode and constantly and recklessly exposed himself in the face of the enemy. In November 1942 he was promoted to *Hauptmann*. Von der Heydte took him on as his *III Bataillon* commander in March 1944, looking for seasoned commanders. Trebes was caught up in the intense fighting around the US bridgeheads in Normandy following the D-Day invasion in June. He lost his life during an Allied strafing attack on 29 July, south-west of Sainte Lô and is buried at La Cambe, France.

LEUTNANT FRANZ-PETER WEIXLER

The photographer who filmed the brutal massacre at Kondomari on 2 June 1941.

After the reprisal Weixler had prints made from the original film by a friend in Athens. These he kept, alongside a copy of the division reprisal order, despite signing an official statement to the contrary. On return to Germany he was dismissed from the Wehrmacht that summer for political reasons. When he tried to publicize the massacre in 1943 he was arrested by the Gestapo and incarcerated in Munich's Neudeck Prison in January 1944 awaiting trial. Because his files in Berlin and Nuremberg had been destroyed by air raids he was kept in Gestapo custody as a *Toteskandidaten*, earmarked for execution. He narrowly escaped being shot before Munich was occupied by the Americans on 30 April 1945. Weixler submitted his affidavit, which was used during Göring's war crimes trial. During the post-war period Weixler re-engaged with CSU Christian-Democratic politics. He even returned to Crete in 1957 as an act of contrition, meeting with Georgios Galanis, the sole survivor of the massacre. Despite being received with customary hospitality he was asked to leave when he admitted he was the photographer. Weixler died on 23 April 1971 aged 71 at Bad Reichenhall. His negatives were unearthed in 1980 at the *Bundesarchiv* in Koblenz by a Greek journalist, who publicized the incident.

MAJOR REINHARD WENNING

Commanded a Ju 52 Air Transport wing dropping Stentzler's parachute troops around Hill 107 and later landing at Maleme aerodrome under artillery fire.

Wenning's group flew back to the Reich in June and in 1942 he was appointed Operations Officer with an Italian Air Force staff. The remainder of his war was uneventful, taken up with staff and administrative appointments including as an instructor on army staff course training. In April 1944 he was promoted to *Oberstleutnant*, and by June was on the staff of *Luftflotte 3* in a liaison capacity. He seems to have survived the war.

Table of German Military Ranks

Feldwebel	Sergeant
General	General
Generalfeldmarschall	Field Marshal
Generalleutnant	Lieutenant General
Generalmajor	Major General
Generaloberst	General
Hauptmann	Captain
Jäger	Private
Kapitänleutnant	Lieutenant Commander
Konteradmiral Süd-Ost	Vice Admiral South East
Leutnant	Lieutenant
Major	Major
Oberfeldwebel Senior	Sergeant
Oberjäger	NCO
Oberleutnant	Lieutenant
Oberst	Colonel
Oberstabsarzt	senior medical officer
Oberstleutnant	Lieutenant Colonel
Unteroffizier	Lance Corporal

Notes

PROLOGUE

1 Krug, quoted in G. Forty, *The Battle of Crete*, p. 100.
2 Sturm, quoted in C.N. Hadjipateras and M.S. Fafalios, *Crete 1941: Eyewitnessed*, p. 243.
3 Rechenberg, *Fallschirmjäger im Osten, Korinth, Die Wehrmacht 1941*, pp. 200–1.
4 Sturm, quoted in Hadjipateras and Fafalios, p. 243.
5 Gotzel and A. von Roon, 'Fallschirmjäger Einsatz bei Korinth 1941', *DF* 3, Mai/Jun, 1984, pp. 6–8.
6 Rechenberg, *Fallschirmjäger im Osten, Korinth, Die Wehrmacht 1941*, pp. 200–1. Wehrmacht report, *Kreta: Ein Heldenlied unsurer Zeit*, 1942.
7 Von Richthofen Diary, 26 April 1941, quoted in C. Stockings and E. Hancock, *Swastika over the Acropolis*, p. 465.
8 Sturm, in Hadjipateras and Fafalios, p. 243. Rechenberg, p. 201.
9 Krug, quoted in G. Forty, p.100. Rechenberg, p. 201.
10 Oliphant and Battery Commander, quoted in Stockings and Hancock, p. 466.
11 Von Roon, *DF* article, 1984, pp. 6–8. Rechenberg, p. 203.
12 Krug, quoted in G. Forty, p. 100.
13 F. Fink, *Der Komet auf Kreta*, p. 62.
14 Baron Von der Heydte, *Daedalus Returned*, pp. 30–33.
15 Ibid.

THE HILL

CHAPTER I

1 Hargest, letter to wife, 28 Apr 1941.
2 C. Pugsley, *A Bloody Road Home*, p. 100. Mohi, quoted in
W. Gardiner, *Te Mura o te Ahi: The Story of the Maori Battalion*,
p. 58.
3 G. Cox, *A Tale of Two Battles*, p. 33.
4 J. Hetherington, *Airborne Invasion*, p. 11.
5 Cox, p. 56.
6 Bassett, quoted in A. Ross, *23 Battalion*, p. 59.
7 Hetherington, p. 28.
8 Northumberland Hussar, quoted in J. Sadler, *Operation Mercury*,
p. 67.
9 Comd 6 Bde, report 29 Apr 1941, HQ 6 Bde.
10 Cox, p. 33.
11 Pugsley, p. 111; Cox, pp. 67 and 57.
12 Hargest orders, quoted in Ross, p. 62. Cox, p. 48.
13 Battalion soldier, quoted in Ross, p. 62. 21 Bn CO change, J.F.
Cody, *21 Battalion*, p. 83.
14 Cox, pp. 53 and 55. Davin, quoted in P. Monteath, *Battle on
42nd Street*, p. 37. British Report, C. MacDonald, *The Lost Battle*,
p. 147. Leggat, quoted in J. Henderson, *22 Battalion*, pp. 36–37.
J.F. Cody, *28 (Maori) Battalion*, p. 88. Hetherington, p. 24.
15 Aircraft figures, S.W. Mitcham, *Eagles of the III Reich*, p. 73 and
D.M. Davin, *Crete*, p. 85. M. Comeau, *Operation Mercury*, p. 58.
Ditty, T.F. Beel, from C.N. Hadjipateras and M.S. Fafalios, *Crete
1941: Eyewitnessed*, p. 58.
16 Student, quoted in H. Götzel, *Generaloberst Kurt Student and seine
Fallschirmjäger*, pp. 152–53.
17 Göring and Trettner, quoted in MacDonald, p. 4.
18 Trettner, in G. Roth, *Die Deutsche Fallschirmtruppe 1936–1945*,
p. 107. Hitler and Trettner, Götzel, p. 199 and Roth, p. 109.
19 Zei, 14-year-old Athens girl, quoted in J. Käppner, R. Probst and
B. Weidinger, *Die Letzten Augenzeugen*, p. 69.
20 Ringel interview 1960, quoted in W. Ansel, *Hitler and the Middle
Sea*, p. 207.
21 Drakopoulos, quoted in G.C. Kiriakopoulos, *Ten Days to Destiny*,
pp. 38–40.
22 Korten, quoted in Götzel, p. 334.

23 Student's view of airfield, quoted in Ansel, p. 248. Troop figures Maleme, quoted in E.M. Winterstein and H. Jacobs, *General Meindl und Seine Fallschirmjäger*, p. 19.

24 Comeau, p. 58. Pender, quoted in Henderson, pp. 34–35.

25 Observer, Patrick Leigh Fermor, introduction to G. Psychoundakis, *The Cretan Runner*, p. 19.

26 Hetherington, pp. 26–27.

27 Cody, pp. 78 and 85. Johnston, Diary 29 Apr and 7 May, quoted in Ross, p. 59.

28 McAra, letter 9 May 1941, quoted in G. Forty, *Battle of Crete*, pp. 134–35.

CHAPTER 2

1 Von Seelen, *Kriegstagebuch des Einsatzes 'Kreta'*, 23 Apr–20 May 1941 signed Meindl. BA 8A-2025.

2 Seibt, Allied Interrogation Report Genmajor Conrad Seibt, US Army APO 696, 1 Sep 1945.

3 G. Müller and F. Scheuering, *Sprung über Kreta*, p. 5.

4 W. Gericke, *Da Gibt Es Kein Züruck*, pp. 15 and 18. E. Reinhardt, *Memoirs of a Former German Paratrooper*, p. 28.

5 Bosshammer, quoted in J.-Y. Nasse, *Fallschirmjäger in Crete*, pp. 36 and 34. Von der Heydte, *Daedalus Returned*, pp. 27–28. Von Seelen, *Kriegstagebuch*, 29 and 30 Apr, 1 May 1941.

6 PK film, L. Bayer, *Kreta, Ein Heldenlied unsurerer Zeit*, 1942. Meindl, quoted in E.M. Winterstein and M. Jacobs, *General Meindl und seine Fallschirmjäger*, p. 21. F. Fink, *Der Komet auf Kreta*, pp. 52–56.

7 Churchill, quoted in A. Clark, *The Fall of Crete*, p. 48. Fink, pp. 57–58.

8 Reinhardt, p. 11. M. Pöppel, *Heaven and Hell*, p. 46. Von der Heydte, pp. 25–26.

9 Von Seelen, *Tagebuch*, 2–3 and 9 May 1941. Von der Heydte, pp. 34–35. Fink, pp. 65–66, Müller and Scheuering, p. 21. Pöppel, p. 53.

10 Von Seelen, *Tagebuch*, 10 May 1941. Gericke, p. 21. Bosshammer, quoted in Nasse, pp. 36 and 38.

11 Von Seelen, 11–14 May 1941. Gericke, p. 22.

12 PK film, *Deutsche Wochenschau* 561, 4.6.41. Meindl and orders, *Regimental orders for Operation Mercury, Appendix 2, Periodical*

Notes on the German Army No 38, War Office 20 Mar 1942. Fink, p. 82. Von Seelen, *Tagebuch*, 19 May 1941.

13 G. Cox, *A Tale of Two Battles*, p. 57.
14 Andrew, quoted in C. Pugsley, *A Bloody Road Home*, pp. 44–45.
15 Andrew, note to Hargest, quoted in D.M. Davin, *Crete*, p. 55.
16 M. Comeau, *Operation Mercury*, p. 60.
17 Thomas, TV interview in J. Isaacs, *Touch and Go!: The Battle for Crete 1941*, New Zealand TV 1991.
18 Twigg, quoted in C.N. Hadjipateras and M.S. Fafalios, *Crete 1941: Eyewitnessed*, p. 59.
19 Vourexaki-Nikoloudaki, quoted in ibid., p. 78. Kounalakis interview, in C. Epperson (Dir), *The 11th Day*, Archangel Films 2006. G. Psychoundakis, *Cretan Runner*, p. 26. Gerogianni and Veisaki, interviews in Epperson, *The 11th Day*.
20 Intelligence picture, Davin, pp. 77–78.
21 Rutter, quoted in P. Ewer, *Forgotten Anzacs*, pp. 310–11.
22 Comeau, p. 80.
23 Cox, pp. 19–21, 29–30.

CHAPTER 3

1 J. Ringel, *Hurra, die Gams!* pp. 64, 8 and 68.
2 Medical Corporal, Major Flecker and S. Dobiasch, *Gebirgsjäger auf Kreta*, pp. 41–44.
3 Ringel, pp. 68, 46 and 72.
4 Recce reports, according to Student, I. McD. G. Stewart, *The Struggle for Crete*, p. 89. Staff assessments, quoted in Flecker and Dobiasch, pp. 22 and 24.
5 Ibid., p. 30.
6 *Oberjäger* P., and soldier quotes, ibid., pp. 31–32 and 34.
7 Rosenhauer, quoted in J.-Y. Nasse, *Fallschirmjäger in Crete*, pp. 50 and 48.
8 Jäger B. Regt 85, quoted in Flecker and Dobiasch, pp. 34–36.
9 Ringel, p. 67.
10 McAra, letter 9 May 1941, quoted in G. Forty, *Battle of Crete*, pp. 134 and 136.
11 Bn log, 19 May 1941, pp. 21–23. Murphy, letter 9 May 1941, quoted in ibid.
12 Priests, Bn log 19 May 1941.

13 McAra letter to wife, 11 May 1941, quoted in Forty, p. 136.

14 Jackson, Diary 13 May 1941, quoted in Forty, p. 139. Johnson's C Coy, Bn log, 9–19 May 1941. M. Comeau, *Operation Mercury*, p. 80.

15 Comeau, pp. 80–81. Bn log, 9–19 May. McAra, letter to wife, 11 May, quoted in Forty, p. 137.

16 McAra, final letter 11 May, quoted in Forty, pp. 136–37. Galatas village incident, C. MacDonald, *The Lost Battle*, p. 166.

17 Wenning, *Kreta Mai–Juni 1941*, BA RL 10/548.

18 Vassilas, quoted in C.N. Hadjipateras and M.S. Fafalios, *Crete 1941: Eyewitnessed*, pp. 41–42.

19 Heyking, quoted in T. Saunders, *Crete: The Airborne Invasion 1941*, p. 48.

20 Rodenbusch, quoted in Nasse, p. 45.

21 Baron von der Heydte, *Daedalus Returned*, pp. 40 and 43–44.

22 Drakapoulos, quoted in G.C. Kiriakopoulos, *Ten Days to Destiny*, pp. 38–43.

23 Von Seelen, *Kriegstagebuch des Einsatzes 'Kreta'*, 19 May 1941. Gericke, *Da Gibt Es Kein Züruck*, p. 33. Von der Heydte, pp. 47 and 49. Rothert, postcard 13 May 1941, Maleme German Cemetery, Crete.

24 Scheuering, quoted in G. Müller and F. Scheuering, *Sprung über Kreta*, p. 42. Reinhardt, *Memoirs of a Former German Paratrooper*, p. 31. Fink, *Der Komet auf Kreta*, pp. 68–70. Braun change of plan, von Seelen, *Kriegstagebuch*, 19 May 1941.

25 Fink, pp. 94–97. Rauch, quoted in Nasse, p. 58.

26 Student, quoted in W. Ansel, *Hitler and the Middle Sea*, p. 275.

27 Weather and RN scare, Ansel, pp. 275–76 and H. Götzel, *Generaloberst Kurt Student und Seine Fallschirmjäger*, pp. 232–34.

CHAPTER 4

1 Andrew, quoted in D.M. Davin, *Crete*, pp. 92–93. M. Comeau, *Operation Mercury*, p. 83.

2 Johnson, letter HQ NMD, 24 May 1948. Eyewitness, quoted in J. Henderson, *22 Battalion*, p. 41.

3 3,000 bombs, quoted in Henderson, p. 41. Sinclair, letter to Maj Gen Kippenberger, 30 Mar 1948.

4 Andrew, Bn Log, 20 May 07.45, p. 25 and P. Monteath, *Battle on 42nd Street*, P. 95.

5 Eyewitness, quoted in J. Hetherington, *Airborne Invasion*, p. 57.
   Andrew, quoted in Henderson, p. 65. Young, quoted in J. Sadler,
   Operation Mercury, P. 70.
6 Francis, quoted in G. Forty, *Battle of Crete*, pp. 163–64. Comeau,
   p. 85.
7 Howell, quoted in I. McD. G. Stewart, *The Struggle for Crete*,
   p. 148. Comeau, p. 85. Leggat, letter to New Zealand History
   Branch, 17 Jun 1948.
8 Johnson, letter 24 May 1948.
9 Howell, quoted in Stewart, pp. 148–49.
10 Sargeson, quoted in Henderson, p. 41.
11 Twigg, letter to New Zealand War History Branch, 14 Nov 1948.
12 Pemberton, quoted in Henderson, p. 61.
13 Comeau, p. 85.
14 Craig, interview by W.E. Murphy, 17 Feb 1948. Sargeson, quoted
   in Henderson, p. 56.
15 Johnson, letter 24 May 1948. Leggat, letter 17 Jun 1948. Forty,
   p. 164.
16 Twigg, letter to R.D. Hastings, New Zealand War Historical
   branch, 14 Nov 1948.
17 Andrew, log and assessments, Bn Log, 09.00 20 May 1941, p. 26.
18 Glider numbers, quoted in Von Seelen, *Tagebuch*, 17 May 1941.
19 Fink, *Der Komet auf Kreta*, p. 100.
20 Wachter, quoted in M. Cavendish, *Images of War*, Vol 1, p. 157.
   Fink, p. 100.
21 Schuster, quoted in K. Kollatz, *Feldwebel Erich Schuster*, p. 25.
   Fink, p. 102. Wachter, p. 157.
22 Fink, p. 104.
23 Wachter, p. 157. G. Cox, *A Tale of Two Battles*, p. 85.
24 Glider losses, *Vorlaufiger Erfahrungsbericht XI Fliegerkorps, Einsatz
   Kreta*, 11 Jun 1941. BA RL 33/116.
25 Archer, Diary Athens 20 May 1941, *Balkan Journal*, p. 217.
26 Süssmann's glider mishap, H. Götzel, *Generaloberst Student und
   Seine Fallschirmjäger*, pp. 244–45. G.C. Kiriakopoulos, *Ten Days to
   Destiny*, pp. 105–7. C. Shores, B. Cull and N. Malizia, *Air War for
   Yugoslavia and Greece*, p. 341.
27 Student, *Gefechtsbericht XI Fl. Korps – Einsatz Kreta*, BA RL
   33/98.

28 Rieckhoff, *Erfahrungsbericht, Anlage 1 an KG.2,* 1 Jun 1941, pp. 18–20 and 26. BA RL 8/243.

29 Wachter, p. 157.

30 Schuster, quoted in Kollatz, p. 25. Wachter, p. 157. Fink, pp. 105, 108 and 110.

31 Fink, pp. 111 and 114–15. Wachter, p. 157.

32 Koch's After-Action Report, *Gefechtsbericht I/Sturmregiment,* p. 51 para 3 and p. 54, LL/LTS Fachbibliotech Altenstadt Germany.

33 Wachter, p. 157.

34 Haddon, TV interview in J. Isaacs, *Touch and Go!: The Battle for Crete 1941,* New Zealand TV 1991.

35 Howell, quoted in Stewart, pp. 149–50.

36 Sinclair and 15 Platoon, Letter to Maj Gen Kippenberger 30 Mar 1948 and Henderson, p. 40.

37 Johnson, letter to HQ NMD 24 May 1948.

38 Craig, interview, by W.E. Murphy, 17 Feb 1948.

39 Sherry, quoted in P. Ewer, *Forgotten Anzacs,* p. 314. Minson, TV interview, *Touch and Go!.*

40 Butler, quoted in Sadler, p. 73.

41 Ashworth, quoted in C.N. Hadjipateras and M.S. Fafalios, *Crete 1941: Eyewitnessed,* pp. 85–86.

42 Johnson, letter 24 May 1948. Andrew, Bn Log 09.30 20 May 1941, pp. 27–28. Sargeson, quoted in Henderson, pp. 56–57.

43 Sinclair, letter 30 Mar 1948. Johnson, letter 24 May 1948. Comeau, p. 88. Hetherington, p. 58. Butler, quoted in Sadler, p. 73.

CHAPTER 5

1 R. Wenning, *Kreta Mai–Juni 1941,* p. 5. BA RL 10/548.

2 Von Schutz, TV interview in J. Isaacs, *Touch and Go!: The Battle for Crete 1941,* New Zealand TV 1991. Grande photos, personal album Lt Grande, *Foto-Archiv* Band 3, p. 8.

3 Baron von der Heydte, *Daedalus Returned,* pp. 52–53. Wenning, p. 6.

4 Wenning pp. 6–7. Von Heyking, quoted in C.N. Hadjipateras and M.S. Fafalios, *Crete 1941: Eyewitnessed,* pp. 68–69, Maue, quoted in J.-Y. Nasse, *Fallschirmjäger in Crete,* p. 58.

5 Student, *Vorläufiger Erfahrungsbericht des XI Fliegerkorps*, p. 2, BA RL 33/116.

6 Wenning, p. 8.

7 Wenning, ibid. Von Könitz, quoted in A.D. Steinweg, 'Wir Holen Ihn Heraus!' *Deutsche Fallschirmjäger*, Issue 3, Mai/Jun, 1982.

8 Maue, quoted in Nasse, p. 58. Von Schutz, TV interview, *Touch and Go!*.

9 Wenning, pp. 8–9.

10 Leggat, letter to WEM War History Branch, 17 Jun 1948. Gordon, TV interview, *Touch and Go!*. Comeau, *Operation Mercury*, p. 88 and 97. Hanton, J. Henderson, *22 Battalion*, p. 63, Slade, ibid., pp. 71–2, 11 Pl Comd, Ibid, p. 72.

11 Andrew figures, Bn log 09.30 20 May 1941, p. 28 and 10.55 report recorded in 5 Bde War Diary. Comeau, p. 88.

12 Chittenden and Croft, quoted in Henderson pp. 63–64.

13 Andrew, quoted in I. McD. G. Stewart, *The Struggle for Crete*, pp. 170–71.

14 Twigg, letter to New Zealand War History Branch, 14 Nov 1948. Leggat, letter 17 Jun 1948.

15 Fleet Air Arm officer, T. Saunders, *Crete: The Airborne Invasion 1941*, p. 77. Comeau, p. 92. Twigg, letter 14 Nov 1948.

16 Leggat, letter 17 Jun 1948 and Twigg, letter 14 Nov 1948.

17 Andrew, Bn log 20 May 09.30–12.00 pp. 28–29 and Henderson, p. 69.

18 Comeau, p. 95. Sinclair, letter to Maj Gen Kippenberger, 30 Mar 1948.

19 Twigg, letter 14 Nov 1948. Andrew comment, Johnson letter to HQ NMD, 24 May 1948. Andrew's concerns, Bn Log 20 May 1941, 09.30–1200, pp. 28–33.

20 Meindl, quoted in F. Kurowski, *Der Kampf um Kreta*, p. 38.

21 Lingg, quoted in J.-Y. Nasse, *Green Devils! German Paratroopers 1939–45*, p. 45. W. Gericke, *Da Gibt es Kein Zurück*, p. 38.

22 Fink, *Der Komet auf Kreta*, p. 120. Von der Heydte, pp. 59–60.

23 Gaerte, TV interview 1991, *Ultimate Blitzkrieg: Battle of Crete*, Episode 1 *Invasion*, Pilot Productions, 2019.

24 Gericke, p. 53.

25 Lingg entanglement, Nasse, *Green Devils!*, pp. 45–47.

26 Craig, interview by W.E. Murphy, 17 Feb 1948. Gericke, p. 42.

27 Fink, p. 131.
28 Radios, *Funkverkehr des Regt-Stabes während des Einsatzes Kreta von 20–27.5.41.* BA RL 33/34.
29 Fink, pp. 138 and 140.
30 Lingg, quoted in Nasse, *Green Devils!* p. 47.
31 Mürbe episode, eyewitness account provided by Josef Rettinger, private correspondence with author, Dec 1993.
32 Fink, p. 165. Lingg, quoted in Nasse, *Green Devils!* p. 47.

CHAPTER 6

1 Wikiriwhi, quoted in J.F. Cody, *28 (Maori) Battalion*, p. 90.
2 Irving, TV interview in J. Isaacs, *Touch and Go!: The Battle for Crete 1941*, New Zealand TV 1991.
3 W.B. Thomas, *Dare to be Free*, p. 13.
4 Watson, quoted in D.M. Davin, *Crete*, pp. 122–23.
5 Gibbons, quoted in P. Monteath, *Battle on 42nd Street*, p. 20. New Zealand soldier, quoted in I. McD. G. Stewart, *The Struggle for Crete*, p. 151.
6 Thomas, p. 15 and TV interview, *Touch and Go!*. Dummy trial, H.-O. Muhleisen, *Kreta 1941*, p. 46 note 90. Also F. Fink, *Der Komet auf Kreta*, p. 37.
7 Davin, quoted in Monteath, p. 93. Thomas, interview, *Touch and Go!*.
8 Follas, interview by W.E. Murphy, 12 Feb 1948. Cunningham, quoted in A. Ross, *23 Battalion*, p. 65.
9 Thomas, pp. 16–18.
10 Leckie's signal, M. Comeau, *Operation Mercury*, p. 180.
11 Follas, interview by W.E. Murphy, 12 Feb 1948. Irving, TV interview, *Touch and Go!*.
12 Dawson and Cunningham, quoted in A. Ross, p. 66.
13 Fink, p. 147.
14 Aircraft mounting plan, *Verladeplan 1 Welle*, Muhlleisen, p. 90. Breuing and Rothert, display boards from Maleme War Cemetery Crete.
15 Witzig and Wenzel background, J.E. Mrazek, *The Fall of Eben Emael*, p. 111 and O. Gonzales, T. Steinke and I. Tannahill, *The Silent Attack*, p. 165.

16 Goltz background, Comeau, pp. 88–89.
17 H. Wenzel, 'Auszug aus Meinem Tagebuch von Damals', *Der Deutsche Fallschirmjäger*, No. 5, Sep/Okt 1983, p. 10.
18 Ibid. Witzig, quoted in H. Götzel, *Generaloberst Kurt Student und seine Fallschirmjäger*, p. 239.
19 Kienzen, quoted in J.-Y. Nasse, *Fallschirmjäger in Crete*, p. 47. R. Wenzel, Diary *Kreta Mai–Juni 1941*, BA RL 10/548.
20 Aircraft returns, W. Ansell, *Hitler and the Middle Sea*, p. 296. K.-H. Golla, *The German Fallschirmtruppe*, p. 438 and C. Shores, B. Cull and N. Malizia, *Air War for Yugoslavia, Greece and Crete 1940–41*, p. 344.
21 Rothert, Maleme German War Cemetery. Eyewitness, quoted in H. von Dach, 'Der Luftandeangriff auf Kreta', *Schweizer Soldat*, Special Issue, 1971, p. 44.
22 Zollinger, *Funkverkehr des Regts-Stabes während des Einsatzes Kreta von 20–27.5.41*, 8 Jul 1941, BA RL 33/34.
23 Koundouras, quoted in C. MacDonald, *The Lost Battle: Crete 1941*, p. 176.
24 Tzitzikas and Peterakis, interviews, C. Epperson (Dir), *The 11th Day*, Archangel Films 2006.
25 Kastelli massacre, J. Rettinger, letter to author, Dec 1993. C. MacDonald, p. 177. G.C. Kirakpoulos, *Ten Days to Destiny*, pp. 129–32.
26 Kapetanakis, Ninolakis and Papagiannakis, interviews, *The 11th Day*.
27 Doulakis, quoted in C.N. Hadjippateras and M.S. Fafalios, *Crete 1941: Eyewitnessed*, p. 80. Mourellos, *The Battle of Crete*, p. 85. G. Yiannikopoulos, *The Greek Forces in the Battle of Crete*, Academia Paper website. Marridakis, interview, *The 11th Day*.
28 Marridakis, interview, *The 11th Day*.
29 Markantonaki, quoted in Hadjippateras and Fafalios, p. 80.
30 Tzitzikas, interview, *The 11th Day*. G. Psychoundakis, *The Cretan Runner*, pp. 25 and 27.
31 Papagiannakis, interview, *The 11th Day*.
32 Guerilla fighters' comment, quoted in *Teil II Gefechtsbericht des XI Fliegerkorps – Einsatz Kreta*, p. 5. BA RL 33/98. Student, ibid., Feindbeurteilung, *Anlagen zum Gefechtsbericht XI Fl.Korps – Einsatz Kreta* 11.6.41 BA RL 33/99, pp. 8–9.

33 Woman fighter, quoted in E. Papagiannakis, *Military History Magazine*, pp. 24–25. G. Yiannikopoulos, *Greek Forces in the Battle of Crete May 1941*, Academia Paper website.

34 G.L. Soubassis, *Civilian Resistance in Crete 20 May 1941– 15 May 1945*, USMC Command and Staff College Paper, Academia website. Data on missing, total missing was 395 men, *Gefechtsbericht Sturm Regt 7.6.41.* BA RL 33/31.

CHAPTER 7

1 M. Comeau, *Operation Mercury*, p. 104.

2 Bn Log 20 May 1941, 12.00 to 21.00, p. 34.

3 Comeau, p. 180. Johnson, letter to HQ NMD Auckland, 24 May 1948.

4 Andrew/Hargest signal exchange, Comeau, p. 182. Johnson, letter, 24 May 1948.

5 Johnson, letter, 24 May 1948. Donald, quoted in C. Pugsley, *A Bloody Road Home*, p. 147 and interview, M. Hutching, *Kiwi Oral Accounts*. Andrew, 22 Bn Log, p. 35. Sinclair, letter to Maj Gen Kippenberger, 30 Mar 1948.

6 Johnson, letter, 24 May 1948. Donald, quoted in Pugsley, p. 147.

7 Johnson, letter, 24 May 1948. Andrew, 22 Bn Log 20 May 41, 21.00, pp. 36–37.

8 Andrew signal, Comeau, p. 183.

9 G. Cox, *A Tale of Two Battles*, p. 68.

10 Hargest under fire, D.M. Davin, *Crete*, pp. 131–32. Cox, p. 68–69.

11 Dawson and Hargest, quoted in I. McD. G. Stewart, *The Struggle for Crete*, p. 178.

12 Moss, quoted in Pugsley, p. 137.

13 Inglis, quoted in Stewart, p. 196. Puttick told, quoted in Pugsley, p. 137. Freyberg, quoted in Stewart, p. 170.

14 Andrew, 22 Bn Log, 20 May 1941, 07.45, p. 25. Cox, p. 111.

15 Andrew and Hargest, quoted in Comeau p. 183.

16 Hotel details, Baron von der Heydte, *Daedalus Returned*, p. 110 and L. Archer, *Balkan Journal*, p. 209.

17 Radio traffic, *Funkverkehr des Regiments – Stabes während des Einsatzes Kreta vom 20.–27.5.1941. Erfahrungsbericht XI Fliegerkorps 11.6. 41.* BA. RL 33/34 (henceforth *Funkverkehr Kreta*). All

timings one hour ahead of Allied time. 12.15 Gr West an XI, 16.20 and 19.10, 20 Mai 1941. HQ portrait, von der Heydte, pp. 110 and 112.

18 Aircraft losses, C. Shores, B. Cull and N. Malizia, *Air War for Yugoslavia, Greece and Crete 1940*, Losses chart p. 404.

19 J. Ringel, *Hurra, die Gams!*, p. 84.

20 Staff officer, quoted in von der Heydte, p. 112. Student, quoted in J. Sadler, *Operation Mercury*, p. 124.

21 Student, quoted in A. Clark, *The Fall of Crete*, p. 101.

22 *Funkverkehr Kreta*, 22.35 20 Mai 1941.

23 Student on Kleye, quoted in Sadler, p. 125.

24 Student, testimony to French historian R. Cartier Kathimerini Athens, 2 Jun 1985, quoted in C. Hadjipateras and M. Fafalios, *Crete 1941: Eyewitnessed*, p. 101.

CHAPTER 8

1 *Funkverkehr Kreta* 8.50 and 18.32 German time.

2 W. Gericke, *Da Gibt es Kein Zurück*, pp. 54 and 58–59.

3 F. Fink, *Der Komet auf Kreta*, pp. 238–39 and 252–53.

4 Schuster, quoted in K. Kollatz, *Feldwebel Erich Schuster, Landser*, No. 351. Baron von der Heydte, *Daedelus Returned*, p. 97.

5 H. Wenzel, 'Auszug aus mein Tagebuch von Damals', *Deutsche Fallschirmjäger*, No. 5 Sep/Oct 1983, p. 10.

6 Fink, p. 240. Gericke, p. 74.

7 Tank attack, Gericke, pp. 74, 59 and 67. Fink, p. 257.

8 Schuster, quoted in Kollatz, p. 34. Gericke, pp. 65 and 75. Counter-attack comment, quoted in C. MacDonald, *The Lost Battle: Crete 1941*, p. 202.

9 Wenzel, *Tagebuch*. Schuster, quoted in Kollatz, p. 34.

10 *Funkverkehr Kreta*, 22.35 20 Mai 1941, German time.

11 Craig, interview W.E. Murphy, 17 Feb 1948. Johnson, letter to HQ NMD Auckland, 24 May 1948.

12 Johnson, ibid. Donald, interview Megan Hutching.

13 Rutter, quoted in P. Ewer, *Forgotten Anzacs*, p. 318.

14 Twigg, letter to R.D. Hastings, 14 Nov 1948.

15 Cpl Andrews and Crarer, quoted in J. Henderson, *22 Battalion*, p. 74.

16 Andrew, quoted in C. Pugsley, *A Bloody Road Home*, p. 149.

17 McAra, quoted in Henderson, p. 73 and A. Ross, *23 Battalion*, p. 68. Letter, G. Forty, *The Battle of Crete*, p. 138.
18 Comeau and Fraser, quoted in M. Comeau, *Operation Mercury*, p. 118.
19 Craig, interview W.E. Murphy, 17 Feb 1948. Campbell, quoted in J. Henderson, *22 Battalion*, pp. 62–64.
20 Johnson, letter to HQ NMD Auckland, 24 May 1948.
21 Neumann, quoted in MacDonald, p. 202.
22 *Funkverkehr Kreta*, messages 23.00, 20 Mai 41, 01.10 and 01.45, 21 Mai German time.
23 Wenzel, *Tagebuch.*
24 Gericke, p.76.
25 Wenzel, *Tagebuch.*
26 Witness, Gericke, pp.76–77. Citation, for KC and Ramke's comment, K. Kollatz, *Dr Heinrich Neumann, Landser*, No. 553, p. 50.
27 Wenzel, *Tagebuch.*
28 Gericke, pp. 78–79. Fink, *Der Komet auf Kreta*, pp. 293–94.

CHAPTER 9

1 B. Ramcke, *Vom Shiffsjünger züm Fallschirmjäger-General*, pp. 203–4.
2 Strauch and Pöppel and situation at Topolia airfield, quoted in R.J. Kershaw, *Skymen*, p. 126. Ramcke, pp. 208–9.
3 Von Könitz, quoted in A.D. Steinweg, 'Wir Holen Ihn Heraus!' *Deutsche Fallschirmjäger*, Mai/Jun, 3/1982.
4 Student, *Vorläufiger Erfahrungsbericht des XI Fliegerkorps: Einsatz Kreta. 11.6.41*, BA RL 33/98.
5 Von Richthofen, quoted in W. Ansel, *Hitler and the Middle Sea*, pp. 316–17. Ringel, *Hurra die Gams!* pp. 87 and 88.
6 Radio report, *Funkverkehr Kreta, 21 Mai 01.10* [German time].
7 Rzeha, quoted in J.-Y. Nasse, *Fallschirmjäger in Crete*, p. 74 and 76. R. Wenning, *Kreta Mai–Juni 1941*, BA RL 10/548.
8 Rzeha, quoted in Nasse, p. 78 and Wenning, *Kreta Mai–Juni 1941*, BA RL 10/548.
9 Ramcke, pp. 209–10. Fink, *Der Komet auf Kreta*, p. 335.
10 Fink, pp. 383–85.
11 Andrew and Hargest, diary entries 20–21 May, 5 New Zealand Brigade files. C. Pugsley, *A Bloody Road Home*, pp. 154–55.

12 Puttick and Gentry, quoted in Pugsley, p. 155. Official history, J. Henderson, *22 Battalion*, pp. 74–75.
13 M. Comeau, *Operation Mercury*, p. 122. W.B. Thomas, *Dare to be Free*, p. 19.
14 Comeau, p. 121. 22 Battalion Log, 21 May 1941, p. 47. Thomas, p. 19.
15 Dawson, quoted in Pugsley, p. 156.
16 G. Cox, *A Tale of Two Battles*, p. 75. Anderson, quoted in D.M. Davin, *Crete*, p. 188–9. Dyer, quoted in Davin, p. 190.
17 Battalion Log, 22 May 1941, p. 51.
18 Cox, p. 80. J. Hetherington, *Airborne Invasion*, p. 101.
19 Buchholz, Germany 1960, quoted in Ansel, p. 321.
20 Major Flecker and S. Dobiasch, *Gebirgsjäger auf Kreta*, p. 37. Ringel, pp. 91 and 88.
21 Buchholz, quoted in A. Morris, *German Airlift During the Battle of Crete*, p. 8. Schuster, quoted in K. Kollatz, *Feldwebel Erich Schuster*, p. 38.
22 Raither, quoted in Flecker, p. 55. Moutain Soldier, Davin Papers, I. McD. G. Stewart, *The Struggle for Crete*, p. 322.
23 Raither, quoted in Stewart, p. 56. Pfefferkorn, quoted in C.N. Hadjipateras and M.S. Fafalios, *Crete 1941: Eyewitnessed*, pp. 147–48.
24 Fink, pp. 326–29. Cox, pp. 80–81.
25 Mountain Gefreiter, quoted in Flecker, p. 58–59.
26 Bartels, quoted in Ringel, p. 113.
27 Baron von der Heydte, *Daedalus Returned*, pp. 108–9.

CHAPTER 10

1 Ehal's ship pronunciation, quoted in J. Ringel, *Hurra die Gams!* p. 102. Convoy contents, 'Die Tragödie auf See', *Deutsche Fallschimjäger*, Mär/Apr, 1982, p. 16.
2 Schmidt, quoted in *Bericht über den Untergang der S105 am 21.5.41*, dated 26 May 1941. BA RH 28-5/89. Greek crew, quoted in Ringel, p. 108.
3 Staubwasser, quoted in *Bericht über das Unternehmen Merkur in der Zeit von 19.5.–24.5.41*. BA RH 28-5/89. Schmidt, quoted in Major Flecker and S. Dobiasch, *Gebirgsjäger auf Kreta*, p. 66.
4 Schmidt, ibid., p. 67.

5 Linder Kriegstagebuch des II/GJR 85 vom 10.2.41 – 3.6.41, quoted in *Bericht*. Schmidt, quoted in *Bericht über den Untergang der S105 am 21.5.41*, dated 26 May 1941. BA RH 28-5/89.

6 Kerstens, quoted in T. Saunders, *Crete: The Airborne Invasion 1941*, p. 184. Sigrist, quoted in *Gefechtsbericht*, 21.5.41, dated 26 May, BA RH 28-5/89. Bracht, quoted in C.N. Hadjipateros and M.S. Fafalios, *Crete 1941: Eyewitnessed*, p. 124.

7 Staubwasser, *Bericht*, 26 Mai. Hörmann, quoted in W. Ansel, *Hitler and the Middle Sea*, pp. 331–32.

8 Schmidt, quoted in Flecker and Dobiasch, p. 68.

9 Riep and Stribny, quoted in A.M. de Zayas, *Die Wehrmacht-Untersuchungsstelle*, pp. 382 and 383.

10 Staubwasser, *Bericht*, ibid. RN losses, D.M. Davin, *Crete*, p. 247.

11 Kerstens, article *Deutsche Fallschirmjäger* Magazine, Mär/Apr 1982, p. 18. Würz, quoted in G. Stein article in *Crete 1941: Eyewitnessed*, p. 125. Losses, W. Ansel, p. 337 and *DF* Magazine, Mär/Apr 1982, p. 18.

12 Hargest Diary and Gentry, quoted in C. Pugsley, *A Bloody Road Home*, p. 159.

13 Marshall, quoted in J. Sadler, *Operation Mercury*, p. 131.

14 Farran, quoted in T. Saunders, *Crete: The Airborne Invasion 1941*, pp. 182–83.

15 G. Cox, *A Tale of Two Battles*, pp. 82 and 83.

16 Brown, quoted in R. Campbell Begg and P. Liddle, *For Five Shillings a Day*, p. 129. Carr, quoted in P. Monteath, *Battle on 42nd Street*, p. 110.

17 Hargest, quoted in Davin, p. 215.

18 Burrows, quoted in G. McLean, I. McGibbon and K. Gentry, eds, *New Zealanders at War*, pp. 292–93. Carr, quoted in Monteath, pp. 110–111.

19 Farran, quoted in Saunders, p. 186. Beel, quoted in Hadjipateros and Fafalios , p. 98.

20 Rzeha, J.-Y. Nasse, *Fallschirmjäger in Crete*, p. 80.

21 Farran account, quoted in C. MacDonald. *The Lost Battle: Crete 1941*, p. 223. Saunders, pp. 189–90 and I. McD. G. Stewart, *The Struggle for Crete*, pp. 326–27.

22 Beel, quoted in Hadjipateros and Fafalios, p. 98.

23 Young, quoted in J. Sadler, *Operation Mercury*, p. 136.

24 Dyer, quoted in Davin, p. 220. Upham, quoted in Pugsley, p. 163.

25 Elliot, quoted in Pugsley, p. 165.

26 Hargest messages, Davin, pp. 229–30.

27 Freyberg, diary entry, Pugsley, p. 165.

28 Jumper analogy, Pugsley TV interview, *Ultimate Blitzkrieg: Battle of Crete*, Episode 1 *Invasion*. Pilot Productions 2019.

29 F. Fink, *Der Komet auf Kreta*, p. 367.

30 Flecker, quoted in Flecker and Dobiasch, p. 63.

31 *I/85* take-off, *Kriegstagebuch des Gebirgsjäger Regiment 85*, p. 26, BA RH 37/2154.

32 Baron von der Heydte, *Daedalus Returned*, pp. 139–40. Von Richthofen, *Sammelung Luftkrieg 1939/45 Balkan Greichenland*, p. 34 and 45, BA R L8/239. Löhr, quoted in W. Ansel, p. 362.

33 K. Neher, *Kampf um den Englischen Stutzpunkt Kreta*, pp. 2–4. Wenning, personal diary, *Kreta Mai–Juni 1941*, p. 12, BA RL 10/548. Aircraft losses 22 May, A. Morris, *German Airlift During the Battle of Crete*, pp. 105–6.

34 Neher, pp. 4–5. Wenning, p. 13. Eyewitness, von der Heydte, pp. 114–15.

35 *Gefreiter* O., Flecker extracts, quoted in Flecker and Dobiasch, pp. 60 and 62.

36 Flecker and Dobiasch, pp. 63–64. Ringel, pp. 128 and 134.

37 Flecker and Dobiasch, pp. 87 and 64 and 66.

38 Ringel, pp. 130–32. Neher, pp. 8–9.

39 Casualties, Pugsley, p. 178, Ansel p. 419, *After the Battle*, issue 47, p. 24. N. Crookenden, *Airborne at War*, p. 58, *Gefechtsbericht Gruppe West 7.6.41*, p. 16, BA 8A-2025. RL 33/31. Von der Heydte, TV interview in J. Isaacs, *Touch and Go!: The Battle for Crete 1941*, New Zealand TV 1991.

40 Hitler, quoted in Ansel, pp. 420–21.

41 Churchill, quoted in R.J. Kershaw, *Skymen*, p. 77.

POSTSCRIPT

1 Weixler Report, Göring (War Crimes) Case, Krailling near Munich, 11 Nov 1945.

2 Student and Ringel and reprisal measures, K. Margry, 'Reprisal at Kondomari', *After the Battle*, Issue No. 181, pp. 37–38.

3 Weixler Report, Göring War Crimes Case. Trebes, quoted in Margry, p. 43.
4 Weixler Report and Margry p. 43. Weixler Photos: *Bundesarchiv Bild 1011-166 to 0525 – 0332 and 0527-03A-04A.*
5 Weixler Report.
6 Ibid.
7 Margry, pp. 44–45.
8 Kondomari and aftermath, Margry, pp. 36–49. S.D. Yada-McNeal, *Franz-Peter Weixler: The Invasion of Greece and Crete by the Camera of a Propaganda Photographer.* See appendix for subsequent events.

THE KEY DECISION-MAKERS AND TAKERS

1 Letter to wife, New Zealand official biography.
2 Lange, quoted in J. Mrazek, *The Fall of Eben Emael,* p. 174.
3 Meindl and Ursula Meindl letter, quoted in G. Roth, *Die Deutsche Fallschirmtruppe 1939–1945,* pp. 285 and 160.

Bibliography

GENERAL

Ansel, W., *Hitler and the Middle Sea*, Duke University Press, 1972.

Antill, P.D., *Crete 1941*, Osprey, 2005.

Beevor, A., *Crete: The Battle and the Resistance*, Penguin, 1992.

Cavendish, M. *Images of War*, Vol 1

Clark, A., *The Fall of Crete*, Anthony Blond Ltd, 1962.

Crookenden, N., *Airborne at War*, Ian Allan, 1978.

Davin, D.M., *Crete*, War History Branch Dept of Internal Affairs New Zealand, 1953.

Ewer, P., *Forgotten Anzacs*, Scribe, 2016.

Forty, G., *The Battle of Crete*, Ian Allan, 2009.

Gonzalez, O., Steinke, T. and Tannahill, I., *The Silent Attack*, Pen and Sword, 2015.

Grundelach, K., *The Battle for Crete 1941*, from H.-A. Jacobsen and J. Rohwer, eds, *Decisive Battles of World War II: The German View*, Andre Deutsch, 1965.

Kershaw, R.J., *Skymen*, Hodder and Stoughton, 2010.

Kurowski, F., *Der Kampf um Kreta*, Efstathiadas, 1994.

MacDonald, C., *The Lost Battle: Crete 1941*, Papermac, 1993.

Mitcham, S.W., *Eagles of the III Reich: Men of the Luftwaffe in WWII*

Monteath, P., *Battle on 42nd Street*, Newsouth, 2019.

Morris, A., *German Airlift during the Battle of Crete*, US Army Comd and Staff College, June 2014.

Mrazek, J.E., *The Fall of Eben Emael*, Robert Hale, 1970.

Muhleisen, H.-O., *Kreta 1941*, Rombach Verlag, 1968.

Rechenberg, *Fallschirmjäger im Osten, Korinth, Die Wehrmacht 1941*

Sadler, J., *Operation Mercury*, Pen and Sword, 2007.

Saunders, T., *Crete: The Airborne Invasion 1941*, Pen and Sword 2008.

Shores, C., Cull, B., Malizia, N., *Air War for Yugoslavia, Greece and Crete*, Grub Street, 1987.

Soubassis, G., *Civilian Resistance in Crete 20 May 1941–15 May 1945*, USMC Comd and Staff College.

Stewart, I. McD. G., *The Struggle for Crete*, Oxford University Press, 1991.

Stockings, C. and E. Hancock, *Swastika over the Acropolis: Reinterpreting the Nazi Invasion of Greece in World War II*, Brill, 2013

Yada-Mc Neal, S.D., *Franz-Peter Weixler: The Invasion of Greece and Crete by the Camera of a Propaganda Photographer*, 2018

Yiannikopoulos, G., *The Greek Forces in the Battle of Crete May 1941*, Academia Paper website, accessed 2021

Zayas, A.M. de, *Die Wehrmacht-Untersuchungsstelle*, Heyne Bücher, 1981.

BIOGRAPHIES, PERSONAL ACCOUNTS, DIARIES AND LETTERS

German

Fink, F., *Der Komet auf Kreta*, Gelka-Druck Verlag.

Flecker, Major and Dobiasch, S., *Gebirgsjäger auf Kreta*, Wilhelm Limpert Berlin, 1942.

Gericke, W., *Da Gibt Es Kein Zurück*, Fallschirmjäger Verlag, 1955.

Götzel, H., *Generaloberst Kurt Student und seine Fallschirmjäger*, Podzun-Pallas Verlag, 1980.

Heydte von der, Baron, *Daedalus Returned: Crete 1941*, Hutchinson, 1958.

Käppner, J., Probst, R. and Weidinger, B., *Die Letzen Augenzeugen*, Suddeutsche Zeitung, 2010.

Kiriakopoulos, G.C., *Ten Days to Destiny*, Avon Books, 1985.

Kollatz, K., *Feldwebel Erich Schuster, Der Landser* Grossverband, Nr 351.

Müller, G. and Scheuering, F., *Sprung über Kreta*, Gerhard Stalling Verlag, 1944.

Nasse, J.-Y., *Fallschirmjäger in Crete*, Histoire and Collections, 2002.

Neher, K., *Kampf um den Englischen Stutzpunkt Kreta*, Alltenstadt-Schongau LL Museum, 1942.
Pöppel, M., *Heaven and Hell: The War Diary of a German Paratrooper*, Spellmount, 1988.
Ramcke, B., *Vom Schiffsjungen züm Fallschirmjäger-General*, Wehrmacht Verlag, 1943.
Reinhardt, E., *Memoirs of a Former German Paratrooper*, Self-published Fallingbostal, 1984.
Ringel, J., *Hurra, die Gams!* Leopold Stocker Verlag 8th Edition.
Uruena, G., *Generalfeldmarschall Wolfram Freiherr von Richthofen*, Corner History German Army Publishers, 2016.
Winterstein, E.M. and Jacobs, M., *General Meindl und seine Fallschirmjäger*, Ladstetter GmbH.

New Zealand, British and Greek
Archer, L., *Balkan Journal*, W.W. Norton and Co., 1944.
Campbell Begg, R. and Liddle, P., *For Five Shillings a Day*, Harper Collins, 2000.
Comeau, M., *Operation Mercury*, Patrick Stephens, 1991.
Cox, G., *A Tale of Two Battles*, William Kimber, 1987.
Hadjipateras, C.N. and Fafalios, M.S., *Crete 1941: Eyewitnessed*, Efstathiadis Group, 1989.
Hetherington, J., *Airborne Invasion*, George Allen and Unwin, 1944.
McLean, G., McGibbon, I. and Gentry, K., eds, *New Zealanders at War*, Penguin, 2009.
Psychoundakis, G., *The Cretan Runner*, Efstathiadis, 1991.
Thomas, W.B., *Dare to be Free*, Cassel, 2005.

UNIT ACCOUNTS

Cody J.F., *21 Battalion*, History Branch, Wellington, New Zealand, 1953.
Cody, J.F., *28 (Maori) Battalion*, History Branch, Wellington, New Zealand, 1956.
Gardiner, W., *Te Mura o te Ahi. The Story of the Maori Battalion*, Reed Books, 1995.
Golla, K.H., *The German Fallschirmtruppe 1936–41*, Helion, 2012.

Henderson, J., *22 Battalion*, History Branch, Wellington, New Zealand, 1958.

Nasse, J.-Y., *Green Devils! German Paratroopers 1939–45*, Histoire and Collections, 1997.

Pugsley, C., *A Bloody Road Home*, Penguin, New Zealand, 2014.

Ross, A., *23 Battalion*, History Branch, Wellington, New Zealand, 1959.

Roth, G., *Die Deutsche Fallschirmtruppe 1936–45*, Mittler & Sohn, 2010.

DOCUMENTS

(German unpublished. BA Bundesarchiv)

Gruppe West
Flugplatzbereich Maleme.
Funkverkehr des Sturm Regiments – Stabes wahrend des Einsatzes Kreta vom 20–27.5.1941.
Gefechtsbericht I/Sturm Rgt BA 8H-1658.
Gefechtsbericht der 3/Sturm Rgt. Einsatz Kreta. Zeit von 20–28.5.1941.
Gefechtsbericht der 4/Sturm Rgt 15.8.1941.
Gefechtsbericht der Gruppe West fur den Einsatz Kreta von 20–28.5.41.
Signed Ramcke Chania 7.6.41.
Sturm Rgt 8 Jul 1941. BA RL33/34.
Tagebuch 23.4. –20.5. und 29.5–13.7 und Rgt Gefechtsbericht 20.5–28.5.
Signed Meindl 11.9.41. BA H 8905.
Wenning, R., Diary, *Kreta Mai–Juni 1941*, BA RL 10/548.

XI Fliegerkorps
Anlagen zum Gefechtsbericht XI Fl.Korps – Einsatz Kreta 11.6.41. BA RL 33/99.
Gefechtsbericht XI Fliegerkorps – Einsatz Kreta 11.6.41. BA RL 33/98.
Vorläufiger Erfahrungsbericht des XI Fliegerkorps 11.6. 1941. Einsatz Kreta.
Luftwaffe, BA RL 33/98.
Anlage 1 zu K.G. 2 Ia 1.6.41.
Einführung zum balkanfeldzug des VIII Fliegerkorps, unter benutzung der Tagebucher des Generalfeldmarschalls Frhr von Richthofen. RL8/239.

Erfahrungsbericht über das Unternehmen Merkur. BA RL8/243.
Gefechtsbericht des L.G.1 Gen Kdo des VIII Fliegerkorps 22 &23.5.41.

German Army
Kriegstagebuch des II/GJR 85 vom 10.2.41–3.6.41 Griechenland und Kreta.
  BA RH 37/2150.
Kriegstagebuch des Gebirgsjäger Regiment 85. Signed Krakau Iraklion
  15.7.41. BA RH 37/2154.

Unpublished German – General
Seibt, C., Interrogation Report, APO 696 US Army 1 Sep 1945, UK
  Airborne Museum.
Student and Bassinger interrogation, 24 Sep 1945, UK Airborne Museum.
Weixler Report (statement), Göring (War Crimes) Case, Krailling, near
  Munich 11 Nov 1945.

New Zealand
22 Battalion Diary 20–23 May 1941 (hand written). 22 New Zealand
  Battalion website, http://www.22battalion.org.nz/, accessed 2021.

MAGAZINE ARTICLES

(*Deutsche Fallschirmjäger* Magazine = *DF*)
Dach, H. von, 'Der Luftangriff auf Kreta', *Schweizer Soldat* Nr 8 & 11.
'Die Tragödie auf See', *DF* 2, Mär/Apr 1982 and Mai/Jun, 3/1982.
Gotzel and A. Von Roon, 'Fallschirmjäger Einsatz bei Korinth 1941',
  DF 3, Mai/Jun, 1984.
'Major I.G. Trettner Ia. Generalstab XI Fliegerkorps vor Funfzig Jahren
  Unternehmen Merkur', *DF* Magazine, 2/1991.
Margry, K., 'Reprisal at Kondomari', *After the Battle*, Issue No. 181, 2018.
Pallud J-P., 'Crete 1941', *After the Battle*, Issue No. 47, 1985.
Plowman, J., Grieve, M. and Wilson, M., 'Matilda Tanks on Crete',
  After the Battle, Issue 175, 2017.
Steinweg, Hpt A.D., 'Wir Holen Ihn Heraus!', *DF* 3, Mai/Jun, 1982.
Valasiadis, N., 'A Staged Surrender in Crete', *After the Battle*, Issue 189,
  2020.
Wenzel, H., 'Auszug aus Meinum Tagebuch von Damals', *DF* 5, Sep/
  Okt, 1983.

FILM, TV AND MEDIA INTERVIEWS

Amiard, C. and D. Ablin, *Hitler's Steel Beast*, 909 Productions Dec 2016.

Bayer, L., Film, *Kreta, Ein Heldenlied unserer Zeit*, Ref 561 04.06.41.

Deutsche Wochenschau, Nr 561 4.6.41.

Die Deutschen im Zweiten Weltkrieg, Teil 2, SWF & ORF German TV 1985.

Epperson, C., Film, *The 11th Day*, Archangel Films 2006.

Isaacs, J., *Touch and Go!: The Battle for Crete 1941*, New Zealand TV 1991.

Ultimate Blitzkrieg World War 2, Battle of Crete, Episode 1 *Invasion*, Pilot Productions 2019.

Index

Page numbers in **bold** refer to maps.